BOOKS BY NORMAN BEIM

NOVELS

Hymie And The Angel

PLAYS

Six Award Winning Plays

Plays At Home And Abroad

My Family The Jewish Immigrants

Giants Of The Old Testament

Infamous People

Comedy Tonite!

Women Laid Bare

FOR MY GUARDIAN ANGELS,

Marvin Hayes & Frank Bara

Women
Laid Bare

NORMAN BEIM

NEW CONCEPT PRESS
425 West 57 Street Suite 2J
New York, NY 10019
212-265-6284
Fax: 212-265-6659
newconpres@aol.com

CAUTION: These plays are fully protected in whole, in part, or in any form under copyright laws and are subject to royalty. All rights, including professional, amateur, motion pictures, radio, television, recitation and public readings are strictly reserved. All inquiries for performance rights should be addressed to:

Samuel French, Inc.
45 West 25th Street
New York, New York 10010

Library of Congress Control Number: 2006910837

Beim, Norman
   Women laid bare/Norman Beim
       p. cm.
   Contents: A kingdom by the sea-The liberation of linda dworkin-An audience of one-Lulu in babylon-The disintegration of della longstreet-I went to a marvelous party-Dancing in the dark

ISBN: 978-0-931231-13-1 / 0-931231-13-2 (Alk. paper)
  1. Drama   I. Title

812'.54--dc22

Special thanks to LARRY ERLBAUM, FRANK BARA, MARVIN HAYES and last, but not least MARTY BEIM.

Front Cover design by HOMER GUERRA

Printed in the United States of America
10 9 8 7 6 5 4 3 2 1

CONTENTS

Kingdom By The Sea	1
The Liberation Of Linda Dworkin	71
An Audience Of One	185
Lulu In Babylon	261
The Disintegration Of Della Longstreet	333
I Went To A Marvelous Party	411
Dancing In The Dark	501

KINGDOM BY THE SEA

A Play in Two Acts

"I was a child and she was a child,
In this kingdom by the sea,
But we loved with a love that was more than love...
I and my Annabel Lee...
With a love that the winged seraphs of heaven
Coveted her and me..."

EDGAR ALLAN POE

CAST OF CHARACTERS

Terry Helenski

Brian Wood

Craig Wood

SCENE

A room in Brian Wood's summer home

ACT I

Scene 1

The den of BRIAN WOOD's summer home. The furniture is covered with dust sheets. Classical music is being played on a transistor radio. TERRY HELENSKI enters from the interior of the house and removes the dust sheets, folding them neatly.

RADIO ANNOUNCER: We interrupt this program for an important news bulletin. A patient has escaped from the Brooks Mental Institute. He is dressed in a raincoat and is approximately six feet tall. This man is armed and dangerous. Repeat. This man is armed and dangerous. Anyone seeing a man answering this description please call the police at once. We repeat this announcement.

(TERRY has stopped folding the sheets and turns off the radio. SHE stands listening for a moment, looks about the room and sights a hunting rifle on the wall over the fireplace. SHE walks quickly to the fireplace, takes down the weapon and faces the French doors. A figure can be seen approaching.)

TERRY: Who's there? Who's there?

(TERRY raises the gun to her shoulder as the French doors are opened and BRIAN WOOD enters in a raincoat. HE holds up his hands.)

BRIAN: I'm yours.

TERRY: You scared me to death.

BRIAN: I came around the back. It's closer to the garage. That gun isn't loaded, by the way. *(HE steps out and returns with two shopping bags.)* What are you so upset about?

TERRY: A bulletin just came over the radio. Someone's escaped from the Brooks Mental Institute. Is that far from here?

BRIAN: It's down the road about a mile or so.

KINGDOM BY THE SEA

TERRY: What sort of a place is it?

BRIAN: It's a hospital for the criminally insane.

TERRY: Good lord!

BRIAN: There's nothing to worry about. They never get very far. I'll put this stuff in the kitchen.

> *(BRIAN goes off. TERRY puts down the gun, closes the French doors then stands looking out into the gloom. BRIAN reenters.)*

TERRY: Do they escape very often?

BRIAN: Not really, no.

TERRY: It looks pretty dismal out there.

BRIAN: The rain has stopped, for the moment. Have there been any calls?

TERRY: No, not yet? What time are Craig and his lady friend due?

BRIAN: I was expecting them last night.

TERRY: The radio said something about the roads being flooded.

BRIAN: Spring in New England. I'm sorry about the electricity. I usually don't come up here this early.

TERRY: Well, as long as the phone is working, we can always call for help.

BRIAN: Oh, come now.

TERRY: How far are we from civilization?

BRIAN: There are houses all around us.

KINGDOM BY THE SEA

TERRY: I didn't see any last night.

BRIAN: Well, there are. I bought some extra candles, just in case.

(*TERRY finishes folding the dust sheets.*)

BRIAN: Here, let me help you.

TERRY: I'm just about done. Do you come up here every summer?

BRIAN: I used to, until my wife and I split up. Here, I'll put them away. (*HE puts the dust sheets in a drawer.*)

TERRY: Maybe we ought to load that gun, just in case.

BRIAN: If it'll make you feel any better. I think there are still some shells here somewhere. Ah, here we are. Well, if we're going to load the gun, maybe I'd better clean it first. It hasn't been used in quite some time. (*HE takes some cleaning material out of a drawer and proceeds to clean the rifle.*) Have you ever fired a rifle?

TERRY: As a matter of fact, I'm an excellent shot. I worked in a shooting gallery once...when I was in high school.

BRIAN: Did you really?

TERRY: I had all sorts of crazy jobs along the way.

BRIAN: I hope I didn't offend you last night. I didn't mean to rush things.

TERRY: No harm done.

BRIAN: Beneath that calm exterior there lurks a very calm exterior. Or is there really a sea of passion churning within that nubile body of yours?

TERRY: Nubile?

BRIAN: Whatever.

KINGDOM BY THE SEA

TERRY: I'll have to look that up.

BRIAN: You're a strange little creature, Terry Helenski.

TERRY: Little?

BRIAN: Figuratively speaking.

TERRY: Meaning?

BRIAN: I don't know. There's something wild and untamed about you. Like the geese we used to hunt in the Spring.

TERRY: I see. And you're the great white hunter.

BRIAN: Not really, no.

TERRY: Then what's that rifle doing over your fireplace?

BRIAN: It belonged to my father. He loved to hunt. Actually he was a very gentle man in some ways. "Genteel," I suppose would be more accurate. In his own quiet way, however, he was something of a tyrant. We came from, what used to be called, "old money." As a matter of fact, he was furious when I went took over Beechwood Press. "Radical, left wing Bohemians! I forbid it."

TERRY: Beechwood?

BRIAN: Yes, well it's changed quite a bit over the years. So have I, I suppose. We all go through that phase, do we not? At one time or another. My father was not very understanding, nor very supportive. That's why I'm cursed with this awful inferiority complex?

TERRY: You could have fooled me.

BRIAN: Why do you think I always look so busy?

TERRY: I'll bite. Why?

KINGDOM BY THE SEA

BRIAN: I live in constant fear that someone's going to come up to me and say, "And what do you do here, young man?" So I'm always ready with, "Well, you see, sir, I'm checking out these reports." or "I'm just going over our latest figures."

TERRY: Oh come now, Brian, you happen to be an excellent business man, and you know what you're doing every minute of the day.

BRIAN: I'm not really. I just happen to be an excellent judge of character. I choose my staff so well that Beechwood Press could run itself very efficiently if I should happen to disappear one of these days.

TERRY: Yes, well, I'm not so sure about that.

(There is a loud clap of thunder.)

BRIAN: It's inescapable, you know.

TERRY: What's that?

BRIAN: Women turn into their mothers...

TERRY: And men turn into their fathers?

BRIAN: Despite their shortcomings. It's amazing how much more intelligent our parents become as we grow older.

(There is a clap of thunder.)

TERRY: What a dreary day! This house must hold all sorts of memories for you.

BRIAN: Ah, yes indeed. My grandmother died of a heart attack in this very room. She couldn't sleep and she took to wandering about the house at night. We found her here one morning, sitting upright in that chair over there, staring into the sun. *(After a moment)* I was standing in that doorway when I received the news of my daughter's death. I can still hear the ticking of the grandfather clock in the hallway, and my wife's footsteps on the stair. "What is it, Brian?" she asked. She must have noticed how pale I was, and she said, "It's Craig, isn't it?" "No," I said, "it's Prue. She's drowned...in the pond." I caught her just in time. She would have hit her head on the bannister. And things were never the same between us.

TERRY: Why do you come here, if your memories are so painful?

BRIAN: It's my home, or one of then, at any rate. And pain is pain, no matter where you are. Craig was born here in this house. Upstairs, in the master bedroom. We hadn't planned it that way, but he was very insistent, and he's had his way ever since. I suppose you must have gathered by now that Craig has been somewhat of a disappointment to me.

TERRY: And you, to him?

BRIAN: My wife insists that I didn't take enough interest in him.

TERRY: Did you? Do you?

BRIAN: I believe in giving people space.

TERRY: You're very wise in your relationships, aren't you?

BRIAN: "'Tis a consummation devoutly to be wished." And you? Are you wise in your relationships?

TERRY: God, no! I'm like the geese, remember? Wild and untamed.

BRIAN: *(HE finishes loading the gun.)* There we are. All safe and sound. I put the safety catch on, so there's no danger of an accident. *(HE places the rifle back on the wall.)* Do you want to check out the food?

TERRY: Good idea.

(TERRY goes off. BRIAN looks about.)

BRIAN: Have you seen...? Never mind. *(HE picks up his attaché case from the floor, sits in a chair near the window, opens the case and takes out some papers. HE changes his mind, goes to the phone, picks it up and dials.)* It's me. Have you heard anything from Craig, by the way? Well, he's not here yet. It's probably the weather. Any more headaches? Edith... Edith, for God sakes, I was not being sarcastic...I... *(HE listens for a moment, holds the phone away from his ear, then slams it down.)* Stupid bitch! *(HE heaves a sigh, goes back to his attaché case and takes out some papers.)*

(The telephone rings.)

BRIAN: *(HE picks up the phone.)* Hello? Yes, Edith. That's quite all right. I understand. We're all on edge these days. I'm sure there's nothing to worry about. I'll have him call you as soon as he gets in. I'm doing fine. Thank you for asking. Well, as long as there are schools that need textbooks Beechwood Press will always be in business. Yes, dear. I'll have him call you. Good-bye.

(BRIAN hangs up as TERRY reenters.)

TERRY: Was that the phone?

BRIAN: That was Edith, my ex-wife. I don't know why it is, but every time we speak we end up at each others throat.

TERRY: Is there anything wrong?

BRIAN: Actually I called her. I just thought she might have heard from Craig.

TERRY: And?

BRIAN: No, not a word.

TERRY: I'm sure it's the weather. I've never met him, have I? I mean at the office perhaps.

BRIAN: Good lord, no! At "the market place?" No, I haven't seen the prodigal since after my divorce became final.

(The phone rings. BRIAN answers it.)

KINGDOM BY THE SEA

BRIAN: Hello? Yes, well I think I'm here. Where are you? We'll expect you shortly then. What's that? I see. All right. Good-bye. *(HE hangs up.)* I guess I've forgotten what it was like to be a son, but it couldn't have been more difficult than being a father. *(HE puts the papers back in the case.)*

TERRY: Where is he?

BRIAN: He's right nearby, in the village. He'll be here any minute.

TERRY: How long has it been since you've seen him?

BRIAN: Two...three years. He came into some money my father unwisely left him, and he's been having himself a ball ever since.

TERRY: I imagine the divorce couldn't have been easy for him.

BRIAN: Maybe not. He seems to think I deserted her in her time of need. The truth of the matter is Edith has never had a time of need. She has always been self-sufficient. I hope I'm not boring you. As a matter of fact, I've never talked this much about myself to anyone.

TERRY: That was the general idea, wasn't it? For us to get to know one another.

BRIAN: Yes. Yes, it was. Is there enough food?

TERRY: Enough to feed an army. There will only be the four of us, I gather.

BRIAN: Three.

TERRY: What happened to his lady friend?

BRIAN: That's yet to be determined. Excuse me. I've got to dig up some towels.

(BRIAN picks up his raincoat and goes off. TERRY walks about the room, studying the pictures on the wall. SHE wanders over

KINGDOM BY THE SEA

toward the French doors and stands looking out into the mist. CRAIG WOOD enters from the outside. HE wears a raincoat and carries an overnight bag. Unheard by TERRY, HE stands studying her.)

CRAIG: The mysterious Terry Helenski, I presume.

(TERRY whirls about.)

CRAIG: I'm sorry. I didn't mean to startle you.

TERRY: Don't you believe in doorbells?

CRAIG: This *is* my home.

TERRY: I'm sorry. I guess I'm a little on edge.

CRAIG: That's quite understandable. This place does have a way of getting under one's skin.

TERRY: There happens to be a lunatic wandering about somewhere.

CRAIG: Not that unusual.

TERRY: Do they ever get away?

CRAIG: I get the feeling they never want to get away. None of us really want to leave the womb, do we?

TERRY: You haven't answered my question.

CRAIG: I thought I had. Helenski....Helenski...that's

TERRY: Lithuanian.

CRAIG: Craig Wood, white, Anglo-Saxon, Presbyterian. In other words...WASP.

TERRY: How do you do.

KINGDOM BY THE SEA

(THEY shake hands.)

CRAIG: Gloomy, isn't it? *(HE throws down his bag and takes off his raincoat.)*

TERRY: There's no electricity.

CRAIG: He's forgotten to turn it on again.

TERRY: We do have plenty of candles though.

CRAIG: How is the old geezer? Never mind. There's no rush. The prodigal son is not the least bit anxious to be welcomed back into the fold. The place hasn't changed a bit. Sort of spooky, really. Wars have come and wars have gone. People have been born and people have died, and the good old homestead remains the same. The grandfather clock in the hallway ticks on. The furniture has been dusted. The floors have been polished; the brass knocker on the portal shined till it gleams. Hark! Is that the sound of horses I hear at the gate? There's the muffled steps of the servant on the stairs. They're always muffled, you know, and the servant always speaks in a whisper. There's no one at home, and someone leaves his calling card. There's no such thing as prejudice or class. You can be sure of that, since the town crier tells us so.

TERRY: Is that what it was like when you lived here?

CRAIG: I never lived here. I spent my childhood summers here. My little sister drowned out there in the pond...out there in the murky mist.

TERRY: I'm sure your childhood was a very comfortable one, in spite of all that.

CRAIG: My childhood was a lie. It was sugar-spun candy and lemonade, and a pony all my own. The pony was supposed to help me forget the loss of my alter ego. That's what she was, you know---my conscience, my lovely burden, my twin---even though she was a few years younger. We made mischief together, and I was always the culprit. She was the devilish angel and she was called to heaven because God loved her so. What a selfish god, what a merciless god to break so many hearts so casually, because he fancied my pretty little sister! He must have been a Roman god, don't you think? The Greeks had a sense of nicety that the Romans, try as they might, never found.

TERRY: This was quite some time ago, I believe.

CRAIG: Obviously you've never lost anyone close.

TERRY: I lost a brother.

CRAIG: Yes, of course. I'm sorry. Philip Helenski, wasn't it?

TERRY: Yes.

CRAIG: I should like to drink a toast to the dear departed. That's quite all right. I know where they hide the liquor. *(HE goes to a cabinet, opens it and pours a drink.)* Won't you join me? It's very good Scotch. Only the best.

TERRY: Thank you, no.

CRAIG: Then I must drink alone. To our mutual ghosts. *(HE raises his glass than tosses off the drink.)* Now it's your turn to say, "It's rather early in the day, don't you think?" Or the more subtle approach, "Why don't we wait until after lunch?" Or the real zinger, "Did you know that whiskey actually destroys the little grey cells, to say nothing of what it does to one's liver?"

TERRY: "I burn my candle at both ends,/ It will not last the night;/ But, ah, my foes, and oh, my friends...,/ It gives a lovely light!"

CRAIG: What a pleasant surprise! A kindred spirit. Well, well, well. And you actually work for Beechwood Press? How long have you and pa-PAH been...shall we say...friends?

TERRY: And what makes you so sure that your father and I are..."shall we say friends?"

CRAIG: I see.

KINGDOM BY THE SEA

TERRY: Your father's been worried about you. I think it might be considerate of you to let him know that you've arrived safely.

CRAIG: By all means. Let's not keep the old boy in suspense any longer. *(HE goes to the doorway.)* Brian? Brian?

(BRIAN enters.)

CRAIG: The prodigal has returned. Where is the fatted calf?

BRIAN: Good afternoon.

CRAIG: Now that's what I call a welcome. Your only son and heir has returned after three years among the fleshpots and all pa-PAH has to say is "Good afternoon."

BRIAN: It is after one. Are you hungry?

CRAIG: Now that's more like it.

BRIAN: Are you?

CRAIG: Not really, no. Nor am I thirsty. I've been fortifying myself along the way.

BRIAN: Well, I am starved.

TERRY: Lunch should be ready any minute. *(SHE goes off to the kitchen.)*

CRAIG: Congratulations. She's quite attractive, in a humorless sort of way. She must be rather grim in bed though. "Bad form, bad form!" Unless, of course, you haven't been to bed with her, which would have been very remiss of you. Have you been to bed with her?

BRIAN: Where is your lady friend?

CRAIG: Gone. The way of all flesh.

KINGDOM BY THE SEA

BRIAN: I'm sorry. I should like to have met her.

CRAIG: Pamela Stratton?

BRIAN: Pamela? Is that whom you're seeing?

CRAIG: Was. Past tense.

BRIAN: I didn't know that she was the one.

CRAIG: We've been seeing each other for almost a year now...on and off. And now it's off. I must have written you about it.

BRIAN: On one of your indecipherable picture postcards?

CRAIG: Didn't I?

BRIAN: If you had, I would have remembered it. I'm not senile yet.

CRAIG: Okay, okay. Another demerit.

BRIAN: What happened, may I ask? Between you and Pamela?

CRAIG: Incompatibility. Isn't that what they call it?

BRIAN: You're supposed to call your mother, by the way.

CRAIG: I just spoke to her.

BRIAN: When?

CRAIG: Last Wednesday, I believe.

BRIAN: Since she is expecting your call I think it would be considerate of you to phone her.

CRAIG: That is the key word of the day, is it not? Considerate.

BRIAN: Do you know the number?

KINGDOM BY THE SEA

CRAIG: Yes, Brian, I think I do. *(HE picks up the phone.)* Is there room for me in the garage?

BRIAN: Yes, of course.

(BRIAN goes off. Craig dials.)

CRAIG: Ah, the magic of this electronic age! I dial a number and at once my ear is bathed with the dulcet tones of Alma Gluck and Rosa Ponselle...to say nothing of Lotte Lehman. What are you reading! Good Lord! That is a far cry from Henry James. I'm fine. Yes, well the roads are pretty bad. Mother, I have no intention of going anywhere at the moment. Pamela has decided to remain in Gotham. New York, my dear, New York. Yes, I was planning to call you on Monday. Shall we plan on lunch? Dinner then. I'll give you a ring in the morning. Till then, cara mia. Yes. Yes, I will.

(CRAIG hangs up and goes out the front door. There is a pause. The telephone rings several times. BRIAN reenters and picks up the phone.)

BRIAN: Hello? Oh, Sam. Yes, I'm here. No, just for the week-end. That must have been Craig. Yes, he's here too. He's fine. Oh, yes, he's quite the young man. How are you doing? Yes, I heard about it on the radio. I see. Thank you for letting me know. Well, I do have the rifle.

(TERRY enters.)

BRIAN: Yes, I most certainly will. How's the wife, by the way? Good, good. Drop by for a drink, if you have the time. Thank you, Sam. I'd appreciate that. Good-bye. *(HE hangs up.)* That was the sheriff. He's a friend of the family. Apparently the man that escaped was seen in the area.

(The French doors are thrown open and CRAIG enters, carrying a tennis racquet.)

CRAIG: Tennis, anyone?

KINGDOM BY THE SEA

BRIAN: Would you mind closing the door?

CRAIG: That's exactly what I'd planned on doing. *(HE closes the door.)* It's started to rain again.

BRIAN: Sam Barton just called. A man has escaped from the institute.

CRAIG: What else is new?

BRIAN: He's been sighted in the area.

CRAIG: Well, that should certainly add to the festivities. I assume I'm in my own room.

BRIAN: You assume correctly.

CRAIG: In case you haven't noticed, it's rather gloomy in here. I think a ray of light might be in order.

BRIAN: You'll find some candles in your room.

CRAIG: Thank you, sir. *(HE picks up his bag and goes off.)*

BRIAN: The prince has spoken.

TERRY: It is rather gloomy. I'll get some candles.

> *(TERRY goes off. BRIAN stands looking out the French doors. TERRY reenters with two candles which she places in the candlesticks on the mantlepiece. SHE lights the candles. BRIAN closes the drapes across the French doors. TERRY looks at him questioningly.)*

BRIAN: There's no need to extend an invitation.

> *(CRAIG reenters carrying a lighted candle in a candlestick.)*

CRAIG: The haunted house of Usher.

KINGDOM BY THE SEA

BRIAN: Every house is haunted that has been lived in for a while.

TERRY: Where would you like to eat? The breakfast room or the dining room?

BRIAN: The breakfast room would be fine.

TERRY: I'll set the table.

BRIAN: You know where everything is?

TERRY: Yes, I know. *(SHE goes off.)*

BRIAN: I laid out some towels for you.

CRAIG: The perfect host. We could use a fire.

BRIAN: There is no wood.

CRAIG: "How much wood would a woodchuck chuck, if a woodchuck could chuck wood?" Today's her birthday, you know.

BRIAN: It's tomorrow.

CRAIG: Isn't that odd?! I always get the date mixed up. I remember that last party of hers. Mother insisted that she wear her pink dress, the one with the ribbons. She hated it. And the decorations were "pukey." That was her favorite word at the time. And, to top it all off, in all the excitement her best friend hadn't been sent an invitation. I remember your saying, in that unctuous tone of yours, "After all, my dear Prue, this is not your wedding day. It's just another birthday, my dear." But it wasn't, was it, just another birthday?

BRIAN: Is it all over between Pam and you?

CRAIG: It is as far as I'm concerned.

BRIAN: May I ask why?

KINGDOM BY THE SEA

CRAIG: Because I am sick to death of emotional blackmail. When and if I ever join the "Establishment" it will be of my own volition.

BRIAN: I see.

CRAIG: "It will be the day of my castration, when I have no further use for love. It will be the day that beauty dies and the money changers begin to count the rising and the setting of the sun."

BRIAN: That sounds vaguely familiar.

CRAIG: It's from "The Fair Winds Return," a memoir in the form of a novel by one Craig Wood.

(TERRY reenters.)

TERRY: Lunch is ready. It's simple, I must warn you.

BRIAN: Simple is fine. *(To Craig.)* Won't you join us?

CRAIG: Why? Are you coming apart?

BRIAN: Those, I'm afraid, are the jokes.

CRAIG: A touch of humor is always welcome. It alleviates the gloom. I'd better wash up. *(HE goes off.)*

BRIAN: Good idea. Shall we?

(BRIAN starts off. TERRY is about to follow him when SHE stops. The drapes billow out. SHE stands frozen.)

BRIAN: What is it? What's the matter? *(HE notices the drapes.)* It's just the wind. *(HE pulls open the drapes. The French doors are wide open. HE closes them.)* Are you all right? You look so pale.

TERRY: It's this godawful weather. I'm used to the sun.

BRIAN: It rains in California as well.

KINGDOM BY THE SEA

TERRY: I keep thinking about that man out there, the one that escaped. Do we know anything about him?

BRIAN: I don't think so. Why do you ask?

TERRY: I keep wondering what he's like? What he's doing out there in the cold and the rain? And why was he there in the first place? In that institute, I mean. And where's his family? Where are the people that loved him once? Is he all alone in the world, with no one to care whether he lives or dies?

BRIAN: Subject for a novel. You're not crying, are you?

TERRY: That's all right. I cry at weddings.

BRIAN: That I can understand. It's really coming down. *(He draws the drapes.)* Come on. Let's have some lunch.

> *(BRIAN approaches TERRY and puts his arm around her shoulder. SHE stiffens. HE withdraws his arm. TERRY goes off. BRIAN sighs and follows her off.)*

Scene 2

(An hour later. There is a rumble of thunder in the distance. CRAIG enters from the interior and walks restlessly about the room. HE lounges on a chair, rises, then picks up the phone and dials.)

CRAIG: Pam, did I leave my manuscript in your apartment? Would you look on the table near the sofa? Thank you. What's that? No. There's no need. Just leave it downstairs with the doorman. No, we haven't discussed it yet. Aren't you being a little premature? I'm not asking for your opinion. That's a lot of nonsense. Look...

(CRAIG stands listening for a moment, then slams the phone down as BRIAN enters.)

BRIAN: Was that the phone?

CRAIG: Wrong number.

BRIAN: Which wrong number was that?

CRAIG: Why can't people mind their own business? People are always telling me what to do.

BRIAN: That's never bothered you before, since you always end up doing exactly as you please.

CRAIG: Oh, really? And how did I end up at Yale?

BRIAN: You were lucky enough to be accepted.

CRAIG: And why was I accepted?

BRIAN: Probably because your grandfather and I contributed handsomely to the Alumni Fund.

CRAIG: Exactly.

BRIAN: Craig, I had no objection to your going to any university that would have you. As I recall, your grades were not very good.

KINGDOM BY THE SEA

CRAIG: My grades were acceptable, and I wanted to go to Northwestern.

BRIAN: Did you apply to Northwestern?

CRAIG: You know perfectly well that I didn't.

BRIAN: Why didn't you?

CRAIG: Because Mumsie forbade me to, that's why. She said it would break your heart.

BRIAN: That was your mother's doing, not mine.

CRAIG: She put it into words, that was the only difference.

BRIAN: Craig, whatever you do with your life is fine with me, just so long as you're really happy doing it.

CRAIG: And suppose I told you that I've decided to be a writer, a novelist to be specific?

BRIAN: There's always room for another Hemingway, or another F. Scott Fitzgerald.

CRAIG: What about Jack Kerouac? Or another Henry Miller?

BRIAN: If you're going to be a novelist, why not the best?

CRAIG: Henry James, perhaps? Or William Makepeace Thackery?

BRIAN: Why not Craig Wood?

CRAIG: "Barkus is willing." You still haven't told me what you think of my novel?

BRIAN: When have I had the chance?

CRAIG: Dad, I submitted the novel to you over three months ago.

KINGDOM BY THE SEA

BRIAN: Your whereabouts for the past three years, to say nothing of the past three months, have been a deep dark secret.

CRAIG: Well, I'm here now.

(BRIAN picks up his attaché case, rummages through it and pulls out a manila folder which he hands to CRAIG.)

CRAIG: What's this?

BRIAN: I've had several of our editors read your novel. These are their reports.

CRAIG: You mean you never even bothered to read it yourself?

BRIAN: I read it the first week-end after I received it.

CRAIG: Is your report in there as well?

BRIAN: I haven't written a report?

CRAIG: You didn't think it was important enough to bother with.

BRIAN: I didn't write a report because it would have been impossible for me to be objective.

CRAIG: I see.

BRIAN: As a matter of fact, I removed your name from the manuscript. I didn't want anyone to know that the author was my son. However, I will say this: I was very impressed and very proud of all the effort that went into this book.

CRAIG: In other words, the only thing you found commendable about it was the fact that I actually sat down and took the trouble to write it.

BRIAN: There were portions of your book that were extremely well written, which came as no surprise to me since you do have a way with words. Which is to say, since the day you learned to speak you have been anything but inarticulate.

CRAIG: Are you interested in publishing it?

BRIAN: Not in it's present form, no. What are you smiling at?

CRAIG: Of course, it's really not the sort of thing you publish.

BRIAN: Then why did you give it to me?

CRAIG: Because it was turned down by Harcourt-Brace, by Random House, by Viking and by Doubleday.

   (TERRY enters.)

TERRY: I'm sorry. Am I interrupting?

CRAIG: That's quite all right. It was nothing of importance. *(HE bows deeply, folder in hand, and strides off.)*

TERRY: Has he always been that dramatic?

BRIAN: He fancied himself as an actor once, until he learned that you actually had to memorize your lines and then repeat them night after night. That was an excellent lunch, by the way.

TERRY: You're being kind.

BRIAN: No, really.

TERRY: Actually I am good at whipping things up, when I have the time and all the ingredients.

BRIAN: We have all week-end.

TERRY: Yes, I know.

BRIAN: You've been so tense since we got here. Are you still chilly?

KINGDOM BY THE SEA

TERRY: I've been chilly ever since I came East.

BRIAN: Would you like a sweater?

TERRY: No, that's all right. Were you discussing Craig's novel when I came in?

BRIAN: I was trying not to. I gave him all the reports.

TERRY: Including mine?

BRIAN: Yours was the only really good one.

TERRY: I wish you hadn't done that.

BRIAN: Why not?

TERRY: It wasn't meant for the author.

BRIAN: I'm sure he'll be very grateful to you.

TERRY: What happened to his lady friend?

BRIAN: The romance is over apparently. It's a pity.

TERRY: Do you know the girl?

BRIAN: Her name is Pamela Stratton. I've watched her grow from a gawky little girl with braces, to a lovely, intelligent young woman. It's ironic.

TERRY: Why do you say that?

BRIAN: They loathed each other as children.

(There is a loud clap of thunder.)

BRIAN: What a dreary week-end!

KINGDOM BY THE SEA

TERRY: Oh, come now, Brian! The week-end's just begun. The rain may stop any minute now. The clouds may drift away, and the world may be flooded with sunshine.

BRIAN: Well, I'm glad to see your spirits have recovered.

TERRY: You're the eternal optimist.

BRIAN: At the moment, I do not feel very optimistic. Come, sit beside me and tell me all about yourself.

TERRY: What would you like to know?

BRIAN: Everything...from the moment you saw the light of day till...*(HE looks at his watch.)*...two fifteen this afternoon.

TERRY: If the bridge is flooded, how do we get out of here?

BRIAN: Don't change the subject.

TERRY: No, really.

BRIAN: The highway is less than two miles away and easily accessible. Now...

TERRY: What do you want to know?

BRIAN: I know nothing about you really, except that you're dedicated to your work. There must be more to you than that.

TERRY: Not really, no. I'm not very interesting.

BRIAN: Let me be the judge of that.

TERRY: I have no social graces, no small talk. My only interest is books.

BRIAN: You have no social life whatsoever?

KINGDOM BY THE SEA

TERRY: Oh, I do have some friends, I suppose. Writers, editors, people in the business...and not many of those. I think I'm very lucky though.

BRIAN: In what way?

TERRY: Most people wander through life not knowing what they want. It seems to me I've always known.

BRIAN: And that's it? No family, no husband? No children?

TERRY: I would like a child some day, I suppose. I don't know when I'd find the time to raise it though. My plate is full as it is.

(CRAIG reenters with the manila folder which he hands to BRIAN.)

CRAIG: Thank you.

BRIAN: You've read them all?

CRAIG: It's not exactly "War And Peace."

BRIAN: You may keep them if you like. I had them run off especially for you.

CRAIG: They're not the sort of thing I would paste in my scrapbook, if I had a scrapbook, that is. *(HE draws open the drapes and stands looking out.)* It's pouring.

(There is silence.)

TERRY: What was that?

BRIAN: I didn't hear anything.

TERRY: I thought I heard someone knocking. There it goes again.

(A faint knocking sound is heard.)

KINGDOM BY THE SEA

BRIAN: Someone's at the front door. *(HE starts off.)*

TERRY: Brian...

BRIAN: Yes? What is it?

TERRY: Be careful.

CRAIG: Do you want me to go?

BRIAN: If you're worried about the madman, I don't think he would bother to knock. *(HE goes off.)*

CRAIG: The master has spoken.

(After a moment BRIAN reenters.)

BRIAN: There was no one there.

(The knocking is heard again.)

CRAIG: It's the back door.

BRIAN: I'll go. *(HE goes off.)*

TERRY: I'll be glad when this week-end is over.

CRAIG: It's this house. It has a way of closing in on you.

(After a moment BRIAN reenters carrying his raincoat.)

BRIAN: I think it's the elm. Every once in a while a branch breaks off and beats against the roof. *(HE goes off.)*

TERRY: Do you believe in predestination?

CRAIG: What do you mean by predestination?

TERRY: I mean that our lives are all laid out before we're even born?

KINGDOM BY THE SEA

CRAIG: You mean there's no such thing as free will?

TERRY: I was just asking.

(CRAIG goes to the French doors and opens them.)

CRAIG: The rain has stopped.

(CRAIG steps out onto the terrace. BRIAN reenters. The telephone rings and BRIAN picks it up. CRAIG comes back into the room and closes the French doors.)

BRIAN: Hello? Oh, Sam. Yes? What is it? Where are you? I'll be right over. *(HE hangs up.)*

CRAIG: What is it?

BRIAN: It's Sam Barton. He's stuck in the mud near the Jefferson place. I'll be right back.

TERRY: Brian?

BRIAN: Yes? What is it?

TERRY: That noise?

BRIAN: It's the elm. I'll take care of it when I get back. *(HE goes off.)*

TERRY: Shall we turn on the radio? There may be some news.

(CRAIG turns on the radio. Classical music is heard.)

CRAIG: The news usually comes on at three. *(HE turns down the volume.)* You're not really worried, are you? With two strapping men to protect you? How long have you been with Beechwood Press?

TERRY: It's been almost a year.

CRAIG: Do you like it there?

KINGDOM BY THE SEA

TERRY: Like it?

CRAIG: Are you comfortable there? Are you happy there?

TERRY: I never thought about it. I have a job to do and I do it.

CRAIG: Do you always see eye to eye with paPAH?

TERRY: No, of course not. But we do agree enough of the time.

CRAIG: You are T. H., aren't you?

TERRY: When I wrote that report... Never mind.

CRAIG: That's not fair.

TERRY: Your father never should have shown you my report.

CRAIG: Why not?

TERRY: He never told us who the author was.

CRAIG: Would you have written it differently if you had known?

TERRY: It's been quite some time since I wrote that report.

CRAIG: What you wrote was...and I quote: "This author shows promise. I think he should be encouraged. With certain revisions..."

TERRY: Yes, I remember.

CRAIG: Did you mean it?

TERRY: Why would I write something I didn't mean?

CRAIG: Well, you are in the minority. No, I take that back. One report said, "Not entirely without talent." I suppose that was meant as a compliment.

KINGDOM BY THE SEA

TERRY: I would certainly take it as such. Don't forget, we read hundreds of books.

CRAIG: I've been toying with the idea of embarking on a writing career. That is to say, I'm thinking of revising it. What do you think?

TERRY: It's a personal decision.

CRAIG: I'm asking you for your opinion.

TERRY: I wrote my opinion.

CRAIG: Then you would encourage me to go on.

TERRY: No.

CRAIG: Why not?

TERRY: The life of an artist is not an easy one.

CRAIG: Then you would not encourage me to go on.

TERRY: I would not encourage anyone to be a writer, unless it's something he absolutely had to do. Unless, writing for him or her was compulsive. And it wouldn't hurt if one happened to be independently wealthy, which may be the case with you.

CRAIG: Unfortunately not. In case you haven't heard, I am a spendthrift, a wastrel, a ne'er-do-well and I haven't a penny to my name.

TERRY: I'm sure you can find something else to do with your life.

CRAIG: Ah, but you see, doctor, that's my problem. I can't do anything else. Except, perhaps, play a good game of tennis. Not good enough, however, to be a pro. I'm awfully good at making love. Unfortunately that's hardly a proper career...for a man, at any rate.

TERRY: But suitable for a woman?

KINGDOM BY THE SEA

CRAIG: Love is a woman's destiny. Well, sort of.

TERRY: What did you have in mind when you wrote that book?

CRAIG: Nothing. I just felt like writing a book. I've always been more of a doer than a thinker. I guess it's the thinkers that are at a premium.

TERRY: True originality is rare.

CRAIG: What, exactly, is originality?

TERRY: I think it's a way of looking at things that is peculiarly one's own. It's putting into words something all of us have thought but never quite articulated. One thing it is not, is being different merely for the sake of being different.

CRAIG: And that's what you think of my book?

TERRY: I never said that.

CRAIG: Do you think "The Fair Winds Return" is original?

TERRY: No.

CRAIG: Then that settles that. You're really very irritating. One minute you say one thing. The next you say another. What do you really think?

TERRY: What difference does it make what I think?

CRAIG: I'd like to know.

TERRY: And your decision to continue with your writing would be based on what I think?

CRAIG: Well, no, not exactly.

TERRY: Then what difference does it make what I think?

KINGDOM BY THE SEA

CRAIG: Are you putting me on? You're testing me, aren't you? You really ought to smile more often. What makes you tick, Miss Helenski?

TERRY: I thought we were discussing your book.

CRAIG: We were. And now we're discussing you.

TERRY: Let's stick to the book.

CRAIG: I find you an enigma.

TERRY: I'm very flattered.

CRAIG: I think you're afraid of me.

TERRY: Now why should I be afraid of you?

CRAIG: I don't know. Perhaps I can reach a part of you that no one's ever reached before.

TERRY: You're very sure of yourself, aren't you?

CRAIG: On the contrary. That's my appeal. Little boy lost. No, seriously. We're all of us born with a smattering of talent, aren't we? It's a gift we're given as a child. Most people don't pursue it though. Or perhaps when they decide to pursue it it's too late. If I decide to be a writer I'd want to be the best, otherwise what would be the point? You do agree with that, don't you? May I ask you a personal question?

TERRY: That all depends.

CRAIG: Why did you decide to become an editor?

TERRY: I don't have the talent to be a writer.

CRAIG: Your report is very well written.

KINGDOM BY THE SEA

TERRY: Oh, I can be quite articulate when it comes to someone else's work. I seem to be blessed, or cursed, with the mind of a critic. I wish I could turn if off.

CRAIG: But that, in itself, is a gift.

TERRY: It's a burden.

CRAIG: I suppose I don't have anything profound to say, but I would like to share what I've experienced with others. Of course, as you say in your report, the book has no structure and yet it cries out for one and, maybe if I worked long and hard, I could find it. You look so sad. Did I say something to offend you?

TERRY: No. You remind me of someone.

CRAIG: A lover? Your brother? What happened to him? Do you mind talking about it?

TERRY: He died very young.

CRAIG: I understand...

TERRY: Yes, he took his own life.

(The knocking sound is heard.)

CRAIG: You're trembling.

TERRY: I'm chilly.

(CRAIG leans over and kisses her.)

CRAIG: I'm sorry. I shouldn't have done that.

TERRY: *(SHE rises and walk about.)* I keep thinking of him, lying out there in the cold and the rain. He couldn't stand to be cooped up.

CRAIG: It's hard to let go.

KINGDOM BY THE SEA

TERRY: I don't like New York. It's a cruel city. All those pale, lonely faces...lost, wandering about. Huddling for shelter in doorways, and no one seems to care. They step over people lying in the street. Some of them are deeply disturbed, I know that. And they're filthy and they smell, and they can be nasty to boot. But they weren't always like that. And I wonder, how did they lose their way? Why did they give up? I wake up at night sometimes and I lay there, thinking...all that human debris...

CRAIG: How old was your brother when he died?

TERRY: Twenty six.

CRAIG: What about your mother and your father?

TERRY: What about them?

CRAIG: Are they still alive?

TERRY: I don't know.

CRAIG: Aren't you in touch with them?

TERRY: My brother and I disowned them a long time ago.

CRAIG: It's usually the other way around.

TERRY: When we were young, they were terrifying monsters. Now they're just a couple of pitiful drunks. Have you ever been locked up?

CRAIG: You mean in prison?

TERRY: My parents used to lock us up in the closet, my brother and I, for safe keeping they said. He was younger than I was and very sensitive. I came home from school one afternoon and found him chained to the radiator. The heat was on and Phil was lying on the floor, soaking wet.

CRAIG: How awful!

KINGDOM BY THE SEA

TERRY: We ran away once. And once...I almost killed my father. I tried to stab him with a bread knife. And I would have, if I hadn't been stopped. That was after he'd beaten my brother in a drunken rage. He broke his arm and fractured his ribs. The police came and they called for an ambulance. They let me ride with Phil to the hospital. He was in terrible pain and I kept reciting our favorite poem, over and over. "It was many and many a year ago,/ In a kingdom by the sea,/ That a maiden there lived whom you may know/ By the name of Annabel Lee."

CRAIG: "I was a child and she was a child,/ In this kingdom by the sea,/ But we loved with a love that was more than love...I and my Annabel Lee."

TERRY & CRAIG: "And neither the angels in heaven above,/ Nor the demons down under he sea,/ Can ever dissever my soul from the soul/ Of the beautiful Annabel Lee."

TERRY: Edgar Allan Poe was our favorite poet. We spent every moment that we could in the public library. We would read everything...poetry, history, novels, biographies. And we vowed that when we grew up we would dedicate our lives to literature. Phil would write great books...poetry and novels...and I would be his inspiration, his guide, his muse.

CRAIG: Why did he kill himself?

TERRY: He worked for years on this one novel. He put his heart and his soul into it. It was to be his masterpiece. When it was accepted we were both delirious. And then there was a delay, and another, and another. And finally it was decided that they wouldn't publish it.

CRAIG: And that's why he killed himself? One disappointment? At the age of twenty six?

TERRY: How did you feel when your book was rejected?

CRAIG: I was disappointed, of course, and depressed. But if you're dead, that's the end. There's no chance of improving it, or writing something else.

KINGDOM BY THE SEA

TERRY: My brother felt that he'd been judged and found wanting, and if he couldn't be a great writer...well, there wasn't any point in going on.

CRAIG: *(After a moment)* I could use some coffee. How about you?

TERRY: It'll give us something to do, at any rate.

> *(THEY look at one another. TERRY turns away and heads toward the kitchen. CRAIG follows her off. After a moment the French doors open slowly and a breeze seems to sweep through the empty room.)*

ACT II

(An hour later. The French doors are still open. The rain has stopped. BRIAN enters from the front of the house. HE closes the doors and looks about.)

BRIAN: Craig? Craig?

(CRAIG enters.)

BRIAN: Have you been outside?

CRAIG: No. Why?

BRIAN: The door was wide open.

CRAIG: It must have been the wind.

BRIAN: Where's Terry?

CRAIG: She's upstairs, lying down. She's got a slight headache. Would you like some coffee?

BRIAN: I would love some coffee.

(CRAIG goes off. BRIAN takes off his raincoat and tosses it onto a chair. HE stands looking out the French doors. CRAIG reenters with a mug of coffee which he hands to BRIAN.)

BRIAN: Thank you.

CRAIG: Has there been any news?

BRIAN: Not that I know of.

CRAIG: What was her brother like?

BRIAN: Phil? Why do you ask?

CRAIG: Apparently they were very close.

KINGDOM BY THE SEA

BRIAN: Phil was, what we used to call in the thirties, a "Bohemian."

CRAIG: And what, exactly, is a Bohemian?

BRIAN: A Bohemian was someone who thought he was above it all. Most of them were just plain lazy.

CRAIG: He did write some books, didn't he?

BRIAN: There was one slim volume of poetry, which he published himself.

CRAIG: Did you read it?

BRIAN: I skimmed through it once. Fancy paper, ten or twelve words to a page. Pretentious dribble, as far as I was concerned. And then there was his novel. Novella, actually. It ran less than ninety pages.

CRAIG: Which you thought good enough to publish.

BRIAN: Not really, no.

CRAIG: You took it on, didn't you?

BRIAN: At the insistence of Adam Brandt. He threatened to quit if I didn't. I'm afraid that Adam was more enamored of the boy than he was of his literary gifts. I took an option on the book, on the condition that there were to be major rewrites.

CRAIG: You don't usually do that, do you?

BRIAN: Adam was the best in the business. I didn't want to lose him. Oh, I suppose the boy did have something to offer. I don't know. At any rate, I'm not even sure that he was aware of the conditions. Adam was very protective. And the boy could certainly turn on the charm. I will say that for him. As a matter of fact, he was quite witty at times. We later found out he was hooked on heroin.

CRAIG: Did Terry know that?

KINGDOM BY THE SEA

BRIAN: I really don't know.

CRAIG: How well did you get to know him?

BRIAN: We met for lunch a few times, the three of us...Adam, Phil and myself. There was something too eager about the boy, almost feverish. One minute he was begging for your approval. The next he was insulting you.

CRAIG: That might have been the dope.

BRIAN: Quite possibly. At any rate, there were no rewrites, to speak of, that is. I think he may have changed a comma or two. Finally, I lost patience and I dropped the option.

CRAIG: And he committed suicide. Have you ever talked to her about him?

BRIAN: Not really, no. I met her for the first time when she came East for the funeral. I found out that she was looking for a job and I offered her one.

CRAIG: Out of guilt?

BRIAN: No, not out of guilt. She seemed highly intelligent and very efficient. And we had an opening. Adam retired after Phil killed himself.

CRAIG: Or because you were attracted to her?

BRIAN: I do not hire people on the basis of physical attraction.

CRAIG: Do you believe in mental telepathy?

BRIAN: Terry claimed she knew the minute her brother died. As a matter of fact, it was her call that prompted Adam to look in on him.

CRAIG: Is he the one that found him?

BRIAN: Yes. I've got to change. I'm soaked through.

KINGDOM BY THE SEA

CRAIG: Dad...

BRIAN: Yes, Craig? What is it?

CRAIG: I've decided to go ahead with my book. My novel.

BRIAN: Good luck.

CRAIG: The only problem is I just happen to be broke.

BRIAN: There's always a job waiting for you at Beechwood Press.

CRAIG: I'm aware of that. I was hoping...

BRIAN: What?

CRAIG: That you might sponsor me. While I worked on the rewrites.

BRIAN: I see. And how long would you say these rewrites would take?

CRAIG: I don't know. A year, maybe less. It took me about a year or so to write the book...on and off, that is.

BRIAN: So, you want me to support you for a year. Is that it?

CRAIG: Maybe less.

BRIAN: And then what? After you've finished the rewrites?

CRAIG: The book is published and it becomes a best seller.

BRIAN: Well, just for the sake of argument, mind you, suppose no one wants to publish your book?

CRAIG: Why argue?

BRIAN: Craig, there is that very remote possibility that no one will buy your book after it is rewritten.

KINGDOM BY THE SEA

CRAIG: Why don't we cross that bridge when we come to it?

BRIAN: Do you know how many books are written every year, compared to the number that are published? As I understand it, you wrote that book in your spare time? Is that correct?

CRAIG: You want me to continue to work on my book in my spare time. Is that it? While I held down a full time job?

BRIAN: It has been done, you know. Herman Melville...

CRAIG: I know all about Herman Melville. The answer is no. Is that what you're trying to tell me?

BRIAN: I cannot back a project that I don't believe in.

CRAIG: You don't believe in me, is that it?

BRIAN: I believe in your potential, Craig.

CRAIG: But not as a writer.

BRIAN: If you have the makings of a writer, it will out.

CRAIG: You took on Phil Helenski, didn't you?

BRIAN: Exactly.

CRAIG: A perfect stranger? As I recall, Brian, you didn't make it on your own.

BRIAN: It just so happens that Beechwood Press was a going concern when I took it over.

CRAIG: But not going well.

BRIAN: Craig, your grandfather left you five hundred thousand dollars. I offered to invest it for you, but no, you insisted on enjoying life while you were still young. That was your decision and, for all I know, maybe it was the right one.

CRAIG: It was closer to four hundred and fifty thousand.

BRIAN: And, as far as Beechwood Press is concerned, I did not get the money from my father. He refused to lend it to me. I took out a bank loan, and I went into debt.

CRAIG: So, because your father turned you down, you're going to turn me down, is that it? Oh, come on, Dad, you have it. You have it to spare. I'm your only son and heir. You yourself have said so, I don't know how many times. Okay, okay. Forget it. I'll go to Mumsie.

BRIAN: I wish you wouldn't.

CRAIG: Why not?

BRIAN: For one thing, she doesn't have it. The fact of the matter is your mother, against my advice, made some very bad investments. She lives comfortably. I've seen to that. As a matter of fact, I don't think she's fully aware of the extent of her losses, and there's really no need for her to know, at this point.

CRAIG: When did all this come about?

BRIAN: A year or so ago.

CRAIG: Why wasn't I told?

BRIAN: For one thing, you weren't here. And if you had known what would you have done? At any rate, I hope you will spare your mother the embarrassment of having to turn you down. And now, if you will excuse me, I would like to change.

> (BRIAN goes off. CRAIG paces about. The telephone rings. CRAIG picks it up.)

KINGDOM BY THE SEA

CRAIG: Yes? Oh. What is it? *(HE listens. After a moment)* Pamela, what is it you want of me? Hello? Hello?

(HE slams down the phone, heaves a sigh, hesitates, picks up the phone, changes his mind and puts it down again. HE sits tensely. The knocking sound is heard.)

CRAIG: Oh, shut up!

(The knocking sound is heard again. CRAIG claps his hands over his ears. The knocking grows louder. HE rises and goes off to the kitchen, reentering with a saw. TERRY enters in an attractive house coat.)

TERRY: Where are you going?

CRAIG: That branch is driving me crazy.

TERRY: It seems to have stopped.

CRAIG: For the moment.

TERRY: You're not going out like that?

CRAIG: It's stopped raining, and it's not that cold.

TERRY: You'll get yourself all dirty.

CRAIG: I don't have any other clothes.

TERRY: Maybe your father has some overalls he can lend you.

(CRAIG sits with a sigh.)

TERRY: Have you spoken to him?

CRAIG: Oh, yes.

TERRY: And?

KINGDOM BY THE SEA

CRAIG: He offered me a job. He's never encouraged me, never.

TERRY: Maybe if I had a talk with him.

CRAIG: Forget it. I squandered my inheritance, and Daddy's going to teach me a lesson.

TERRY: Maybe he's just testing you.

CRAIG: You don't know Brian. "Some day, Son, you're going to thank me for this. This hurts me more than it hurts you."

TERRY: Maybe he's right.

CRAIG: That's not the real reason.

TERRY: What is the real reason?

CRAIG: He's afraid that I'm going to succeed where he has failed. Ah, you didn't know that did you? As a matter of fact, no one does. Brian Wood wrote a novel once. Not one, but two.

TERRY: How do you know that?

CRAIG: I came across them in the attic, quite by accident. Two manuscripts in a box, with an envelope full of rejections slips. It's a deep dark secret. Even my mother doesn't know.

TERRY: I guess all of us are frustrated writers, when it comes right down to it.

CRAIG: Brian Wood is a cold-hearted son-of-a-bitch. He destroyed my mother. Oh yes, he did. He just stopped loving her, just like that. He blamed her for my sister's death, because she was the only one in the house at the time that it happened. The truth of the matter is the fault was his, not hers. We were not allowed to go swimming in the pond by ourselves. That was the law, and my sister knew that. But she was Daddy's darling. She could do as she pleased. He spoiled her to death. That's what he did. And what about your brother?

KINGDOM BY THE SEA

TERRY: What about him?

CRAIG: He knew how sensitive he was. He knew how much that novel meant to him, and he just cut him off, just like that. *(After a moment)* I suppose you think I'm wrong to go ahead with the novel.

TERRY: I told you what I thought.

CRAIG: Not really, no. You've never really told me what you thought my chances were.

TERRY: Of what?

CRAIG: Of being a success as a writer.

TERRY: I think you know full well that no one can predict what's going to sell. You asked me if I thought you were a writer, and I said yes, I thought you were. And as far as your father is concerned, I don't think he's going to cut you off without a cent. And if he does...

CRAIG: Then what?

TERRY: And if you're really serious about working on your book...

CRAIG: Then what?

TERRY: I'll sponsor you.

CRAIG: Oh?

TERRY: I have large, lovely loft with an extra room, at the moment full of junk. It'll take me a couple of hours to clean it out...and voila, you've got a room to work in or live in...or whatever. And, as far as food is concerned, I can always throw an extra chop on the pan. You can look upon it as a loan.

CRAIG: Do you make it a habit of sponsoring all the promising writers you come across?

KINGDOM BY THE SEA

TERRY: I don't come across that many. And I can assure you that your chastity will be perfectly safe, if that's what you're concerned about.

(The sound of the knocking is heard again.)

CRAIG: That branch is driving me out of my mind.

(CRAIG rises, picks up the saw and starts off. BRIAN enters in fresh clothes.)

BRIAN: Where are you off to?

CRAIG: I'm going to cut off that branch.

BRIAN: I'd better give you a hand.

CRAIG: I don't need your help.

TERRY: Don't you have something for him to wear?

BRIAN: There's a pair of overalls in the kitchen closet.

(CRAIG goes off to the kitchen.)

BRIAN: That's a very becoming outfit.

TERRY: Thank you, sir. Has there been any news?

BRIAN: Not really, no.

TERRY: Do you mind if I turn on the radio?

BRIAN: Go right ahead.

(TERRY turns on the radio. Loud jazz is heard. SHE changes the station. There's static. SHE turns the radio off.)

BRIAN: Terry...

KINGDOM BY THE SEA

TERRY: Yes? What is it?

BRIAN: If you want to leave, we can. This whole week-end has been a bust. What with the weather and all.

(CRAIG reenters wearing a pair of overalls. HE picks up the saw.)

BRIAN: I'd better give you a hand.

CRAIG: It won't be necessary. *(HE goes off.)*

TERRY: *(After a moment.)* I understand you don't approve of Craig going on with his novel.

BRIAN: Is that what he told you?

TERRY: Am I wrong?

BRIAN: I simply told him that I had no intention of sponsoring him.

TERRY: Why not?

BRIAN: Because I think it's about time that boy came down to earth. You may not be aware of it, Terry, but Craig has always been irresponsible. He always opted for the easy way out.

TERRY: Oh, come now, Brian, you and I know perfectly well that writing a novel can be very hard work.

BRIAN: You and I may be aware of it, but I don't think that sonny boy is. My son is under the impression that being a novelist means attending cocktail parties and giving interviews and appearing on talk shows.

TERRY: I think you're doing him a great injustice.

BRIAN: Terry, Craig has been spoiled from the cradle...by his mother, by his grandfather, by his aunts, by all his adoring relatives.

KINGDOM BY THE SEA

TERRY: He's resentful of the fact that you've never showed him any affection.

BRIAN: Yes, well Craig is very adept at arousing sympathy in the bosom of all the women he comes in contact with.

TERRY: Do you really think he's that manipulative?

BRIAN: When you have children of your own, you will find that it comes natural to them.

TERRY: In case you haven't noticed it, Craig is not a child any longer.

BRIAN: I beg to differ with you. Craig is Peter Pan and Huckleberry Finn and Little Lord Fauntleroy all rolled into one. Not that I blame him. Being an adult isn't all fun and games.

TERRY: I've told him that if you're not willing to help him out, that I would.

BRIAN: I hope that doesn't mean you're going to ask for a raise.

TERRY: I've offered him the use of my loft. I do have that spare room.

BRIAN: I see. And you're offering it to him to work in?

TERRY: Or live in, or both. I'm gone all day, and the place is certainly large enough for the two of us, without our getting in each other's way.

BRIAN: I wish you wouldn't do that, Terry.

TERRY: Why not?

BRIAN: I'm in love with you, Terry. I have been since the day we first met.

TERRY: Really, Brian...

KINGDOM BY THE SEA

BRIAN: It's true. I haven't spoken sooner... Well, for one thing, I think you may still be trying to come to terms with your brother's death, and...

TERRY: And...?

BRIAN: And I think that, perhaps, you may hold me responsible.

TERRY: I've never said that, Brian.

BRIAN: Not in so many words, perhaps. God knows, I never meant your brother any harm. But it is true I offered him hope when, in my heart of hearts, I really didn't believe in his book.

TERRY: Then why did you take it on?

BRIAN: Because of Adam.

TERRY: And that's why you won't help Craig, because you don't want to give him any false hope? Is that it?

BRIAN: That's one of the reasons.

TERRY: It's all a game of chance, isn't it? Chance. Luck. Call it what you will. The only thing we have to go on is our instinct.

BRIAN: And your instinct tells you that Craig has the makings of a writer? Terry, please, I beg of you, don't mess up our lives for the sake of a foolish boy.

TERRY: What are you afraid of, Brian? That I'm going to hop into bed with a foolish boy?

BRIAN: Craig may have the mind of a boy, but his body is that of a healthy young male.

TERRY: It is a dilemma, is it not? A dilemma that is easily solved.

BRIAN: Now who's being manipulative?

KINGDOM BY THE SEA

TERRY: I believe in the novel, Brian, and I think Craig needs my help.

BRIAN: He needs a good, swift kick in the ass.

(CRAIG reenters.)

CRAIG: The damned handle came off. Don't we have an axe around here somewhere?

BRIAN: We did have. I lent it to the Jeffersons, and they never returned it.

CRAIG: I thought I saw one in the garage.

BRIAN: There is no axe in the garage.

CRAIG: I'll double check. *(HE goes off.)*

BRIAN: If Craig has any talent at all, it's a talent for having his own way. If you don't mind my saying so, Terry, you're making the same mistake you made with your brother.

TERRY: And what mistake was that?

BRIAN: Reading into Craig things that are simply not there. We both of us know that it takes a hell of a lot more than talent to make an artist.

TERRY: You're jealous of him, aren't you? I don't mean only in regard to me. I'm talking about that novel of yours. The one you have buried in your attic.

BRIAN: How do you know about that?

TERRY: What difference does it make?

BRIAN: I was never really serious about my writing.

TERRY: Then why did you write, not one, but two novels?

KINGDOM BY THE SEA

BRIAN: One and a half.

TERRY: Which you submitted to a number of publishers.

BRIAN: I submitted just the one.

TERRY: And how many publishers did you submit it to?

(CRAIG reenters, wearing his raincoat.)

CRAIG: I'm going into town. I'm going to pick up an axe.

BRIAN: It's almost four o'clock.

CRAIG: Richards is open until six, as I recall.

BRIAN: In this weather?

CRAIG: The rain has stopped. Would you care to come with me, Terry?

TERRY: As a matter of fact, I could use some air. Give me a couple of minutes to change.

CRAIG: Take your time.

(TERRY goes off.)

BRIAN: The roads are not very good.

CRAIG: I'll drive carefully.

BRIAN: As a matter of fact, they're predicting a thunderstorm.

CRAIG: We'll be back in twenty minutes. Why don't you come along? This house is so depressing. I can't understand why you insist on holding onto it.

BRIAN: It's my home, and yours as well.

KINGDOM BY THE SEA

CRAIG: This house is full of decay and death.

BRIAN: Aren't we all?

CRAIG: We are getting morbid in our old age. Sorry, old boy. Middle age.

BRIAN: Craig...

CRAIG: Yes, Dad? What is it?

BRIAN: I understand that Terry has offered to...sponsor you.

CRAIG: Yes. Isn't that generous of her?

BRIAN: Are you going to accept?

CRAIG: I told you, Dad, I'm broke.

BRIAN: And you're going to let a woman keep you?

CRAIG: Isn't that awful?!

BRIAN: I don't want you to move in with her.

CRAIG: Why not?

BRIAN: Because I happen to be in love with her. And I intend to marry her.

CRAIG: Does she know that?

BRIAN: Well, sort of.

CRAIG: And how does she feel about it?

BRIAN: I think, in time, she'll come around.

CRAIG: Then there's nothing to worry about.

KINGDOM BY THE SEA

BRIAN: We're not married yet. As a matter of fact...we're not even lovers.

CRAIG: And you're afraid that if I move in with her, she'll succumb to my manly charms. Is that it? Well, that shows very little faith in the woman you intend to make your wife.

BRIAN: Terry is very vulnerable at the moment. She still hasn't gotten over the death of her brother. I don't want to see her hurt again.

CRAIG: I assure you, Dad, I have no intention of going to bed with a woman that you happen to be in love with.

BRIAN: She takes you seriously...as a writer, that is.

CRAIG: Isn't it a pity one has to turn to the kindness of strangers?!

BRIAN: Okay, okay. How much are you asking?

CRAIG: Oh, come on Dad!

BRIAN: All right, let me put it in another way. How long do you think it will take you to finish your rewrites?

CRAIG: I don't know. One month, two. Maybe six. I don't know.

BRIAN: And how much money do you think you will need to live on? Per week. Don't forget, you can live here, or you can share my apartment. I've got two bedrooms.

CRAIG: Five hundred.

BRIAN: Make it three. Three hundred dollars a week, until you finish your rewrites.

CRAIG: As long as it takes?

BRIAN: As long as it takes.

KINGDOM BY THE SEA

CRAIG: Three hundred dollars?

BRIAN: You won't be giving any parties, I assume.

CRAIG: No, of course not.

BRIAN: And you won't be paying any rent.

CRAIG: But three hundred dollars?

BRIAN: I'm not going to quibble. I'll write you a check every week, to cover your expenses. You can consider it an advance on your book. And Beechwood Press will have first refusal.

CRAIG: It's a deal. Well, this calls for a drink. Scotch?

BRIAN: Nonsense. This calls for champagne. I have some in the fridge.

(BRIAN goes off. CRAIG sits, lost in thought. The knocking sound is heard. CRAIG rises and paces about. TERRY reenters wearing a dress and a raincoat.)

TERRY: All set. Where's Brian?

CRAIG: He's in the kitchen. There's been a change of plans.

TERRY: Oh?

CRAIG: He's going to sponsor me after all.

TERRY: How did that come about?

CRAIG: What difference does it make? He's going to foot the bills, until I've finished my book. And, in exchange, he wants first refusal. Which is only fair, don't you think? There are times, you know, when I have been sort of hard on the old man. My mother is not the easiest person to get along with. And, now that I think about it, he has been more than patient with her. He's jewed me down to three hundred dollars a week, but he's not going to quibble.

KINGDOM BY THE SEA

(BRIAN reenters with champagne and three glasses on a tray.)

BRIAN: Here we are. Have you heard the good news?

TERRY: Yes, I have.

BRIAN: I thought you'd be pleased.

TERRY: What made you change your mind?

BRIAN: I've had second thoughts. I must admit your arguments have been most persuasive.

TERRY: Which arguments are those?

CRAIG: It's not important. The important thing is the old boy has come to his senses. He finally realizes how absolutely brilliant I am.

TERRY: I'm sorry to disappoint you, Craig. It's not your book your father's interested in.

CRAIG: What difference does it make?

TERRY: It makes all the difference in the world. Your father took on my brother's book because he wanted to hold on to Adam Brandt. Don't you see? He's making the same mistake all over again. The truth of the matter is your father has no intention of publishing your book.

BRIAN: That isn't true.

TERRY: Do you believe in the book or don't you?

BRIAN: In it's present form, no.

TERRY: And do you really believe that Craig is capable of whipping it into a form that's acceptable to you?

BRIAN: I don't see why not.

KINGDOM BY THE SEA

CRAIG: There you are? Now, what's the matter?

TERRY: Nothing, Craig. You are perfectly free to accept your father's offer.

CRAIG: Then we can go ahead as planned.

TERRY: Not we, my dear. You.

CRAIG: Why not?

TERRY: Because I couldn't possibly work with you under those conditions?

CRAIG: What conditions? What are you talking about?

TERRY: If your father's going to publish the book, fine. Are you going to publish it, Brian?

BRIAN: That all depends...

TERRY: Not good enough.

CRAIG: But I need you, Terry. You're the only one that understands. You understand the book better than I do.

BRIAN: There's no need to decide right now. Why don't we open the champagne while it's still cold?

TERRY: I thought we were going into town.

CRAIG: That's right. We'd better get going before the store closes.

BRIAN: Terry, I'd like you to stay. There's something I'd like to discuss with you.

TERRY: Don't you think we've had enough discussion for one afternoon?

BRIAN: It's about your brother. Why don't you go on ahead, Craig.

KINGDOM BY THE SEA

(CRAIG looks at TERRY. SHE looks away.)

CRAIG: Okay, okay. But don't you two do anything I wouldn't do. It's a joke, kids. It's a joke. I'll be back in a jiffy.

BRIAN: Drive carefully.

CRAIG: Yes, PaPAH.

(CRAIG goes off. There is a clap of thunder. The candles flicker.)

BRIAN: I hope we have enough candles.

TERRY: There are plenty of candles, Brian.

BRIAN: Why don't we have some champagne?

TERRY: What is it you wanted to talk to me about?

BRIAN: There's something I think you ought to know.

TERRY: Well?

BRIAN: Your brother left a suicide note.

TERRY: A suicide note?

BRIAN: Adam and I decided not to show it to you. As a matter of fact, he and I are the only ones that have seen it.

TERRY: Why wasn't I told?

BRIAN: I'm going to have some champagne. Won't you join me?

TERRY: Thank you, no.

BRIAN: Then I'll have to drink alone. *(HE opens the bottle, pours a glass and takes a sip. After a moment.)* You know, of course, that your brother was hooked on dope.

KINGDOM BY THE SEA

TERRY: He smoked "pot" now and then.

BRIAN: It was far more serious than that.

TERRY: He may have sniffed cocaine once. He didn't care for it though.

BRIAN: He was shooting heroin. And he was deep in debt.

TERRY: I know that, Brian. I'm still paying them off.

BRIAN: Many of them were paid before you even got here.

TERRY: By you?

BRIAN: No, by Adam. He was keeping your brother.

TERRY: What are you trying to prove?

BRIAN: I don't want to hurt you, Terry, but I think it's about time you knew the truth.

TERRY: And what might that be?

BRIAN: Your brother gave up the ghost long before he took his own life.

TERRY: What is that supposed to mean?

BRIAN: He was interested only in this image he had of himself, that you had of him. He was not prepared for, nor was he really interested in, rolling up his sleeves and sitting down at his typewriter and putting in a day's work.

TERRY: Are you trying to say that Phil was a dilettante, a phoney?

BRIAN: I wouldn't put it that way.

TERRY: How would you put it?

BRIAN: I know it's hard for you to accept, but...

KINGDOM BY THE SEA

TERRY: Phil was a human being. He got depressed, from time to time, like all of us do. He needed love. He needed encouragement, like all of us do from time to time. Like your son does now. I don't expect you to understand. You were born with a silver spoon in your mouth. You were never faced with the harsh realities of life.

BRIAN: That's not true.

TERRY: Have you ever gone hungry, Brian? Have you ever really come in contact with poverty, with cruelty, with all the ugliness in the world? Yes, Phil was weak. Don't you think I know that? How strong would you have been if you had been beaten before you could even walk? If you had gone without a decent meal for days at a time? Yet we survived, Phil and I. We came through unscathed...inside...where it really mattered.

BRIAN: Maybe you did, Terry.

TERRY: What do you know about the pain an artist goes through, the agony he suffers to produce the merchandise that you sit in your comfortable office and peddle?

BRIAN: I never claimed to be more than a business man. But, at least, I'm an honest one.

TERRY: It pays to be honest, doesn't it?

BRIAN: And I face the facts.

TERRY: And what facts are those?

BRIAN: You've been fooling yourself, Terry. You've painted this idyllic picture of you and your brother, two twin souls united against the world.

TERRY: What are you trying to say? That Phil and I loved one another? Of course, we did. Our relationship was a special one. Oh, we may have had lovers, from time to time, but none of them ever competed with the special bond that the two of us had. None of them ever came close.

BRIAN: When and if you read that note...

KINGDOM BY THE SEA

TERRY: I don't care about any note. He was probably depressed when he wrote it. He was never satisfied with what he put down on paper. It never lived up to his vision. A true artist's work never does. Rewriting was painful for him.

BRIAN: There were no rewrites, Terry. That's what I'm trying to tell you. And, besides, it wasn't the rewrites he was troubled by.

TERRY: What was it then?

BRIAN: It was that compact the two of you made when you were children, that oath that the two of you signed in blood. He was afraid if you knew that he'd broken that pact, that he would lose you. And that was something your brother could never face.

TERRY: In other words you're holding me responsible for my brother's death. Is that it?

BRIAN: We knew you might think that. That's why we never showed you the note.

TERRY: I know Phil. He would never give up. It was you that gave up on him. You rejected him just when he needed you the most. Phil lived for his art. That was all he lived for. And if that failed him, there was no reason for him to go on living. My brother and I inhabited a world that you could never understand. The stark simplicity of his work, his economy, his imagery, the delicacy of his vision... Phil never wrote a sentence, a word that wasn't true, that wasn't filtered through the agony of his existence.

BRIAN: Okay, Terry...

TERRY: He was everything that you are not. In two or three years time...maybe sooner, if I can raise the money, I'm going to publish a memorial edition of his work. And then, maybe he will receive the recognition that he so richly deserves, the recognition that you denied him.

KINGDOM BY THE SEA

BRIAN: *(After a moment)* Terry, the only genuine thing about your brother was his love for you. And Craig is your brother all over again. For the moment, perhaps, he's swept away by the things you wrote in your report, by your enthusiasm. Inside of a month, I promise you, my son is going to miss all the parties, all the fun, all the luxuries of life that he's become accustomed to.

TERRY: It all comes down to money, does it not?

BRIAN: Not really, no.

TERRY: You know perfectly well that it does. But after you're gone, he's going to come into it anyway, isn't he? Isn't he?

BRIAN: Yes, of course.

TERRY: Well, then?

BRIAN: He's just going to have to wait until then, I'm afraid.

TERRY: I see.

(There is a pause. Suddenly TERRY looks about.)

BRIAN: What is it?

TERRY: What was that?

BRIAN: What?

TERRY: I thought I heard a noise. Out there, on the terrace. There it is again.

BRIAN: I didn't hear anything.

TERRY: There's someone out there, Brian. I'm sure of it.

BRIAN: Stand over there. Out of the way.

KINGDOM BY THE SEA

(BRIAN takes down the rifle and starts toward the French doors. TERRY blows out the candles. BRIAN opens the French doors and steps out onto the terrace.)

BRIAN: There's no one out here.

TERRY: There is. I'm sure of it.

BRIAN: Okay, okay. I'll take a look around.

TERRY: You're not going to leave me here alone?

BRIAN: *(HE comes back into the room and hands the rifle to TERRY.)* The safety catch is on, just in case. *(HE starts off.)*

TERRY: Brian!

BRIAN: What is it?

TERRY: Your raincoat. It's starting to rain again. *(SHE hands him his raincoat.)*

BRIAN: I'll be right back.

(BRIAN puts on his raincoat and goes off to the terrace. TERRY releases the safety catch and stands facing the French doors. There is a long pause. SHE raises the rifle as BRIAN comes through the door and fires twice. HE falls to the floor. SHE walks over to him and looks down. Seeing he is dead SHE sets down the rifle. SHE drags the body out onto the terrace then comes back into the room. SHE picks up the rifle, sits and waits. SHE sets down the rifle, paces about. SHE hears something, picks the rifle up again and sits. CRAIG enters.)

CRAIG: The store was closed. I guess they close early on Saturday. *(HE glances from TERRY to the open door.)* What is it? What's the matter? What's happened?

TERRY: There was an accident.

KINGDOM BY THE SEA

CRAIG: What happened?

TERRY: We thought there was someone out there. Your father went out to look. He handed me the rifle. And then I saw this man in a raincoat... It was dark. And I panicked.

CRAIG: Is he...?

TERRY: I'm afraid to look.

(CRAIG goes out onto the terrace and then comes back in.)

TERRY: Is he...?

CRAIG: He's dead. How did it happen?

TERRY: I just told you.

CRAIG: Yes. Yes, of course. I'd better call the sheriff. *(HE looks up a phone number then dials.)* Hello? Mrs. Barton? It's Craig. Craig Wood. Is your husband there? There's been a terrible accident. It's my father. He's dead. Thank you. Could you tell Mr. Barton when he does call in? Thank you. *(HE hangs up.)* We can't leave him out there in the cold.

(TERRY rises.)

CRAIG: That's all right. I can manage.

(CRAIG goes out onto the terrace. TERRY walks over to the fireplace and hangs the rifle on the wall. BRIAN drags the body into the house and lays him out in the middle of the room.)

CRAIG: He's heavier than I thought.

TERRY: Don't you think we ought to close his eyes?

CRAIG: *(HE closes BRIAN's eyes.)* He looks so young. Actually he was still in his fifties. Fifty nine, I think. Or was it fifty eight?

KINGDOM BY THE SEA

TERRY: We ought to cover him.

(TERRY gets a dust cloth from the cupboard and brings it to CRAIG.)

TERRY: Craig...

CRAIG: Oh. Thank you. Maybe we better put him on the sofa. Do you mind?

(SHE sets down the dust sheet.)

CRAIG: If you'll get his legs.

(TERRY takes hold of BRIAN's legs. CRAIG lifts the upper part of his body and THEY place him on the sofa. CRAIG covers the body with the dust cloth.)

CRAIG: It's so dark in here.

TERRY: I'll get some matches.

(TERRY goes off. CRAIG sits, lost in thought. TERRY reenters with the matches. SHE lights one but her hand is trembling badly. SHE blows out the light.)

CRAIG: Here. Let me. *(HE lights the candles.)* Are you all right?

TERRY: I just can't believe that it happened. It was all so quick.

CRAIG: Yes, of course. It was an accident. *(HE sits)* I knew he'd leave us one day, but not like this. It's this damned house. It's cursed. Poor Dad. In spite of everything, however, he really was a happy man. I remember the first time I visited him at Beechwood Press. I couldn't believe it. He was a different man. There was a twinkle in his eye, something I'd never seen before. It occurred to me that the man actually had a sense of humor. And he was so well liked. I looked around at the office, at the people around him and I said to myself, "This is his home, his real home." I should call my mother. *(HE picks up the phone and dials.)* No answer. *(HE hangs up.)* I'm the head of the family now. Isn't that a kicker?

TERRY: What will you do?

CRAIG: I don't know.

TERRY: I guess you won't have to worry about a place to stay. Of course, he did come around in the end. What I mean to say is, he was going to sponsor you after all.

CRAIG: Ironic, isn't it?

TERRY: Yes, isn't it.

CRAIG: He left everything to me, you know. He kept telling me that he would. Beechwood Press as well.

TERRY: That's another thing you won't have to worry about. He's often said that Beechwood Press could run itself.

CRAIG: I doubt it. He was the heart and soul of that place. He resented his dependence on textbooks, you know. He always said he wanted to publish more fiction, literature, poetry even. And most of all he wanted to discover new writers.

TERRY: Perhaps our first discovery will be you. That would be a fitting memorial, wouldn't it?

CRAIG: Quite possibly. Under the circumstances, however, I'm going to have to put the novel aside, for a while at any rate. There's the estate, and the lawyers and all that sort of thing.

TERRY: Knowing Brian, I'm sure he made the necessary arrangements.

CRAIG: And, of course, there's still Beechwood Press. I'll have to take over, for a while, at least. At least until things run smoothly. I'll need your help, of course.

KINGDOM BY THE SEA

TERRY: Yes, of course.

CRAIG: It might even be fun, you know. He certainly seemed to get a kick out of being a publisher. It's odd, you know.

TERRY: What's that?

CRAIG: I think I knew even then, that this was going to be my destiny. He was one of the few people I know that really enjoyed doing what he did, and I envied him. I've always had this energy, this drive and no place to put it. Wouldn't it be ironic if that place was right under my nose? It's funny all the phases a kid goes through. First you want to be a fireman, then a policeman, then a cowboy.

TERRY: Yes, well, that was a long time ago.

CRAIG: I'm really a very silly young man, when you come right down to it. And actually I'm not that young anymore.

TERRY: What about your novel?

CRAIG: You know something, Terry. As a publisher I'm not quite sure I would take it on. Isn't that a kicker?

TERRY: Just because you're taking over Beechwood Press, if that's what you're planning, there's really no reason to give up on your novel, Craig.

CRAIG: Oh, I'm not giving up on it. I'll get back to it one of these days, when I have a more mature outlook on life. I forget who it was... but someone once said one should never write anything until one was thirty. And remember what you said about being a writer?

TERRY: What was that?

CRAIG: That one shouldn't be a writer unless you absolutely had to be, unless it was compulsive. While I was driving into town I was thinking, "I'm a writer now. I'm a writer now." And I saw myself sitting in front of my typewriter with that blank piece of paper staring me in the face. And suddenly I got that awful feeling in the pit of my stomach. How am

KINGDOM BY THE SEA

I going to fill that blank piece of paper? Oh, I love the idea of being a writer, but I wonder if I'm really ready to pay the price. Of course, what really teed me off was that my own father didn't have enough faith in me.

TERRY: But even before that, Craig, you wanted to go on with your book.

CRAIG: It was your report that really did it. And then when you said that you're be willing to back me up. It was like a dream come true. The only trouble with dreams is you've got to wake up eventually. Oh, I've always been a little in love with books, but not enough to marry them, I guess.

TERRY: And now it's time to get married? Is that it?

CRAIG: Do you know Pamela Stratton? In a way you're very much like her. I was amazed to find out how strong she is. I guess I don't have the courage to work without a net. And that's what it takes, I think. That sort of courage. Are you all right?

TERRY: Yes, I'm fine.

CRAIG: You look so sad.

TERRY: Do I?

CRAIG: What are you thinking?

TERRY: I'm thinking...

CRAIG: Yes?

TERRY: The world is full of pygmies.

CRAIG: Not while you're around. You are a giant, Terry.

TERRY: Ah, but you see, there is no room in the world for giants.

CRAIG: The first thing I'm going to do is to sell this house.

KINGDOM BY THE SEA

TERRY: I hope you get a good price for it, Brian. What?

CRAIG: You called me Brian.

TERRY: Did I?

(The sound of the knocking is heard.)

CRAIG: I'd better call my mother. I just did, didn't I? Excuse me. *(HE goes to the phone and dials.)* Hello? Don't hang up on me, please. I've got to talk to you. It's my...Dad. He's dead. *(HE begins to weep.)*

(TERRY, unseen by CRAIG, takes the rifle down and goes off through the French doors.)

CRAIG: What's that? No, it was an accident. I can't believe it. It's like the world has come to an end. My world, at any rate. You don't have to. If you really want to... But drive carefully, the roads...

(A shot is heard. CRAIG looks around.)

CRAIG: Pam... Pam, I'll call you right back. *(HE hangs up and goes to the French doors.)* Terry? *(HE looks out.)* Terry? Oh, Jesus!

(A breeze blows the drapes. The golden rays of the setting sun light up the room. The knocking sound is heard again, gently, as if from a distance. Silence.)

THE LIBERATION OF LINDA DWORKIN

A Comedy In Two Acts

CAST OF CHARACTERS

Linda Dworkin

Bernie Dworkin

Melanie Dworkin

Sherry Dworkin

Fran Jackson

Sam Sotherby

Gloria Nussbaum

Sylvia Dworkin

Dan Dworkin

SCENE

The home of Linda and Bernie Dworkin, somewhere in the Midwest, not too long ago. There are two levels. Visible on the lower level are the den and the living room, separated by the vestibule. Visible on the upper level are Melanie's room and Sherry's room.

ACT I

Scene 1

The phone in the vestibule rings. LINDA DWORKIN, an attractive woman in her early forties, enters and picks up the phone.

LINDA: Hello? Fran? Where are you? Now listen, you're staying with us. I don't want to hear any arguments. Well, bring her along. Him, then. We've got plenty of room.

(MELANIE DWORKIN, age fifteen, and SHERRY DWORKIN, age thirteen, enter from the outside carrying books. THEY kiss LINDA and march up the stairs to their rooms where THEY deposit their books.)

LINDA: Well, Bernie is still in the office, otherwise he'd pick you up. You have the address. We'll see you soon. Good-bye.

(LINDA hangs up and stands lost in thought. MELANIE and SHERRY come down the stairs.)

LINDA: Did you wash?

MELANIE & SHERRY: Yes, Mother.

(The GIRLS go off to the kitchen. LINDA picks up the phone and dials.)

LINDA: Hello, Glenda. Is the doctor busy? *(To the GIRLS in the kitchen.)* Don't touch the cheese cake! *(Into the phone.)* Bernie? This won't take a minute. Fran is here. Fran Jackson, my old roommate. I just wanted to let you know, that's all. She'll be staying with us...and a friend of hers. Yes.

(MELANIE and SHERRY enter with glasses of milk and cookies.)

LINDA: *(To the GIRLS)* Don't get crumbs on the floor.

MELANIE & SHERRY: Yes, Mother.

THE LIBERATION OF LINDA DWORKIN

LINDA: *(Into the phone)* Yes, yes. Good-bye. *(SHE hangs up.)*

MELANIE: How long will she be here?

(The doorbell rings.)

SHERRY: I'll get it. *(SHE dashes off.)*

LINDA: Don't run, Sherry.

MELANIE: How long will she be here?

LINDA: Who, dear?

MELANIE: Fran Jackson.

LINDA: I don't know.

(SHERRY enters with GLORIA NUSSBAUM, a woman in her early forties.)

MELANIE: Hello, Mrs. Nussbaum.

GLORIA: Hello, dear.

LINDA: What's it like out?

GLORIA: Haven't you been out?

LINDA: Today's my wash day.

GLORIA: You let them eat in the living room?

MELANIE: We're very clean.

LINDA: Don't be fresh, dear.

MELANIE: I wasn't being fresh. Honestly...!

THE LIBERATION OF LINDA DWORKIN

LINDA: That's enough. Where are you going?

MELANIE: I'm going to wash my glass. I don't want to leave any dirt. *(SHE goes off to the kitchen.)*

SHERRY: We're not animals. We're human beings. *(SHE goes off to the kitchen.)*

GLORIA: I'm sorry.

LINDA: It's not your fault. What's the matter? Have you got a headache?

> *(MELANIE and SHERRY reenter.)*

LINDA: Please bring me a couple of aspirins and a glass of water.

> *(MELANIE and SHERRY go off. GLORIA starts to sob uncontrollably. MELANIE and SHERRY reenter. MELANIE hands LINDA the aspirins and SHERRY the water. LINDA shoos them off.)*

GLORIA: I don't want any aspirins. I just want to die.

LINDA: Now stop it!

GLORIA: I just can't go on.

LINDA: Don't be ridiculous. You've got your whole life ahead of you.

GLORIA: I have nothing to live for, absolutely nothing. One minute I'm a wife and a mother. Now I'm nothing.

LINDA: You still have Irving.

GLORIA: He doesn't need me anymore. He's out on his own.

LINDA: He needs you more than ever.

THE LIBERATION OF LINDA DWORKIN

GLORIA: And what about me? What am I gonna do with my days? Not to mention my nights.

LINDA: Gloria, you're still young. You'll find someone else.

GLORIA: I don't want someone else. I'll never get married again, never. Let this be a warning for you. Don't put all your eggs in one basket. Jerry was perfectly healthy and then boom. If Bernie should die, God forbid, that's the end. And as for our children, they're passing through, that's all, just passing through.

(MELANIE and SHERRY reenter carrying books and start off.)

LINDA: Where are you going?

MELANIE: For our piano lessons.

LINDA: I thought you had Hebrew school today.

SHERRY: That's afterwards.

LINDA: And come right home. You hear me?

MELANIE: Mother, you've been acting very strangely lately.

(MELANIE and SHERRY go off.)

GLORIA: I don't even have a daughter to talk to.

LINDA: You have a sister.

GLORIA: In Florida. And besides, have you ever tried talking to Frances? I'll take that aspirin after all. *(SHE takes the aspirins and swallows them down with water.)* Are those new curtains?

LINDA: No. I just had them cleaned. Would you like some coffee?

GLORIA: I need something.

THE LIBERATION OF LINDA DWORKIN

LINDA: Tea? Milk? Soda? Seltzer?

GLORIA: Keep going.

LINDA: Would you like something to <u>drink</u>? Gloria!

GLORIA: Please. I'm not turning into a lush. I take a drink once in a while.

LINDA: Brandy?

GLORIA: Let it be brandy.

LINDA: Apricot brandy? If you want something stronger...

GLORIA: Linda, apricot brandy will be fine.

LINDA: I'm not a prude, but it is the middle of the day.

> *(LINDA goes to the bar in the den. GLORIA inspects the curtains. LINDA brings the brandy to GLORIA.)*

GLORIA: You sure you can spare it?

LINDA: If you want some more, you can have it.

> *(The doorbell rings and SYLVIA DWORKIN, Linda's mother-in-law, enters carrying a large bag. SYLVIA and LINDA kiss.)*

LINDA: What are you doing here?

SYLVIA: I brought you some meatballs.

LINDA: Thank you. You remember Gloria.

SYLVIA: Yes, of course. I'm sorry to hear about your loss.

GLORIA: Thank you.

THE LIBERATION OF LINDA DWORKIN

SYLVIA: How's your son?

GLORIA: He's fine. Thank you for asking. He's in college now. He's going to Michigan.

LINDA: Excuse me. *(SHE goes off with the meatballs.)*

SYLVIA: *(Calling to LINDA)* When you heat them up, be sure to put a little water in. *(To GLORIA)* Isn't this a lovely home? Every time I come here I just "kvell."

GLORIA: Linda is an excellent housekeeper. She puts us all to shame.

(LINDA reenters.)

LINDA: Would you like some coffee?

SYLVIA: We don't have time. We're invited to dinner.

LINDA: Where's Dan?

SYLVIA: He's parking the car.

(DAN DWORKIN enters and kisses LINDA.)

DAN: How's my favorite daughter-in-law?

LINDA: Fine. How are you feeling?

DAN: So so. Where are the kids?

LINDA: They went for their piano lessons.

SYLVIA: The minute he steps in the door.

DAN: They're my granddaughters. I have a right to ask about them, don't I?

GLORIA: You have every right.

THE LIBERATION OF LINDA DWORKIN

DAN: How are you?

SYLVIA: Gloria lost her husband.

DAN: I know.

LINDA: Have you seen Bernie?

DAN: We just came from the office. I broke a tooth. That's why we're here. Excuse me. *(HE goes off.)*

SYLVIA: He's not well.

LINDA: What's the matter with him? Has he seen a doctor?

SYLVIA: Three of them.

LINDA: What do they say?

SYLVIA: They don't know. And he's sick.

GLORIA: They're bloodsuckers, everyone of them.

SYLVIA: You're telling me?

GLORIA: It costs more money to die than to live. My poor Jerry suffered so. May they rot in hell.

(Dan reenters.)

SYLVIA: Why do you keep going to the bathroom? Will you tell me?

DAN: I think I have to go, and then when I get there...I don't.

GLORIA: You should see a doctor, a good one. If you can find one.

DAN: Good doctors, like good women, are hard to find.

SYLVIA: Enough with the jokes already?

THE LIBERATION OF LINDA DWORKIN

LINDA: *(To DAN)* Would you like some tea?

SYLVIA: We really have to go.

LINDA: But you just got here.

DAN: What time do the kids get home?

SYLVIA: Again with the kids. You'd think they were the only two people in the world.

LINDA: They won't be home for, at least, a couple of hours.

SYLVIA: You'll see the girls on the week-end. Did you ever see anything like it? He lives for those two girls.

GLORIA: What else is there?

SYLVIA: But there's a limit. It's Melanie did this and Sherry said that. I mean after a while people get bored. Believe me, I'm just as proud of my grandchildren as he is, but I don't talk about them all the time. I think they're the most beautiful girls in the world, and the cleverest, but there are other topics of conversation.

DAN: You're worse then I am.

SYLVIA: I can't help it. I love them, and I'm not ashamed of it.

GLORIA: And you have every right to be proud of them. Linda and Bernie are doing a wonderful job bringing up those girls. If I had daughters of my own, I would want them to be exactly like Melanie and Sherry. *(SHE stifles a sob.)*

SYLVIA: *(Empathizing)* "Oy, Gottenyou!" *(SHE dabs her eyes.)*

LINDA: Excuse me. *(SHE goes off to the kitchen.)*

SYLVIA: We've got to be going.

THE LIBERATION OF LINDA DWORKIN

(The doorbell rings.)

SYLVIA: Linda...!

LINDA: Coming.

SYLVIA: It's the doorbell. I'll get it.

(SYLVIA goes off. LINDA enters from the kitchen. FRAN JACKSON, a beautiful woman in her early forties, enters from the outside, followed by SAM SOTHERBY, a hulking, not unattractive man in his forties, followed by SYLVIA.)

FRAN: Linda! Oh, my dear!

(FRAN and LINDA embrace.)

FRAN: Let me look at you.

LINDA: Well, say it.

FRAN: Well, Poopsie, you were never really chic, but I think you're aging beautifully. You've got character in your face.

LINDA: I've always had character in my face.

FRAN: Character, my dear, is nothing to be ashamed of. I can't wait till I get some character. I love your house, that is...

LINDA: You hate it.

FRAN: This is Sam Sotherby.

SAM: How do you do. *(HE shakes hands with LINDA.)*

LINDA: This is my mother-in-law, Mrs. Dworkin, and this is my father-in-law.

SAM: How do you do.

THE LIBERATION OF LINDA DWORKIN

LINDA: And this is a friend of mine, Gloria Nussbaum.

FRAN: Where are your little girls?

LINDA: They're taking their piano lessons.

DAN: Sylvia...

>(SYLVIA motions for DAN to be quiet. She's not ready to go.)

LINDA; Would you like to wash up?

FRAN: I'd love to.

LINDA: Come along.

>(LINDA leads FRAN off.)

SYLVIA: Tell me Mr. Sotherby, why is there so much violence in your pictures?

SAM: My dear lady, I don't make them. I just appear in them.

SYLVIA: I don't approve of violence.

GLORIA: Neither do I.

DAN: Sylvia, he said he doesn't make them.

SYLVIA: He appears in them.

SAM: I abhor violence myself, but it is a part of our lives.

SYLVIA: Maybe your life, but not ours.

>(MELANIE and SHERRY enter from the outside. MELANIE is carrying all the books, while SHERRY holds a bloody handkerchief to her knee.)

THE LIBERATION OF LINDA DWORKIN

SYLVIA: My God! What happened?

MELANIE: She fell.

SHERRY: I was pushed. George Martin pushed me.

SYLVIA Let me see. All right, all right. It's nothing. Linda! Linda!!

(LINDA has just come down the stairs.)

DAN: Sylvia, she's right here.

LINDA: What happened?

SYLVIA: The child is bleeding to death.

MELANIE: Oh, Grandma, for heaven sakes! It's just a bloody knee.

LINDA: All right, Melanie. That's enough.

MELANIE: For heaven sakes!

LINDA: Take her upstairs.

MELANIE: Come on, clumsy.

SHERRY: It wasn't my fault.

(MELANIE and SHERRY go off.)

LINDA: Knock on the door. There's someone in the bathroom.

SYLVIA: "Oy Gottenyou!" My nerves. I can't take it.

DAN: All right, Sylvia. Calm down, calm down.

SYLVIA: Did you see that handkerchief? It was full of blood. And she looked as white as a sheet. Maybe you ought to take her to a doctor.

THE LIBERATION OF LINDA DWORKIN

LINDA: She'll be all right.

SYLVIA: I think I'm going to be sick.

LINDA: Sylvia, it was nothing. It happens every day.

SYLVIA: That knee was scraped to the bone.

> *(BERNIE DWORKIN, a pleasant looking man in his early forties, enters from the outside.)*

BERNIE: I thought you had a dinner date. What's the matter?

SYLVIA: It's Sherry.

LINDA: She's all right. She scraped her knee.

BERNIE: Where is she?

LINDA: Melanie is taking care of her. Bernie, this is Sam Sotherby.

SAM: How do you do.

BERNIE: My pleasure.

> *(THEY shake hands.)*

GLORIA: I'd better be going. Do you want me to pick up those things for you?

LINDA: I hate to bother you.

GLORIA: I'm going shopping anyway.

LINDA: I have them written down. *(SHE goes off to the kitchen.)*

GLORIA: I've enjoyed your performances very much.

SAM: Thank you.

THE LIBERATION OF LINDA DWORKIN

(LINDA returns with the list which SHE hands to GLORIA.)

GLORIA: I'll drop them off in about an hour or so. *(SHE goes to the foot of the stairs.)* It was nice meeting you, Miss Jackson. Good-bye everybody.

(LINDA sees GLORIA off and comes back on.)

BERNIE: Would anyone care for a drink? Dad?

DAN: No, thank you.

BERNIE: How about you, Sam?

SAM: I wouldn't mind one.

BERNIE: Come with me.

(BERNIE and SAM go to the bar in the den.)

DAN: Have you got any aspirins?

SYLVIA: What's the matter?

DAN: You're getting a headache.

LINDA: I'll get you some.

SYLVIA: I don't want any aspirins.

DAN: Do me a favor, Sylvia, take some aspirins.

SYLVIA: Dan, please.

DAN: All right. let's go.

SYLVIA: I'm not going.

DAN: What do you mean, you're not going?

THE LIBERATION OF LINDA DWORKIN

SYLVIA: I'm not up to having dinner with Helen tonight.

DAN: But they're expecting us.

 (The phone rings.)

LINDA: Excuse me. *(SHE picks up the phone.)*

DAN: If you take some aspirins now, by the time we get back...

LINDA: Hello? Yes, Miss Bradford. Sherry fell and hurt her knee and Melanie brought her home.

DAN: So what do you want to do?

LINDA: I'll pay for the lessons, of course.

DAN: Do you want me to phone Helen and tell her that we're not coming?

LINDA: Same time next week? Thank you, Miss Bradford. Good-bye. *(SHE hangs up.)*

DAN: Sylvia, what do you want to do?

 (FRAN comes down the stairs with MELANIE and SHERRY, who wears a band-aid on her knee.)

DAN: I'm going to get a drink. *(HE goes into the den.)*

SYLVIA: Dan, don't drink! Dan! You hear me? He's not supposed to drink.

MELANIE: Mother, we've got to phone Miss Bradford.

LINDA: She just called.

MELANIE: Can she take us tomorrow?

THE LIBERATION OF LINDA DWORKIN

LINDA: Do you have to limp like that?

SHERRY: It hurts.

MELANIE: Mother...?

LINDA: Yes, dear? What is it?

MELANIE: Can Miss Bradford take us tomorrow?

LINDA: I told her you'd come next week.

MELANIE: But I was supposed to get a new piece today. I've had this same old piece for almost a month already.

LINDA: And you still don't know it. Sherry, will you please stop walking like that?

SYLVIA: Where is it written that you're not supposed to kiss your grandmother?

   (SHERRY and MELANIE kiss SYLVIA.)

SYLVIA: Boy, what a kiss!

MELANIE: Oh, Grandma!

SYLVIA: That's all right. I didn't bring you a present today, so you don't have to kiss me.

MELANIE: Really, Grandma!

SYLVIA: Really, what? Well?

MELANIE: Nothing.

LINDA: You'd better get ready for Hebrew school.

MELANIE: Do we have to go?

THE LIBERATION OF LINDA DWORKIN

SYLVIA: You're not gonna send... *(SHE stops herself.)* I won't say a word.

MELANIE: We still have plenty of time.

LINDA: You can walk slowly.

SHERRY: My knee hurts.

LINDA: Bring down Sherry's books.

MELANIE: Yes, Mother. *(SHE goes upstairs.)*

SHERRY: Do you think I'll have a scar?

LINDA: I doubt it.

SYLVIA: Excuse me.

>*(SYLVIA goes into the den. MELANIE comes down the stairs with the books.)*

MELANIE: We'll get there too early.

LINDA: Then you can study your lessons. You haven't looked at your Hebrew books all week.

MELANIE: That isn't true. *(SHE hands a book to SHERRY.)* Here. You didn't hurt your arm.

SHERRY: Some sister. You didn't even protect me.

MELANIE: I didn't know you were being attacked.

>*(SYLVIA comes into the living room with DAN.)*

SYLVIA: We'll be going. We'll drop the kids off.

MELANIE: We'll get there early as it is.

THE LIBERATION OF LINDA DWORKIN

SHERRY: Well, I can't walk.

(SHERRY limps off. SYLVIA kisses LINDA.)

SYLVIA: *(To FRAN)* It was nice meeting you. Maybe we'll see each other again.

DAN: *(HE kisses LINDA.)* Good-bye, Sweetie. *(To FRAN)* It's been a pleasure meeting you. *(To MELANIE)* Come on, Princess.

MELANIE: Oh, Grandpa!

LINDA: When do you see the doctor again? *(To FRAN)* Would you excuse me for a minute?

FRAN: Sure.

SYLVIA: We'll call you tomorrow.

> *(MELANIE, SYLVIA, DAN and LINDA go off. FRAN walks about, examining the living room. SHE picks up a piece of china, examines it and sets it down, then looks about with amusement. LINDA reenters.)*

LINDA: Jewish modern. Don't say it. I'm everything I swore I wouldn't be.

FRAN: As long as you're happy.

LINDA: You look absolutely magnificent. Are you and Sam...?

FRAN: We're fucking friends. I've shocked you.

LINDA: No. No, of course not. What about your husband?

FRAN: That prick? We're still friends.

LINDA: And your little girl?

THE LIBERATION OF LINDA DWORKIN

FRAN: That's why we're friends. He's a pig. He still lives in the Middle Ages. He can, but She can't. It's so good to see you again, Poopsie.

LINDA: Poopsie! Oh, God! *(SHE laughs.)*

FRAN: That's better. That's the old Linda Shirley Shapiro.

LINDA: Linda Shirley Shapiro. I'll never forget the expression on your face when I told you my name.

(BERNIE enters from the den.)

BERNIE: Would you ladies care for a drink?

LINDA: This is my husband, Bernie. Fran Jackson.

BERNIE: Yes, of course. Pleased to meet you.

FRAN: You never told me your husband was so attractive.

BERNIE: Ho ho! You said the magic word, and for that you get a glass of our best Scotch.

FRAN: Do you have any sherry?

BERNIE: The only wine we have is Manischewitz, left over from Passover. The Passover before last.

FRAN: I'll try it.

BERNIE: It's sweet, I'm warning you. Straight or on the rocks?

FRAN: Straight.

BERNIE: How about you, Honey? A little Southern Comfort?

LINDA: Maybe just a little.

BERNIE: That's all there is. *(HE goes to the bar.)*

THE LIBERATION OF LINDA DWORKIN

LINDA: *(After a moment)* Where are your bags?

FRAN: They're at the airport. I don't want to inconvenience you.

LINDA We're got plenty of room. You can have Sherry's room. There are twin beds in Melanie's room which Sherry often uses. And Sam can sleep in the den. The sofa opens up. It's very comfortable.

> *(BERNIE enters, carrying two glasses, followed by SAM, carrying two glasses.)*

BERNIE: Manischewitz for the movie star and Southern Comfort for Sexpot here. *(To FRAN)* If you don't like it, you can have something else. If you do, you can have the rest of the bottle.

FRAN: It is sweet.

BERNIE: How about a highball?

FRAN: No, no. It's fine.

BERNIE: Whiskey Sour? Martini? Gin and tonic? There's no extra charge.

LINDA: Bernie, she'll drink the wine.

BERNIE: If she doesn't like it, why should she drink it?

FRAN: I love it, I love it.

BERNIE: How about a Black Russian? That's...

FRAN: I know what a Black Russian is.

LINDA: Bernie, why don't you drive Sam down to the airport and pick up their bags?

FRAN: Linda, I...

THE LIBERATION OF LINDA DWORKIN

BERNIE: Sure. Let's go. Do we need any food?

LINDA: I don't think so.

> *(BERNIE goes off. SAM polishes off his drink and follows him off.)*

FRAN: I'd better call the hotel and cancel our reservation.

LINDA: It's right over there.

FRAN: *(SHE picks up the phone and dials.)* What's the number of the Blake Hotel, please? Thank you.

> *(FRAN hangs up and dials again. LINDA picks up the dirty glasses and goes into the kitchen.)*

FRAN: Hello? This is Fran Jackson. I'd like to cancel the reservations made for Mr. Sotherby and myself. Hello? That's right. I'm terribly sorry, but other arrangements have been made for us. We'd be glad to... That's very kind of you. Thank you. Good-bye. *(SHE hangs up, takes a sip of the wine, makes a face and sets it down.)*

> *(LINDA reenters.)*

LINDA We're having steak for dinner. Will that be all right?

FRAN: You're still as sexy as ever. What's the matter?

LINDA: Nothing.

FRAN: You're sure this is all right? I mean the two of us barging in on you like this?

LINDA: I want you to stay. Please. We've got so much to catch up on.

FRAN: Are you sure?

LINDA: Yes, I'm sure. So, how was your trip?

THE LIBERATION OF LINDA DWORKIN

FRAN: It is sort of stuffy in here. Let's get some air. Why don't you show me around the neighborhood?

LINDA: I've got so much to do.

FRAN: I need some air. Do you mind if I take a little walk?

LINDA: No. No, of course not.

> *(FRAN kisses LINDA on the cheek. LINDA stiffens and blushes.)*

FRAN: Relax, Poopsie. It's just old Fran. *(SHE starts off.)*

LINDA: Fran...

FRAN: Yes?

LINDA: It's good to see you.

> *(FRAN goes off. LINDA stands lost in thought for a moment, then goes off to the kitchen.)*

Scene 2

(An hour or so later. SAM and BERNIE enter from the outside, each carrying a suitcase. LINDA enters from the kitchen.)

LINDA: Fran? Oh, you're back already. Why don't you put the suitcases in the den for now.

BERNIE: Why don't we bring them upstairs?

SAM: Okay. Which room?

LINDA: Put them in the room at the end of the hall, to the left.

(SAM goes up the stairs with his suitcase and places it in Sherry's room. BERNIE starts to follow him.)

LINDA: Bernie...

BERNIE: Yes, Honey?

LINDA: They're not married.

BERNIE: I thought they were. Don't they have a little girl?

LINDA: Fran has a little girl. She's married to someone else.

(SAM comes down the stairs.)

SAM: I'll take it.

BERNIE: What's that? Oh, yes.

(SAM takes the other suitcase and goes up the stairs and places it in Sherry's room.)

BERNIE: We'll settle it later. Do you need any help?

LINDA: No, no.

BERNIE: I'm gonna wash up. Did you take the steaks out of the freezer?

THE LIBERATION OF LINDA DWORKIN

(LINDA nods and BERNIE goes up the stairs. LINDA walks about the living room, straightening things out absent-mindedly. SAM comes down the stairs.)

SAM: This is a very comfortable house.

LINDA: Thank you.

SAM: I hope we're not putting you to any trouble.

LINDA: It's our pleasure.

SAM: What does one do for fun around here?

LINDA: Fun?

SAM: Kicks. You know.

LINDA: Not very much, I'm afraid.

SAM: We'll find something. *(HE goes into the den.)*

LINDA: There's a newspaper on the coffee table.

(LINDA starts for the kitchen. FRAN enters from the outside.)

LINDA: I thought you'd gotten lost.

FRAN: Not me, Honey.

LINDA: When do your meetings start?

FRAN: Friday. Friday afternoon. At five. Are you coming?

LINDA: I don't think so.

FRAN: Why not?

LINDA: I'm not very political.

THE LIBERATION OF LINDA DWORKIN

FRAN: You used to be.

LINDA: Not really.

FRAN: I remember...

LINDA: I've got things to do in the kitchen.

> *(LINDA goes into the kitchen. FRAN goes into the den. SAM embraces FRAN and nuzzles her.)*

SAM: Love me?

FRAN: No. Mmmmm. Sam, not here.

SAM: Why not?

FRAN: The kids are liable to walk in any minute.

SAM: Which ones?

> *(FRAN breaks away.)*

SAM: What's the matter with you? I want you, Baby. Let's go upstairs.

FRAN: Not now.

SAM: *(Nuzzling her passionately.)* Oh, Jesus!

FRAN: Now stop it. We'll make up for it tonight.

SAM: Oh, Baby...

FRAN: Sam, please.

SAM: I'm almost ready to pop.

FRAN: You are a horny old thing.

THE LIBERATION OF LINDA DWORKIN

SAM: You know what I'd like to do?

(SAM whispers into FRAN'S ear and SHE giggles. BERNIE comes down the stairs. A noise is heard in the kitchen.)

BERNIE: Linda?

(BERNIE goes into the kitchen. FRAN and SAM wrestle on the sofa. LINDA comes into the living room, sits on the sofa and dries her eyes. In the den FRAN and SAM do some heavy necking and groping. BERNIE enters the living room and sits beside LINDA.)

BERNIE: What's the matter, Honey?

LINDA: I don't know. I guess I'm just tired.

BERNIE: Why did you ask them here? You've been acting strangely for the past few weeks.

(SAM keeps trying to pull down his trousers while FRAN keeps pulling them up. The doorbell rings.)

SAM: Oh, God!

BERNIE: I'll get it.

(BERNIE goes toward the front door, passing the den in time to see SAM pulling up his trousers and buckling his belt. HE does a double-take, hesitates then goes off and returns with GLORIA, holding a bag.)

SAM: Come in, come in.

(BERNIE guides GLORIA past the den, practically shoving her.)

GLORIA: Please, Bernie, this bag is heavy.

THE LIBERATION OF LINDA DWORKIN

BERNIE: I'm sorry. *(HE takes the bag.)* What have we got in here? *(HE goes into the kitchen with the bag.)*

GLORIA: *(SHE goes into the living room.)* What's the matter? Have you been crying?

LINDA: I got something in my eye.

GLORIA: Ah, yes. We can't live with them and we can't live without them. I don't know what the answer is. Jerry and I used to fight all the time. It's all a part of being married, I guess.

LINDA: Excuse me, Gloria. I've got to change. *(SHE goes up the stairs.)*

GLORIA: Yes, of course.

> *(BERNIE enters the living room.)*

BERNIE: Where did Linda go?

GLORIA: She went upstairs to change. Be patient with her, Bernie. Women are complicated creatures.

BERNIE: I've noticed that. Excuse me.

> *(BERNIE goes up the stairs. GLORIA stand lost for a moment, sighs and starts for the front door. BERNIE comes back into the living room.)*

BERNIE: I'm sorry, Gloria. How much do we owe you?

GLORIA: Fourteen dollars and ninety-five cents.

BERNIE: Can you break a ten?

GLORIA: Let me see. I've got the five cents.

> *(BERNIE raps on the doorpost next to the den.)*

THE LIBERATION OF LINDA DWORKIN

BERNIE: Excuse me. Can you break a ten?

SAM: *(Remaining seated, HE looks into his wallet.)* Sorry, old boy.

FRAN: I never carry any cash.

BERNIE: *(To GLORIA)* I'll see if Linda has a five. *(HE goes up the stairs.)*

> *(The phone rings and GLORIA picks it up.)*

GLORIA: Hello? Yes. Just a moment. *(SHE sets down the receiver.)* Bernie, it's your mother.

> *(BERNIE comes down the stairs.)*

BERNIE: Here you are dear. Thank you. *(HE picks up the phone.)* Hello? Where are you? Stay there. Mother, will you listen to me? Just stay where you are, and I'll pick you up. Ma, I know where it is. Yes. I'll start out right now. There's no need to get hysterical. I'll be there in a couple of minutes. Good-bye.

> *(BERNIE hangs up as LINDA comes down the stairs in a pair of attractive hostess pajamas.)*

LINDA: What's the matter?

BERNIE: They almost had an accident.

LINDA: Who?

BERNIE: My parents.

LINDA: Where are they?

BERNIE: A few blocks from here. They're waiting for me to pick them up. *(HE goes into the den.)* Sam, can you drive?

SAM: Why, yes.

THE LIBERATION OF LINDA DWORKIN

BERNIE: Would you mind coming with me, please? My mother and father almost had an accident. They're waiting for me to pick them up. I'll need someone to drive my car back.

SAM: Yes, of course.

(SAM starts to rise, then stuffs his hand into his pockets. FRAN turns away to conceal her smile.)

FRAN: Are they all right?

BERNIE: Yes, they're fine.

LINDA: Drive carefully.

BERNIE: Linda, please.

(BERNIE goes out the front door, followed by SAM.)

LINDA: Bernie...

(LINDA goes out the front door. FRAN comes into the living room.)

GLORIA: Her father-in-law shouldn't be driving if he doesn't feel well.

(LINDA reenters.)

GLORIA: I was just telling Miss Jackson...

FRAN: Please, call me Fran.

GLORIA: I was just telling Fran that Dan shouldn't be driving if he doesn't feel well. Is that new?

LINDA: No. I've had it for quite a while.

GLORIA: I've never seen it. It's a lovely outfit. Isn't it, Fran?

THE LIBERATION OF LINDA DWORKIN

FRAN: What? Oh. Yes, very nice.

GLORIA: What's the matter with you, Linda?

LINDA: I'm worried about the girls. They'll be waiting at the Hebrew school. Bernie usually picks them up.

GLORIA: Would you like me to get them?

LINDA: I hate to bother you.

GLORIA: Just let me put my frozen things in your refrigerator. *(SHE goes out the front door.)*

FRAN: She's very helpful.

LINDA: What's that? Yes, she is.

(GLORIA reenters with a bag.)

LINDA: *(SHE takes the bag.)* I'll take care of them. Thank you, Gloria. They're usually waiting on the corner.

(GLORIA goes out the front door.)

LINDA: Excuse me. *(SHE goes into the kitchen and reenters shortly.)* Did you enjoy your walk?

FRAN: Are you going to tell me what's wrong, or do I have to guess?

LINDA: I don't know. *(SHE starts to cry.)* I'm sorry. I don't know what's the matter with me. I think maybe I ought to see a psychiatrist.

FRAN: You're talking to one...almost. I've been in analysis so long I think I know everything there is to know about everything.

LINDA: I have a wonderful marriage. Two lovely girls. There's no reason on earth why I shouldn't be happy.

THE LIBERATION OF LINDA DWORKIN

FRAN: And you're not.

LINDA: I don't know. I keep thinking...

FRAN: What?

LINDA: I keep thinking that there ought to be more.

FRAN: Maybe there ought to be.

LINDA: But what? If I knew what I wanted I wouldn't be so upset. I feel like an absolute fool even talking about it, and I haven't spoken to anyone about it...up until now.

FRAN: Not even Bernie? Maybe you ought to discuss it with him.

LINDA: How can I expect anyone else to understand, when I don't understand it myself. Do you understand?

FRAN: Yes, I do. You have no identity.

LINDA: I don't know what you're talking about? What do you mean, I have no identity?

FRAN: Who are you?

LINDA: I'm Linda Shapiro...or rather...

FRAN: No, no, no. Stop right there. Who are you? Linda Shapiro or...Linda...

LINDA: Dworkin. But people grow up. They get married.

FRAN: Oh, Honey, people never grow up. And marriage is a trap.

LINDA: Don't you believe in marriage?

FRAN: Not in the conventional sense, no.

THE LIBERATION OF LINDA DWORKIN

LINDA: What about children?

FRAN: I have a lovely daughter. She's growing up remarkably well, and she's certainly much happier than when Andre and I were together, and at each others throats all the time.

LINDA: Does she live with Andre?

FRAN: Yes, and I see her often. We have a wonderful relationship. We're actually friends.

LINDA: But I love Bernie, I really do.

FRAN: Apparently, Poopsie, Bernie's not enough for you.

LINDA: What do you mean?

FRAN: Honey, one's first obligation is to oneself.

LINDA: But this is my life...here, with Bernie. I don't know what else I would do.

FRAN: Will you do me a favor? Will you come to the meeting with me this week-end?

LINDA: Oh, Fran...

FRAN: Linda, Women's Lib is not a joke. These meetings are being held for your benefit.

LINDA: Okay.

FRAN: You're a beautiful woman. You always have been, and I want to see you fulfilled.

LINDA: Well, I'm certainly not a movie star.

FRAN: I'm not speaking of physical beauty.

THE LIBERATION OF LINDA DWORKIN

(MELANIE and SHERRY enter.)

MELANIE & SHERRY: Shalom.

LINDA: Shalom. Did Mrs. Nussbaum pick you up?

MELANIE: We walked. Daddy said he had to pick up Grandma and Grandpa. Can I visit Rhoda after dinner?

LINDA: What about your homework?

MELANIE: I could do some of it now, and we plan to do our history together, if it's all right with you.

SHERRY: What about the dishes? It's your turn tonight.

MELANIE: We could switch.

SHERRY: I'll think about it.

MELANIE: Do you need any help?

LINDA: No, no. Go do your homework.

(The phone rings.)

SHERRY: That's for me. *(SHE picks up the phone.)* Hello? Just a moment. *(SHE hands the phone to MELANIE.)* It's for you.

MELANIE: Hello?

LINDA: *(To SHERRY)* Don't you have any homework?

MELANIE: *(On the phone)* Yes.

SHERRY: No. But I do have some reading to catch up on. Excuse me. *(SHE goes up the stairs.)*

THE LIBERATION OF LINDA DWORKIN

MELANIE: *(On the phone)* Yes. Good-bye. *(SHE hangs up.)* Oh, Miss Dworkin, may I speak to you for a moment?

(MELANIE follows SHERRY up the stairs. DAN enters, followed by SYLVIA.)

DAN: Sylvia, please, leave me alone.

SYLVIA: But you're sick. What are you gonna do? Wait until you drop dead?

DAN: I'm seeing the doctor on Monday.

(BERNIE enters.)

SYLVIA: Bernie, look at him. Does he look well to you?

DAN: Sylvia, will you stop already? I've had these attacks before.

SYLVIA: All right. I won't say another word.

BERNIE: Let me call Paul Geller.

LINDA: Excuse me.

(LINDA goes into the kitchen. BERNIE picks up the phone and dials.)

FRAN: *(To SYLVIA)* What kind of an attack did he get?

DAN: It's not good.

BERNIE: *(On the phone)* Hello, Ruth? Bernie Dworkin. Is Paul in? Can I speak to him for a minute? It's important. Hello, Paul? Fine, fine. Listen, my father's been getting these attacks. Can you take a look at him? How long will you be in? We'll be right over. Thank you, Paul. *(HE hangs up.)* His office is right around the corner. Let's go.

(SAM enters.)

THE LIBERATION OF LINDA DWORKIN

BERNIE: We're taking my father to this friend of mine. He's a doctor.

SAM: Do you want me to come along?

BERNIE: That's all right. Thank you.

SYLVIA: From here on in, I'm not going to say another word.

DAN: Sylvia, please.

>   *(BERNIE, SYLVIA and DAN go off. LINDA comes in from the kitchen.)*

LINDA: Where did they go?

FRAN: To see your doctor friend.

LINDA: Oh, Paul.

FRAN: Linda's coming to the meeting on Friday.

SAM: Oh, great.

FRAN: Would you...like to wash up, Sam?

SAM: What? Oh, sure. I'd love to wash up.

FRAN: I'll show you where the bathroom is.

>   *(FRAN and SAM go up the stairs and into Sherry's room. In the darkened room they proceed to make out. The doorbell rings and GLORIA enters.)*

GLORIA: I couldn't find them. Have they come home?

LINDA: They're here. I'm sorry, Gloria.

GLORIA: That's all right. As long as they're all right.

THE LIBERATION OF LINDA DWORKIN

(The phone rings.)

LINDA: Excuse me. *(SHE picks up the phone.)* Hello? Ma? Is everything all right.

(SHERRY comes down the stairs.)

SHERRY: Mother, may I read in your room, please?

LINDA: *(Into the phone.)* Just a moment. *(SHE looks up at SHERRY.)* What is it, Sherry?

SHERRY: May I read in your room, please?

LINDA: Yes, you may. *(Into the phone.)* I'm sorry, Mother.

SHERRY: Hello, Mrs. Nussbaum.

GLORIA: What are you reading, dear?

LINDA: *(On the phone.)* I meant to call you this morning, but this was my wash day and I got all involved.

SHERRY: It's about a girl who grew up as an orphan. *(SHE runs up the stairs.)*

LINDA: Sherry, don't run! I'm sorry, Mother. How is your back? Well, what did the doctor say?

(MELANIE comes down the stairs.)

MELANIE: Mother...

LINDA: Melanie, please. I'm talking long distance.

MELANIE: My goodness!

GLORIA: It's your grandmother, dear.

THE LIBERATION OF LINDA DWORKIN

MELANIE: I just wanted to know if we had any light bulbs.

LINDA: You know where we keep the light bulbs.

(MELANIE goes into the kitchen.)

LINDA: *(On the phone.)* I'm sorry, Mother. No, no. Everything's just fine. The children are fine. Bernie is fine. My stomach?

(MELANIE reenters.)

MELANIE: I don't see any.

LINDA: Then we don't have any. *(Into the phone.)* Well, we may be out at the end of the month. There's a three day week-end coming up.

(MELANIE goes up the stairs.)

LINDA: *(On the phone.)* Fran Jackson is visiting us. That's right. I'll write you a long letter on the week-end. Give my love to Dad. All right. Good-bye. *(SHE hangs up.)*

GLORIA: How are your parents?

LINDA: All right, I guess. Did Melanie find a light bulb?

GLORIA: No. What you need is a vacation.

LINDA: From what? I have your things in my freezer. *(SHE goes into the kitchen.)*

GLORIA: That's all right.

(SHERRY comes down the stairs with a book and stretches out on the sofa in the living room. LINDA reenters with GLORIA's bag of groceries.)

GLORIA: Thank you.

THE LIBERATION OF LINDA DWORKIN

LINDA: Thank you. Sherry, if you're going to put your feet on the sofa, take off your shoes.

SHERRY: What do we have plastic for?

LINDA: Not for dirty shoes.

GLORIA: Are you playing Mah Jong on Friday?

LINDA; I don't think so. Fran has asked me to come to one of the meetings.

GLORIA: Women's Lib? Well, I certainly don't think that's the answer.

LINDA: Gloria, at this point I'm not even sure what the question is.

GLORIA: The trouble with you is you take things too seriously. Bernie has a wonderful sense of humor. Look on the bright side of things. I'm just telling you for your own good.

LINDA: You know what, Gloria? When I want your advice I'll ask for it.

GLORIA: Well...pardon me. *(SHE stalks off.)*

SHERRY: You told her.

LINDA: I thought you liked to read in the privacy of your own room.

SHERRY: Fran and her boy friend are in my room.

LINDA: What about my room?

SHERRY: Melanie's in your room. Her lamp doesn't work. Mother, can I ask you something?

LINDA: What?

SHERRY: Do people often have sex in the daytime?

THE LIBERATION OF LINDA DWORKIN

LINDA: I beg your pardon?

SHERRY: I said, do people often have sex in the daytime?

LINDA: What brought that on?

SHERRY: Well, Melanie said that Fran and her boyfriend are having sex.

LINDA: How would she know that?

SHERRY: Well, she started to go into my room to borrow a bulb and she said it looked like they were having sex.

LINDA: I'm sure she's mistaken.

SHERRY: I doubt it. Melanie is very perceptive when it comes to that sort of thing.

LINDA: I see.

SHERRY: You still haven't answered my question.

LINDA: Which one was that?

SHERRY: Do people often have sex in the daytime?

LINDA: It has been known to happen.

SHERRY: I don't know why you get so embarrassed when I talk about sex.

LINDA: Well, Sherry, it is a sensitive subject.

SHERRY: I don't see why. It's just a bodily function.

LINDA: Who told you that?

LINDA & SHERRY: Melanie.

THE LIBERATION OF LINDA DWORKIN

LINDA: Well, Melanie's wrong. Sex is an act of love, performed by two people after they've been married.

SHERRY: Are Fran and her boyfriend married?

LINDA: They have been married, yes. And her boyfriend's name is Sam Sotherby.

SHERRY: I know his name, Mother. I've seen him in the movies.

LINDA: Then why do you keep calling him Fran's boyfriend?

SHERRY: Well, he is her boyfriend, isn't he? Isn't he?

LINDA: Well, yes. But he does have a name. How would you like it if I kept referring to you as my daughter?

SHERRY: Don't you?

LINDA: No, I don't. I refer to you as Sherry. You do have an identity of your own.

SHERRY: One would never know it.

(SHERRY picks up her shoes and her book and goes into the den, spreading out on the sofa there. LINDA follows her.)

LINDA: What did you mean by that?

SHERRY: What?

LINDA: That you have no identity.

SHERRY: That's not what I said, Mother. You're the one that has no identity. If it weren't for me and Melanie...Melanie and I...what would you be? Absolutely nothing.

LINDA: That isn't true.

THE LIBERATION OF LINDA DWORKIN

SHERRY: Isn't it? You just think about it for a while. And now, I'd like to go back to my reading, if you don't mind.

LINDA: You're the one that started this conversation, not me. *(SHE goes off to the kitchen.)*

SHERRY: Not true!

>*(SHERRY goes back to her book, puts the book aside and buries her head in her arms, spread out on the sofa. BERNIE enters from the outside, goes into the den and sits beside SHERRY.)*

BERNIE: Are you asleep?

SHERRY: Nope.

BERNIE: What are you thinking about?

SHERRY: Sex.

BERNIE: Anyone I know?

SHERRY: Oh, Daddy!

BERNIE: What is there you want to know about sex and were afraid to ask?

SHERRY: Do people often have sex before they're married?

BERNIE: Honey, haven't we been through all that?

SHERRY: Have you and Mother ever had sex with anyone else? I mean after you were married?

BERNIE: No.

>*(LINDA enters the living room and sits on the sofa, thinking.)*

BERNIE: Why do you ask?

THE LIBERATION OF LINDA DWORKIN

SHERRY: Fran Jackson and Sam Sotherby have sex.

BERNIE: How do you know that?

SHERRY: Well, don't they?

BERNIE: Sherrilah, I just met them today, and so did you, so how can you be sure they have sex?

SHERRY: That's what they're doing right now, having sex in my room.

BERNIE: As long as they don't fight. Where's your mother?

SHERRY: I don't know.

> (*SHERRY buries her head in her arms. BERNIE goes into the living room.*)

LINDA: How's your father?

BERNIE: Paul's putting him into the hospital for tests. He thinks it may be his gall bladder. Listen, Linda, these friends of yours... We've got to do something about them.

LINDA: What do you mean?

BERNIE; I mean that they're having sex all over the house. What are they, some kind of nymphomaniacs? I mean, as far as I'm concerned, they can screw all they want to, but we have kids in the house. I mean, they're not kids anymore. They're young ladies, at a very impressionable age.

LINDA: They're only going to be here for a few days, Bernie.

BERNIE: Well, if you don't say something to them, I will. (*HE goes into the kitchen and then comes out again.*) Hey, Sherry, how about giving me a hand with those steaks?! (*HE goes back into the kitchen.*)

SHERRY: Honestly, I don't know what the two of you did before we were born.

THE LIBERATION OF LINDA DWORKIN

(SHERRY goes into the kitchen. LINDA sits lost in thought.)

Scene 3

That evening. SYLVIA enters the foyer from the kitchen, picks up the phone and dials.

SYLVIA: So? How are you doing? Please, Dan!

(BERNIE enters the foyer from the kitchen.)

BERNIE: How is he?

SYLVIA: *(To BERNIE)* He was asleep.

BERNIE: *(HE takes the phone from SYLVIA.)* How are you doing, Pop? How's the food?

SYLVIA: He hardly touched a thing. Let me speak to him. *(SHE takes the phone.)* Dan, if you sleep now, you won't be able to sleep tonight.

BERNIE: Tell him I'll see him tomorrow around noon.

SYLVIA: *(Into the phone.)* Bernie'll be in to see you tomorrow noon. I'm sleeping at Gloria's. They have guests. I'll talk to you tomorrow. Yes. I'll talk to you tomorrow. Good-bye.

(SYLVIA hangs up. The doorbell rings. BERNIE goes off and returns with GLORIA.)

BERNIE: You didn't have to come over.

GLORIA: Listen, what are friends for? How's your husband, Mrs. Dworkin?

(SYLVIA shrugs and sighs.)

GLORIA: Whatever it is, if you catch it in time, you've got a fighting chance.

SYLVIA: I'll get my pocketbook. *(SHE goes upstairs.)*

THE LIBERATION OF LINDA DWORKIN

BERNIE: You don't have to leave right away.

(LINDA comes in from the kitchen.)

LINDA: Did you call your father? How is he?

BERNIE: He seems to be resting comfortably. *(HE goes upstairs.)*

LINDA: I'm sorry I snapped at you this afternoon.

GLORIA: Look, you don't have to apologize to me. I'm a lonely old busy-body, and if I stuck my nose where it didn't belong you had a right to tell me off.

(SYLVIA and BERNIE enter Melanie's room.)

BERNIE: Look, Ma...

SYLVIA: Did I say a word?

BERNIE: You don't have to.

SYLVIA: Bernie, please don't make me angry. It's your house. If there's no room, that's all there is to it.

BERNIE: What do you want me to do, kick them out?

SYLVIA: No, Bernilah, never. Better you should kick me out.

(BERNIE leaves Melanie's room. SYLVIA takes a Kleenex from the bureau and dabs her eyes. BERNIE enters the living room.)

BERNIE: Linda, can I talk to you for a minute? Would you excuse us, please?

(BERNIE takes LINDA into the den.)

LINDA: What do you want me to do? I told her she could stay here.

THE LIBERATION OF LINDA DWORKIN

BERNIE: Did you ask her?

LINDA: Where is she?

BERNIE: She's in Melanie's room.

(LINDA goes up the stairs. BERNIE goes into the living room.)

GLORIA: If there's anything I can do...

BERNIE: No, no, Gloria please! Don't do anything.

(LINDA enters Melanie's room.)

LINDA: Are you all right? Mother, you know you're welcome to stay here.

SYLVIA: No, no, Linda. Why should I put you through all that trouble?

LINDA: It's no trouble.

SYLVIA: Besides, Gloria's place is right near the hospital. I can walk over there in the morning. It's ridiculous. Gloria has an empty house. Why should we all crowd in here?

(SAM enters the living room from the kitchen.)

SAM: That was the best fuckin' steak I ever had. Bernie boy, you've really got it made out here.

GLORIA: Good evening.

SAM: Cool, Honey, cool.

LINDA: As long as you know that you're welcome.

SYLVIA: Linda, dear, you don't have to tell me that. There are times, to tell you the truth, when I feel closer to you than I do to Bernie.

THE LIBERATION OF LINDA DWORKIN

(SYLVIA and LINDA leave Melanie's room.)

GLORIA: It must be very exciting, making movies.

SAM: It's a lot of hard work. I often wonder what I would have done, if I hadn't made it as an actor.

(LINDA and SYLVIA enter the living room.)

LINDA: What would you have done?

SAM: I probably would have gone back to the farm. That's where I was raised, you know, on a farm. *(To BERNIE)* Did you ever fuck a sheep? Man, that is great.

SYLVIA: I was looking for my pocketbook.

LINDA: It's in the den. I'll get it. *(SHE goes into the den.)*

SYLVIA: That's all right. *(SHE follows LINDA into the den.)* I don't like that kind of talk. If Dan were here he would put a stop to it.

LINDA: He doesn't mean any harm.

SYLVIA: It's disrespectful. And besides, Melanie and Sherry are still children. Even if he is a movie star. And she's no better. I'm sorry, Linda. Maybe she's your friend, but that's how I feel. And maybe I'm old fashioned, but a lady is still a lady.

(LINDA picks up the pocketbook from the bar and hands it to SYLVIA.)

BERNIE: How about an after dinner drink, Sam?

SAM: Okay.

BERNIE: How about you, Gloria?

GLORIA: No, thank you.

THE LIBERATION OF LINDA DWORKIN

(LINDA and SYLVIA enter the living room.)

BERNIE: Would you like a drink, Honey?

LINDA: Not right now.

BERNIE: Ma?

SYLVIA: No, thank you.

(BERNIE and SAM go into the den.)

BERNIE: I've got something here you will really like.

(SHERRY and FRAN enter from the kitchen.)

SHERRY: Can I watch your television set, Mother? It's only nine o'clock. *(To FRAN)* Do you know Carol Burnett?

FRAN: Not really. I know Lucille Ball. I've had dinner with her.

(SHERRY goes upstairs.)

LINDA: She likes Carol Burnett.

BERNIE: Look, Sam, I don't mean to be a prude, but I wish you'd watch your language around the kids.

SAM: Sure, Bernie, sure. I understand.

FRAN: Don't they have any classes on sex education here in the schools?

LINDA: I'm afraid we're not that far advanced.

SYLVIA: Since when do they teach sex in school?

LINDA: That's been going on for a long time now.

SYLVIA: I know it's been going on, Linda. I didn't think they taught it.

THE LIBERATION OF LINDA DWORKIN

FRAN: It's better than learning it in the streets.

SYLVIA: My grandchildren don't go in the streets.

FRAN: Oh? Really?

SAM: I don't suppose you go in for group sex around here.

BERNIE: Oh, sure. But it's so hard to get a group together.

SAM: How about the four of us, and maybe Gloria?

BERNIE: I was only kidding. We're Jewish Democrats, Sam. That's about it.

SAM: Pity.

FRAN: Excuse me. *(SHE goes upstairs.)*

GLORIA: She's very pretty. Even prettier in person than in the movies.

SYLVIA: You think so?

> *(FRAN enters Sherry's room, closes the door behind her and heaves a sigh of relief. SHE takes out some "pot," rolls a cigarette and smokes it.)*

SAM: Did you ever have sex with a man?

BERNIE: I got blown in the army once. Does that count?

SAM: I'm not gay, or anything like that...but a good tight ass, Bernie...

BERNIE: How about a game of ping pong?

SAM: Man, that's a great idea. I haven't played ping pong since I was a kid.

BERNIE: You can take your drink with you.

THE LIBERATION OF LINDA DWORKIN

(BERNIE and SAM enter the living room.)

BERNIE: Honey, Sam and I are gonna play some ping pong.

SYLVIA: I'm really very tired. Will you be going soon?

GLORIA: Yes, of course. Any time you like.

BERNIE: What time will you get to the hospital?

SYLVIA: I'll be there first thing in the morning.

BERNIE: Give me a ring and let me know how Dad is doing.

LINDA: We'll see you tomorrow.

BERNIE: Thank you, Gloria.

GLORIA: Don't mention it.

SYLVIA: Say good night to the children for me.

BERNIE: We will.

> *(LINDA goes out the front door with SYLVIA and GLORIA. BERNIE and SAM go off to the basement. There is a knock at the door to Sherry's room. FRAN waves away the smoke.)*

FRAN: Oh, the hell with it!

> *(FRAN opens the door, cigarette in hand. SHERRY enters.)*

SHERRY: I'm sorry to bother you. I'd like to get my pajamas.

FRAN: Help yourself.

SHERRY: *(SHE gets her pajamas from the drawer.)* Are you smoking "pot?"

THE LIBERATION OF LINDA DWORKIN

FRAN: Why, yes. Have you ever smoked it?

SHERRY: No, but I've read about it.

(SHERRY picks up her slippers and leaves her room. FRAN shuts the door and takes a deep drag on the cigarette. LINDA reenters and goes up the stairs. FRAN puts her bag on the bed and opens it. There is a knock at the door. FRAN opens it. LINDA enters. FRAN unpacks.)

LINDA: What is that smell?

FRAN: It's "pot."

LINDA: Are you smoking it?

FRAN: Do you object? The children?

LINDA: Well, you know how they are. They're like monkeys. They imitate everything.

FRAN: It's really less harmful than ordinary cigarettes, to say nothing of liquor.

LINDA: That has yet to be proven.

FRAN: I'll just finish this joint.

LINDA: How long have you been smoking it?

FRAN: For years. And I'm perfectly healthy.

LINDA: I'm sorry about separating you and Sam.

FRAN: Maybe it was a mistake, our staying here.

LINDA: You're disappointed in me, I know.

THE LIBERATION OF LINDA DWORKIN

FRAN: Poopsie, what difference does it make what this old movie star thinks?

LINDA: I was never ambitious like you.

FRAN: Honey, being a housewife is a perfectly honorable career.

LINDA: I've seen every one of your movies. You've certainly come a long way. What I mean to say is, you've improved a great deal.

FRAN: I should hope so. Whatever happened to your musical career? I thought you were an excellent pianist.

LINDA: I was never that good.

FRAN: And your writing career. That wonderful short story that you wrote.

LINDA: That's just it. A jack of all trades and a master of none.

FRAN: It takes years of hard work to become a master.

> (SHERRY, in pajamas, enters Melanie's room and tries to turn on a lamp. It doesn't work. SHE tosses her clothes on one of the beds, goes out of the room and comes down the stairs.)

FRAN: Remember that poem we recited in class? How did it go?
"The world is too much with us; late and soon.
Getting and spending, we lay waste our powers:
Little we see in Nature that is ours."

LINDA: "We have given our hearts away, a sordid boon!
This sea that bares her bosom to the moon:
The winds that will be howling at all hours,
And are upgathered now like sleeping flowers."

FRAN: "For this, for everything, we are out of tune:

FRAN & LINDA: "It moves us not...Great God!

THE LIBERATION OF LINDA DWORKIN

I'd rather be a Pagan suckled in a creed outworn;
So might I standing on this pleasant lea,
Have glimpses that would make me less forlorn:
Have sight of Proteus rising from the sea;
Or hear old Triton blow his wreathed horn."

> *(LINDA bursts into tears. FRAN embraces her.)*

FRAN: Oh, my dear, my dear.

> *(LINDA breaks away and leaves Sherry's room. Meanwhile SHERRY has gone through the living room, down the cellar and come back up with BERNIE. THEY go into Melanie's room and BERNIE examines the desk lamp. Since it still doesn't work HE turns on a floor lamp.)*

BERNIE: There, that throws a little light on the subject.

SHERRY: Very little.

BERNIE: You're a little girl. How much do you want to see? I'll fix it tomorrow. Do you smell something funny?

SHERRY: I think Fran is burning incense.

BERNIE: *(With a Jewish accent)* Verry fency!

SHERRY: Oh, Daddy, we've burned incense. Remember?

BERNIE: I don't remember it smelling like that.

> *(BERNIE leaves Melanie's room. SHERRY shuts the door and lies on the bed, reading. FRAN goes into a Yoga exercise, and meditates. LINDA comes down the stairs and into the den, carrying bed clothes. SHE is followed by BERNIE.)*

BERNIE: Do you smell something funny?

LINDA: No.

THE LIBERATION OF LINDA DWORKIN

BERNIE: It smells like incense.

LINDA: I don't smell a thing.

> *(LINDA opens the sofa and makes the bed. SAM comes up from the cellar into the foyer.)*

SAM: Bernie?

> *(BERNIE enters the foyer.)*

SAM: Are we going to finish the game?

BERNIE: How about a rain check? I'm kind of pooped.

SAM: Okay. Where's Fran? Do you know?

BERNIE: I think she's up in her room.

SAM: Right.

> *(SAM goes up the stairs. BERNIE goes back into the den. SAM enters Sherry's room, closing the door behind him. HE rolls a cigarette and sits, smoking "pot.")*

BERNIE: Have you spoken to them?

LINDA: About what?

BERNIE: Linda, please. Don't play games with me. I've had a long day.

LINDA: And what the fuck do you think I've had?

BERNIE: What's the matter with you? Are you sick?

LINDA: Yes, I'm sick...sick and tired.

BERNIE: You can sleep late tomorrow.

THE LIBERATION OF LINDA DWORKIN

LINDA: I don't want to sleep late tomorrow.

BERNIE: What do you want to do?

> *(MELANIE enters from the outside, carrying books, and goes into the den.)*

MELANIE: Mrs. Hendricks said to say hello.

BERNIE: What time is it?

MELANIE: It's exactly ten o'clock. *(SHE goes up the stairs into her room.)*

BERNIE: She's quite a character, this friend of yours.

MELANIE: *(To SHERRY)* You've certainly made yourself comfortable.

BERNIE: And what a wierdie that Sam is. That's what I've been smelling!! They're smoking "pot," the both of them! He is, I'm sure of it. That man's in another world. You mean to tell me that you didn't smell something in the hall?

LINDA: Oh, Bernie, what difference does it make?

BERNIE: What difference does it make? Possession of marijuana is a criminal offense. We could all go to jail. What the hell has gotten into you?

LINDA: I don't know, Bernie, I really don't know.

SHERRY: *(To MELANIE, quite casually)* They're smoking "pot," you know.

MELANIE: Who is?

SHERRY: Fran Jackson and Sam Sotherby.

MELANIE: How do you know?

THE LIBERATION OF LINDA DWORKIN

SHERRY: She was smoking it when I went into my room to get my pajamas.

MELANIE: Did she say it was "pot?" My God!

SHERRY: Didn't you smell it?

BERNIE: You knew it was "pot" all along. Why did you lie to me? I'm asking you, Linda. Why did you lie to me? *(HE goes up the stairs.)*

LINDA: Bernie! Bernie, what are you going to do? *(SHE goes to the foot of the stairs and stands looking up.)*

MELANIE: A lot of people smoke "pot." So what?

SHERRY: But right here, in the house!

> *(There is a knock at the door to Sherry's room. SAM opens the door. BERNIE enters and closes the door behind him.)*

BERNIE: Is that "pot" you're smoking?

SAM: Would you like some?

> *(LINDA goes up the stairs.)*

BERNIE: Sam, we have kids in the house. *(HE looks at FRAN.)* What is she doing?

SAM: That's her yoga exercise. I do them, too. They're really great.

> *(LINDA enters Sherry's room. FRAN comes out of her meditation.)*

LINDA: Is everything all right?

FRAN: I'm sorry. I should have said something to Sam.

SAM: About what? Oh, the "pot." Sure, Bernie, sure. I understand.

THE LIBERATION OF LINDA DWORKIN

LINDA: I've made your bed, Sam. Down in the den.

SAM: My bed? Oh, that's all right. We can manage okay.

FRAN: Sam, dear...

SAM: *(HE looks from one to the other.)* You're kidding. Well, tell the kids we're married or something.

MELANIE: Rhoda had sex. Did you know that?

SHERRY: Rhoda? But she's so ugly.

MELANIE: You don't have sex with your face.

SHERRY: It's possible.

SAM: You see, I have this thing about sleeping alone.

BERNIE: I'm sorry...

SAM: Ever since my divorce... You see...

FRAN: Sam... *(SHE motions for him to be quiet.)*

BERNIE: It's just for a couple of nights. I mean, we're trying to bring up our kids the best we know how.

SAM: Sure, Bernie, sure. I understand. But you see...

FRAN: It's okay.

BERNIE: It's not that we're prudes, or anything like that...

FRAN: No sweat, Bernie. Forget it.

BERNIE: There's a bathroom downstairs you can use. It's right off the den.

THE LIBERATION OF LINDA DWORKIN

LINDA: If you need anything, just let us know. *(SHE starts off.)* Bernie...

SAM: You're not going to bed now, are you?

BERNIE: Well, I've had a pretty rough day at the office, and I've got to get up pretty early. And today was Linda's wash day, so we're both pretty tired. You can sleep as late as you want. We'll keep the kids quiet in the morning.

> *(LINDA and BERNIE leave Melanie's room, leaving the door ajar.)*

MELANIE: I'm going to brush my teeth.

SHERRY: Big deal.

> *(MELANIE leaves her room. BERNIE reenters Sherry's room.)*

BERNIE: You want me to help you move your things downstairs?

SAM: That's all right, Bernie. I can manage. Thank you.

> *(BERNIE leaves Sherry's room. FRAN goes up to SAM and bites him on the ear.)*

FRAN: I'll be down later.

SAM: But...

FRAN: Screw 'em!

SAM: Oh, baby!

FRAN: I'm gonna take a shower.

SAM: You want me to do your back?

FRAN: Later.

THE LIBERATION OF LINDA DWORKIN

(FRAN takes her terry robe and goes off. SAM gathers his things together. MELANIE enters her room.)

MELANIE: I think they're gonna sleep together.

SHERRY: Who?

MELANIE: Fran Jackson and Sam Sotherby.

SHERRY: I told you that.

(SAM leaves Sherry's room, goes down the stairs and into the den. HE opens his suitcase and takes out his pajamas.)

MELANIE: I was the one that told you.

SHERRY: Same difference. Are you going to have sex before you're married?

MELANIE: I haven't decided yet.

SHERRY: You mean you're considering it?

MELANIE: I haven't even decided if I'm going to get married.

(SAM goes off to the bathroom off the den with his pajamas.)

SHERRY: You mean you're just going to have affairs?

MELANIE: The important thing is to be in love. What difference does a piece of paper make?

SHERRY: You think Mother and Daddy are in love?

MELANIE: I don't know. Sometimes I think they are, and sometimes I think they're not.

SHERRY: What did Rhoda tell you?

THE LIBERATION OF LINDA DWORKIN

MELANIE: Not very much.

SHERRY: Didn't she tell you what it was like?

MELANIE: I don't think she enjoyed it very much.

SHERRY: How do you know?

MELANIE: Just the way she talked about it.

SHERRY: What did she say?

MELANIE: It's not what she said. It was the way she said it.

SHERRY: How did she say it?

MELANIE: I don't know. She tried to sound very casual.

SHERRY: Did he hurt her?

MELANIE: She didn't say.

SHERRY: I just can't imagine it. The whole thing sounds so peculiar. It's like an invasion of one's privacy, and one certainly gets very little of that.

MELANIE: What?

SHERRY: Privacy, dummy.

MELANIE: Well, you're still young.

SHERRY: I'm not that young.

MELANIE: I mean emotionally.

(BERNIE enters Melanie's room.)

BERNIE: You kids okay?

THE LIBERATION OF LINDA DWORKIN

SHERRY: Fine, Daddy.

BERNIE: Good night, Honey. *(HE kisses SHERRY.)*

SHERRY: Good night, Daddy.

BERNIE: Good night, Melanie. *(HE kisses her.)*

MELANIE: Good night, Daddy.

BERNIE: How would you like to go on a picnic this Sunday?

SHERRY: That would be fine, Daddy.

BERNIE: How about you?

MELANIE: I'm not sure yet.

BERNIE: Okay, we'll see. Sleep tight.

> *(BERNIE leaves Melanie's room, goes down the stairs into the living room. SAM enters the den in his pajamas, carrying his clothes, which he sets down on a chair. BERNIE enters the den.)*

BERNIE: You okay?

SAM: Fine, Bernie, fine.

BERNIE: Good night.

SAM: Good night, Bernie.

> *(BERNIE goes into the living room, shuts the light then goes up the stairs. SAM picks up a script and reads.)*

SHERRY: You think Mom and Dad are happy together?

MELANIE: No one's happy all the time. There's more to life than being in love.

THE LIBERATION OF LINDA DWORKIN

SHERRY: You mean sex?

MELANIE: No, stupid.

SHERRY: Then what?

MELANIE: A career, for one thing.

SHERRY: You wanna be a career woman?

MELANIE: I haven't decided yet.

> *(LINDA, in pajamas and robe, enters Melanie's room. SHE sits and looks at the girls.)*

LINDA: What would you two do if I were to disappear one day?

SHERRY: Oh, Mother!

LINDA: I'm perfectly serious. What would you do?

MELANIE: Are you going somewhere?

LINDA: I haven't decided yet.

> *(FRAN enters Sherry's room in her terry robe.)*

MELANIE: Where would you go? Aren't you happy here?

SHERRY: Oh, Melanie!

MELANIE: You haven't answered my question.

LINDA: You haven't answered mine.

MELANIE: We'd do the same thing we're doing now, I suppose.

LINDA: Would you miss me?

THE LIBERATION OF LINDA DWORKIN

SHERRY: Of course, we would!

MELANIE: Are you feeling sorry for yourself again?

LINDA: No, no. I'm tired of feeling sorry for myself.

> *(FRAN opens the door of Sherry's room, looks out then goes off, closing the door behind her.)*

MELANIE: Where would you go?

> *(FRAN goes down the stairs and into the den.)*

LINDA: That's just it. Where would I go? What would I do?

> *(SAM shuts the light in the den and HE and FRAN get into bed.)*

MELANIE: Then you're not going anywhere.

LINDA: I don't know.

MELANIE: If you're dissatisfied with your life, why don't you change it? You don't have to go anywhere to do that. It's all a matter of one's mental attitude.

LINDA: You're quite right.

MELANIE: So what are you going to do about it?

LINDA: Right now, I'm going to bed. Good night, dear. *(SHE kisses MELANIE.)* Good night, Honey. *(SHE kisses SHERRY.)* Sleep tight. Don't read too late.

> *(LINDA leaves Melanie's room. A moment later there is a knock at the door of Sherry's room. The door is opened and LINDA looks in.)*

LINDA: Fran? Fran? *(SHE turns on the light)* Oh, what the hell!

THE LIBERATION OF LINDA DWORKIN

(LINDA turns the light off and leaves Sherry's room, closing the door behind her. MELANIE opens the door of her room and looks out.)

SHERRY: What are you doing?

MELANIE: Shhh. I'm going downstairs.

SHERRY: For what?

MELANIE: A glass of milk.

(MELANIE leaves her room, closing the door behind her. SHE goes down the stairs, into the foyer and stops at the sound of FRAN's voice.)

FRAN: Ouch. You bit me.

(MELANIE goes into the kitchen. SHERRY turns off the lamp in Melanie's room, opens the door and looks out. SHE leaves the room, closing the door behind her. MELANIE enters the living room with a glass of milk and sits on the sofa. SHERRY comes down the stairs.)

SHERRY: What are you doing?

MELANIE: Shhh!

SAM: Ouch! What was that for?

(MELANIE motions for SHERRY to be silent. BERNIE, dressed in pajamas and robe, enters Melanie's room.)

BERNIE: Sherry? Melanie? *(HE turns on the lamp. Seeing the room is empty HE comes down the stairs.)* What are you kids doing down here? *(HE turns on the light.)* What's going on?

SHERRY: We're drinking milk.

THE LIBERATION OF LINDA DWORKIN

BERNIE: Get upstairs, the both of you.

MELANIE: Daddy...

BERNIE: I said, get upstairs.

(LINDA comes down the stairs.)

LINDA: What's the matter? What's going on?

BERNIE: That's what I'd like to know.

SHERRY: We were just sitting here.

BERNIE: With a glass of milk? In the dark? *(To MELANIE)* What are you doing down here?

MELANIE: I thought I heard something.

BERNIE: Finish your milk and go upstairs.

MELANIE: I don't want any milk. *(SHE sets the glass down and goes upstairs.)*

SHERRY: Neither do I.

(SHERRY follows MELANIE up the stairs. BERNIE goes into the den, followed by LINDA.)

LINDA: Bernie, don't make a scene.

(BERNIE turns the light on in the den. SAM sits up in bed. FRAN peeks out from under the covers. SHERRY and MELANIE appear at the foot of the stairs and listen.)

BERNIE: I'm afraid I'll have to ask you to leave.

SAM: Now?

THE LIBERATION OF LINDA DWORKIN

LINDA: I'm sorry. Please, stay the night.

FRAN: I'm not going back upstairs.

LINDA: There's no need to. We'll talk in the morning.

>*(SHERRY and MELANIE dash up the stairs. LINDA turns off the light in the den and goes into the living room. SHE picks up the glass of milk. BERNIE enters the living room.)*

BERNIE: Are you coming upstairs?

>*(LINDA doesn't respond. BERNIE goes up the stairs. LINDA stands irresolutely.)*

ACT II

Scene 1

(Two days later. The doorbell rings. SHERRY enters from the kitchen, goes to the front door and reenters with SYLVIA and GLORIA.)

SYLVIA: Is your mother ready?

SHERRY: She hasn't come down yet?

(MELANIE enters from the kitchen.)

MELANIE: Good morning, Grandma.

GLORIA: Don't we look lovely this morning.

MELANIE: Oh, it's just a little something I picked up.

SYLVIA: That color is very becoming.

MELANIE: How's Grandpa?

(SYLVIA shrugs and sighs.)

MELANIE: What did the doctor say?

SYLVIA: He's coming along.

MELANIE: How long will he be in the hospital?

SYLVIA: Who knows?

GLORIA: He did seem to have a little more color.

MELANIE: Dr. Geller is a very good doctor.

(BERNIE enters from the kitchen.)

BERNIE: Good morning. Would anyone like a cup of coffee?

THE LIBERATION OF LINDA DWORKIN

GLORIA: Not for me, thank you.

BERNIE: How about a bagel, with lox and cheese? Some scrambled eggs? You don't know what you're missing.

SYLVIA: We're late already. Isn't Linda up yet?

BERNIE: I'll see what's keeping her. *(HE goes upstairs.)*

SYLVIA: Are you two ready? You better put on a sweater. It's chilly outside.

>*(MELANIE and SHERRY go upstairs. MELANIE enters her room. SHERRY stands in the doorway.)*

SHERRY: What are you going to wear?

MELANIE: My new coat.

>*(MELANIE chooses a light coat. SHERRY goes to her room and does the same.)*

GLORIA: How's your arthritis?

SYLVIA: It's killing me.

>*(BERNIE enters Melanie's room.)*

BERNIE: Your mother's not going.

MELANIE: Why not?

BERNIE: I don't know. Tell Grandma. *(HE leaves Melanie's room.)*

SYLVIA: When Dan has no appetite you can be sure that something's wrong.

>*(SHERRY enters Melanie's room.)*

THE LIBERATION OF LINDA DWORKIN

MELANIE: Mother's not going.

SHERRY: Why not?

MELANIE: I don't know.

(MELANIE leaves her room, followed by SHERRY.)

GLORIA: Well, you know he's getting the best of care. And they do know that it's his gall bladder.

SYLVIA: He's not a young man.

GLORIA: I'm sure they won't have to operate.

SYLVIA: I'm not a well woman myself. How much can a person take?

GLORIA: You've just got to hold on, that's all.

SYLVIA: I didn't sleep a wink last night.

GLORIA: Why didn't you tell me? I could have given you one of my sleeping pills.

SYLVIA: That's all I need is another pill. It's very difficult for me to sleep in a strange house, in a strange bed. Not that I don't appreciate your hospitality, God forbid.

GLORIA: I know, I know. There's nothing like one's own home.

(SHERRY enters the living room.)

SHERRY: Mother's not going.

SYLVIA: Why not?

SHERRY: I don't know.

SYLVIA: Is she sick? That's all I need.

THE LIBERATION OF LINDA DWORKIN

(MELANIE enters the living room.)

SYLVIA: What's the matter with your mother?

MELANIE: She's not going.

SYLVIA: I know she's not going. Why isn't she going?

MELANIE: She has a previous engagement.

SYLVIA: What do you mean, she has a previous engagement? She knew about the Bas Mitzvah over a year ago.

MELANIE: She said to go without her.

SYLVIA: She must be sick.

(BERNIE enters the living room.)

SYLVIA: What's the matter with Linda?

BERNIE: She's not going.

SYLVIA: Bernie, please... *(SHE gets up, starts for the stairs then stops.)* Oh! *(SHE grabs her side.)* Please. Please, I'm all right. *(SHE sits down again.)*

GLORIA: I'll go up and talk to her.

(GLORIA rises as LINDA enters the living room.)

LINDA: Good morning. *(SHE goes off to the kitchen.)*

SYLVIA: I thought you said she was sick.

BERNIE: I never said she was sick.

SYLVIA: She can't do this to Carol. She doesn't realize what she's doing. Carol would never forgive her.

THE LIBERATION OF LINDA DWORKIN

GLORIA: After all, Carol did come to both Melanie's and Sherry's Bas Mitzvah.

BERNIE: Don't tell me, tell her.

MELANIE: If she doesn't want to go, she doesn't want to go.

SYLVIA: Shut up! This has nothing to do with you.

MELANIE: It has nothing to do with anyone, except Mother.

BERNIE: Melanie!

MELANIE: Don't I have a right to say anything? I'm tired of being told to shut my mouth every time I open it. I'm fifteen years old.

BERNIE: But you're not too big to spank.

MELANIE: Oh....bull!!

BERNIE: You come back here. I want you to apologize to Grandma.

SYLVIA: Leave her alone.

MELANIE: I apologize, Grandma. I apologize to all of you for living. *(SHE runs up the stairs, into her room and throws herself on her bed.)*

SHERRY: I think you're being very unfair. *(SHE runs up the stairs into Melanie's room.)* You'll wrinkle your dress.

MELANIE: *(SHE sits up.)* Everybody's organizing except us. I'm talking about children. We are the most oppressed minority of all. We have no right to think. We have no right to feel. I'll be so glad when I leave this place.

SHERRY: Where are you going?

MELANIE: To college, Dummy. It's like being in a prison.

THE LIBERATION OF LINDA DWORKIN

(LINDA enters the living room from the kitchen, sipping a cup of coffee.)

LINDA: Didn't Bernie tell you I wasn't going?

SYLVIA: Why aren't you going?

LINDA: I have a meeting.

SYLVIA: What meeting?

LINDA: A conference, rather.

GLORIA: You went to the conference last night.

LINDA: Gloria Steinem is going to speak.

GLORIA: Don't you think your friendship for Carol is more important than hearing Gloria Steinem speak?

LINDA: I'm hoping Carol will understand.

GLORIA: Well, frankly, Linda, I don't understand myself. After all Carol has done for you... What shall I tell her if she asks me?

LINDA: Tell her I'll call her this evening.

GLORIA: Frankly, Linda, I think you're making a big mistake. This conference is going on all week-end.

SYLVIA: We're gonna be late.

GLORIA: Well, I'm ready.

SYLVIA: Bernie, will you please call the children?

(BERNIE goes up the stairs into Melanie's room.)

BERNIE: May I come in?

THE LIBERATION OF LINDA DWORKIN

MELANIE: It's your house.

BERNIE: As long as you act like a child, you'll be treated like a child.

MELANIE: As long as I'm treated like a child, I'm forced to act like a child.

LINDA: How's Dad this morning?

SYLVIA: He looks the same to me. I don't see any improvement.

MELANIE: I have an opinion just like anyone else, and I don't see why I'm not allowed to say what I think. How dare Grandma tell me to shut up?! How dare she!! What am I? Some sub-human? And then for you to make me apologize to her! She's the one that should apologize to me.

BERNIE: All right. I'm sorry. I apologize. Does that make you happy? If you're so grown up, then you ought to realize that even adults are human and they lose their temper.

SHERRY: After all, we are the future.

BERNIE: God help us!

MELANIE: I don't think that's funny, Daddy. And, as far as Mother is concerned, I'm glad she's found an interest outside the house, and I think she ought to be encouraged.

BERNIE: Am I objecting to her attending those meetings?

MELANIE: You're not encouraging her.

SYLVIA: *(At the foot of the stairs.)* Melanie! Sherry!

LINDA: Bernie was at the synagogue last night, so we were represented.

GLORIA: Carol was very hurt that you weren't there. She was convinced that you were sick.

THE LIBERATION OF LINDA DWORKIN

BERNIE: Are you going to the synagogue or not?

(MELANIE rises and marches down the stairs, followed by SHERRY. BERNIE trails after them. MELANIE kisses LINDA and marches out the front door. SHERRY does the same.)

SYLVIA: If I live through this, I'll live forever. *(SHE goes out the front door.)*

GLORIA: Linda, I think we both know how important friends are. Think twice before you do this to Carol. *(SHE goes out the front door.)*

BERNIE: What time did you get in last night?

LINDA: Three o'clock.

BERNIE: Aren't you tired?

LINDA: No. I'm wide awake.

BERNIE: Was it an interesting evening?

LINDA: It was an eye-opener. Bernie dear, sit down. I have something to tell you.

BERNIE: *(HE sits.)* You're gonna bomb City Hall.

LINDA: I don't expect you to understand. I think Melanie does, though. Bernie, I've got to have my freedom.

BERNIE: You wanna divorce?

LINDA: Don't be ridiculous. All I ask is that you be patient with me and try to understand.

BERNIE: What do you want me to do?

LINDA: I don't want you to do anything. I want to go away for a while.

THE LIBERATION OF LINDA DWORKIN

BERNIE: Where do you want to go?

LINDA: Fran said that she could use a secretary.

BERNIE: You're going to Hollywood?

LINDA: She's going to Washington first. After that, I don't know.

BERNIE: How long will you be gone?

LINDA: I don't know.

BERNIE: Is it anything I've done? Anything I've said?

LINDA: No.

BERNIE: What is it then?

LINDA: It's what we are, or rather what I am, or rather what I'm not.

BERNIE: What do you want to be?

LINDA: That's what I've got to find out.

BERNIE: And what about us?

LINDA: Bernie, I'm on the verge of a nervous breakdown. At least, I was up until a couple of days ago. I'm an intelligent woman. I'm Phi Beta Kappa. I have a master's degree in English literature, and how have I been spending my life? Cleaning and cooking and taking out the garbage. I am wasting away.

BERNIE: Is that how you look on our marriage? As a waste?

LINDA: Not our marriage, Bernie. My position in Society.

BERNIE: We can afford help. You can sit and eat chocolates all day, if you want to. I don't care.

THE LIBERATION OF LINDA DWORKIN

LINDA: I've got to break out.

BERNIE: It's Fran, isn't it? She's put a bug up your ass.

LINDA: Please!

BERNIE: What you mean, please? You can say "fuck" and I can't even say a bug up your ass?

LINDA: This has nothing to do with Fran. I've been unhappy for a long time.

BERNIE: Why haven't you said something?

LINDA: It's something I couldn't put into words.

BERNIE: And Fran has found the words for you. Is that it?

LINDA: No, it is not.

BERNIE: What is it then?

LINDA: I've come to see that my problem isn't unique. As a matter of fact, it's very common. I've accepted a secondary position in life, when all the while I've been preparing myself...

BERNIE: For what?

LINDA: For something more?

BERNIE: What more do you want? You want to go into politics? There's plenty of politics right here. Whatever you're looking for, you can find it right here.

LINDA: Fran is going to Washington to lobby for this bill. Tell me something. How much do you pay Glenda?

BERNIE: I pay her two hundred dollars a week.

THE LIBERATION OF LINDA DWORKIN

LINDA: And you think that's a living wage?

BERNIE: All she does is answer the phone and make appointments.

LINDA: And help you with your patients and run errands and...

BERNIE: All right, all right. I'll give her a raise. I was going to give her a raise anyway. So that settles that. You've done your bit for Women's Lib.

LINDA: Everything is a joke with you.

BERNIE: No, Linda, I do not consider you a joke. You and the girls are my life.

LINDA: You have a career.

BERNIE: What kind of a career? I'm a dentist.

LINDA: You play a role in Society.

BERNIE: Linda, you <u>are</u> Society. You're a wife. You're a mother. You are the foundation.

LINDA: I don't wanna be a foundation. I wanna be me.

BERNIE: When are you planning on leaving?

LINDA: Tomorrow.

BERNIE: And this is for how long? You don't know.

LINDA: It'll do us both good. We need a vacation from each other.

BERNIE: And what about the girls?

LINDA: I think we've done a pretty good job, don't you? I think they're quite capable of looking after themselves.

THE LIBERATION OF LINDA DWORKIN

(The doorbell rings.)

LINDA: That must be Fran. Would you get the door please?

(LINDA gulps down the rest of her coffee and goes into the kitchen with her cup and saucer. BERNIE goes off and reenters with FRAN.)

BERNIE: Would you care for some coffee? Or something to eat?

FRAN: We don't have that much time. Is Linda up?

BERNIE: Oh, yes indeed. How are the meetings going?

FRAN: Quite well.

BERNIE: Getting lots of recruits?

(LINDA enters from the kitchen.)

LINDA: All set.

FRAN: It's chilly out.

LINDA: I'll get a coat. *(SHE goes upstairs.)*

BERNIE: Linda tells me she's going to work with you for a while.

FRAN: Isn't it wonderful!

(The doorbell rings. BERNIE goes off and reenters with SAM.)

SAM: How you doing, Bernie?

BERNIE: Fine, just fine.

SAM: Where are those beautiful girls of yours?

BERNIE: They went to the synagogue.

THE LIBERATION OF LINDA DWORKIN

SAM: That's right. Today's the Sabbath. Beautiful religion, Bernie, beautiful. I almost converted once. This girl I was...going with... I love Jewish girls.

(LINDA comes down the stairs with her coat.)

BERNIE: Are you going to Washington, too?

SAM: There's a lot of work to be done there, Bernie. This Women's Lib is not only for women. It works both ways.

BERNIE: I'm sure it does. What are you two doing for dinner tonight? Linda, why can't they join us? Do you like chili?

SAM: I could live on chili.

BERNIE: I make the best chili this side of the Mississippi. How about it?

FRAN: You two might want to be alone, your last night.

BERNIE: I'm sure it's not going to be our last night, and it may be the last chance I get to see the two of you.

SAM: It's okay with me. And Fran and I promise not to screw in your den.

BERNIE: Sammy boy, you can screw in any room you want to. The girls won't be here tonight. They're going to a pajama party.

SAM: Oh? Where is that?

LINDA: Why don't you come?

FRAN: Fine with me. We'd better get going.

SAM: Why don't you join us, Bernie?

BERNIE: I'll see you this evening.

THE LIBERATION OF LINDA DWORKIN

SAM: Take care.

(FRAN and LINDA go out the front door, followed by SAM. BERNIE sits, lost in thought.)

Scene 2

(That evening. SHERRY and MELANIE enter from the kitchen, go up to their respective rooms and proceed to pack an overnight bag. SHERRY leaves her room and enters Melanie's room, absentmindedly holding her toothbrush.)

MELANIE: What's the matter?

SHERRY: Nothing.

(SHERRY goes back to her room and sits, holding her toothbrush. MELANIE goes into Sherry's room.)

MELANIE: Hey, wake up. You're not sick, are you?

SHERRY: I've got a headache.

MELANIE: Take an aspirin.

SHERRY: I don't want an aspirin.

MELANIE: I wish you'd stop acting like a child.

SHERRY: I am a child.

(LINDA enters from the kitchen, goes up the stairs and looks into Melanie's room. Seeing it empty SHE goes into Sherry's room.)

LINDA: What's the matter?

MELANIE: She's got a headache.

(LINDA sits beside SHERRY and puts her arm around her. SHERRY lays her head on Linda's shoulder. LINDA strokes Sherry's head.)

MELANIE: Oh, really! What a baby she is!

LINDA: She has a right to act like a baby.

THE LIBERATION OF LINDA DWORKIN

MELANIE: She's thirteen years old.

SHERRY: So what?

MELANIE: If Barbara saw you now, she would never have invited you. This is an adult pajama party. Mr. Blum is going to be here any minute now. Well, I'm going to finish packing. *(MELANIE goes back to her room.)*

LINDA: You don't have to go, if you don't want to.

SHERRY: You weren't even going to tell us that you were leaving.

LINDA: Of course, I was, dear.

SHERRY: Why do you have to leave tomorrow?

LINDA: Because that's when Fran is leaving.

SHERRY: I think we need you more than she does.

LINDA: That's not the point.

SHERRY: What is the point?

(MELANIE enters Sherry's room, carrying her bag.)

MELANIE: I'll be waiting downstairs.

LINDA: All right, Melanie.

(MELANIE goes downstairs into the den.)

LINDA: Do you remember the other day we were speaking of identity, and you said that if it weren't for you and Melanie, I would have no identity whatsoever.

SHERRY: That's ridiculous.

THE LIBERATION OF LINDA DWORKIN

LINDA: No, dear. It was very wise of you to see that, and it's true. But I did have an identity once, and I intend to find it again.

SHERRY: In Washington?

LINDA: Quite possibly.

SHERRY: Suppose you never find it? Does that mean you'll never come home again?

LINDA: Of course not.

(SAM enters the den.)

SAM: There was a girl named Melanie,/ Who once committed a felony./ She stole my heart and ran away...

MELANIE: And that's a lot of belany.

SAM: Belany?

MELANIE: That's short for baloney.

SAM: So young and already so cynical.

SHERRY: And what about Daddy?

LINDA: What about him?

SHERRY: Won't he miss you?

LINDA: Of course, he will, and I'll miss him. But then maybe we'll appreciate each other all the more.

SHERRY: Don't you appreciate each other now?

SAM: I have a little girl, you know. She's almost as old as you are.

MELANIE: Where is she now?

THE LIBERATION OF LINDA DWORKIN

SAM: She's with her mother.

MELANIE: You mean your first wife?

SAM: I've only had one wife.

SHERRY: And what about our heart to heart talks?

LINDA: Sherry, I'm not leaving you forever. We'll write each other. We'll talk on the phone, and we'll be seeing each other.

SHERRY: When? And for how long? And men are fickle, you know. Daddy may get himself a mistress.

LINDA: Well, if your father is that fickle then...he deserves what he gets.

SHERRY: Men can't help themselves.

LINDA: Where did you get all this information about men?

SHERRY & LINDA: From Melanie.

LINDA: Well, Melanie's wrong. Men can be just as faithful as women. Maybe even more so.

SHERRY: Well, if I were you I would not take Daddy for granted. After all, he is a handsome man.

MELANIE: Do you flirt with every female that you meet?

SAM: Why, yes. I suppose I do.

MELANIE: Why?

SAM: I don't know. I guess I can't bear not to be loved.

> *(FRAN and BERNIE enter the living room from the kitchen. A car horn is heard.)*

THE LIBERATION OF LINDA DWORKIN

MELANIE: Excuse me. *(SHE goes into the living room.)* Mr. Blum is here. *(SHE goes to the foot of the stairs.)* Mr. Blum is here!

BERNIE: Melanie, please don't shout.

(MELANIE goes up the stairs into Sherry's room.)

MELANIE: Mr. Blum is here. Are you ready or not?

SHERRY: This is Mother's last night at home.

MELANIE: So what are you going to do, sit and hold her hand? Mother has guests to entertain. And it's not as if she's going away forever. Well, I'm going.

LINDA: Melanie, just a minute.

(The car horn is heard.)

BERNIE: *(To FRAN)* Excuse me. *(HE goes out the front door.)*

LINDA: Do you want to go to the party, or don't you?

SHERRY: I suppose so.

MELANIE: Are you ready or not?

SHERRY: Yes, I'm ready.

LINDA: Have a good time, dear.

> *(SHERRY picks up her bag and follows MELANIE into the living room. LINDA trails after them.)*

FRAN: Have a good time.

MELANIE: Thank you.

> *(BERNIE reenters.)*

THE LIBERATION OF LINDA DWORKIN

BERNIE: You ready?

MELANIE: Good night, Daddy.

SHERRY: Good night, Daddy. *(To LINDA)* Remember what I said.

(MELANIE and SHERRY go off.)

BERNIE: What did she say?

LINDA: I don't remember.

(MELANIE reenters.)

MELANIE: I forgot my tape recorder.

(MELANIE runs up to her room and looks around.)

BERNIE: What time does your plane leave tomorrow?

FRAN: Nine o'clock.

BERNIE: In the morning?

FRAN: I'm afraid so.

(MELANIE runs down the stairs.)

MELANIE: Has anyone seen my tape recorder?

(The car horn is heard.)

MELANIE: Oh, never mind. *(SHE runs off.)*

BERNIE: *(To LINDA)* Do you plan to see my mother and father before you leave?

LINDA: Your mother invited herself to breakfast.

THE LIBERATION OF LINDA DWORKIN

BERNIE: What about Dad? He doesn't even know you're leaving.

LINDA: I could see him tonight, I suppose. *(To FRAN)* Would you mind?

FRAN: No, of course not. Sam can drive you over. I'll let him know. *(SHE goes into the den.)*

LINDA: I'll get my coat. *(SHE goes up the stairs.)*

FRAN: Sam, dear...? What's the matter, Honey? You're depressed. You've been down all evening. You're thinking about your little girl.

SAM: She's not so little anymore, and we're almost strangers.

FRAN: Honey, people can live together all their lives and still be strangers. Look at Linda and Bernie.

SAM: No foundation all the way down the line.

FRAN: Come on, Sotherby!

SAM: You are something, Baby. You're made of steel.

FRAN: Don't say that.

SAM: Doesn't anything get you down?

FRAN: You know me better than that.

(LINDA comes down the stairs in her coat.)

BERNIE: I love you, Tiger.

LINDA: I love you too, Sexy.

BERNIE: Are you gonna miss me?

THE LIBERATION OF LINDA DWORKIN

LINDA: Bernie, don't make more of this than it really is. You're my husband, and you always will be.

BERNIE: And suddenly I'm not enough for you. All right, all right.

(LINDA goes into the den, followed by BERNIE.)

LINDA: I hate to impose on you, Sam.

FRAN: Would you mind driving Linda to the hospital? She'd like to see her father-in-law before she leaves.

SAM: My pleasure.

BERNIE: You know how to get there?

SAM: I think so.

(BERNIE goes out the front door with SAM and LINDA. FRAN walks about, picks up a small tape recorder from the bookshelf. SHE punches a key.)

MELANIE'S VOICE: "So live, that when thy summons comes to join that innumerable caravan which moves to that mysterious realm where each shall take his place in the silent halls of death, thou go not like the quarry slave at night, scourged to his dungeon; but, sustained and soothed by an unfaltering trust, approach thy grave like one who wraps the drapery of his couch about him and lies down to pleasant dreams."

(BERNIE has reentered the den. FRAN turns off the tape recorder.)

BERNIE: What was that?

FRAN: "Thanatopsis" by William Cullen Bryant. Why is it that the older we get the less we think about death?

BERNIE: Linda thinks she doesn't need us anymore.

THE LIBERATION OF LINDA DWORKIN

FRAN: I don't think she thinks that at all.

BERNIE: She's going to find out differently. She's not like you.

FRAN: What is that supposed to mean?

BERNIE: You have a career, and that means more to you than anything else.

FRAN: You're wrong about me too. I'm a woman first, and then an actress. You remind me so much of my father. He thought he was so modern, so sophisticated.

BERNIE: Don't you believe in anything?

FRAN: I believe in the dignity of man. I believe in beauty, and I believe in freedom.

BERNIE: And what about responsibility?

FRAN: One's first responsibility is to oneself.

BERNIE: That sounds familiar. We've got a good marriage, Fran. And there are not many of those around. *(HE sighs.)* Would you care for a drink?

FRAN: Not right now. Thank you. You're a good man, Bernie.

BERNIE: But?

FRAN: You function only from the neck down.

BERNIE: You mean I'm not an intellectual.

FRAN: They're just as bad. We've got a body and we've got a mind. That's what I used to love about Linda. She functioned on all levels. Bernie, my dear. You're in a prison, too. Don't you see that? What does your life consist of? Getting up and going to work, and then going back to bed. In between, you eat and have sex. Or do you?

THE LIBERATION OF LINDA DWORKIN

BERNIE: Our sex life is just fine, thank you.

FRAN: Didn't you have any dreams as a kid?

BERNIE: Sure I had dreams.

FRAN: Like what?

BERNIE: I dreamt about Hedy LaMarr.

FRAN: I'm serious.

BERNIE: Yes, I had dreams. I dreamt about being a great neurosurgeon.

FRAN: What stopped you?

BERNIE: Money, for one thing. And...

FRAN: And what?

BERNIE: I guess I just wasn't that dedicated.

FRAN: So you took the easy way out.

BERNIE: I wanted a home, and I wanted a family. And I like being a dentist...most of the time. I like being a husband. I like being a father. I'm a happy man. Or I was...

FRAN: Until I came along.

BERNIE: Maybe it's not your fault. I don't know.

FRAN: Do you think you're being fulfilled?

BERNIE: Things could always be better, I suppose.

FRAN: What are you afraid of?

BERNIE: I'm not afraid of anything.

THE LIBERATION OF LINDA DWORKIN

FRAN: Right now your heart is beating faster. You feel warm all over.

BERNIE: I don't know what the hell you're talking about.

FRAN: I suppose you wouldn't like to go to bed with me.

BERNIE: I'd like to go to bed with a lot of women.

FRAN: But you're tied to Linda.

BERNIE: I'm not tied to Linda. I love her. She's my wife.

FRAN: Is that any reason to give up the world?

BERNIE: What the hell are you talking about? You mean I should just hop into bed with any woman that comes along? And don't think I haven't had the opportunity.

FRAN: What's stopping you?

BERNIE: What's stopping me? Linda, that's what's stopping me. If I cheat on her then she has every right to cheat on me.

FRAN: Aren't you cheating on yourself right now? And isn't Linda cheating on herself?

BERNIE: Is this what Women's Lib is all about? No wonder Sam is hot for Women's Lib.

FRAN: Making love is beautiful, Bernie. It doesn't have to be done in the dark.

BERNIE: Are you propositioning me?

FRAN: Bernie, Bernie, Bernie. Love is something that just happens. It has nothing to do with words.

THE LIBERATION OF LINDA DWORKIN

BERNIE: Well, sometimes words like "yes" and "no" help to clear things up. Have you discussed this with Linda? I mean this bit about sexual freedom?

FRAN: We used to talk about it all the time.

BERNIE: And she agrees with you? I can't believe that. She's the original green-eyed monster. She has me going to bed with every woman I meet.

FRAN: Linda's eyes have been opened...to many things.

BERNIE: Then as far as she's concerned it's all right for me to have an affair with another woman.

FRAN: She doesn't think in those terms anymore. Join us, Bernie.

BERNIE: What are you talking about? I have a practice. I have a home.

FRAN: You have week-ends.

BERNIE: I don't see myself trailing after Linda like some lost puppy.

FRAN: But it's all right for her to trail after you.

BERNIE: You really are a ball-breaker. You know that?

FRAN: Does that frighten you, Bernie? Do I intimidate your virility?

BERNIE: I've never had any trouble with my virility. You're a fucking bitch.

FRAN: You're like a little boy, stumbling in the dark. Take my hand, Bernie.

BERNIE: You're a nut.

FRAN: You beautiful, dumb cluck. *(SHE takes his hand and kisses it.)*

BERNIE: Are you for real?

THE LIBERATION OF LINDA DWORKIN

FRAN: *(SHE kisses him on the lips.)* The world is yours for the taking, Bernie.

BERNIE: Don't play games with me.

(SHE starts to unbutton his shirt.)

BERNIE: Okay, okay. I believe you. Let's go upstairs.

(SHE starts to lead him off.)

BERNIE: Give me a minute. I'll just turn off some of these lights. Go ahead, go ahead.

(FRAN goes off to the foot of the stairs. BERNIE turns off a lamp. He then picks up the tape recorder, pushes a button and, holding the tape recorder behind his back, HE joins FRAN at the foot of the stairs.)

FRAN: That's what I love about you. You're so down to earth.

BERNIE: Sure. Why not? And you really think that Linda would have no objection?

(FRAN takes his free hand and leads him up the stairs.)

Scene 3

(The following morning. LINDA comes down the stairs with a suitcase, an overnight bag and a topcoat over her arm. SHE sets the bags down in the living room and tosses the topcoat onto the sofa. BERNIE enters from the kitchen.)

BERNIE: Aren't you having any breakfast?

LINDA: I had some juice.

BERNIE: You're really leaving, aren't you?

LINDA: Mildred will be coming in every day to make lunch and clean the house, except for the week-ends, of course. She'll take care of the laundry and the shopping. If you need anything let her know. And I told her we'd pay her a hundred and fifty dollars a week, which is pretty cheap, I think. The girls can make their own breakfast, and I don't think dinner will be a problem.

BERNIE: And what about after dinner? Specifically bed time? Have you made any arrangements in that department?

LINDA: We can get together on week-ends. Washington is not that far away.

BERNIE: And what about Hollywood?

LINDA: Let's take it one step at a time.

BERNIE: Look, if I've been unreasonable, I'm sorry. As far as bringing up the girls is concerned...we've always been in agreement about that, haven't we? You've been just as strict as I've been. Even more so. You're the one that wanted them to go to Hebrew school, and you're the one that wanted them to be bas-mitzvahed.

LINDA: I know that, Bernie.

BERNIE: And you're the one that doesn't want them to see certain movies, and you're the one that keeps an eye on the books they read.

THE LIBERATION OF LINDA DWORKIN

LINDA: I've never denied that.

BERNIE: But you act as if I'm some sort of dictator. Would you smoke "pot"? Would you let the girls smoke "pot"? Would you want the girls to watch Sam and Fran make love?

LINDA: Of course not.

BERNIE: And yet you're acting as if I were the villain.

LINDA: Bernie, I am not leaving because you kicked Fran and Sam out of the house.

BERNIE: I am open-minded, Linda. I'm always willing to learn. I try to keep up with things. I read the Dental Journal every month. I read Time Magazine. Don't we get the New York times every Sunday? We're involved in practically every cultural activity in town. What more do you want from me?

LINDA: It's not you, it's me. I've told you that.

BERNIE: I need you, Linda. I love you. I can't handle the girls all by myself. What the fuck is all this for? My whole life is built around you. You can have anything you want. You can do anything you want. When have I ever stopped you?

LINDA: You're trying to stop me now.

BERNIE: I'll be lost without you, Linda.

LINDA: And I'll be lost if I stay here.

   (The doorbell rings.)

LINDA: That must be Fran.

   (BERNIE goes out the front door and returns with FRAN.)

FRAN: Good morning.

THE LIBERATION OF LINDA DWORKIN

LINDA: Good morning.

FRAN: I'd love some coffee. That's all right. I can help myself. *(SHE goes into the kitchen.)*

LINDA: I forgot my watch.

>*(LINDA goes upstairs. BERNIE sits, looking forlorn. FRAN enters sipping coffee.)*

FRAN: Bernie...Honey, it's not the end of the world.

BERNIE: It is for me. I just don't understand. All of this, our whole way of life...it's all her doing.

>*(The doorbell rings. FRAN sets down her coffee.)*

FRAN: That's Sam. I'll get it.

>*(FRAN goes out the front door and reenters with SAM.)*

SAM: Good morning. *(HE glances at BERNIE.)* Maybe not. Are these Linda's bags. I'll put them in the trunk. Where's Linda?

BERNIE: She's upstairs.

SAME: It's a beautiful day. *(HE picks up the bags and goes out the front door.)*

FRAN: We'll take good care of her.

BERNIE: That's what I'm afraid of. *(After a moment)* Have you told her about last night?

>*(LINDA comes down the stairs.)*

LINDA: Where are my bags?

FRAN: Sam is putting them in the trunk.

THE LIBERATION OF LINDA DWORKIN

LINDA: I'd like to hold on to my overnight bag. *(SHE goes out the front door.)*

BERNIE: Are you going to tell her or shall I? And if you're planning to deny it, forget it, because I have proof?

FRAN: Proof? *(SHE laughs.)* What kind of proof?

BERNIE: You don't believe me? *(HE goes to a drawer and takes out the tape recorder.)*

FRAN: You're not serious?

BERNIE: Try me.

(LINDA, holding her overnight bag reenters, followed by SAM.)

LINDA: What's the matter? What are you doing with Melanie's tape recorder?

FRAN: I think Bernie wants to play something for you? Bernie?

BERNIE: I wanted to spare you both.

LINDA: *(Laughs)* You put it on tape?

BERNIE: You know?

LINDA: *(Laughs.)* Oh, Bernie, Bernie, Bernie! *(SHE kisses him.)*

BERNIE: She told you? I bet she didn't tell you the whole thing?

LINDA: She tried to seduce you. And you refused to be seduced. I told her.

BERNIE: You told her what? You mean to say that you planned this whole thing, the two of you?

LINDA: No, we didn't plan it.

THE LIBERATION OF LINDA DWORKIN

BERNIE: What then?

LINDA: Fran thought you were very sexy. And I told her to forget it. I guess I sort of bet her. I didn't think she would take it seriously.

BERNIE: I see. And suppose you lost your bet?

LINDA: That's all right. I didn't bet any money.

BERNIE: Very funny. I guess I'm just a great big joke to you.

(SHERRY and MELANIE enters with their overnight bags.)

SHERRY: Mama! (SHE throws her arms around LINDA.) I was afraid you'd be gone.

LINDA: Of course not, Honey. I wouldn't leave without saying good-bye.

MELANIE: I told her. Mrs. Blum wants you to call her.

LINDA: I don't have time. I'll write her.

MELANIE: Are you leaving right now?

LINDA: I did want to say good-bye to Grandma. She was supposed to be here for breakfast. Do you want to call her, Bernie?

(BERNIE picks up the phone and dials.)

SHERRY: When will you be back?

LINDA: I don't know, Honey. I'll call you tonight.

MELANIE: Could we come down to Washington to visit you?

LINDA: I don't see why not. Maybe next week-end.

SHERRY: We've never been to Washington.

THE LIBERATION OF LINDA DWORKIN

MELANIE: We have too.

BERNIE: *(HE hangs up.)* There's no answer. They must be on the way.

LINDA: How was the party?

MELANIE: It was okay.

LINDA: Didn't you have any fun?

SHERRY: She had a fight with one of the girls.

MELANIE: What's my tape recorder doing here? I was looking all over for it.

BERNIE: I was using it.

MELANIE: What for?

BERNIE: I was helping Fran rehearse a scene.

MELANIE: For a movie?

BERNIE: Well, sort of.

MELANIE: Can we listen to it? Fran?

FRAN: That's up to your father.

BERNIE: Well, it's not the kind of scene...

MELANIE: Oh, Daddy! Can we listen to it, Mother?

SAM: I'd like to hear it, too.

(The doorbell rings.)

BERNIE: I'll get it.

THE LIBERATION OF LINDA DWORKIN

(BERNIE goes off and reenters with SYLVIA and GLORIA.)

SYLVIA: You're going somewhere?

LINDA: I'm going to Washington.

SYLVIA: What's in Washington?

FRAN: The government, for one thing.

SYLVIA: How long will you be gone?

LINDA: I don't know. Gloria, will you look in on the girls for me?

GLORIA: Yes, of course.

MELANIE: Really, Mother. We're not children.

SYLVIA: Isn't this rather sudden?

LINDA: *(SHE kisses the girls.)* Good-bye, dear. Good-bye, Honey. I want you to listen to your father. And don't give him any trouble.

(SHERRY starts to cry.)

MELANIE: Oh, for heaven sakes!

LINDA: Oh, Honey, there's nothing to cry about. You're a big girl now.

MELANIE: Hah!

SHERRY: I want to go with you.

LINDA: What about school?

SHERRY: I don't care about school. I want to go with <u>you</u>.

SYLVIA: How long will you be gone?

THE LIBERATION OF LINDA DWORKIN

MELANIE: Until she finds herself.

SYLVIA: I didn't know she was lost. *(To BERNIE)* And you're gonna let her go?

BERNIE: What am I supposed to do?

FRAN: Don't worry. He's tried. We really should be going.

SHERRY: No!

LINDA: Now, Sherry.

SHERRY: You don't care about us.

SAM: Now, Sherry honey, distance has nothing to do with being apart. Right now, I'm far away from my little girl, but I think about her all the time, and she thinks about me. And that's what really matters, doesn't it? You want the best for your mother, don't you?

SHERRY: Read "The Blue Bird!" They found what they were looking for right in their own backyard.

SAM: Yes, dear, but everyone has their own way of looking for things.

LINDA: I'll call you tonight. *(SHE kisses SHERRY, picks up her overnight bag and goes off goes off quickly.)*

SYLVIA: I've never heard of such a thing.

SAM: *(HE kisses SYLVIA.)* Good-bye, Sylvia. It's been real. *(HE goes off.)*

SYLVIA: *(To FRAN)* This is all your doing.

FRAN: Tell you what? I'll share the blame, fifty-fifty. Bernie... *(SHE blows him a kiss.)* Good-bye, kids. Take care of Daddy. Good-bye, Gloria. Good luck. *(SHE winks at GLORIA and goes off.)*

THE LIBERATION OF LINDA DWORKIN

(BERNIE goes out the front door.)

SYLVIA: She didn't even say good-bye to Dan.

MELANIE: She did, too. Last night.

(MELANIE picks up her overnight bag and her tape recorder and goes upstairs into her room, followed by SHERRY.)

SYLVIA: What do you think of all this?

GLORIA: Linda has always been a very intelligent woman.

SYLVIA: But to leave her children like this...and her husband.

GLORIA: I'm sure she has a very good reason.

(BERNIE reenters.)

BERNIE: Where are the girls? Where...? *(HE goes up the stairs.)*

(MELANIE holds up the tape recorder.)

SHERRY: Do you think we should?

MELANIE: Mother said we could.

SHERRY: No, she didn't. She said it was up to Daddy.

(MELANIE pushes a button and we hear BERNIE'S VOICE.)

BERNIE'S VOICE: Now, look Fran...

FRAN'S VOICE: Yes, dear?

(BERNIE bursts into the room, picks up the tape recorder and hurls it to the floor, breaking it into pieces.)

MELANIE: How dare you?!!

THE LIBERATION OF LINDA DWORKIN

(MELANIE slaps BERNIE.)

MELANIE: I'm sorry, I'm sorry.

(BERNIE takes MELANIE over his knee and proceeds to spank her.)

MELANIE: I said I'm sorry.

SHERRY: Leave her alone. Stop it.

(SHERRY beats on BERNIE as he spanks MELANIE. The phone rings downstairs. SYLVIA picks it up.)

SYLVIA: Hello? What is it? All right, all right. *(SHE puts the phone down and goes to the foot of the stairs.)* Bernie? Bernie, it's Dr. Geller.

SHERRY: *(Beating on BERNIE)* You brute! You tyrant!

BERNIE: *(HE stops spanking MELANIE.)* Shut up!

SYLVIA: Bernie! It's Dr. Geller. He wants to speak to you.

BERNIE: Don't you leave this room. *(HE goes downstairs.)*

MELANIE: I said I was sorry. *(SHE picks up the pieces of the tape recorder and drops them into the wastebasket.)*

BERNIE: *(HE picks up the phone.)* Hello? Yes, Paul. I'll be right over. *(HE hangs up.)* They're going to operate on Dad.

SYLVIA: Oy, Gottenyu!

BERNIE: Now take it easy, Ma. It's a very simple operation.

SYLVIA: He's not a young man.

GLORIA: You go on ahead. I'll take the girls.

THE LIBERATION OF LINDA DWORKIN

SYLVIA: Oh, Bernie, Bernie!

BERNIE: Now take it easy.

SYLVIA: He'll never live through it.

> *(BERNIE and SYLVIA go out the front door. GLORIA goes to the foot of the stairs.)*

GLORIA: Melanie? Sherry?

MELANIE: Yes? What is it?

GLORIA: Come downstairs. I can't yell.

> *(MELANIE sighs and comes down the stairs, followed by SHERRY.)*

MELANIE: Yes, Mrs. Nussbaum. What is it?

GLORIA: Your grandfather is being operated on. We're going over to the hospital.

SHERRY: Does Mother know?

GLORIA: Your mother is gone.

MELANIE: Is he all right?

GLORIA: I'm sure he will be.

> *(MELANIE goes out the door.)*

GLORIA: You should put on a sweater.

> *(SHERRY runs out the door.)*

GLORIA: Don't run, dear.

THE LIBERATION OF LINDA DWORKIN

(GLORIA goes out the front door.)

Scene 4

Four weeks later. Voices are heard from the kitchen. Silence. LINDA enters from the outside. SHE looks about. Seeing no one SHE walks into the living room, looks about, runs her fingers over some furniture to test for dust. Voices are heard. SHE listens, sighs and sits, then rises. GLORIA enters from the kitchen.)

GLORIA: Linda!? How long have you been here? When did you get in?

LINDA: Just now.

GLORIA: How are you?

LINDA: Fine. Just fine.

GLORIA: Does Bernie...?

LINDA: No.

GLORIA: You look wonderful. Have you lost weight?

LINDA: A little maybe. How are the girls?

GLORIA: They're fine, just fine. They missed you. We're having a cookout, on the patio.

(DAN comes down the stairs.)

DAN: Hey! Princess!

LINDA: Dan!

(THEY embrace.)

LINDA: How are you doing?

DAN: I'm here. How are you doing?

LINDA: It's good to see you.

THE LIBERATION OF LINDA DWORKIN

DAN: You're just in time for dinner.

LINDA: How long have you been out of the hospital?

DAN: It's almost two weeks already. And I'll tell you something, I don't miss that gall bladder one little bit.

SYLVIA: *(Offstage)* Gloria...? *(SHE enters from the kitchen.)* Gloria.... Linda! When did you get in?

LINDA: Just now.

    (SYLVIA goes over to her and THEY embrace.)

SYLVIA: So...how was Washington? And Hollywood?

GLORIA: I'll let Bernie know that you're here. *(SHE goes off to the kitchen.)*

SYLVIA: *(After a moment.)* I hope it was worth it.

    (SHERRY enters from the kitchen.)

SHERRY: Mother! Oh, Mother!

    (THEY embrace.)

LINDA: Did you miss me?

    (MELANIE enters from the kitchen.)

LINDA: Melanie...

MELANIE: Are you home for good?

DAN: Of course, she's home for good. What a question!

SHERRY: Melanie had a date last week.

THE LIBERATION OF LINDA DWORKIN

MELANIE: Big deal!

LINDA: With who?

SHERRY: And Daddy bought Melanie a new tape recorder.

MELANIE: You're a walking newspaper.

SHERRY: It's not supposed to be a secret, is it?

MELANIE: It if were, it wouldn't be for long.

SHERRY: Oh, really! She's gotten so snooty.

(BERNIE enters from the kitchen.)

BERNIE: Hello, Sexy.

LINDA: Hello, Tiger.

BERNIE: Welcome home.

LINDA: Thank you.

SHERRY: Are you home for good?

SYLVIA: Sherry, dear, let your mother catch her breath.

SHERRY: You're just in time for Parents' Day. It's Monday afternoon.

MELANIE: And Miriam Geller is getting married.

SHERRY: She knows that.

MELANIE: And I got a new dress for the wedding.

SHERRY: So did I.

MELANIE: Gloria helped me pick it out.

THE LIBERATION OF LINDA DWORKIN

SHERRY: She asked us to call her Gloria.

SYLVIA: The food is getting cold. You must be hungry.

LINDA: I just had my dinner, on the plane.

SYLVIA: Come on, let's eat. You'll talk to your mother later.

SHERRY: You're not going away again, are you?

SYLVIA: Sherry, dear?

MELANIE: Come on, Blabbermouth.

SHERRY: Oh.....bull!

(MELANIE and SHERRY go off to the kitchen.)

DAN: We've got a lot to catch up on. *(HE kisses her and goes off to the kitchen.)*

SYLVIA: No one can take your place. You know that.

LINDA: Thank you.

(SYLVIA goes off to the kitchen.)

BERNIE: Why didn't you let me know you were coming? I could have picked you up at the airport. So, where do we stand?

LINDA: Did you miss me?

BERNIE: What do you want, a testimonial?

LINDA: You're still angry with me, aren't you? I never thought that Fran would take it seriously.

BERNIE: That's not what I'm talking about?

THE LIBERATION OF LINDA DWORKIN

LINDA: What then?

BERNIE: I didn't know we had secrets from each other.

LINDA: What secrets?

BERNIE: You never told me that you were unhappy.

LINDA: I wasn't unhappy.

BERNIE: What then?

LINDA: I was frustrated, and I didn't know why.

BERNIE: And now you know?

LINDA: I know a little more.

BERNIE: About what?

LINDA: About myself.

BERNIE: What do you know?

LINDA: I know why I left.

BERNIE: All right. I'm waiting.

LINDA: I don't know how you're going to feel about this.

BERNIE: There's only one way of finding out.

LINDA: You know that Fran and I were roommates at college. Well, there was always this physical attraction between us. Nothing ever came of it and I'd forgotten all about it. And then when she called and said she was coming into town, it started up again. And then, when I saw her...I couldn't ignore it anymore. We just had to see it through.

BERNIE: I see. And?

THE LIBERATION OF LINDA DWORKIN

LINDA: We had an affair.

BERNIE: You went to bed together. And you didn't enjoy it.

LINDA: I wouldn't say that. After a week or so, however, we saw that there was really no future for the two of us. This attraction between us was just sex, and nothing more. Not that we didn't respect one another, and not that we couldn't be friends. And then I realized that what was really bothering me was something...bigger, something much more important.

BERNIE: Women's Lib.

LINDA: To some extent. One aspect of it, at any rate.

BERNIE: I understand that the bill didn't pass.

LINDA: No, but passing the bill wasn't really as important as we thought it was. Just the fact that we got together, that was the important thing. And the bill is calling attention to things that have to be done.

BERNIE: All right. So where do we stand? I mean you and me, now that you've gotten that out of your system. Or have you?

LINDA: It isn't as simple as that?

BERNIE: I see. There's more to it than that.

LINDA: I've come to see that...I'm a work in progress.

BERNIE: Oh, great.

LINDA: I've been doing a lot of thinking.

BERNIE: And?

LINDA: I've come to see that I've really accomplished a great deal, so far. With your help, I've produced two wonderful human beings. I have a wonderful marriage. I have a lovely home.

THE LIBERATION OF LINDA DWORKIN

BERNIE: But that isn't enough.

LINDA: I have so much more to offer, Bernie.

BERNIE: Like what?

LINDA: I don't know.

BERNIE: You still don't know?

LINDA: No. But I intend to find out.

BERNIE: I see. And where are you off to now?

LINDA: Nowhere. That is, if you'll have me. When the girls were growing up I needed to be here full time. I wanted to be here full time, for them. But now that they don't need me anymore.

BERNIE: They will always need you, Linda.

LINDA: Quite possibly. But not as much as they did before. As a matter of fact, I'm beginning to make a pest of myself, and I've got to find a place for all this energy. At one time I really had great promise as a pianist. It may be too late for that, I suppose. But I also had talent as a writer, and I've been thinking about a novel.

BERNIE: Fine.

LINDA: I will need help with the housework though.

BERNIE: You could have had it all along.

LINDA: I know, I know. But I've always believed that if you want something done well, you've got to do it yourself. I guess I'm a perfectionist.

BERNIE: No kidding. Where are your bags?

LINDA: They're outside, on the porch.

THE LIBERATION OF LINDA DWORKIN

BERNIE: You weren't planning to stay?

LINDA: I wasn't sure how you'd feel

BERNIE: As a matter of fact, I've been giving a great deal of thought to our marriage.

LINDA: Oh? And? What conclusion have you come to?

BERNIE: I'm not quite sure. I'm beginning to think it's a work in progress. *(HE kisses her.)* Mmmm. You smell so good. I'll get your bags.

(HE goes off. After a moment MELANIE enters from the kitchen.)

MELANIE: Aren't you going to eat something?

(BERNIE reenters with Linda's bags.)

BERNIE: I'll put them upstairs. *(HE goes upstairs with the bags.)*

LINDA: Can we be friends?

MELANIE: I'd like that.

LINDA: You will be patient with me.

MELANIE: Do I have a choice?

(THEY go off to the kitchen, their arms about one another.)

AN AUDIENCE OF ONE

A Bittersweet Comedy

CAST OF CHARACTERS

Ida Greenberg

Helen Greenberg

Joel Shapiro

Maud Harris

Carl Morgan

Christine Greenberg

Mark Shapiro

(Joel and Mark Shapiro should be played by the same actor.)

SCENE

An apartment in Greenwich Village in New York City

ACT I

Scene 1

(HELEN GREENBERG is on the phone.)

HELEN: How's your leg? Did you take your pill? Don't give me that stuff. Take the pill. It's an apartment, an apartment in Greenwich Village. That says it all. She's too young to be out on her own. Years have nothing to do with it. She's still a child. Look, Morris, you gave her your blessing. I had nothing to say. Oh, never mind. Did you take the chops out of the freezer? All right. I'll be home soon. Soon is soon. Good-bye.

(HELEN hangs up as IDA GREENBERG enters from the outside, carrying a shopping bag with groceries.)

HELEN: What took you so long?

IDA: I had to stand in line.

HELEN: That's all you bought?

IDA: They're delivering the rest.

HELEN: It's not too late to change your mind.

IDA: Mama...

HELEN: All right, all right. I'm not gonna argue with you. But just remember I tried to talk you out of it.

IDA: How could I forget?

HELEN: I don't blame you. I blame your father. He spoiled you from the day you were born. I was hoping that one day, when you grew up, we might be friends. That's what mothers and daughters are supposed to be. Maybe it's my fault. I don't know. Maybe I neglected you.

IDA: You didn't neglect me.

AN AUDIENCE OF ONE

HELEN: I spend so much time in the store. But if I didn't, we'd starve to death. You could have gone to college. You're a bright girl. It wouldn't have been easy, but we would have managed.

IDA: I know that, Mama.

HELEN: I never had the opportunity.

IDA: I don't wanna go to college. I'm tired of going to school every day, all day long. I wanna start my life. Besides, I'll be taking courses all my life anyway.

HELEN: What do you expect to happen? You expect Prince Charming to come along and sweep you off your feet. This boy you're seeing. Is he gonna move in with you? I'm asking you. What is he? A musician?

IDA: He's a composer. At least that's what he wants to be. He's very talented. He plays the piano. You should hear him, Mama.

HELEN: He's a student, isn't he?

IDA: He's in his final year. And he's Jewish.

HELEN: Are you having sex? All right. If you wanna ruin your life I can't stop you. I just hope you come to your senses before it's too late. And don't come crying to me. You're a foolish girl, Ida. You're a dreamer.

IDA: Didn't you have dreams when you were young?

HELEN: Everyone has dreams, when they're young. You read fairy tales. But then you grow up and come down to earth. I wanted to be a dressmaker.

IDA: You are very good with your hands.

HELEN: I thought one day I would have my own dress shop. But things were different in those days. I met your father. We got married. He opened a shop, but it wasn't a dress shop. What's the use of complaining?

AN AUDIENCE OF ONE

But I was hoping you might do better than me. Does he wanna get married, this friend of yours?

IDA: We haven't even thought about marriage.

HELEN: You're twenty years old. Almost twenty one. When I had you...

IDA: You were twenty two.

HELEN: You could have Harry Gold, if you wanted him. He's not exactly a brain surgeon, but he earns a good living...and you're not exactly a beauty, my dear.

IDA: Thank you, Mama. Did you call Daddy? How's his leg?

HELEN: Your father's not a well man. I just hope he doesn't need an operation.

IDA: Can we afford it?

HELEN: If he has to have it we'll have to afford it.

IDA: Well, now that I'm working...

HELEN: Keep it. You'll need it.

IDA: You don't have to worry about me.

HELEN: You can't even boil an egg.

IDA: So I'll learn.

HELEN: When are these people due back?

IDA: Next fall.

HELEN: Then what? If I was just starting out I'd want my own furniture at least. Okay, okay. I've said enough. When will I see you again?

AN AUDIENCE OF ONE

IDA: Mama, I'm twenty minutes away on the subway.

HELEN: Send me a New Years card, at least.

(HELEN kisses her. IDA embraces her.)

HELEN: Okay, okay. Let's not get sloppy. And call me. I think you know the number.

IDA: Yes, Mama.

(HELEN goes off. IDA sighs, looks about the room then starts for the kitchen. The phone rings. SHE hesitates, puts down the bag and answers the phone.)

IDA: Hello? They're in Europe now. Italy. I have an address for them, if you want it. They'll be gone for a year. I'll tell her you called. What's your name again? How do you spell that? (SHE writes on a pad.) Me? I'm sixty years old, and I have three grandchildren. Do you really? Well, I like young people. Good-bye.

(SHE hangs up, picks up the bag and goes into the kitchen. JOEL SHAPIRO enters a moment later.)

JOEL: Ida? Ida, where are you?

(IDA reenters.)

IDA: What is it? What's the matter? You're pale as a ghost. What's the matter?

JOEL: *(HE sits.)* I'm sick.

IDA: What's the matter?

JOEL: You don't care. You don't care whether I live or die.

IDA: The concert is cancelled.

AN AUDIENCE OF ONE

JOEL: Worse.

IDA: You've been replaced.

JOEL: Worse.

IDA: What? Tell me. What?

JOEL: I've got to conduct.

IDA: You're not gonna play?

JOEL: I've got to conduct and play at the very same time.

IDA: Oh, Joel! That's wonderful.

JOEL: "Vus meer" wonderful? I've never done that before.

IDA: You've conducted.

JOEL: Once. Besides, this is a major concert. And anyway, I've never played and conducted at the very same time. That idiot Clarence has the flu, and I'm the only one that knows the score. Well enough to conduct, at any rate.

IDA: Well, there you are!

JOEL: One rehearsal!

IDA: That's all you need.

JOEL: You don't understand. This is a piano concerto by Beethoven, no less. It's not "Bei Mir Bist Du Schoen." There are VIPs out there. Important people.

IDA: Look, Joel, you said yourself, you're a composer. Piano playing, conducting...it's frivolous. Of minor importance. You said so yourself.

JOEL: Well, one of these days I would like to conduct my own work.

AN AUDIENCE OF ONE

IDA: And you will, one day.

JOEL: Not if I fuck this up. A chance like this comes once in a lifetime. Tomorrow evening may be my key to obscurity. This concert is going to be reviewed.

IDA: By the school newspaper.

JOEL: No. I understand there may be someone there from the New York Times.

IDA: And what if there is? You're not a professional...yet. You're still a student. They expect you to show promise, that's all.

JOEL: This was all a mistake.

IDA: What?

JOEL: Music. I should never have gone to Julliard. I should have gone into the furniture business. That would make my father happy. That would make...well, maybe not my mother...but my brother.

IDA: Your brother?

JOEL: Yes, my brother. He's envious of me. He wants me to fail.

IDA: Nonsense. He's very proud of you.

JOEL: That's what he says, publicly. But privately, he's praying that I'll fail. He thinks that just because he went into the family business I should too. Just because he's a nonentity he wants me to be a nonentity, too.

IDA: I don't think so, Joel.

JOEL: You don't know him like I do. Oh, he's very charming, and lovable. I love him, too. And that's what hurts. Can I help it if I'm a god? Tell me that. Did I choose to be a god? No. It was thrust upon me. I don't trust anyone. I really don't. People don't want you to succeed. Success makes them uncomfortable. It's true. The world is full of envy.

AN AUDIENCE OF ONE

And a Jew besides. "Oy Gottenyu!" You're a sweet, innocent child. You don't know what the world is like. But nothing is going to stand in my way. Nothing and no one. I'm warning you here and now. If I hurt you one day, if I crush you like a bug, you have my apology right here and now. I'm really a monster.

IDA: I thought you were a god.

JOEL: Gods, monsters...they're all the same. You won't desert me, will you? If you were to walk out on me I think I would die.

IDA: I'm not going to walk out on you. Have you had your lunch?

JOEL: I don't remember. I did have breakfast, didn't I?

IDA: When's your rehearsal?

JOEL: At five.

IDA: I'll make you a sandwich.

JOEL: There isn't time. Besides, I'm not hungry.

IDA: Joel, you've got to eat something. I bought some yogurt.

JOEL: Let it be yogurt.

(SHE goes off to the kitchen.)

JOEL: Where's that recording?

IDA: It's on top of the phonograph.

(JOEL locates the record, places it on the phonograph and plays it loudly. IDA reenters with two cups of yogurt and two spoons.)

JOEL: Listen to that.

IDA: It's beautiful.

AN AUDIENCE OF ONE

JOEL: What?

IDA: I said it's beautiful.

JOEL: Beautiful?! He's butchering it. Listen. Listen. The clarinets were late. The tempo...it's too slow, too slow. Ah! That's interesting. What's that?

> *(HE turns to IDA. SHE holds out the yogurt and JOEL takes it and starts eating.)*

JOEL: And that's the great Ormandy, God help us all. He's been fooling the public for years.

IDA: Joel.

JOEL: What? What did you say?

IDA: Can you turn it down?

> *(HE turns down the volume and continues to eat.)*

JOEL: I'm hungry. What else have you got?

IDA: I bought some fruit. A banana?

JOEL: Perfect.

> *(SHE goes off and returns with a banana, which JOEL promptly devours.)*

IDA: What would you like for dinner? Joel?

JOEL: What? Anything.

IDA: I thought I'd cook something nice while you're at rehearsal.

JOEL: No.

AN AUDIENCE OF ONE

IDA: No, what?

JOEL: No dinner. I want you in the audience.

IDA: I'm coming to the performance.

JOEL: I want you at the rehearsal.

IDA: You said you didn't want me at the rehearsals.

JOEL: That was yesterday.

IDA: I've got so much to do. The kitchen is a mess.

JOEL: Are you a cleaning lady or are you my paramour? I want you to sit where I can see you.

IDA: Joel, how can you play the piano, conduct the orchestra and watch the audience?

JOEL: Just knowing that you're there, just knowing that there's someone there on my side, just knowing that someone there is rooting for me... You don't know what it's like out there. It's dog eat dog. Do you know how many people in my class would like to be in my place?

IDA: No. How many?

JOEL: Everyone in that orchestra. I think I'm gonna throw up. Maybe I shouldn't have eaten that banana.

IDA: You want some Alka Seltzer?

JOEL: Just hold my hand.

> (SHE takes his hand. THEY sit on the sofa. HE places his head in her lap and SHE caresses him.)

JOEL: What would I do without you? Oh, I know, I know. You're going to leave me, just like all the others?

AN AUDIENCE OF ONE

IDA: What others? What are you talking about?

JOEL: Hazel, for one. She left me for the captain of the football team. Women are so fickle. You won't ever leave me, will you?

IDA: Not unless you want me to.

JOEL: I shall dedicate my performance tomorrow to you, my rock, my soul, my everything. Suppose I called in sick? That would solve everything. They'd have to postpone the concert and, by that time, Clarence would be over the flu and then I'd just have to play.

IDA: You could do that.

JOEL: And disappoint all those people? I couldn't do that. They're all waiting for me to fall on my face. Ida?

IDA: Yes, dear?

JOEL: You don't want to get married, do you?

IDA: It's up to you.

JOEL: There's one thing that I do not want, is children. As soon as there's children the man of the house is second or third or fourth. Especially in Jewish families. I want you all to myself. I want you to be my mother, my lover and my friend.

IDA: You have a mother.

JOEL: Artists are children. They need constant attention. Listen to that. Listen.

IDA: What?

JOEL: Either that piano needs tuning or it's the record. Oh, God! Look at the time. We'd better get going.

IDA: I ought to change.

AN AUDIENCE OF ONE

JOEL: You look fine. Let's go.

IDA: Let me put the groceries away. All right, all right.

JOEL: Feel my head. Do you think I have a fever?

    (SHE feels his head.)

JOEL: Well, what do you think?

IDA: I think you'll live.

JOEL: How can I possibly play in this condition? All right, all right. Let's go. You lead the way.

IDA: *(SHE takes his hand then let's it go.)* Oh, my God!

JOEL: What? What?

IDA: Your hands are like ice. I'm only joking. Come on, let's go.

    (SHE takes his hand again and leads him off. A moment later HE runs back on and turns off the phonograph.)

JOEL: *(HE looks about the room.)* Good-bye, little table. Good-bye, little chair. Good-bye, little room. We may never meet again.

    (HE runs off. As the lights come down the concerto is heard.)

Scene 2

(The music fades as the lights come up. Three weeks later. The doorbell rings. IDA enters from the kitchen and goes off to answer the door.)

IDA: *(Offstage)* Mama!? Come in, come in.

(IDA reenters with HELEN.)

IDA: I wasn't expecting you. Is everything all right?

HELEN: Is your boyfriend here?

IDA: His name is Joel.

HELEN: I know what his name is. What have you got to drink?

IDA: You want some coffee? Juice? Something stronger? I've got some wine. Someone gave us a bottle of cognac.

HELEN: Give me some cognac.

IDA: Are you sure?

(IDA produces the cognac, goes off to the kitchen, returns with a glass and pours a drink. HELEN takes a sip and grimaces.)

IDA: I never saw you take a drink before.

HELEN: You never saw lots of things. You're looking good. Living in sin seems to agree with you. Is he gonna marry you?

IDA: We haven't talked about it.

HELEN: Well, you're still young. But when the children come...

IDA: Is there something wrong?

(HELEN starts to weep.)

AN AUDIENCE OF ONE

IDA: Mama, what is it?

HELEN: Before you know it, it's all over. The hours drag on, but the years fly by. I used to think that you were weak. It just goes to show you. You give birth to a child. You watch them grow up, and you're still strangers. I thought I was the strong one.

IDA: Mama, what's wrong?

HELEN: He's got cancer.

IDA: How do you know?

HELEN: They took X rays, and they found it...by accident.

IDA: How bad is it?

HELEN: He saved all that money to go to Israel. He wanted to see it before he died.

IDA: Mama? How bad is it?

HELEN: A month. Two months. Three, if he's lucky.

IDA: You should get a second opinion.

HELEN: That is a second opinion.

IDA: Where is he now?

HELEN: He's in the hospital. But they're not gonna keep him. They say there's nothing they can do for him. And even if they did, we couldn't afford it.

IDA: What about an operation?

HELEN: It's too late for that.

IDA: He was never that sick, was he?

AN AUDIENCE OF ONE

HELEN: He was sick, he was sick. He was just too stingy to spend the money. I kept telling him, see a doctor. I don't know what I'm going to do. I can't take care of him and take care of the store. All the money we saved... I don't know how I'm going to manage.

IDA: I'll take a leave of absence.

HELEN: You're only subleasing anyway.

IDA: No, the apartment is mine. I signed a lease. They're not coming back.

HELEN: Are you still taking those courses?

IDA: I'm studying composition. Music composition.

HELEN: What happened to the singing?

IDA: I never took it seriously.

HELEN: So what's the point?

IDA: I love music.

HELEN: So now you're gonna be a composer?

IDA: Not really, no. Joel's a composer. He's working on this piano concerto.

HELEN: It's your life, my dear. I'm not gonna tell you what to do. You won't listen to me anyway. But just remember this. Family is what's important. That's what's wrong with the world today. That's why there's so much drugs, so much killing. There's no respect. There's no loyalty. There's no love. And by love, I don't mean hopping into bed with the first man you meet. I've got to go. Myrna's watching the store till I get back.

IDA: How is she?

AN AUDIENCE OF ONE

HELEN: She's fine. But she's only a cousin, a third one at that. And besides she's got a houseful of kids. If you could come in for a few hours a day...

IDA: Mama, I said I would take a leave of absence. I'll give you as much time as you need.

HELEN: What about your boyfriend?

IDA: He's busy during the day anyway. Excuse me. I'm cooking something.

HELEN: What are you cooking?

IDA: I'm making cookies.

HELEN: Can I use your phone?

IDA: Yes, of course.

> *(IDA goes off to the kitchen. HELEN picks up the phone and dials.)*

HELEN: Myrna? I'm on my way. I'm at Ida's now. She's gonna take a leave of absence. Did you sell anything? Well, that's better than nothing. I'll be there in half an hour.

> *(HELEN hangs up as JOEL enters from the outside.)*

JOEL: Oh. Hello, Mrs. Greenberg.

HELEN: Good afternoon.

JOEL: How's everything?

> *(IDA reenters.)*

IDA: Hi.

AN AUDIENCE OF ONE

JOEL: Hi.

HELEN: I've gotta go. *(To JOEL)* How's your music coming?

JOEL: Fine.

HELEN: That's good.

>   *(HELEN goes off followed by IDA. JOEL paces about. HE notices the bottle on the table, picks it up and looks at it. HE sniffs the air, puts the bottle down and goes off to the kitchen. IDA reenters.)*

IDA: Joel?

>   *(JOEL enters eating a cookie.)*

IDA: You'll spoil your dinner.

JOEL: What did your mother want?

IDA: My father's sick.

JOEL: Oh? What's the matter with him?

IDA: It's cancer.

JOEL: How bad is it?

IDA: Pretty bad.

JOEL: What are they gonna do? Are they gonna operate?

IDA: It's too late for that.

JOEL: I see.

IDA: I've offered to help out.

AN AUDIENCE OF ONE

JOEL: How?

IDA: In the store.

JOEL: How are you gonna manage that?

IDA: I'll take a leave of absence.

JOEL: Just like that?

IDA: If I can manage it, I'll work part time. If not... It's my father. What can I do? What did Mr. Montalbo want? Joel? What did Mr. Montalbo want?

JOEL: It's not important.

IDA: You're not gonna tell me?

JOEL: I said it's not important.

IDA: All right.

JOEL: If you must know, he offered me a job.

IDA: What sort of a job?

JOEL: Conducting.

IDA: Where?

JOEL: What difference does it make? I'm not gonna take it.

IDA: Why not?

JOEL: It involves a tour. A five month tour. And now that your father's sick...

IDA: What kind of a tour?

AN AUDIENCE OF ONE

JOEL: Zurickman is getting old.

IDA: Otto Zurickman? The Otto Zurickman?

JOEL: *(Sarcastically)* No. Shmuel Zurickman.

IDA: I don't understand.

JOEL: I've just told you. Zurickman is old and frail. He can't handle an entire evening, and they want me to conduct the first half of the concert.

IDA: Oh, my god! What an honor!

JOEL: I'm sure they'll understand.

IDA: Understand what? You can't turn this down because of me. And besides they wouldn't allow me along anyway. We're not even married.

JOEL: What has that got to do with it? Anyway, I told them I couldn't leave without you.

IDA: And what did they say?

JOEL: Nothing. As a matter of fact...

IDA: As a matter of fact...what?

JOEL: They offered to increase my per diem, so I could take you along.

IDA: I see. Of course, you wouldn't have time to work on your concerto.

JOEL: I'd have plenty of time. More time than I have right now.

IDA: Then you've got to accept.

JOEL: I'm not going alone. I'll tell them I changed my mind, that's all.

IDA: Don't do this to me, Joel, please.

AN AUDIENCE OF ONE

JOEL: What?

IDA: You know I can't let you turn this down because of me.

JOEL: That's up to you.

IDA: Joel, my father is dying.

JOEL: So what? Are you gonna cure him?

IDA: They need me. My mother can't take care of my father and run the store.

JOEL: Why can't they hire somebody? Or let them get a nurse.

IDA: They can't afford it.

JOEL: I'll be getting a thousand dollars a week, plus a per-diem. We could live on the thousand, and then some. I'll send them my per diem.

IDA: It's not only the money. Joel, would you really want me to go, under those circumstances?

JOEL: Yes! Yes! Yes! They're old. They've had their life. We're just starting out. We've got our whole life ahead of us. What are they? Two peasants? Somewhere in the wilds of Brooklyn they sell cheap ties and underwear. Will they ever write a symphony? Will they ever create a work of art? What contribution have they ever made to Society? The only thing they've ever done with their life is you. And it's up to you to do something worthwhile. All right, I'm a shit. I'm vain. I'm selfish. I'm demanding. But so was Wagner. So was every artist that ever lived. Oh, Honey, I know it's a terrible thing I'm asking of you, but I wouldn't ask anything of anybody that I wouldn't ask of myself. And besides, these things can go on for years. My uncle was given six months to live. He's still around, and he's gonna outlive us all. And besides, my lovely Jewish madonna, this is the twentieth century. There are airplanes and telephones and busses. You can speak to them every day.

IDA: They'd never forgive me. I'd never forgive myself.

AN AUDIENCE OF ONE

JOEL: Your mother's like an ox. She could take on a whole football team.

IDA: That's what I used to think. But today, for the first time I realized how vulnerable she is.

JOEL: Okay, okay. I understand. *(HE picks up the phone.)*

IDA: Who are you calling?

JOEL: Montalbo. I'll just tell him that I can't go.

(SHE takes the phone from JOEL and sets it down.)

JOEL: What is that supposed to mean?

IDA: I need time to think.

JOEL: What is there to think about. No. No, you're right. I have no right to ask this of you.

IDA: You'll go then?

JOEL: No. I'm not a conductor. I'm a composer. I need time to work on my concerto.

IDA: But you said yourself you'd have plenty of time. And working with Zurickman... I mean this puts you in another category. You might even be able to conduct your own concerto when it's finished.

JOEL: These cookies are delicious. And you say that you haven't got any talent. *(HE goes off and reenters eating another cookie.)*

IDA: All right. I'll go.

JOEL: Are you sure?

IDA: I said I would go.

AN AUDIENCE OF ONE

JOEL: Oh, Baby, you won't regret it. I promise you. And when that concerto is finished, I'm gonna dedicate it to you.

IDA: You better.

JOEL: Oh, Honey, just think of it. We're gonna see America. America? We're gonna see the world, and we're gonna see it in style.

IDA: Meanwhile I've gotta start dinner.

JOEL: Forget it. We're eating out. Put on your best bib and tucker. We're going to the Russian Tea Room.

> *(JOEL goes off. IDA hesitates then picks up the phone.)*

IDA: Hello, Myrna. It's Ida. I'm fine, fine. Is my mother back yet? Well, as soon as she gets in will you have her call me please?

> *(IDA hangs up and stands lost in thought. As the lights come down symphonic music is heard.)*

Scene 3

(The music fades as the lights come up. Five months later. JOEL is on the phone.)

JOEL: Yes, I just picked it up. I should get in around ten, your time. You don't have to. I'll see you then. I can't talk now. No, I haven't told her yet. Good-bye.

(HE hangs up as IDA enters from the outside.)

JOEL: Hi.

IDA: Hi.

JOEL: What did the doctor say? Ida?

IDA: I'm fine. It's nothing. My stomach. Nothing to worry about. Was that for me? The phone call?

JOEL: No. It was Irene. Irene Manners. She's offering me her cottage to work in.

IDA: That's very generous of her.

JOEL: There's no need for you to be sarcastic. She's anxious for me to finish my concerto.

IDA: When do you leave?

JOEL: I said I'd speak to you first.

IDA: Are you asking my permission?

JOEL: That's an odd way of putting it? I don't know what's come over you, Ida. Permission!

IDA: I'm sorry. I used the wrong word.

JOEL: Are you sure the doctor said that you're all right?

AN AUDIENCE OF ONE

IDA: I'm fine. I've just gotta watch my diet, that's all.

JOEL: You're getting too heavy. I've told you that. I know you don't like Irene, but she thinks very highly of you.

IDA: We hardly know each other.

JOEL: I've spoken to her about you many times, and she knows how much you mean to me. It would be nice to get away for while. Not from you.

IDA: I know what you mean. And it is lovely out there. How long will you be gone?

JOEL: I don't know.

IDA: Until it's finished, of course. The concerto, I mean.

JOEL: She is on the board of the Los Angeles Philharmonic.

IDA: So you've said.

JOEL: And she has all sorts of contacts.

IDA: And money.

JOEL: For your information, she started out as a chorus girl. And there is absolutely nothing phoney about her. The money means nothing.

IDA: It's what she can do with it.

JOEL: Exactly. And she's devoted to the arts. Especially music. If it wasn't for her the Los Angeles Philharmonic would not exist. What did Charley have to say? Can you get your old job back?

IDA: Quite possibly. I don't know yet.

JOEL: What do you mean, you don't know?

AN AUDIENCE OF ONE

IDA: Is there any ginger ale left?

JOEL: I think so.

> (SHE goes off to the kitchen. JOEL paces about. SHE reenters with a glass of ginger ale.)

JOEL: Aren't you gonna take off your coat?

IDA: I'm a little chilly.

JOEL: Are you sure you're all right?

IDA: Joel, I am fine. I'm a little tired, that's all. It's been a long trip. Tour. Whatever.

JOEL: Well, I'm sure you enjoyed it just as much as I did. And please don't pretend that you didn't.

IDA: Of course, I enjoyed it.

JOEL: What did your mother want? She called this morning, didn't she? What did she want?

IDA: She didn't say.

JOEL: She called for no reason at all?

IDA: She said she'd be dropping by.

JOEL: I thought she disowned you.

IDA: She didn't disown me.

JOEL: That's what you said.

IDA: She's very hurt, that's all. She barely talked to me at the funeral.

JOEL: Well, you got there, didn't you?

AN AUDIENCE OF ONE

IDA: Not really, no. I was too late. The flight was delayed.

JOEL: You paid your respects. And that's the important thing. And there's no reason on earth for you to feel guilty about it. Life goes on. Where are you going?

IDA: I'm gonna lie down for a while.

JOEL: I think we oughta talk.

IDA: About what?

JOEL: About what? I am leaving in a couple of hours. I don't know how long I'll be gone. Do you need any money? There's eight hundred dollars in the bank.

IDA: That'll be fine.

JOEL: Are you sure? Okay, okay.

IDA: Is there anything else?

JOEL: You don't really care, do you? You don't care if I live or die. You're like a lump of clay. I don't know, Ida, maybe you're the lucky one. Nothing bothers you. I just hope to hell...

IDA: What?

JOEL: You're so gullible. You're so naive. The world is full of sharks, my dear. Not that I want you to sit around and mope.

   (The doorbell rings.)

JOEL: That'll be your mother. I don't want to see her. Besides I've still gotta pack. Let me know when she leaves.

   (JOEL goes off to the bedroom. IDA goes off and returns with HELEN.)

AN AUDIENCE OF ONE

HELEN: I won't stay long.

IDA: You're welcome to sit down.

HELEN: Don't be sarcastic with me, young lady.

IDA: What do you want, Mama?

HELEN: Where's your boyfriend?

IDA: He's busy right now.

HELEN: How long you been back?

IDA: A couple of days.

HELEN: *(SHE studies her for a moment.)* Does he know you're pregnant? Well, if he walks out on you, don't come running to me. You're not...

IDA: What?

HELEN: Never mind. I don't wanna know about it. But just remember, you're still Jewish. I'm still trying to figure out who you take after. No one on my side, that's for sure. And no one on your father's side, as far as I know. He left you some money, incidentally. Not very much, so don't get your hopes up. You should be getting a check in a couple of weeks.

IDA: If you need it...

HELEN: He left it to you. It's yours. Here. *(SHE hands her an envelope.)*

IDA: What's this?

HELEN: Your father asked me to give it to you.

IDA: What is it?

AN AUDIENCE OF ONE

HELEN: It's addressed to you. I didn't open it. He worshipped you, you know.

IDA: He didn't worship me.

HELEN: You know what his very last words were? "Where is Ida?"

IDA: Mama, I came as soon as I could.

HELEN: He waited and waited. The man was dying and he still held on. He held on to the very last minute.

IDA: The flight was delayed. I told you that.

HELEN: I'm not talking about the funeral.

IDA: What then?

HELEN: I'm talking about your phone call.

IDA: What phone call? I don't know what you're talking about?

HELEN: You forgot all about it. I spoke to your boyfriend. As soon as I knew the end was near I called you. Your father wanted to say good-bye. Your boyfriend said he would give you the message. Maybe he forgot, too. What difference does it make? He's gone now. Your father is gone. But I will never forgive you. As long as I live, I will never forgive you.

IDA: Mama, I swear to you, I never got the message. Of course, I would have called.

HELEN: You're still young, and you've got a lot to learn. Boy, have you got a lot to learn. And as far as this kid of yours is concerned, if you don't want it, I'll take it. It is, after all, your father's grandchild. I'll take the kid, if you want me to, but you're not welcome in my house. Not ever.

AN AUDIENCE OF ONE

(*HELEN takes one last look and goes off. A door slam is heard. IDA sits with a sigh and opens the envelope. A snapshot falls to the floor as she removes a note. SHE picks up the snapshot, looks at it, then reads the note. JOEL looks cautiously into the room, then enters.*)

JOEL: Is she gone?

IDA: Obviously.

JOEL: What did she have to say?

IDA: She brought me this note from my father.

JOEL: (*HE picks up the snapshot.*) That's you, I gather.

IDA: In my graduation dress.

JOEL: Your father was nice looking when he was young. What does he say in the note?

IDA: He says good-bye, and that he loves me. You didn't tell me my mother called.

JOEL: Of course, I did.

IDA: Two days before he died?

JOEL: It must have slipped my mind. All right, I didn't want to upset you.

IDA: That was the night you played the Hollywood Bowl, wasn't it?

JOEL: Ida, there was nothing you could do. What was the point?

IDA: I could have said good-bye, for the very last time.

JOEL: How in the world was I supposed to know? All right, I'm sorry. Maybe I should have told you. I apologize. I thought it was the right

AN AUDIENCE OF ONE

thing to do. Boy, I thought we musicians were melodramatic! Well, I'm all packed. I gotta get to the bank before it closes. Ida...

IDA: Yes, dear?

JOEL: You know I love you.

IDA: Yes, dear, I know.

> *(HE kisses her and goes off. SHE sits lost in thought, rubs her belly automatically, then picks up the snapshot and studies it as the lights come down.)*

ACT II

Scene 1

(Five years later. There is an easel with a stool in front of it, together with painting materials in one corner of the room. There is one painting on the wall. A number of paintings, wrapped for shipment are stacked against the wall. MAUD HARRIS is in the process of packing a painting. The phone rings and MAUD answers it.)

MAUD: Hello? She's not in right now. I don't know when she'll be back. I said I didn't know. Are you deaf or something? The same to you.

(SHE slams the phone down and returns to her packing. IDA enters from the outside.)

IDA: What are you doing?

MAUD: What does it look like?

IDA: I said I would help.

MAUD: So you did.

IDA: The exhibition isn't until the twentieth.

MAUD: They're picking up the stuff on Friday.

IDA: This is only Monday.

MAUD: I know what day it is. Where were you?

IDA: I ran into Carl Morgan.

MAUD: Purely by accident.

IDA: He's your friend, Maud, not mine.

MAUD: He's not my friend. He's merely an acquaintance.

AN AUDIENCE OF ONE

IDA: Well, you're the one that introduced us.

MAUD: What is that supposed to mean?

IDA: I can see you're in one of your moods.

MAUD: You're so naive. He's trying to get you into bed.

IDA: I thought he was gay.

MAUD: Carl? He's a womanizer, and a lush. Not all of my friends are gay.

IDA: Would you like some tea?

MAUD: Didn't you have tea with Carl?

IDA: We didn't have anything. I ran into him in the park, and we just sat and chatted. I'll put on the kettle. *(SHE goes into the kitchen.)*

MAUD: *(After a moment)* Arthur called.

IDA: *(SHE appears in the doorway holding a kettle.)* Arthur Chandler?

MAUD: How many Arthurs do you know?

IDA: What did he want?

MAUD: How should I know?

IDA: Didn't you take a message?

MAUD: I am not your secretary. If it's important, he'll call again.

IDA: He's the accompanist at the ballet school. I asked him to watch Christine. I wanted to know how she's doing.

MAUD: Don't you talk to her teacher?

AN AUDIENCE OF ONE

IDA: I wanted a second opinion. And I trust his judgement.

MAUD: Don't you trust her teacher?

IDA: Madame Sloviova seems to be enthusiastic about all her pupils.

MAUD: Well, you have my opinion. She's much too young to be studying ballet.

IDA: She's made up her mind. She's gonna be a dancer.

MAUD: She's five years old.

IDA: You'd never know it, to talk to her. You must admit, she's very bright.

MAUD: She'll still a child, a baby.

(IDA goes back into the kitchen.)

MAUD: Did you hear what I said? Ida?

IDA: Yes, I heard you. *(SHE reenters.)*

MAUD: You're so naive.

IDA: Now what?

MAUD: I'm referring to Carl. Carl Morgan.

IDA: What about him?

MAUD: I told you. He's trying to get you into bed.

IDA: He knows I'm with you.

MAUD: He doesn't take our relationship seriously.

IDA: I never led him to think...

AN AUDIENCE OF ONE

MAUD: What?

IDA: That I didn't.

MAUD: Maybe he can read between the lines.

IDA: I love you, Maud.

MAUD: As far as I'm concerned you are perfectly free to do as you please.

IDA: No one is perfectly free to do as they please.

MAUD: Well, I'm not stopping you. If you want to move in with Carl, go right ahead. But you know nothing about him.

IDA: I know he's a novelist, and he's talented. What do you know about him?

MAUD: For one thing, he is not a novelist. He wrote a book of short stories that received some good reviews. That was three years ago. He's written nothing since.

IDA: That's not true. He's working on a novel right now.

MAUD: Everything he's written since then has been rejected. He drinks like a fish. He's divorced, and he's always getting into fights. But maybe he can give you what I can't.

IDA: Are we gonna start that again? Sex is not that important to me.

MAUD: Well, it is to me. And you act like a martyr.

IDA: Now you know that's not true.

MAUD: Isn't it? The fact of the matter is you're still in love with Joel. Well, aren't you?

AN AUDIENCE OF ONE

IDA: What difference does it make how I feel about Joel? Joel is not a part of my life.

MAUD: But you'd take him back in a minute, wouldn't you? Wouldn't you? If he called right now and asked you to join him...wherever he is you'd hop on the next plane out of here. He gave a concert in New York and he didn't even bother to call you. Why didn't you let him know about Christine?

IDA: I told you. He doesn't want children.

MAUD: The least he could do is pay for her support. And when are you gonna tell Christine who her father is? Don't you think she has a right to know?

IDA: When she's old enough, and she really wants to know, I'll tell her.

MAUD: He's making shitpots.

IDA: I don't need his money.

MAUD: And apparently he's changed his mind about children.

IDA: I'm not gonna run after him.

MAUD: He's divorced, you know.

IDA: What are you driving at? You want me to get together with him? Is that what you want?

MAUD: Maybe he can make you happy.

IDA: If there's anyone here that's unhappy, Maud, it's you. Not me. Oh, Jesus. The tea! *(SHE runs off to the kitchen.)*

MAUD: I told you to get a new tea pot.

> *(MAUD finishes wrapping the picture and places it up against the wall next to the others. SHE sits and lights up a cigarette.)*

AN AUDIENCE OF ONE

MAUD: Oh, shit!

(MAUD puts out her cigarette as IDA reenters with the tea pot and two mugs on a tray.)

IDA: You're not...

MAUD: No, I am not. I just forgot, that's all.

IDA: Why do you carry them around?

MAUD: If I want your advice, I'll ask for it.

IDA: You are in a mood. Do you want some pie? Maud?

MAUD: If you want some pie, have some.

IDA: It's fat free. *(Indicating the picture on the wall)* What about that one?

MAUD: I'm not showing that one.

IDA: Why not?

MAUD: Because it's yours. I gave it to you.

IDA: There's no reason why you can't exhibit it, is there? Aren't you excited?

MAUD: About what?

IDA: Your show! I mean...it is the Rosenfeld Gallery. It's what you've always wanted. What you've dreamed about for years. I should think you'd be delighted.

MAUD: Excited! Mr. Rosenfeld asked me, "Aren't you enjoying all this attention, Maud?" "Enjoying it?" I'm forty five years old, and they're first beginning to notice me. I said to him, I said, "If you put a meal in front of a starving man, do you ask him if he's enjoying it?"

AN AUDIENCE OF ONE

IDA: Look at it this way. Suppose it wasn't happening? What then?

(THEY drink their tea.)

IDA: You never told me about Zoe.

MAUD: What about her?

IDA: You said she left you.

MAUD: She did.

IDA: You never told me she took her own life.

MAUD: What difference does it make?

IDA: How did it happen?

MAUD: Why do you want to know?

IDA: She was a part of your life. She was a painter too, wasn't she?

MAUD: A very talented one, and a very troubled one. I'd rather not talk about it. I suppose Carl filled your ears. What did he tell you?

IDA: That she committed suicide.

MAUD: And he blamed me.

IDA: Not really.

MAUD: What did he say?

IDA: Nothing much, really. He said that she had mental problems. I'm gonna have some pie.

> *(IDA goes into the kitchen. MAUD sits drinking her tea. IDA reenters with a slice of pie on a plate and sits beside her.)*

AN AUDIENCE OF ONE

IDA: Was she pretty?

MAUD: She was beautiful, and demented. This was in Paris. Montmarte. It was all very romantic, and exciting and lovely, except for her jealous rages.

IDA: What was she jealous of?

MAUD: Me. If I looked at another woman, or a man. Once she climbed out onto the roof and threatened to jump, just because I spent some time talking to this girl at some party. And it wasn't only that. I sold a painting once. She insisted that the man wanted to buy her painting but that I persuaded him to take mine instead. I don't know. Maybe I was to blame. I loved to tease her. We were both very young, and very insecure. Sometimes I'd flirt with someone I knew she didn't like, just for the hell of it. She came at me with the bread knife, and then she threatened to stab herself.

IDA: Why didn't you take her to a psychiatrist?

MAUD: Psychiatrist? We didn't have the money to pay the rent. *(After a moment)* It was Christmas Eve. I used to dread the holidays because we drank too much, and there were those awful rows. But this Christmas was different. We were at a party. It was a very quiet party for a change. She said she had a headache. She left early and she urged me to stay on. So I did. But after a while, I got worried. She'd been so quiet all evening. So I ran home. The place was in shambles. She'd slashed two of my paintings. And she was gone. It was the middle of winter. It was freezing. We spent all night looking for her. We finally gave up, and I went to bed. Days passed by and no sign of Zoe. Then one morning the police knocked on my door. They asked me to come down to the morgue to identify a body. Sure enough, it was Zoe. They'd found her in the Seine. She wanted to be cremated. So I had her cremated. They put her in a box. Her family lived in Cincinnati. I was tired of Paris. So I came back to the states, with Zoe in a box and I delivered her to her family in Cincinnati. And that was the end of Zoe.

IDA: Was it? Is it?

AN AUDIENCE OF ONE

MAUD: You don't stop loving someone just because they're dead. And how could I forget poor, demented, lovely Zoe? And lately...

IDA: What?

MAUD: I've been thinking about Paris. How'd you like to move to Paris?

IDA: Permanently?

MAUD: Permanently! What does that mean, permanently? What is permanent? Who is permanent?

IDA: I never thought about Paris. Except to visit, of course. And there is Christine.

MAUD: I think I'll have some pie, after all. Just a sliver.

(*IDA goes into the kitchen.*)

MAUD: Just a sliver!

IDA: (*Offstage*) I heard you.

(*IDA reenters with the pie and THEY sit eating.*)

IDA: I wish you'd exhibit that painting. You can mark it "not for sale."

MAUD: It's your favorite, I know.

IDA: Maybe it's because that's how we met. You were so snippy. Why I stuck around, I don't know. It was a cold, windy day. I guess I thought that anyone that talented couldn't be all bad. Why did you decide to give it to me?

MAUD: Since you liked it so much, I thought you would make a nice home for my "baby."

IDA: You acted so strangely. I couldn't figure you out.

AN AUDIENCE OF ONE

MAUD: I was afraid of you.

IDA: Afraid of me? Why?

MAUD: Because I was in love with you, right then and there. And I was still nursing my wounds, and besides I didn't know if you were gay or not.

IDA: I wasn't. As a matter of fact, I never thought I could love another woman like that.

MAUD: Suppose I hadn't come along? What then?

IDA: I wasn't looking for love. I had Christine. And the way she took to you, and you took to her. I guess that settled it. I think she likes you better than she does me.

MAUD: That's because I don't lay down the law.

IDA: Someone has to.

MAUD: Well, you're the mother.

IDA: So why does everyone think she's your daughter?

MAUD: She looks like me.

IDA: She doesn't look like you at all. *(After a moment)* Do you really want to go to Paris?

MAUD: Yes, I do.

IDA: I bought a new dress, for the show.

MAUD: Where is it?

IDA: It needs some alteration.

MAUD: I think you're gonna get more of a kick out of this than I am.

AN AUDIENCE OF ONE

IDA: I'm very proud of you.

MAUD: It's all so phony. The whole art world.

IDA: But you're not. That's the important thing.

MAUD: People go to these shows just to be seen, or to eat and drink. Or to pick up a trick. I should know.

IDA: But there will be some buyers there.

MAUD: I've sold some already. It'll be nice to have some money for a change.

IDA: And some recognition. I admire you so. The way you've stuck to it.

MAUD: I'm a painter. That's what I do.

IDA: Not everyone's so dedicated.

MAUD: That's my curse.

IDA: Or your blessing. Some people go through life not knowing what to do with it. Like me.

MAUD: Well, we've got to have an audience, don't we?

IDA: I wish I had your talent.

MAUD: No you don't. Besides, you've made your contribution, and a lovely one at that.

IDA: I don't know what I would do without her. She keeps me sane.

MAUD: But, for God's sake, don't become a professional mother.

IDA: There's no danger of that. Not with you around.

AN AUDIENCE OF ONE

MAUD: I may not always be around. What's the matter?

IDA: Christine! I've got to pick her up. You wanna come with me?

MAUD: I've got some things to do.

IDA: What do you want for supper? I've got some lamb chops in the freezer.

MAUD: No cooking. I'm taking us out tonight. Where would you like to go? I know. The Russian Tea Room.

IDA: Not the Russian Tea Room.

MAUD: Why not?

IDA: I've been there. I'd like to go someplace I haven't been.

MAUD: Lutece? Le Cirque? Twenty One? Tavern On The Green?

IDA: You need a reservation for all those places. What's wrong with The Pub? I love their food.

MAUD: Okay, okay. We'll go to The Pub. And I'll order champagne.

IDA: That'll be lovely. And we'll take Christine.

MAUD: No. We'll dump her in the garbage can.

IDA: *(SHE kisses her.)* I love you.

MAUD: Yeah, yeah.

> *(IDA runs off. MAUD finishes her tea. She sits thinking for a moment, then goes to the phone. SHE looks up a number in the phone book and dials.)*

AN AUDIENCE OF ONE

MAUD: Hello? Yes. I'm planning to fly to Paris in about two weeks. Let's say the twenty-fifth. Just one. No. One way. Early afternoon. Around one, say.

(The lights fade.)

Scene 2

(Three years later. In a corner of the room there is a table set up as a desk with a typewriter. CARL MORGAN is discovered at the typewriter. HE types a few lines, stops and reads what he's written, then rips the sheet out and throws it on the floor next to several other pieces of paper. HE rises, paces about then turns on the radio. Popular standards are heard. HE sits and listens, then rises, turns off the radio and returns to the typewriter. HE sits thinking for a moment, then starts typing, stops, tears out the sheet and throws it on the floor. HE picks up a magazine, leafs through it, throws it down and goes to the bookcase. HE removes a book from the shelf then produces a bottle which was hidden behind it. Hearing a noise, HE quickly replaces the bottle and the book and returns to the typwriter. IDA enters from the outside, carrying a small parcel. SHE stands watching him. HE turns around.)

IDA: Don't stop. I don't want to disturb you.

CARL: That's all right. I need a break.

(HE rises, walks over to her and kisses her. THEY sit on the sofa.)

IDA: How's it going?

CARL: It's not. I don't know why I bother.

IDA: I brought you something.

CARL: Am I supposed to guess?

IDA: Open it.

(SHE hands him the parcel. HE tears off the wrapping.)

CARL: Where did you find it?

IDA: At the Strand.

AN AUDIENCE OF ONE

CARL: Wouldn't you know it! Together with all the other remainders.

IDA: It's brand new.

CARL: Probably a review copy, which the reviewer never read. How much did you pay for it?

IDA: Ten dollars. Plus tax.

CARL: Well, at least I'm worth ten dollars.

IDA: Plus tax.

CARL: How was your day?

IDA: A day like any other day, only I was there. And yours.

CARL: I arrived at National Packing at nine pm. I loaded trucks till one. I ate my lunch, which you were kind enough to prepare for me. I sat down at two thirty and tried to start a new novel. I used up...I'd say thirteen sheets of paper. And that was my day.

IDA: Have you heard from your agent?

CARL: She's decided to put it aside. She's submitted it to ten publishers and that's it. Oh, yes. I had a lovely chat with your daughter. She told me all about the "Nutcracker." She's going to play the plum fairy, or was it the cherry fairy? She asked me if I knew the source of the Nile River. She's studying Egypt in geography. I asked her where the Nile River was.

IDA: You're all tensed up. Sit up. Let me rub you.

(HE sits erect and SHE kneads the back of his neck.)

CARL: I should have been a carpenter, or a farmer.

IDA: Or a brick layer.

AN AUDIENCE OF ONE

CARL: No. That would take some talent. Oh, that feels good. I don't know why I became a writer. I have nothing to say. Absolutely nothing.

IDA: Then give it up.

CARL: I've thought about it.

IDA: And...?

CARL: What would I do with my life? That's all I've thought about. That's all I've dreamed about. That's it. I'm a phoney. I became a writer for all the superficial reasons. The glamor of being a celebrity. Of reading about myself in the columns. Of seeing my book in the window of a fancy book store on Fifth Avenue. Of being interviewed on television. Of receiving the Pulitzer Prize. And eventually, of course, the Nobel Prize. Of traveling about the world and being greeted as a literary lion in all the capitals of Europe.

IDA: What's wrong with that?

CARL: Nothing. Come to think of it.

IDA: You could start by autographing my copy of this fascinating collection of short stories.

CARL: How do you know they're fascinating?

IDA: I've read them.

CARL: When?

IDA: In the library. Don't you remember? The second book is always the hardest.

CARL: I've written the second book.

IDA: The third then.

CARL: This is the fourth.

AN AUDIENCE OF ONE

IDA: And you say you've got nothing to say.

CARL: Well, let's put it this way. Whatever I've got to say, nobody wants to listen to. Uh, oh. I ended a sentence with a preposition. Very well, I will autograph this masterpiece. Where is my pen? *(HE rises, gets a pen from the desk and returns to the sofa.)* Now how would you like me to sign it? To Ida, who's fool enough to believe in me.

IDA: No!

CARL: How then?

IDA: To Ida, the most beautiful woman in the world.

CARL: Very well. *(HE writes.)*

IDA: I was only joking.

CARL: Well, you are. In my world, at any rate. There you are.

IDA: Thank you. *(SHE kisses him.)* Now the most beautiful woman in the world is going to start dinner.

CARL: *(HE kisses her hand.)* And soil those lovely hands?

IDA: It's either that or starve. *(SHE rises and places the book on a table.)* Back to work.

> *(SHE kisses him and goes off to the kitchen. HE sighs, rises and sits at the typewriter. HE sits, staring into space. HE rises, picks the book up from the table and starts to leaf through it, puts it back on the table and goes back to his desk. HE sits, thinking for a moment, rises, glances toward the kitchen and walks over to the bookshelf. His eye on the kitchen door, HE reaches behind the books and pulls out the bottle. HE takes quick swig, starts to replace the cap, changes his mind, takes a long swig, replaces the cap and puts the bottle back on the shelf behind the books. HE heaves a sigh and returns to his desk. HE sits for a moment,*

AN AUDIENCE OF ONE

rises, returns to the bookshelf, takes another long swig of Scotch and returns the bottle to the shelf. IDA reenters, catching him at the bookshelf. SHE stands looking at him.)

CARL: What's the matter? Is there anything wrong?

IDA: I don't know.

CARL: What is that supposed to mean? You're so suspicious. There's nothing wrong. What about dinner?

IDA: What about it?

CARL: Is it gonna cook itself? Can't you see I'm working?

IDA: At what?

CARL: What kind of question is that? You have a question?

IDA: I did have. I was gonna ask you if you were gonna pick up Christine.

CARL: Pick up Christine. Pick up Christine. She's almost ten years old. She can certainly take the subway by herself.

IDA: She's only eight. And I don't want her riding the subway by herself.

CARL: Okay, okay. I'll pick her up.

IDA: That's all right. I'll pick her up.

CARL: You don't trust me to pick her up? Suddenly you don't trust me?

IDA: No.

CARL: No! What does that mean...no?

IDA: Carl, you promised.

AN AUDIENCE OF ONE

CARL: Promised? Promised what? To love, honor and obey? Since when? I was married once. That was enough. More than enough. Much more than enough. Enough to last me a lifetime. Go back to the kitchen, woman. I shall pick up your daughter. I shall be honored to pick up your daughter. C'mon, relax. You're so uptight. Everything's fine. So I had a little nip. I deserve some reward.

IDA: Where are you hiding it? Carl?

CARL: Don't start.

IDA: You promised.

> *(HE returns to the table and begins to type. HE stops and looks at her.)*

CARL: I thought you were gonna pick up your precious daughter.

IDA: I will.

CARL: Good.

> *(SHE goes back into the kitchen. HE types then stops and listens. HE types again, then stops. HE gets up and walks over to the bookcase. HE hesitates, reaches behind the books for the bottle and hastily takes a swig, then replaces the bottle and returns to the table.)*

CARL: *(Sings)* "Oh, the monkey wrapped his tail around the flag pole, Around the flag pole, around the flag pole." How ya doing, kid? Hey, Ida. How ya doing? She's not gonna answer me. She's gonna start again. I said, how are you doing? You do understand English, don't you? Or should I say it in Yiddish? Nobody speaks Yiddish anymore. In my neighborhood, where I grew up there was this Yiddish family and they spoke Yiddish all the time. Maybe that's what's wrong with the world. What do you think? I said...Ida, what do you think? You think she thinks? She doesn't think. Hey, Ida!

> *(SHE appears in the doorway.)*

AN AUDIENCE OF ONE

IDA: What do you want?

CARL: C'mon, let's dance.

IDA: I thought you're working.

CARL: All work and no play... You never smile.

IDA: What have I got to smile about?

CARL: Hey! What do you hear from that dyke friend of yours? Is she still in Paris? I know you don't hear from your mother. She won't have anything to do with you. All you've got is your precious little girl. The world rises and sets on your precious little girl. And, of course, there's that great conductor, the great Joel Shapiro. The love of your life. Or was it the dyke? And you think you're so hot. What?

IDA: **You** called **me**.

CARL: I? Called you? You must be dreaming. Why should I call you? I'm trying to write a novel, and all you do is interrupt. And besides, how can anyone concentrate with little twinkle-toes spinning, spinning, spinning?

(IDA goes back into the kitchen.)

CARL: That's right, ignore me. I pay half the rent, you know. I don't want your charity. I'm my own man! That's more than you can say, though you did go to bed with that dyke. That's disgusting. Not that I'm prejudiced. After all, it's a free country, and some of my best friends are faggots. I don't understand it, but that's all right. I am open minded. But when you think about it... What's for dinner? Ida? I said, what's for dinner? She doesn't listen to a word I say. That's all right. She's not alone. I'm gonna call that agent. I am sick and tired... Hey! Hey, Ida. I just thought of something funny. *(HE giggles.)* Ohhhh. *(HE smiles and shakes his head.)* What am I doing here? That's what I ask myself. What am I doing here?

AN AUDIENCE OF ONE

(HE gets up goes up to the painting on the wall. HE stands staring at it, cocking his head to one side, and then to another. IDA appears in the doorway.)

IDA: What are you doing?

CARL: Oh! Oh! I'm looking at her precious painting. I'm looking at the dyke's painting. I'm not gonna hurt your precious painting. Look at the way she looks at me. As if I was gonna attack her precious painting. She hates me. Look at the hate in her eyes.

IDA: I hate what liquor does to you. Don't you realize...?

CARL: Oh! Oh! I thought of something funny. You don't wanna hear it. You're so worried that I'm going to do something to that precious painting of yours. I'm just gonna straighten it, that's all. *(HE adjusts the painting.)* There. There. Now it's straight. Are you happy? Look, look. I'm stepping away from your precious painting. I'm no longer near your precious painting. You can go back to your kitchen now.

IDA: Carl, please. Don't drink anymore. Please. You know what it does to you.

CARL: Do I tell you how to live your life? Do I? I'm asking you. Do I?

IDA: No.

CARL: I rest my case. *(HE approaches the painting, studies it and readjusts it.)* It's a lousy painting. It really is. You can fool some of the people some of the time, and all of the people all of the time. Look at that piece of shit. And she's making shitpots. Well, that figures. You paint shit, you make shitpots. We are not amused. Go back to the kitchen, woman.

(HE returns to the table and starts to type. IDA hesitates, then goes off to the kitchen. CARL continues to type then stops. HE tiptoes over to the painting, takes it off the wall and hides it under one of the pillows on the sofa. HE returns to the table and resumes typing. IDA reenters, takes her coat from the coat rack

AN AUDIENCE OF ONE

and puts it on. SHE is about to leave when SHE notices the absence of the painting. SHE stands quietly for a moment, debating what to do. SHE takes a deep breathe and speaks quietly.)

IDA: Where is it? Carl?

CARL: I beg your pardon?

IDA: Where is it?

CARL: Where is what?

IDA: The painting. Where is it?

CARL: Painting? What painting? Oh, that painting. Isn't that odd! It was there a moment ago.

IDA: Please put it back. Carl.

CARL: What?

IDA: Please put it back.

CARL: In order to put it back, we've got to find it first. Now, where is the painting? If I were a painting where would I go? To the Louvre? All the way over to Paris? Or maybe the Metropolitan Museum of Art. Or maybe the Modern Museum of Art. But if I were a bad painting, where would I go? Where would you go if you were a bad painting? I'm asking you, where would you go? Would you hang it on the wall for everyone to see? God, no! I would hang my head in shame. Or my frame. I would hang my frame in shame. It's a lousy painting. That's my final word.

IDA: That painting is worth a lot of money.

CARL: And here I thought it had a sentimental value.

(SHE goes to the phone and picks it up.)

AN AUDIENCE OF ONE

CARL: Who are you calling? I beg your pardon. Whom are you calling?

IDA: The police. I'm going to report a stolen painting.

> (HE walks over to her, takes the phone from her hand and hangs it up.)

IDA: Are you going to tell me where the painting is?

CARL: It's an ugly painting and it ought to be destroyed.

IDA: If it offends you, I will put it in the drawer. Just tell me where it is. And then...I would like you to leave.

CARL: You're kicking me out?

IDA: We had an agreement. You promised to stop drinking. I'm sorry, Carl, I cannot live with you when you drink. In addition to that I don't want you around Christine when you're in this cohndition. I will help you pack.

CARL: That's it?

IDA: I just can't take it anymore.

CARL: I never laid a hand on Christine.

IDA: If you had, you would have been gone long ago.

CARL: I need a drink. *(HE takes the bottle out from behind the books and sits on the sofa.)* May I have a glass please? I said... Very well, I shall have to be rude. *(HE takes a swig from the bottle.)* Would you care to join me?

IDA: I asked you to leave.

> (HE takes the picture out from under the pillow and puts it back on the wall.)

AN AUDIENCE OF ONE

CARL: Now, are you satisfied? *(HE goes off to the kitchen and reenters with a glass, then sits and pours a drink.)* I thought you were leaving.

IDA: I don't want you here when my daughter returns.

CARL: Your daughter. Fancy, fancy. *(Mimicking)* I don't want you here when my daughter returns. *(Sings)* "Don't put your daughter on the stage, Mrs. Worthington./ Don't put your daughter on the stage!" Let that be a lesson to you. But no, no. My Christine is...queen of the ball. What have you got to offer? Tell me that. You can't dance. You can't sing. You can't paint. You can't write. What have you got to offer? How dare you get on your high horse? You are nothing. A lump of flesh. That's what you are. A lump of flesh. And not a beautiful lump at that. How dare you...? How dare you tell me what to do? How dare you? You ought to kiss the ground I walk on. I have contributed something. I have created something. I have made something out of nothing. I have created beauty where there was nothing.

IDA: Carl...

CARL: Nothing! If I take a drink now and then, what of it? I gotta right. You think it's easy digging down into my guts? Spewing out my soul? For what? So that morons like you can share a moment of beauty, beauty... Oh, what's a use? *(HE finishes the liquor in the glass and pours more in the glass.)*

IDA: You're gonna make yourself sick.

CARL: I am sick. Sick of you. You're not even good in bed, when I can get you into bed with that brat around. You're not kicking me out, baby. I'm leaving...when I'm good and ready. Go on, get out of here. Well, what are you waiting for? Hurry, hurry. Oh! Oh! My little girl is getting on the subway. The big bad subway. Oh! Oh! What? Are you afraid I'm gonna hurt that precious painting of yours? Here, take the fucking thing. Take it with you.

> *(HE takes the painting from the wall and hands it to her. SHE lays the painting down on a table.)*

AN AUDIENCE OF ONE

CARL: I said take the fucking thing! You're not gonna take it? Okay. *(HE goes to the table, picks up a letter opener, picks up the painting and slashes it.)* Okay? You satisfied? Now get the fuck out of here.

>*(HE sits down and drains the glass. HE picks up the bottle and is about to pour another drink when IDA walks over and grabs hold of the bottle. THEY struggle. SHE breaks loose and runs off to the kitchen with the bottle.)*

CARL: You god-damned bitch! I'll kill you. You hear me? *(HE follows her off.)* I'll kill you!

>*(The sounds of a struggle are heard.)*

IDA: *(Offstage)* Carl! Please!

CARL: *(Offstage)* You god-damned bitch!

IDA: *(Offstage)* Carl!

>*(The sounds of a violent struggle.)*

CARL: *(Offstage)* There! And there!

>*(Silence. After a moment CARL staggers on.)*

CARL: I'm going for a walk. I need some air.

>*(HE staggers off. Several moments pass. IDA appears in the doorway, battered and bruised. SHE staggers to a chair and sits, breathing heavily. After a moment SHE rises, then winces in pain. SHE sits again and sobs softly. SHE rises again and staggers to the phone. SHE picks it up and, with difficulty, dials.)*

IDA: Mama, it's Ida. Please. Please, don't hang up. I need you. I need you, Mama. I...

>*(SHE falls in a faint as the lights come down.)*

ACT III

Scene 1

(Seven years later. The outside door is opened and Ida's daughter, CHRISTINE, a slim girl of sixteen enters carrying a suitcase. SHE is dressed in black. SHE sets the suitcase down, looks about the room, then looks back towards the doorway.)

CHRISTINE: Mama?

(IDA enters, dressed in black and carrying a suitcase which SHE sets down.)

IDA: Yes, dear?

CHRISTINE: What happened to Aunt Maud's painting?

IDA: It got damaged.

CHRISTINE: What a shame! How did it happen?

IDA: It's a long story. *(After a moment)* Mama?

IDA: Yes? What is it?

CHRISTINE: Are you sure you're all right?

IDA: Yes. Yes, I'm fine. Why do you ask?

CHRISTINE: Well, you were sick such a long time, weren't you? That was why I came live with Grandma, because you weren't able to take care of me, wasn't it?

IDA: Is that what Grandma told you? Yes, well, I was sick for a while, that's true. I was very sick. I didn't know whether I was going to live or die. I had no one to turn to, and Grandma said she would take care of you, on one condition, that I give her custody, and I don't show my face around the house. I had to agree.

CHRISTINE: Why would Grandma do a thing like that?

AN AUDIENCE OF ONE

IDA: I loved Grandma very much, but she could be very cruel.

CHRISTINE: I asked her once what you were like as a little girl, and she never wanted to talk about you.

IDA: When your grandfather got sick she needed my help and instead of helping her, I went away.

CHRISTINE: Where did you go?

IDA: I went away with your father. He needed me too. And then when your grandfather was dying, he was waiting for me to call, to say goodbye. And I never called.

CHRISTINE: Why not?

IDA: I never got the message.

CHRISTINE: Did you tell her?

IDA: *(SHE nods and shrugs.)* That was your Grandma. Afterwards, when I got better, I consulted a lawyer. He said I didn't have a leg to stand on, since I signed the papers. Besides I wasn't married to your father, and I lived with Uncle Carl, and we weren't married either. And the lawyer said that if I went to court it would be very unpleasant for everyone, especially for you. Grandma finally did agree to write me every once in a while, to let me know how you were doing. And I did go to your graduation.

CHRISTINE: I thought I saw you there. As a matter of fact, I ran out front to look for you. But you were gone. I told Grandma once that I wanted to pay you a visit. She said that it would only upset you. She said that if you saw me you'd want me to come home and live with you, but that you weren't able to take care of me, because you were so sick. Anyway I did come down here once, when I knew you'd be coming home from work. I watched you coming out of the subway, and I followed you home. I wanted to run up to you and hug you, but I was afraid. You didn't look sick but I thought that maybe you were sick, and just didn't show it. *(After a moment)* Mama?

AN AUDIENCE OF ONE

IDA: Yes, dear?

CHRISTINE: Why did you tell me my father was dead?

IDA: What did your Grandma tell you?

CHRISTINE: That my father is Joel Shapiro. Is that true?

(IDA nods.)

CHRISTINE: And you lived with him?

(IDA nods.)

CHRISTINE: Does he know about me?

IDA: No. He didn't want any children, so I never told him.

CHRISTINE: What happened? I mean, did you leave him because of me?

IDA: As a matter of fact, he left me. He met someone else. Someone who could help his career. Your father was very ambitious.

CHRISTINE: I guess it paid off.

IDA: I guess so.

CHRISTINE: Were you in love with him?

IDA: Your father was the love of my life. Does that sound too corny?

CHRISTINE: Oh, no. I think it's beautiful and so sad. He's very good looking, isn't he? I saw him on television the other night. He was so suave.

IDA: Yes, well he wasn't that suave when I knew him. Actually, when I first met him, I didn't like him very much.

CHRISTINE: Why not?

AN AUDIENCE OF ONE

IDA: I thought he was stuck-up.

CHRISTINE: What made you change your mind?

IDA: I heard him play. And then when he spoke about music, he became beautiful. And we both loved music. I was so happy to be with him, and so flattered. I was never a beauty.

CHRISTINE: I think you're beautiful. What are you smiling at?

IDA: I remember how he used to look deep into my eyes, so soulfully. It wasn't until years later that I realized what he saw there.

CHRISTINE: What was that?

IDA: His own reflection.

CHRISTINE: Oh, Mama! Was he really that conceited?

IDA: I wouldn't say conceited.

CHRISTINE: What then?

IDA: He had this terrible insecurity. It was if he didn't exist unless someone paid attention to him. Maybe that's what all artists are like. They need an audience.

CHRISTINE: Why didn't you ever marry?

IDA: Nobody ever asked me.

CHRISTINE: I don't believe it. I don't think I'll ever marry either.

IDA: Why not?

CHRISTINE: Because I am married...to my art.

IDA: What about children?

AN AUDIENCE OF ONE

CHRISTINE: I don't plan to have any children.

IDA: Oh? Well, you may change your mind.

CHRISTINE: I think friends are the most important of all. Lovers can die or they can fall in love with someone else, someone that can help their career. And as far as children are concerned, children grow up and leave. But your art is always there, if you want it.

IDA: What about when you get too old to dance?

CHRISTINE: I'll teach. Anyway I think I'm frigid. It's true. Not that it worries me. In fact, it's a great relief. Sex is really a pain in the neck. I look at some of my girl friends. They're a mess. And all because of some stupid boy. Oh, I'm not saying that I may not fall in love one of these days. But my career will always come first. If I didn't have my dancing, I don't know what I'd do. Not that a dancer's life is easy, but I love it. Did I tell you I've been accepted as a member of the company?

IDA: No. When did this happen?.

CHRISTINE: Two weeks ago. Mr. Davilo called me into the office to tell me. It was the best birthday present anyone ever gave me. When I told Grandma she pretended that it wasn't that important. But I know she was proud of me. And I'm glad she found out before she died. You did get my thank you note, didn't you? For my birthday present. It's a lovely dress.

IDA: Does it fit?

CHRISTINE: It fits perfectly, and I love it. Mr. Davilo told me that, maybe, in a few years from now I might be able to dance Giselle. I couldn't believe it. Aren't you proud of me, Mama?

IDA: Yes, I am. I'm very proud. You must be hungry.

CHRISTINE: I'm stuffed. There was so much food at the funeral.

AN AUDIENCE OF ONE

IDA: How about a cold drink? I'm dying of thirst. I've got some lemonade.

CHRISTINE: Okay.

> *(IDA goes off to the kitchen. CHRISTINE walks about the room inspecting it. SHE picks up a picture and studies it. IDA reenters with two glasses of lemonade. CHRISTINE puts down the picture and accepts the lemonade.)*

CHRISTINE: Mama?

IDA: Yes, dear?

CHRISTINE: What ever happened to Uncle Carl?

IDA: I don't know.

CHRISTINE: Don't you ever hear from him?

IDA: No.

CHRISTINE: He was a writer, wasn't he?

IDA: A very talented one.

CHRISTINE: But he did have a drinking problem, didn't he? I remember once, he came home and he acted very strange. And he smelled terrible.

IDA: He had these demons inside of him. When he was able to control them, he wrote some beautiful stories. Unfortunately, he wasn't always able to control them.

CHRISTINE: I remember one Christmas he dressed up as Santa Claus. And remember the summer he took us to Atlantic City, and we stayed at this fancy hotel? Aunt Maud sent me the most beautiful birthday present. It's a book about all the great ballerinas. There are all these beautiful pictures of Taglioni and Pavlova and Margo Fonteyn. I'll show it to you when we unpack. I guess you never see Aunt Maud anymore.

AN AUDIENCE OF ONE

IDA: I saw her last year.

CHRISTINE: She came to visit you?

IDA: No. I went to visit her.

CHRISTINE: You went to Paris? How exciting! Could we go to Paris sometime?

IDA: I don't see why not.

CHRISTINE: I'd love to go to Paris. One of my friends went to Paris last year and she just loved it. When can we go?

IDA: Maybe in the summer, when I get my vacation. And, of course, it depends on your schedule. Won't you be touring?

CHRISTINE: Not for another year or so.

IDA: Then we'll go this summer.

CHRISTINE: Oh, Mama! *(SHE throws her arms around her and kisses her.)* I'm so glad to be back home. Not that Grandma wasn't good to me in her way.

IDA: Yes, I know.

CHRISTINE: I still can't believe that she could be so cruel. Did you ever notice how when people talk about God and religion they get this mean look on their face? Up until my bat mitzvah I had to go to the synagogue every Saturday, but I went only because I had to. And I don't think that going to the synagogue makes you a better person. As a matter of fact, I don't know...maybe it's sacrilegious but I think that dancing is my religion. I know that it makes me feel good and beautiful and that everything's right with the world. I feel sorry for everyone that doesn't have that in their lives. And the idea that I can make a living doing what I love, I mean that's like dying and going to heaven. And then you look at all these people killing each other in the name of God. *(After a moment)* Mama?

AN AUDIENCE OF ONE

IDA: Yes, dear.

CHRISTINE: Do you think it's possible... I mean one day... For me to meet Joel Shapiro?

IDA: If you really want to...

CHRISTINE: Oh, I do. He's so cool.

IDA: I'm not sure how to get in touch with him. But if you really want to, I guess I could write him...somewhere.

CHRISTINE: Would you? It doesn't have to be right away. Maybe when I dance Giselle. Wouldn't that be something?! Oh, by the way, I hope you don't mind... I'm a vegetarian. I don't eat any meat, or fish or eggs or any living things.

IDA: I think we can manage.

CHRISTINE: I do my own cooking. Grandma let me, so you don't have to bother. And I do Yoga exercises.

IDA: Maybe you can teach me.

CHRISTINE: Oh, I'd love to. Maybe we can start right now.

IDA: What time is it?

CHRISTINE: It's four o'clock.

IDA: I've got to go. I've got a meeting.

CHRISTINE: What kind of a meeting?

IDA: I'm on the arts council. I'd skip it, but I'm the chairman. It's a very important meeting, and I was the one that called it. We can unpack when I get back. I bought a new dresser for you. It's really nice.

CHRISTINE: What time will you be back?

AN AUDIENCE OF ONE

IDA: I should be back by six. Six thirty the latest. And then we'll go out to dinner. There's a lovely vegetarian restaurant right around the corner. It just opened up. Will you be all right?

CHRISTINE: I'll be fine. I can start unpacking.

IDA: Welcome home, Honey.

(THEY embrace.)

IDA: I hate to leave you like this, your first day home.

CHRISTINE: Don't worry about it. Go on, go on. *(SHE kisses her.)*

IDA: I'll be back soon.

(IDA goes off. CHRISTINE sighs, looks around then picks up the suitcases and starts off, then stops. SHE puts down the suitcases, runs over to the phone and dials.)

CHRISTINE: Hi. It's me. Guess where I am. Very funny. I'm in the heart of Greenwich Village. It's cool. It really is. I'll be living with my mother now. I told you. She's fine. Can you believe it? My grandmother lied. It's a long story. Did I tell you what Mr. Davilo said? Well, anyway, it does bear repeating. Oh, Peggy, finally, finally... my life has really begun.

(The lights come down.)

Scene 2

(Three years later. The room is dark. The door is opened and IDA, dressed in black, enters followed by MAUD, dressed in black.)

MAUD: Here we are. *(SHE turns on some lights.)* Sit down. I'll make you some tea.

IDA: Nothing.

MAUD: Ida, you've got to eat something.

IDA: Why?

MAUD: Now stop it! You're still a young woman. You've got your whole life ahead of you.

IDA: To do what?

MAUD: To do whatever you want to do.

IDA: For whom?

MAUD: For yourself. For me. For your friends.

IDA: We were planning a trip to California. She wanted to meet Joel. I was all set to write him a letter. She was so excited.

MAUD: She had a happy life. It was short, I know. But her dream came true. How many people can say that?

IDA: She was just starting out. Oh, Maud, you should have seen her. She was life itself. Like a sunbeam. That son of a bitch!

MAUD: It was an accident. There was ice on the road. It wasn't his fault.

IDA: It's never anybody's fault.

MAUD: You had her for three long years. For more than that. No one can take that away from you.

AN AUDIENCE OF ONE

IDA: My life was so empty for so long. And then when she moved in, it was like starting all over again. I'd forgotten what it was like to really care for someone.

MAUD: I've got this lovely place outside of Paris now. It's a mansion really. Why don't you come over? We could start an art colony, you and I. It's beautiful out there, especially in the summer. You'd love it. Are you listening to me?

IDA: I'm listening.

MAUD: What do you say?

IDA: It's something to think about.

MAUD: I've got an appointment at six. These people have come in from Texas. They want me to do this mural for the lobby of their new office building. We're meeting at the Plaza. They're expecting me to have dinner with them. I've got to meet with them. They're paying me a fortune. But I won't stay for dinner. I'll be back in an hour or so. We can talk more about it. Okay?

IDA: Okay.

MAUD: What are you gonna do?

IDA: What?

MAUD: While I'm gone. What are you gonna do?

IDA: I'm gonna give a concert! How the hell do I know? What I'm gonna do?!

MAUD: All right, all right. Calm down.

IDA: I don't wanna live.

MAUD: Now stop it. I'm gonna call them. I'll postpone the meeting. I can see them tomorrow, in the morning before they leave.

AN AUDIENCE OF ONE

IDA: No don't. I'll be all right. You go on ahead.

MAUD: I hate to leave you like this.

IDA: What can you do? You can't bring her back, can you. Go on. I'll be all right.

MAUD: You sure.? The doctor should have given you something. I have these pills to calm my nerves. *(SHE digs into her bag and pulls out a bottle of pills.)*

IDA: What are they?

MAUD: It's a sedative. They won't upset your stomach. *(SHE gives her one of the pills.)* I'll get you some water.

> *(MAUD puts the bottle back into her bag and goes into the kitchen. IDA hesitates then quickly takes the pill bottle from the bag, empties most of the bottle into her hand then puts the bottle back into the bag. SHE sits down quickly as MAUD reenters with the water.)*

IDA: Is there any ginger ale?

MAUD: I'll see. Would you like some juice?

IDA: Ginger ale is fine. If not you can bring me some juice.

> *(MAUD goes off to the kitchen. IDA hides the pills in a cup on a shelf. MAUD reenters with a glass of juice.)*

MAUD: There was no ginger ale. I brought you some orange juice.

IDA: Fine. *(SHE takes the pill and washes it down with the juice.)*

MAUD: How about something to eat? All right, but when I come back we're going out to dinner. You hear me?

IDA: I hear you, I hear you. Maud...

AN AUDIENCE OF ONE

MAUD: Yes, dear?

IDA: Thank you.

MAUD: For what?

IDA: For everything. For flying out.

MAUD: Don't be ridiculous. I was planning a trip to New York anyway. I want you to take care of yourself. You hear me? You mean a lot to me.

IDA: I envy you, Maud. What kept you going for all those years?

MAUD: Madness.

IDA: I'm serious.

MAUD: I don't know. Stubbornness. Faith.

IDA: In what?

MAUD: In me, I guess. There was nothing else I could do. I burned my bridges. I've got to go. Why don't you lie down for a while? All right, all right. I'll be back in an hour. If you need me call the Plaza. We'll be in the Oak Room. The name of the people I'm meeting is Stanton. Okay? I'm gonna write down the number of the Plaza. *(SHE takes a piece of paper from her bag and writes down the number.)* Here. I hate to leave you like this.

IDA: I'll be all right. Go on. Oh, God. What am I gonna do with her things?

MAUD: When I get back we'll sit down, and we'll talk about it. Okay?

IDA: Okay. I'm sorry. Go on, go on. I'll be all right.

MAUD: Why don't you take a nap? Give me your keys. In case you're asleep I won't have to wake you.

AN AUDIENCE OF ONE

IDA: I'll leave the door unlocked.

MAUD: All right. *(SHE kisses her on the forehead.)* I love you, my dear. Where's my bag?

> *(MAUD goes off. IDA sits forlornly then reaches absentmindedly for the glass. Seeing that there's very little juice left she goes off to the kitchen and returns with a full glass. SHE set the glass on the table then places the cup containing the pills next to it. SHE sits down and as she reaches for the cup the doorbell rings. IDA pauses and waits. A moment later the doorbell rings again.)*

IDA: *(Under her breath)* Go 'way. There's no one here.

> *(There's a knock on the door. IDA shakes her head. The door is opened and MARK SHAPIRO steps into the room.)*

MARK: Hello?

IDA: *(SHE rises shakily and stares at him.)* Joel?

MARK: I'm his son.

IDA: What do you want?

MARK: I'm sorry to barge in on you like this. I was gonna call, but I lost your number. And I was right down the block. May I come in?

IDA: What do you want? Did your father send you?

MARK: Not exactly.

IDA: What is that supposed to mean?

MARK: This is my first time in New York, and I don't know anyone.

IDA: This is a bad time for me. I'm not up to entertaining.

AN AUDIENCE OF ONE

MARK: Yes, I know. I ran into your friend. She told me about your loss. I'm sorry.

IDA: So, if you'll excuse me.

MARK: She asked me to stay with you.

IDA: Well, I'm asking you to leave. Look, Sonny...

> *(SHE accidentally hits the cup with her hand and the pills go flying across the room. MARK goes to pick them up.)*

IDA: Leave them! I said leave them!

MARK: What are you...? *(HE sees the glass, looks at the pills then looks at her.)* I see.

IDA: Go 'way. Please. Leave me alone.

MARK: To do what?

IDA: That's my affair.?

MARK: Is it really that bad?

IDA: I don't know what you're talking about.

> *(HE sits beside her.)*

IDA: What are you doing?

> *(HE takes her hand.)*

IDA: What do you want? What are you looking at?

MARK: My father said you had the most wonderful eyes.

IDA: He talked to you about me?

AN AUDIENCE OF ONE

MARK: He said there was only one person in his life that had never lied to him. That had loved him and never asked for a thing in return. He said that there was only one other person, aside from himself, that he had really loved. He said that if I wanted to locate the real Joel Shapiro I should speak to you.

IDA: Your father was a great one with words.

MARK: Is. Is a great one with words. And he said that there are probably only two people in this world that would consider him a failure. That would be you and himself.

IDA: That's all very interesting.

MARK: You don't believe me?

IDA: Did he send you here?

MARK: No. He said that I might not be welcome.

IDA: Then...?

MARK: I wanted to find out what my father was really like. Besides, I wanted to meet you.

IDA: Well, now that you've seen me you can go back and tell your father you've seen the old bag. And if he thought so highly of me, how come I haven't seen him in almost twenty years?

MARK: Facing you would mean that he'd have to face himself, and that would not be a pleasant experience.

IDA: I see. And you think you have a right to pass judgement?

MARK: I'm not passing judgement. I just use him as a model...for what I don't want to be.

IDA: And what do you want to be?

AN AUDIENCE OF ONE

MARK: A great tenor.

IDA: You sing?

MARK: Good enough to be accepted at Julliard. That's why I came to New York. Isn't that where you and my father met?

IDA: No. It was NYU. I was taking a music course. Hm! So your father talked to you about me, did he?

MARK: Just this once, as I was getting ready to come out here. And suddenly I saw a side of him I'd never seen before, and I almost liked him.

IDA: What about your mother?

MARK: They're divorced, you know.

IDA: Yes, I know.

MARK: That was a great mistake.

IDA: Why do you say that?

MARK: They're too much alike. They both have great compassion for humanity but very little interest in people. My sister's a mess. She's a rebel, you see, but she's not quite sure why or what she's rebelling against.

IDA: And you? What are you rebelling against?

MARK: I'm not rebelling against anything. I think it's a waste of time. I just want to sing. A frivolous pursuit, but at least it doesn't harm anyone, except when I push too hard and I go flat. Where's your husband? Your daughter's father?

IDA: I have no husband.

MARK: I don't mean to pry.

AN AUDIENCE OF ONE

IDA: That's all right. It just so happens that my daughter was your half sister.

MARK: Did my father know that?

IDA: No. I never told him.

MARK: Why not?

IDA: He said he didn't want any children. And, he was on his way to join your mother.

MARK: So you raised her all by yourself? That must have been rough.

IDA: I managed.

MARK: You're quite a lady.

IDA: And you know a lot about ladies.

MARK: Not really. I guess I'm shy.

IDA: Really?

MARK: And young.

IDA: I was like that once.

MARK: I am absolutely starved.

IDA: There's some chicken in the refrigerator.

MARK: Let me take you out to dinner. That's one thing I do have is money. What do you say? You gotta eat, and it is dinner time.

IDA: My friend is coming back.

MARK: Leave her a note.

AN AUDIENCE OF ONE

IDA: *(SHE picks up the paper with the phone number, goes to the phone and dials.)* The Oak Room, please. Hello? Hello? Could you page Maud Harris for me, please? Thank you. Hello? Hello, Maud? No. No, I'm all right. Look, Mark wants to take me out to dinner. So there's no need for you to rush back. Yes. I'll see you later. *(SHE hangs up.)*

MARK: All set?

IDA: I'm not gonna be very good company, I'm afraid.

MARK: That's all right. There's one thing I do have in common with my father. Once I do get started, I talk a lot. Besides, I'd like to hear all about my half sister. What she was like, and all of that. What kind of food do you like?

IDA: You choose.

MARK: I'm easy.

IDA: There's a nice little vegetarian restaurant around the corner.

MARK: Sounds good to me. It's getting cold out there. Where's your coat?

> *(SHE goes off and returns with her coat. HE takes it from her and helps her into it.)*

MARK: They sure move fast here in New York. I'm not used to this frantic pace. Where are they all rushing to?

IDA: That's a good question.

> *(HE goes out the door. SHE follows him and stops at the door.)*

IDA: Just a minute. I forgot my keys! *(SHE goes back into the room, picks up her keys and looks about.)* Here you go again. Ida, my dear, you really are a sucker!

AN AUDIENCE OF ONE

(SHE tosses the keys in the air, catches them and goes off as the lights come down.)

LULU IN BABYLON

A Hollywood Saga In Two Acts

CAST OF CHARACTERS

Lulu Marsh

Her husbands and lovers to be played (preferably) by the same actor:

Wayne Hudson

Randy Tuttle

Myron Zimmer

Rene Germaine, Duke of Saugvernon

Scott Murphy

Senator Barry Sherman

SCENE

Hollywood

ACT I

Scene 1

The song, YOU OUGHT TO BE IN PICTURES, *is heard.*

Subtitle: GARBO TALKS

Subtitle: WILL HAYS ANNOUNCES PRODUCTION CODE

Subtitle: LULU & THE ACTOR

As the song fades the lights come up on the living room of a furnished apartment. WAYNE HUDSON, in pajamas and bathrobe, enters from the kitchen with a mug of coffee. HE sits on the sofa. LULU MARSH, in a pair of men's pajamas much too big for her, follows a moment later with a mug of coffee. SHE sits on a chair.

WAYNE: Must you sit so far away?

LULU: Honey, I need a rest.

WAYNE: You look puzzled.

LULU: I sure am. Are you sure you're a friend of Harvey's?

WAYNE: I was. I am.

LULU: And you roomed together at Princeton?

WAYNE: I know what you're thinking.

LULU: Well, Honey, Harvey's as queer as a three dollar bill. And he said... I mean, I don't care...

WAYNE: Would you marry me?

LULU: Holy cow! Now wait a minute. Back up a little.

LULU IN BABYLON

WAYNE: I know. It sounds crazy, I know.

LULU: Are you putting on a show or something? I mean, if it's for my benefit...

WAYNE: I'll tell you something, Lulu. I'm just as confused as you are. Would you believe that I've never been to bed with a woman before?

LULU: Yeah! I guess that explains it. You were sure trying to make up for lost time. How come...?

WAYNE: You mean, why haven't I been to bed with a woman before? I don't know. Ever since I was a kid I played around with other boys, and I enjoyed it.

LULU: Weren't you ever curious?

WAYNE: I guess so. But in order to go to bed with a woman you have to go through all that rigmarole. Anyway I did try it once, with a prostitute, and that really turned me off.

LULU: What about Harvey?

WAYNE: What about him?

LULU: According to him, you and him...

WAYNE: I'm afraid Harvey took our relationship a little more seriously than I did. I mean, I like Harvey and he's a lot of fun, and we had some good times...but that was about it.

LULU: Well, Harvey's a friend of mine. As a matter of fact, he's one of my best friends. He and I grew up together.

WAYNE: What about last night? Didn't that mean anything? You are attracted to me, aren't you?

LULU: Yeah, well...I think we oughta forget about last night.

LULU IN BABYLON

WAYNE: It didn't mean anything to you?

LULU: Look, Wayne, now that you got a taste of... What I mean to say is you'll meet lots of pretty girls out here. I got a career to think of.

WAYNE: I can help your career. I've got lots of contacts. How do you think I got my contract?

LULU: Yeah, how did you get your contract? It took me three years to get mine, and now they tell me it's not gonna be picked up.

WAYNE: My father's an old friend of Myron Zimmer. Okay, if you won't marry me, can we live together? I can get a bigger apartment.

LULU: Have you read your contract? There's a morality clause. They can drop you just like that.

WAYNE: Are you really serious about this acting business?

LULU: Aren't you?

WAYNE: Not really.

LULU: Then what are you doing out here?

WAYNE: I thought it might be fun. And people kept telling me that I oughta be in the movies. My father's a judge and he wanted me to be a lawyer. My brother's a lawyer and so is my sister. I got my degree just to please him, but after all that I decided that that was not the way to go through life, trying to please others. Actually, it started with Harvey. My father wanted me to stop seeing him, and we had a big fight about that, and I told him to go to hell. And that's when I realized that that's what I'd been doing all my life, trying to please others. And I asked myself, what do I really want to do with my life?

LULU: And what did you decide?

WAYNE: I couldn't decide on anything. All I knew was I didn't want to go into law. And since everyone kept telling me that I ought to be a

LULU IN BABYLON

movie star, I thought the hell with it. Why don't I give it a shot? And then I told Dad that that's what I wanted to be. I wanted to be a movie actor. And believe it or not, he said, "Fine. That's just where you belong, with all those degenerates." And he put in a call to Myron Zimmer, and that was that.

LULU: You're lucky to have a father, period. Especially one with all those connections.

WAYNE: What happened to your father?

LULU: He was run over by a car. That's what they tell me anyway. I was only two years old when it happened. He was a drunk, from what I can gather.

WAYNE: What about your mother?

LULU: I hardly ever see her. The first thing she did was put me in an orphanage, and then I was in a foster home.

WAYNE: You've had a pretty rough life.

LULU: You don't know the half of it.

WAYNE: Where did you meet Harvey?

LULU: In grammar school. We were in the same class together. They used to make fun of him, call him "sissy." And they used to make fun of me. They called me "fatso." So we had something in common. And we got to be good friends. We'd go to the movies together, and then we'd act them out. He'd be Joan Crawford and I'd be Greta Garbo, or sometimes I'd be Charlie Chaplin and he'd be Mary Pickford. We'd make up our own stories. Harvey was good at that. That's how he started writing. We kept a scrapbook together of all our favorites. His mother was real good to me, better than my foster mother. And then when he moved away we'd still keep in touch on the week-ends. And when he went to Princeton we'd write to each other every week. His first book was just published, you know.

LULU IN BABYLON

WAYNE: Yes, I know.

LULU: He must have talked to you about me.

WAYNE: Oh, yes. As a matter of fact he had this picture of you on his desk, but it sure didn't do you justice.

LULU: Yeah, well I lost a lot of weight since then. And I had a couple things done.

WAYNE: What are you gonna do when your contract runs out?

LULU: I'll manage.

WAYNE: Waitressing?

LULU: Yeah. And I've done some modeling. That sort of thing.

WAYNE: If you married me, you wouldn't have to worry about money.

LULU: You don't wanna marry me, Honey. Spending a night in the sack is a little different from getting married.

WAYNE: If you're still worried about Harvey...

LULU: It's not only that.

WAYNE: Because we're nothing more than friends now. As a matter of fact, I think Harvey would approve.

LULU: I've never lived with anyone. Not like that I mean. As a matter of fact, I like my privacy. I couldn't wait to get a room of my own. I mean I've never even had a roommate. And I'm not in love with you, and you're not in love with me.

WAYNE: We like each other, and we had great sex, didn't we? Didn't we?

LULU: Yes, dear.

LULU IN BABYLON

WAYNE: I mean I was okay, wasn't I?

LULU: You were fine.

WAYNE: Well, then?

LULU: Look you went to Princeton. You studied law. I never even finished high school.

WAYNE: That didn't stop you and Harvey from being friends, did it?

LULU: Being friends is a little different from being man and wife. Besides, I'm not ready to be a wife, and then you'll wana have kids.

WAYNE: Not necessarily.

LULU: And you'll want me to take care of the house.

WAYNE: If we get a house, we'll have servants. As a matter of fact, if I got married Daddy would be more than happy to buy me a house. As a matter of fact, Daddy would be more than happy to see me married...period.

LULU: Yeah, well...I don't think he'd approve of me. Besides, acting is my whole life. I live for the movies.

WAYNE: So we do have something in common then, 'cause that's the way I intend to earn my living. I intend to be a motion picture actor. As a matter of fact the studio is sending me to an acting coach. Maybe we can work on scenes together. How about that? And, as far as an education is concerned, if you're really serious about your acting you should think seriously about improving yourself. Suppose someday you have to play some historical figure or a scientist or a professor? You should learn all about art and literature and politics. A serious actor should know about everything. And I could teach you. I mean, have you ever read "A Midsummer Night's Dream?"

LULU: That's by Shakespeare, isn't it?

LULU IN BABYLON

WAYNE: Right. MGM is gonna be making a movie of it. Have you ever read "Of Human Bondage?'

LULU: Is that by Shakespeare?

WAYNE: It's by Somerset Maugham. There's a part in that movie that you could play.

LULU: Is she a waitress?

   (HE nods.)

LULU: You're kidding me.

WAYNE: She's a cockney waitress.

LULU: I could learn cockney. I know this dialogue coach. He's a friend of mine.

WAYNE: And what do you know about the French Revolution? And Charles Dickens? They're making a movie of "A Tale Of Two Cities" with Ronald Colman. That's by Charles Dickens. I could make a reading list for you.

LULU: Oh, I love Ronald Colman. He's so refined, and he has the most beautiful voice. Is there a part in that for me? *(After a moment)* What are you thinking?

WAYNE: I'm think of the part of the waitress in "Of Human Bondage."

LULU: Who's producing it?

WAYNE: Warner Brothers. I bet if I spoke to Mr. Zimmer... Who are you under contract to?

LULU: Paramount. Until the end of the week.

LULU IN BABYLON

WAYNE: 'Cause they're gonna have a hard time casting that role. It's very unsympathetic. Would you mind playing an unsympathetic character?

LULU: Are you kidding? They're the best kind. Is she a real bitch?

WAYNE: Oh, yes. A bitch to end all bitches.

LULU: That'd be right up my alley. Is she a high class bitch or a low class bitch?

WAYNE: She's a cockney waitress.

LULU: Like Garbo in "Anna Christie" maybe. "Gimme a whiskey. Ginger ale on the side. And don't be stingy, baby." And then he says, "Shall I serve it in a pail?" And she says, "That suits me down to the ground." How's that? Of course, I'd have to work on the cockney.

WAYNE: How long would it take?

LULU: A couple of days. I'd have to make sure he was sober.

WAYNE: How much would he charge you?

LULU: He wouldn't charge me nothing. He owes me.

(HE goes to the phone, looks up a number in the pad beside it and dials.)

LULU: Who you calling?

WAYNE: (On the phone.) Hello? This is Wayne Hudson. Can I speak to Mr. Zimmer, please? (To LULU) That was the maid.

LULU: You calling him at home?

WAYNE: Hello, Mr. Zimmer. I hope I'm not disturbing you. No, no. I'm fine. There's someone I'd like you to meet, a friend of mine. Would you be free for lunch tomorrow? Say one o'clock? At the studio? See you then? *(HE hangs up.)* Tomorrow. One thirty. I'll pick you up.

LULU: I've gotta buy a new dress.

(HE shakes his head.)

LULU: What do you mean, no? If I'm gonna meet Mr. Zimmer...

WAYNE: These people have no imagination. Wear your waitress uniform.

LULU: Are you sure?

WAYNE: I'm positive.

LULU: Should I try to speak cockney?

WAYNE: No. Just be yourself. Not that you're a bitch. You're pretty. And he likes a pretty face. Just play it cool. I know what I'm doing. I do think you should know something about the story though.

LULU: Are you auditioning for the picture?

WAYNE: No. I've been cast, in a small role. There's a bunch of interns, at this hospital. What are you smiling at?

LULU: It's so easy, when you know the right people.

WAYNE: Exactly. That's why you can't take it seriously.

LULU: What do you take seriously?

WAYNE: I don't know. The state of the world. That's something serious.

LULU: You mean like government?

WAYNE: And politics. That's something serious. There's also sexual politics.

LULU IN BABYLON

LULU: I think I know what that is. You're really very sweet.

WAYNE: Yes, I know.

LULU: Do you really wanna marry me?

WAYNE: It doesn't have to be forever, if you don't want it to be.

LULU: There's only one thing I want. I wanna be a big star like Norma Shearer or Gloria Swanson or Jean Harlow. Is that so terrible?

WAYNE: Not really. As a matter of fact, you may be the lucky one. 'cause you know what you want. Go on, get dressed. We got things to do.

LULU: Like what?

WAYNE: For one thing, we've got to find a copy of "Of Human Bondage."

LULU: And...? You said things.

WAYNE: And get a marriage license.

> (LULU jumps up, kisses him and starts off. WAYNE, with an affectionate smile on his face, watches her leave as the lights come down.)
>
> *Subtitle:* AND SO THEY WERE MARRIED
>
> *Subtitle:* AND DIVORCED

Scene 2

Song: IF I HAD A TALKING PICTURE OF YOU

Subtitle: WORLDWIDE SEARCH FOR SCARLETT O'HARA

Subtitle: GARBO LAUGHS

Subtitle: LULU & THE DIRECTOR

The lights come up on a den in a posh Hollywood home. The phone is ringing.

LULU: *(Offstage)* Randy? Randy? *(SHE enters in a negligee, hesitates for a moment, then picks up the phone.)* Hello? Hello? *(SHE hesitates, then hangs up.)* Randy? Randy?

(RANDY TUTTLE, wearing a dressing gown and ascot, enters with a breakfast tray.)

RANDY: Good morning, my dear. *(HE kisses her and sets down the tray.)*

LULU: The phone just rang.

RANDY: Did you answer it?

LULU: I thought it might be important.

RANDY: I've asked you not to answer the phone. Who was it?

LULU: I don't know. They just hung up.

RANDY: Drink your tea, like a good little girl.

LULU: Randy...?

RANDY: Yes, my little apple dumpling?

LULU: Who's playing Jessica?

273

LULU IN BABYLON

RANDY: Have you been rummaging in my drawers again?

LULU: I was looking for a handkerchief.

RANDY: I've told you, my dear, I do not like you going into my drawers, unless, of course, they happen to be the ones I'm wearing.

LULU: Why couldn't I play Jessica?

RANDY: For one thing, you happen to be under contract to Warner Brothers.

LULU: I'm sure that Myron would be happy to loan me out.

RANDY: And besides, if they do go ahead with this tawdry little opus...and that's a very big "if"...they will opt for an all star cast, and Jessica, in all probability will go to Rosalind Russell. *(After a moment)* Now what's the matter?

LULU: Nothing. Nothing at all.

RANDY: *(As if addressing an infant)* Ohhhh, we're going to go into our little shell, are we? Now what did I say?

LULU: It's not what you said.

RANDY: What is it then?

LULU: It's what you implied.

RANDY: And what did I imply?

LULU: I may not be a major star. I may not be able to carry a picture, but I'm certainly a name.

RANDY: Of course, you are, and a lovely name it is. What I meant was that if they film this steamy little epic they will be using an all star cast of MGM twinklers, culled from the galaxy that contains more stars than there is in heaven.

LULU IN BABYLON

LULU: And another thing...

RANDY: Yeeees...?

LULU: You are directing the tests for "Gone With The Wind."

RANDY: Paulette Goddard is playing Scarlett.

LULU: I was told Joan Crawford. And besides, everyone in Hollywood is being tested.

RANDY: I'm only directing the tests. I have nothing to do with the casting. Did you hear something?

LULU: No. What?

RANDY: I thought I heard footsteps, in the hallway.

LULU: It's probably Henry.

RANDY: Henry has the day off.

LULU: Well, I didn't hear a thing. You sure have been jumpy these past few days. What's the matter with you?

RANDY: Between those idiots out here and those idiots in New York, I'm on the verge of a nervous breakdown. Incidentally, does Myron know you've been seeing me?

LULU: No one knows I've been seeing you. And even if Myron did, it's none of his business.

RANDY: Aside from the fact that you work for him, he happens to be crazy about you. However, it's very wise of you to keep him at bay. What do you hear from Wayne these days?

LULU: Wayne is busy making speeches.

RANDY: And your little girl?

LULU IN BABYLON

LULU: Suzy is Wayne's little girl, not mine, and Kay's.

RANDY: Don't you ever see her?

LULU: Yes, of course, I see her.

RANDY: You're not the motherly type.

LULU: Can we talk about something else?

RANDY: *(HE drinks his tea.)* You don't happen to know anyone that owns a blue sedan, do you?

LULU: Why?

RANDY: Do you or don't you? If you must know, someone in a blue sedan has been following me about for the past few weeks.

LULU: Why don't you call the police?

RANDY: And tell them what? Are you working today?

LULU: I've got some photo sessions.

RANDY: More cheese cake?

LULU: I don't mind. *(SHE goes off to the bedroom.)* What time is it?

RANDY: Almost time for the sun to come up. God, what a life!

LULU: Will I see you tonight? Randy?

>*(SHE reenters pulling on a dress. SHE presents her back, and HE zips her up.)*

LULU: I'm playing another gangster's moll again. I don't know what to do. It's one little stinker after another.

RANDY: When's your contract up?

LULU IN BABYLON

LULU: In six months.

RANDY: Well, that's not too long, even in your young life.

LULU: What do I do then?

RANDY: Columbia might be better for you.

LULU: What about MGM?

RANDY: You're better off at a smaller studio.

LULU: I can't find my bag.

RANDY: It's probably upstairs in the play room.

> (SHE goes off to the interior of the house. HE picks up the phone and dials.)

RANDY: Did you just call? I asked you not to. You must have gotten the wrong number. There is no one here. Incidentally, do you know anyone with a blue sedan? Never mind. It's not important. I'll see you tonight. *(HE hangs up.)* Who's there? Hello? *(HE goes off to the outer hallway.)* What are you doing here? How did you get in?

> (Several shots are heard, and then the sound of running footsteps.)

LULU: *(From a distance.)* Randy? *(Closer)* Randy? *(SHE enters the room and looks around.)* Randy? *(SHE goes to the door leading to the outer hallway.)* Oh, my God! Randy? *(SHE goes off to the hallway.)* Oh, my God! Oh, my God! Are you all right? *(SHE reappears in the doorway, her hands bloody. SHE goes to the phone, notices the blood on her hands and wipes them clean with a napkin on the breakfast tray. SHE hesitates, not sure whom to call, then picks up the phone and dials.)* Hello? Oh, Kay. Can I speak to Wayne, please? Montana? I thought they didn't start till next week. No. No, never mind. *(SHE hangs up, hesitates, picks up the phone and puts it down again. SHE stands thinking, picks*

LULU IN BABYLON

up the phone, hesitates then dials.) Hello? May I speak to Mr. Zimmer? It's Lulu Marsh. Thank you. Myron? I hate to bother you, but something terrible has happened. I don't know what to do? I'm at Randy Tuttle's. He's been shot. I don't think so. He's still breathing. Thank you. No, I won't touch a thing. *(SHE hangs up and goes to the doorway.)* Randy? Are you all right? *(SHE goes off.)* Randy? Oh, God!

> *(SHE comes back into the room and sits down. SHE rises and paces about, then sits down again, ringing her hands. The lights dim, to denote the passage of time, then come up again. LULU rises.)*

LULU: Myron?

MYRON: Where are you?

LULU: I'm in here.

> *(After a moment MYRON enters from the hallway.)*

MYRON: He's dead.

LULU: I know.

MYRON: The door was wide open. Did you know that?

> *(SHE shakes her head.)*

MYRON: How did it happen?

LULU: I don't know. I was upstairs. I heard these shots. When I came down I found him lying there.

MYRON: You didn't kill him, did you?

LULU: Myron, I swear to you...

MYRON: All right, all right.

LULU IN BABYLON

LULU: Do you think we oughta call the police?

MYRON: What are you crazy? Do you know what this could do to your career? And to the studio? Who do you think could have done it?

LULU: I don't know.

MYRON: Is he into drugs?

LULU: Cocaine, maybe.

MYRON: Have you...?

LULU: No! I don't touch the stuff.

MYRON: Has he been receiving any threats that you know of?

LULU: Not that I know of. He did say...

MYRON: What?

LULU: He said that someone with a blue sedan was following him.

MYRON: A blue sedan?

LULU: What? You know someone?

MYRON: Liz Bentham has a blue sedan, but Liz is a dyke.

LULU: I thought it was purple.

MYRON: Lulu...?

LULU: What?

MYRON: Have you and Liz...?

LULU: Don't be ridiculous.

LULU IN BABYLON

MYRON: Lulu...?!

LULU: Well, she kept pestering me. She couldn't live without me. She was gonna kill herself. What could I do? It was only just once. Well, maybe just three times. I felt sorry for her.

MYRON: And how in the hell did you ever get mixed up with Randy Tuttle? You know his reputation. All right, all right. This is gonna cost me plenty. I'm very disappointed in you, Lulu, very disappointed. I can understand your divorcing Wayne. He is a stuffed shirt, just like his father.

LULU: I thought he was interested in me as an actress. He said he wanted to test me for Scarlett O'Hara. I know, I know. They're using Joan Crawford.

MYRON: According to David it's Bette Davis.

LULU: And then he said he wanted to talk to me about the role of Jessica in "Belle Of The Ball." I'm so tired of playing gangster's molls. I've told you a hundred times.

MYRON: And I've told you to be patient. Why can't you trust me? I have all sorts of plans for you. I've just bought this book about Lucretia Borgia.

LULU: Myron, you know I can't sing. Maybe Grace Moore could dub my voice.

MYRON: Whose doing "Belle Of The Ball?"

LULU: MGM.

MYRON: What's it about?

LULU: It's about this Southern belle. She's just like Scarlett O'Hara. She breaks up her sister's marriage and she stirs up this duel between her brother and her lover, and her brother gets killed and her lover gets

LULU IN BABYLON

typhoid and in the end she redeems herself by killing this spy and then she dies. It's a wonderful part.

MYRON: That's all you think about, isn't it?

LULU: I'm an actress.

MYRON: You're a human being, aren't you?

LULU: Anybody can be a human being. What are you smiling at? All right, I'm not that well educated.

MYRON: Neither am I. Suppose I got you the part of Jessica, and suppose you won an Oscar? Suppose you became as big as Joan Crawford or Bette Davis? What then? You'd still be Lulu Marsh. You'd still have to get up in the morning and brush your teeth. You'd still have to sit down to breakfast and maybe eat it all alone.

LULU: What are you getting at?

MYRON: Love, my dear child, love.

LULU: I don't know what love is.

MYRON: You love your little girl, don't you?

LULU: Yeah, I love my little girl. But she doesn't love me, and she's the only one that...

MYRON: The only one that what?

LULU: The only one that can hurt me.

MYRON: You're gonna go through life afraid of being hurt? Is that a way to live? And besides, aren't you hurt every time you don't get a part that you want?

LULU: Yeah, well, there's always another part.

LULU IN BABYLON

MYRON: There may come a time, my dear, when you'll get tired of running after parts. Maybe Wayne was a mistake. That doesn't mean that...

LULU: What? Are you proposing to me, Myron?

MYRON: Yeah, I guess I am.

LULU: Why? Because you wanna go to bed with me?

MYRON: No. I want more than that. You know what your trouble is? You sell yourself short. You have no self respect. You're better than all these pricks in the business. You're a "mensch." You know what that means?

LULU: I think so.

MYRON: You've got a "yidisha" heart. Sex only lasts a minute. Well, you know what I mean. But friendship, companionship with someone you respect, someone you have something in common with, that's worth thinking about. I'm not trying to buy you, my dear. I'll get Jessica for you, whether you marry me or not.

LULU: Can you?

MYRON: If I said I will, I will. But I wouldn't want you to marry me out of gratitude. I'd like us to spend some time together, and see how we like one another. I'll stop fucking around, but you'll have to too. What's the matter?

LULU: I don't know. It's sort of scary.

MYRON: What?

LULU: You are, I guess. Let me think about it.

MYRON: Good. Let's get out of here.

LULU: What are we gonna do...about Randy?

LULU IN BABYLON

MYRON: Have you got any clothes here? Or any of your things?

LULU: No, but my fingerprints are all over the place.

MYRON: Don't worry about it.

> *(HE takes her by the hand. THEY go off as the lights come down)*

> *Subtitle:* AND SO THEY WERE MARRIED

Scene 3

Song: HOORAY FOR HOLLYWOOD

Subtitle: MRS. MINIVER BREAKS MUSIC HALL RECORD

Subtitle: "PLAY IT AGAIN, SAM. PLAY 'AS TIME GOES BY.'"

Subtitle: LULU & THE PRODUCER

An elegant sitting room in the home of MYRON and LULU. MYRON, wearing a smoking jacket, is seated in a comfortable chair smoking a cigar and reading a script. HE sits erect, puts out the cigar and conceals it, waving the air about to dissipate the odor. LULU enters holding some mail. SHE sniffs the air.

LULU: Myron!?

MYRON: Yes, dear?

LULU: All right. I'm not gonna say a word. Besides, black is very becoming.

MYRON: Very funny.

LULU: Did you take your pill?

MYRON: I did.

LULU: *(SHE sets the mail down on a table, and sits.)* What am I gonna do with you?

MYRON: Christ, if I close my eyes I'm back in the Bronx, and my mother is standing over me. "Why didn't you do your homework, Myron?"

LULU: Well, you are a little boy, still. Why are you home so early? Is anything wrong?

MYRON: I felt a little tired, that's all. How was your afternoon?

LULU IN BABYLON

LULU: I don't know. I do my best.

MYRON: What now?

LULU: I don't like her.

MYRON: She's ten years old.

LULU: Nine. She has all of Wayne's worst qualities. In addition to that, she refers to Kay as "Mother."

MYRON: That isn't right.

LULU: She says that just because I gave birth to her that doesn't mean that I'm her mother. Can you imagine that?

MYRON: What are you then?

LULU: That's what I asked her.

MYRON: And what did she say?

LULU: I'm your wife.

MYRON: I guess there is some sort of logic there somewhere.

LULU: You're gonna take her part?

MYRON: Give her time.

LULU: I don't have to put up with that crap. I did fine without a mother. *(After a moment)* What?

MYRON: Nothing.

LULU: Speaking of which, she called again.

MYRON: What did she want? More money?

LULU IN BABYLON

LULU: She's pathetic.

MYRON: What does she do with it?

LULU: I think she gives it to him, and he really is a sleaze-ball. I told her that I don't have any to give. Which is the truth.

MYRON: I told you to use my broker.

LULU: Yes, Myron.

MYRON: You want me to give her something?

LULU: I really don't feel that I owe her anything. *(SHE sighs.)* I feel sorry for her. She's a mess. I need a drink. *(SHE hesitates.)*

MYRON: That's all right. Go ahead.

LULU: You're sure you don't mind? Anyway, you had your cigar. *(SHE pours herself a drink.)* She insists on calling me Lulu.

MYRON: Who?

LULU: Suzy. My daughter. And she really is a bitch. "I've been reading about you, Lulu," she said. "Have you really?" I said. "Yes, I was reading this article in the Silver Screen. It said that you're box-office poison. What does that mean?" "Look it up in the dictionary," I said. That shut her up.

MYRON: Mark my word. One day the two of you will be buddy buddy. Women always turn to their mothers, eventually.

LULU: What are you reading?

MYRON: You wanna do a comedy, and this is a comedy.

LULU: Is it any good?

LULU IN BABYLON

MYRON: I don't know yet. That's the hardest thing to find, a good comedy. There's a part in it for Wayne.

LULU: Oh, God!

MYRON: It's a professor. He's a stuffed shirt.

LULU: Perfect.

MYRON: Would you mind working with him?

LULU: Why not? Since he married Kay, we get along fine. It's amazing. He was so sweet when I first met him. I think I created a monster.

MYRON: What is that supposed to mean?

LULU: He's running for president of SAG, you know. He wants me to campaign for him.

MYRON: Are you going to?

LULU: I told him I'd let him know.

MYRON: Are you going to?

LULU: No.

MYRON: Why not?

LULU: I don't trust him. He's not the same man I married. Or maybe he is and I never saw that side of him. Maybe it's Kay. The two of them, Macbeth and Lady Macbeth. What's the matter?

MYRON: Nothing.

LULU: Did you take your pill?

MYRON: Yes, I took my pill. If anything happens to me, Lulu...

LULU IN BABYLON

LULU: I don't want to hear it.

MYRON: You'll be well provided for. You'll be a very rich lady.

LULU: I am a rich lady.

MYRON: Even though you're box office poison?

LULU: So what? Greta Garbo and Katharine Hepburn are box office poison, too. It means I've finally arrived. I'll tell you something, Myron. I never thought I'd say this, but I don't care if I never make another picture. I really don't. Unless, of course, I can find a really good comedy. So there! Of course, I would like an Oscar nomination.

MYRON: You had one.

LULU: For a supporting role, how many years ago?

MYRON: What's in the mail?

LULU: Mostly bills.

MYRON: Lemme see.

LULU: *(SHE hands the mail to MYRON.)* I'll get a letter opener.

> *(SHE goes off. MYRON glances through the mail. HE pulls out one envelope, studies it, rips it open and reads its contents. LULU reenters with a letter opener.)*

LULU: What is it? What's the matter?

> *(HE hands the letter to her. SHE reads it.)*

MYRON: Is it true? Tell me the truth.

LULU: Yes.

MYRON: Oh, God!

LULU IN BABYLON

LULU: Do you want an explanation?

MYRON: What good will that do?

LULU: I was told it was going to be soft core. No penetration. No real sex. And then they pulled a fast one on me, and I was all worked up by then. I didn't use my own name, of course.

MYRON: Have you seen it?

LULU: No. And besides, that was before I had my nose done.

MYRON: Your nose? Who's gonna be looking at your nose?

LULU: You're not gonna pay them, are you?

MYRON: We have a choice?

LULU: Let 'em show it.

MYRON: You'll be a laughing stock, and so will I.

LULU: I'm sorry.

MYRON: And they're not playing around. They want the money by tonight.

LULU: Myron, this could go on forever. They've probably made...I don't know how many copies.

MYRON: I cannot let this happen.

LULU: And besides, where are you gonna get all that money on such short notice? It's five o'clock. The banks are closed. Myron, I don't think that anyone will recognize me. My hair was darker then. I looked altogether different. They can't prove it was me. If they use my name we can sue them.

LULU IN BABYLON

MYRON: Oh, great! That's all we need. A law suit. And besides they're threatening to write a letter to Louella Parsons and to Hedda Hopper.

LULU: Hedda is very loyal. And, as far as Louella is concerned... She told me a couple of things when she was in her cups, some things she shouldn't have.

MYRON: Like what?

LULU: Never mind what.

MYRON: You're not gonna tell me?

LULU: I promised her that I wouldn't tell anyone, including you. And, if I should want a favor from her, I better keep my promise.

MYRON: All right, all right. It's that fuckin' Will Hays. How can you make an intelligent movie when you can't even show a man and wife in bed together? Will you tell me that? Oh, shit!

LULU: What now?

MYRON: I forgot to call my mother.

LULU: So call her now.

MYRON: She's in bed by now.

LULU: It's not even nine o'clock in New York

MYRON: She goes to bed early.

LULU: So you'll call her tomorrow.

MYRON: She may be dead by tomorrow.

LULU: Then you won't have to call her.

MYRON: Please don't be disrespectful.

LULU IN BABYLON

LULU: Myron, you're getting all excited. You know what the doctor said.

MYRON: Where's the phone?

LULU: It's right in front of you.

MYRON: *(HE picks up the phone and dials.)* Hello? Barry? Let me speak to your father. Where is he? This is Mr. Zimmer. Have him call me as soon as he gets in. You hear me? As soon as he gets in. It's very important. It's an emergency. *(HE hangs up.)* What now?

   (LULU has opened another letter.)

LULU: Nothing. Nothing important. All right. It's an invitation from Hedda. She's throwing a party for this duke.

MYRON: That phoney?

LULU: He's not a phoney. You don't put anything over on Hedda.

MYRON: And you wanna go.

LULU: I think we should.

MYRON: That's all you're thinking about? A goddamned party? This may be the end of your career.

LULU: I don't think so. As a matter of fact, I think it will help my career.

MYRON: You think the studio will let me use you if this comes out?

LULU: Then I'll go to another studio.

MYRON: You're a dreamer.

LULU: Yes, I am. And my dreams have come true. I've even fallen in love.

LULU IN BABYLON

MYRON: With a sick old man?

LULU: You're not that old. And, if you took care of yourself, you wouldn't be sick.

MYRON: Okay, okay.

LULU: What are you thinking about?

MYRON: You. I'm wondering what's going to happen to you after I'm gone. No one's gonna love you like I do, Baby. That doesn't mean...

LULU: I don't wanna hear this crap.

MYRON: That doesn't mean you shouldn't marry again. But you know what the world is like. It's full of sharks. And you're like a child.

LULU: I'm stupid.

MYRON: No, you're not stupid. You're very intelligent. But, after all these years, after all you've been through you're still naive.

LULU: What brought this on?

MYRON: Oh! A duke, a duke! Royalty. Prince charming. Oh, oh! I'm all excited!

LULU: You think that...?

MYRON: No. Not while I'm still around.

LULU: All right, so I won't marry the duke when you're dead.

(The telephone rings. Myron wheels about.)

LULU: Myron, take it easy.

MYRON: *(He picks up the phone.)* Hello? Henry? It's Myron. I've got a problem. I know I can trust you. All right, all right. Everyone's so sensitive. This is a very delicate situation. No, no, no. It concerns Lulu. Someone's trying to blackmail us. How do you know? That's the first I've heard of it.

LULU: What?

MYRON: *(HE waves at her to be quiet.)* I'm listening, I'm listening. You've seen it?

LULU: He's seen it?

MYRON: Does it look like her? They're not using her name, are they? All right, if that's what you think. Are you sure? All right, if you think so. I'm feeling fine. I'll see you Sunday. Good-bye. *(HE hangs up.)*

LULU: What?

MYRON: He says to forget about it.

LULU: I told you.

MYRON: Apparently the whole world knows about it, except me.

LULU: Maybe I should have told you. They tried to blackmail me years ago. I told them to go to hell. What's the matter?

MYRON: I better take another pill.

LULU: Myron, they're not candy.

MYRON: First you tell me... Oh, never mind. *(HE rises and starts off.)*

LULU: Where are you going?

(At the doorway MYRON stumbles, holds onto the wall for support.)

LULU: Myron!

LULU IN BABYLON

(HE goes off. A crash is heard offstage.)

LULU: Myron?! *(SHE runs off.)* Oh, God! *(SHE runs on, picks up the phone and dials.)* Hello! Please...send an ambulance. It's an emergency. This is Mrs. Myron Zimmer. The address is 3579 Wisteria Drive. Hurry, please. The telephone? 829-6656. Thank you. Yes, yes. Wisteria Drive.

(SHE runs back off as the lights come down.)

Subtitle: MYRON ZIMMER DEAD!

Scene 4

Song: BOULEVARD OF BROKEN DREAMS

Subtitle: ALL STAR CAST FOR "BEST YEARS OF LIVES"

Subtitle: "GENTLEMAN'S AGREEMENT" TOP PIC

Subtitle: LULU AND THE DUKE

Lights come up on the sitting room. RENE GERMAINE, Duke of Sauvergnon, is seated smoking a cigarette. After a moment HE rises, paces about and inspects the furnishings. HE sighs, sits, rises and paces about. LULU enters dressed in black.

LULU: I'm sorry to keep you waiting.

RENE: Perhaps I have come at a very bad time.

LULU: *(After a moment.)* What? You were looking at me rather strangely.

RENE: I'm sorry.

LULU: Do I look pale?

RENE: You look beautiful.

LULU: I wasn't fishing for compliments.

RENE: That wasn't meant as a compliment.

LULU: What was it then?

RENE: It was merely an answer to your question. You asked me if you looked pale. Congratulations on your new picture.

LULU: Have you seen it?

RENE: I was not invited to the screening. However, people are saying it will be a big success.

LULU IN BABYLON

LULU: A picture is a big success if it makes money.

RENE: I suppose that is true of everything here in America.

LULU: And you? Are you a big success? I'm sorry.

RENE: No, I am not a big success.

LULU: That doesn't seem to bother you.

RENE: I have never been interested in being a big success.

LULU: One has to eat.

RENE: As to that, there is a demand for interpreters. I speak four languages...fluently.

LULU: Thank you for the flowers. They must have been very expensive.

RENE: I came here at the suggestion of Miss Hopper. She seems to be concerned about you. I wondered why. Your husband's been dead for over a year now. You have just finished a new picture. But Miss Hopper insisted that you are not doing well. And, I suppose, the fact that you are still wearing black...

LULU: I'm still in mourning.

RENE: Exactly. And Miss Hopper seemed to think that a condolence call, late as it is, might not be unwelcome.

LULU: The attention of an attractive man is never unwelcome.

RENE: As to that, attractive men here in Hollywood are...how do they put it...?

LULU: A dime a dozen. However we don't have many dukes. A lord or two and a count, I believe. Of course, there is John Wayne. That's his nickname, The Duke. What can I do for you?

LULU IN BABYLON

RENE: I beg your pardon.

LULU: How can I help you?

RENE: I think, perhaps, you misunderstand. I did not come here for help. And if you find my visit intrusive...

LULU: Okay, okay. I'm sorry. I'm being a bitch, and I'm sorry. The fact is, I was warned against you.

RENE: By whom?

LULU: By my husband.

RENE: I don't believe...

LULU: No, you never met him. He assumed that you were a fortune hunter.

RENE: You must have loved him very much, and he you.

LULU: Have you ever been in love?

RENE: Continually. You find that amusing?

LULU: No. Would you care for a drink?

RENE: If you will join me.

LULU: It is a little early in the day. Tell me about yourself.

RENE: What would you like to know?

LULU: Whatever you're willing to tell me.

RENE: I fought in the war. When Paris fell I managed to escape. They thought I might be of more use here in America.

LULU: Who is they?

LULU IN BABYLON

RENE: The French Underground. They smuggled me to England and from there I came here. And it's true, I was a fortune hunter...in the service of my country.

LULU: And you've never married?

RENE: Not yet.

LULU: You're not interested in marriage.

RENE: Not really, no. But I will some day, for the sake of the family. I must produce an heir. I am the only remaining male, except for my uncle, but he is old.

LULU: How far back does your family go?

RENE: The fourteenth century. I have a family tree. Perhaps I can show it to you someday.

LULU: And a coat of arms? And a castle?

RENE: The castle, I am afraid belongs to the government. We cannot afford to pay the taxes.

LULU: How much do you owe?

RENE: Fifteen thousand dollars.

LULU: That's not that much.

RENE: It is, if you do not have it.

LULU: You're not homosexual, are you?

RENE: No. *(HE smiles.)* No, I am not homosexual.

LULU: Do you fuck on the first date?

RENE: I beg your pardon?

LULU IN BABYLON

LULU: You heard me.

RENE: I do not fuck, period.

LULU: What do you do?

RENE: I make love. Did I say it wrong?

LULU: No, you said it right. The only thing is I'm not interested in making love. I guess you think I'm crude. Well, I am.

RENE: You come straight...

LULU: To the point. Why do you think Hedda sent you here?

RENE: She is a...procurist?

LULU: A what? Oh, you mean a pimp. I suppose so, among other things.

RENE: Then there has been a big misunderstanding. And now, if you will excuse me...

LULU: No, please don't go. And I thought I was naive. Either that or you're very shrewd.

RENE: A bit of both, perhaps? How long can you mourn your husband? Or is it...?

LULU: What?

RENE: I'm thinking of the word. Self pity.

LULU: That's two words. You're right, of course. But it's more than that.

RENE: No, I understand. You are afraid.

LULU: And tired.

RENE: Tired?

LULU IN BABYLON

LULU: Exhausted. It takes a lot out of you, this rat race. Movies used to be my whole life, and now it's just plain hard work. And I don't need it. I made this last movie because Myron would have wanted me to. And, while I was working, it took my mind off things.

RENE: You have no family?

LULU: None to speak of.

RENE: You have a little girl, no? How old is she?

LULU: Suzy? She's nine. What are you smiling at? Okay, so she's twelve. Going on twelve. I had her when I was very young.

RENE: You are still very young.

LULU: Not inside.

RENE: You never see her?

LULU: She belongs to her father. We don't get along.

RENE: That is sad.

LULU: What's so sad about it? She doesn't need me, and I don't need her.

RENE: Maybe she's afraid of you.

LULU: Afraid of me? Why should she be afraid of me? I'm the one that's afraid of her.

RENE: A little girl?

LULU: She's a monster, created by her father and his current wife.

RENE: Mr. Zimmer is not her father?

LULU IN BABYLON

LULU: No. Her father's Wayne Hudson, my first husband. I'm a two time loser, only the second time wasn't my fault. Or maybe it was. I don't know. I don't know anything anymore. I think you'd better go.

RENE: Do you really want to be alone?

LULU: I don't know. All I know is I was fine until I married Myron.

RENE: He treated you badly?

LULU: On the contrary.

RENE: I see. He taught you what it is to love.

LULU: He taught me to be a "mensch." That means...a whole person. A real person. A decent person. Oh, I know. He was a son-of-a-bitch when it came to business. But that was only part of him. Underneath he was very special.

RENE: In what way?

LULU: He was my father, my friend...and my lover.

RENE: Then you were very lucky.

LULU: Yeah, I guess I was. The only thing is, he spoiled me for anyone else. What am I supposed to do with the rest of my life?

RENE: What would he have wanted you to do?

LULU: I think he wanted me to marry again.

RENE: Well, then?

LULU: And I think he would have been angry at me for letting myself feel sorry for myself.

RENE: Then perhaps you should begin...to live again. To face the world.

LULU IN BABYLON

LULU: When you say "continually," what does that mean? You flit from one love affair to another?

RENE: Flit?

LULU: Like a bee, from flower to flower.

RENE: You are asking if I am fickle.

LULU: Well, yeah.

RENE: It is usually the woman who begins to look elsewhere.

LULU: Why?

RENE: Inevitably there is the question of marriage.

LULU: And you're not interested in marriage.

RENE: Oh, but yes. To the right woman.

LULU: And how will you know which woman is the right woman?

RENE: She must be simpatico...

LULU: And...?

RENE: She must be rich. But money is not everything.

LULU: I see. You're a man of honor.

RENE: You say that with sarcasm, but it is true. But why must we be so serious? We are both young, and there is much joy to be had in life. You are smiling.

LULU: I was just thinking. I think Myron would have liked you.

RENE: I am flattered. And perhaps that means that you like me, too.

LULU IN BABYLON

LULU: I admire your honesty.

RENE: That is a good beginning.

LULU: And what brings you joy in life?

RENE: I like to dance. I am a good tennis player. I am a good horseman. I like good food, good music. I like to read.

LULU: Can you afford all that?

RENE: All of it, no. But what I can afford, I enjoy all the more.

LULU: You're good. You really are. I can see why Hedda's on your team. Why she is your friend. How'd you like to take me to dinner? My treat.

RENE: I can afford to pay for dinner.

LULU: At Ciro's?

RENE: If you like Italian food I know of a charming little restaurant.

LULU: And if I don't?

RENE: What kind of food do you like?

LULU: Is there dancing at this charming little restaurant?

RENE: No, but there is music.

LULU: Do we have to make a reservation?

RENE: It is advisable.

LULU: Why don't you make the reservation while I change?

RENE: There is no need to change.

LULU: I'd like to. The phone's right there.

LULU IN BABYLON

(LULU goes off. RENE picks up the phone and dials.)

RENE: Andre? It's Rene. Dinner for two? An hour or two, perhaps? Good. *(HE hangs up and dials another number.)* Miss Hopper, please. It's Rene. *(After a moment)* Hello? Good evening. I won't be joining you this evening. Yes. Yes. Thank you. Of course.

(HE hangs up as LULU reenters, no longer in black. HE looks at her admiringly.)

LULU: Any problem?

RENE: No problem.

LULU: What? I'm not overdressed, am I?

RENE: No.

LULU: Good. Shall we go?

(RENE nods and follows her off as the lights come down.)

Subtitle: AND SO THEY WERE MARRIED.

Subtitle: INTERMISSION

Subtitle: REFRESHMENTS IN THE LOBBY

ACT II

Scene 1

Song: "LULU'S BACK IN TOWN"

Subtitle: "HIGH NOON" RIDES HIGH

Subtitle: IT'S SWANSON FOR "SUNSET BOULEVARD" OR BETTE DAVIS FOR "ALL ABOUT EVE"

Subtitle: LULU & THE WRITER

Lights come up on the sitting room. SCOTT MURPHY enters followed by LULU.

SCOTT: I need a drink. You want one too, I suppose.

LULU: I'm gonna change.

SCOTT: For the better, I hope.

(LULU goes off. SCOTT pours himself a drink.)

SCOTT: Does anybody out here know what they're doing? We've been shooting this turkey for almost three months now and we're not even half way through. And everyone thinks they're a writer. No wonder Scott Fitzgerald drank himself to death. And talk about acting. You've got one expression, if you can call it that? Are you listening to me? That's a rhetorical question. As if anyone around here listens to me. As soon as we wrap this misbegotten ...whatever it is...I am heading back to New York and sanity.

(The telephone rings. SCOTT answers it.)

SCOTT: Yes, it's me. What's the story? I don't know. The hell with it. They want me to talk, I'll talk. I'll give them an earful. But I'll be damned if I'm gonna name any names. I don't care. No, I'm not gonna take the fifth. Okay, okay. Good-bye.

LULU IN BABYLON

(HE hangs up and stands thinking. LULU reenters in a lounging robe.)

SCOTT: Is that supposed to get me all hot and bothered?

LULU: Was that for me?

SCOTT: No, it was for me.

LULU: May I have a drink? Never mind.

SCOTT: I'll get you the fuckin' drink. Relax.

(HE pours her a drink and hands it to her.)

LULU: Thank you. Maybe it's better that you don't come to the set tomorrow.

SCOTT: Whose idea was that? Herr Director? Or maybe I'm getting in the way of your love life?

LULU: You're making everyone uncomfortable, Scott.

SCOTT: Well, I'll be damned if I'm gonna stand aside and let you tear my script apart.

LULU: It's just that some of your lines...

SCOTT: Are what?

LULU: A little stilted.

SCOTT: Oh, I see. You're an authority on literature now. You made a few movies, and you think you know everything. Just in case you've forgotten, I have won a Pulitzer prize or two. Not that that makes any difference out here in the wilderness. Oh, I'm not blaming you, the fault's all mine. Whatever inspired me to think that I could write a role that you might be proud of playing, that I could write a movie with some class? The fact of the matter is you shook your ass in my face and I was a goner. I mean, what a sap I must have been. You're a tramp. You always were, and you always will be. I say that without any bitterness, without any rancor. How provincial can you get? To expect the queen of the silver screen, the former Duchess of Sauvergnon to be faithful to some "mick" from Brooklyn. The question is, why did you bother to marry me?

LULU: Why did you marry me?

SCOTT: We Irish sometimes like to wallow in the gutter. It's an ethnic thing.

LULU: I'm sorry I hurt your feelings.

SCOTT: Just a pin prick, my dear, just a pin prick. Grist for the mill, so to speak.

LULU: I didn't mean it to happen.

SCOTT: Don't you dare! Don't you dare give me that sophisticated Hollywood crap. You lied to me. You lied to me from the very beginning. The fact of the matter is, you are a monster. I thought at first, maybe it was me. I was insensitive. I was a brute. Poor kid. She's had a miserable childhood. No one understands her. All she needs is love and understanding. Ha! You are a blood-sucking monster. It just so happens that a cousin of mine knows your former mother-in-law, Myron's mother, in case you've forgotten. You left that woman penniless.

LULU: That's not true.

SCOTT: Oh? My cousin's a liar. Is that it?

LULU: Myron's mother gets the same allowance she's always gotten, plus the fact that she owns her own home and a nice portfolio.

SCOTT: And speaking about mothers. Kay Hudson gave me an earful the other day.

LULU: You called Kay Hudson?

LULU IN BABYLON

SCOTT: No, my dear. Kay Hudson called us, that is you. She was throwing a birthday party for your daughter. She thought you might like to attend.

LULU: Why didn't you tell me?

SCOTT: Because you were locked in your trailer, humping away.

LULU: Well, it's no loss. I'm sure my daughter didn't miss me.

SCOTT: It just so happens that she asked Kay to call you. You gave birth to that child. Even an animal cares for its young.

LULU: Suzy asked for me? Are you sure?

SCOTT: Isn't that what I said? According to Kay she keeps a scrapbook with everything that's been printed about you. I suppose you didn't know that. Did you hear what I said?

LULU: No, I didn't.

SCOTT: And why did you lie to me about having children?

LULU: I didn't lie to you Scott.

SCOTT: Why did that count divorce you, or allow you to divorce him?

LULU: You spoke to Rene?

SCOTT: Yes, I spoke to Rene. I wanted to find out the real reason for the divorce.

LULU: And did you?

SCOTT: You lied to him as well.

LULU: Is that what he told you?

LULU IN BABYLON

SCOTT: You knew he wanted an heir and yet you married him letting him think that you could give him one.

LULU: I thought I could.

SCOTT: And you didn't tell Wayne that you didn't want any children? That when you found out you were pregnant you didn't want an abortion, and Wayne didn't talk you out of it? What are you laughing at?

LULU: You really ought to write a detective story.

SCOTT: Is it true or isn't it?

LULU: Yes, it's true. It's also true that I've had two abortions. It's also true that I would really like to have another child. It's also true that you are a cold, self-involved son-of-a-bitch. That nothing else matters to you except your writing. That you know nothing about movie making. That you are a lousy father. You said so yourself. And that if you had been a loving husband I would not have been humping in my trailer.

SCOTT: The fault's all mine, I suppose. I drove you into his arms. Who wrote that line for you?

LULU: Oh, what difference does it make? The fact of the matter is I didn't want to marry you, Scott. You insisted on it. I wanted to have an affair and let it go at that.

SCOTT: Well, that's easy enough, isn't it? Divorces are a dime a dozen out here in la la land. Under the circumstances, I'm sure you'll be glad to get rid of me.

LULU: What circumstances?

SCOTT: As if you didn't know. No, of course not. You've been too busy humping in your trailer, too busy walking through my masterpiece like a zombie. I've got to appear before the House UnAmerican Activities Committee. It's been in all the papers.

LULU: When?

LULU IN BABYLON

SCOTT: I got the call two weeks ago.

LULU: Why didn't you tell me? You're not a Communist, are you?

SCOTT: What difference does that make?

LULU: Then they can't do anything to you.

SCOTT: I attended a couple of meetings.

LULU: There's nothing wrong with that.

SCOTT: There's nothing wrong with being a Communist. It's perfectly legal.

LULU: Then there's nothing to worry about.

SCOTT: Nothing at all, except for the fact that they can crucify me, just like they did Larry Parks. That poor son-of-a-bitch will never work again. They'll insist that I name names.

LULU: And if you don't?

SCOTT: They can put me in jail. This won't help your career any either.

LULU: Everyone knows I'm not political.

SCOTT: What do they care? These people are ruthless. They'd as soon destroy you as look at you. And the bigger you are the bigger the headline. The bigger the headline the more power it brings them. Everyone's running scared. You stand up for your rights and you're a traitor.

LULU: But you're a highly respected writer. You're known all over the world.

SCOTT: Exactly.

LULU: Don't you know anyone on that committee?

LULU IN BABYLON

SCOTT: No, but you do.

LULU: Who?

SCOTT: Barry Sherman.

LULU: Barry? Henry Sherman's son?

SCOTT: He's a senator.

LULU: No kidding. How old is he?

SCOTT: How do I know? He must be around forty, I guess.

LULU: His father was Myron's lawyer, you know.

SCOTT: Yes, I know.

LULU: So Barry's a senator. What do you know! He's a very sweet boy. He was, at any rate. As a matter of fact he had a crush on me once. Why don't we invite him to dinner?

SCOTT: Fuck 'em.

LULU: When do you have to appear?

SCOTT: The week after next. We were supposed to wrap up by then.

LULU: Maybe you can get an extension.

SCOTT: They've given me one already. That's all right. While I'm gone you can rewrite the whole damn picture. The parts that haven't been rewritten already, that is.

LULU: I'll come with you, of course.

SCOTT: Where?

LULU: To Washington. That's where you have to appear, isn't it?

LULU IN BABYLON

SCOTT: You'll have to shut everything down. How will that sit with Herr producer? I need some air. I'm gonna drive over to the gym.

LULU: We have a gym.

SCOTT: You have a gym. This place gives me the creeps. While I'm gone you might spend the time studying your lines, as written. And, incidentally, your ass is getting as big as a house. *(HE goes off.)*

LULU: *(Half to herself)* No matter how big it gets it'll never get as big as your ego. *(SHE refreshes her drink, takes a sip and sets it down. SHE goes to the phone, looks up a number and dials.)* Hello? This is Lulu Marsh. Is Henry in? Thank you. *(After a moment.)* Hello. I'm fine, Henry. How are you? No. No, I don't need any money. I've just learned that Barry is a senator. Yes, well I have been out of the country. Do you have his number handy? Just a minute. *(SHE finds a pencil and paper.)* Okay. His office will be fine. *(SHE writes.)* Thank you. We should. Right now I'm in the middle of shooting. He's a very fine writer. I most certainly will. Give my love to Dinah. *(SHE hangs up, takes a sip of her drink and sets it down. SHE takes a deep breath and dials.)* Hello? This is Lulu Marsh. I'd like to speak to the senator, please. Yes, I will. *(After a moment)* I see. My number? It's area code 818-393-6363. Thank you.

(SHE hangs up and sits in an easy chair sipping her drink. SHE sets down her drink and paces about. SHE starts for the door when the telephone rings. SHE lets it ring three times then picks it up.)

LULU: Hello? Is this the young tennis whiz that I once knew? I'm fine, dear. I'm so proud of you, Barry. Being a senator. Barry, I was out of the country for three years. It just occurred to me. I'm going to be in Washington the week after next. Of course, you must be very busy. Oh? When? Oh, that's very sweet. What anniversary is it? How long will you be in town? Then you must come here for dinner. And bring your wife. Oh, I thought you were. *(SHE laughs.)* Oh, yes. I'm sure you're nursing a broken heart. You're embarrassing me. Well, I am still married. Or married again. If you don't succeed... You must be very busy. I won't keep you any longer. I look forward to it. Good-bye, dear.

LULU IN BABYLON

(SHE hangs up and stands lost in thought as the lights come down.)

Subtitle: SCOTT MURPHY EXCUSED FROM TESTIFYING

Scene 2

Song: STREET OF DREAMS

Subtitle: "SOME LIKE IT HOT" SIZZLES

Subtitle: MILTON BERLE SIGNS WITH NBC-TV

Subtitle: LULU AND THE SENATOR

Lights come up on the sitting room. BARRY SHERMAN is discovered pacing impatiently. The phone rings. HE picks it up.

BARRY: Yes? I can't make it. Tell them anything. Think of something. I don't know. I don't know where she is. Oh, Lord! Well, call it off. You have the guest list don't you? Tell them she's indisposed. A virus. The flu. Use your imagination. Did you send out the mailing? The newsletter. What does he want? Tell him I'm out of town on personal business and as soon as I get back I will look into it. I don't know. Mary, my marriage is hanging in the balance. I didn't want to say anything. I don't know what's come over her. She's out somewhere. Your guess is as good as mine. I think that's her right now. I'll call you later.

(HE hangs up as LULU enters.)

LULU: Oh! When did you get in?

BARRY: Two hours ago.

LULU: Why didn't you let me know that you were coming?

BARRY: Why didn't you let me know that you were leaving?

LULU: Didn't you get my note?

BARRY: After the fact.

LULU: I didn't want to make a scene.

BARRY: You just wanted to give me a heart attack. Honestly, Lulu.

LULU IN BABYLON

LULU: What are you doing here? You're supposed to make your report today. Or was it yesterday?

BARRY: It's today. I'm not the only one on the committee.

LULU: Which committee is it?

BARRY: The environment.

LULU: You're the chairman, aren't you? And you were really looking forward to it. Your moment of glory.

BARRY: My marriage is more important than some committee report. What are you smiling at? Honestly, Lulu, your humor escapes me.

LULU: I know.

BARRY: What? What do you know? You really are an enigma. Have I neglected you? Have I abused you? Tell me.

LULU: It isn't you. It's me.

BARRY: I know I've done something wrong. But I can't change... I can't correct whatever mistake I've made unless I know what it is.

LULU: What it boils down to is the difference in our ages.

BARRY: What? Five years? Six years?

LULU: Seven.

BARRY: Big deal.

LULU: It's not a matter of years.

BARRY: What is it then?

LULU: It's where we're at.

LULU IN BABYLON

BARRY: Oh great! *(After a moment)* Don't you think you owe me an explanation?

LULU: If I told you the truth you wouldn't believe me.

BARRY: Try me.

LULU: I feel like a fish out of water.

BARRY: What are you talking about? They love you. Everyone does. How can you say that? Our dinner parties are the toast of the town. And you're a wonderful hostess.

LULU: At what price?

BARRY: I don't know what you're talking about?

LULU: Barry, I work harder at being your wife than I've ever worked in any of my movies.

BARRY: You don't enjoy being my wife.

LULU: I don't enjoy being a senator's wife.

BARRY: But I am a senator. You want me to give up my career?

LULU: Would you want to give up your career?

BARRY: Are you asking me to?

LULU: Did you ask me to give up my career?

BARRY: No, of course not.

LULU: But I did.

BARRY: It wasn't the first time.

LULU: No, it wasn't. Which goes to prove that I'm not very bright.

LULU IN BABYLON

BARRY: I have no objection to your making movies.

LULU: That means I'd be gone for months at a time. Which means that planning all those dinners and taking part in all those social events might have to be put on hold.

BARRY: Permanently? Can't you manage both?

LULU: After I finish a movie, I need a rest. I'm not as young as I used to be.

BARRY: Who is? There are times when I'd just like to pack it in and take off on a long cruise, or spend a month up in the woods, away from everything. Maybe that's what we both need. The summer's not that far away. As a matter of fact I've never been to France, believe it or not. While you were living there you must have made all sorts of friends. It doesn't have to be France.

LULU: Right now it's difficult for me to make any sort of plans.

BARRY: You've started on a movie? What then?

LULU: My daughter's going through a very bad time.

BARRY: What's the matter with her?

LULU: She got mixed up with the wrong crowd.

BARRY: What about Wayne and his wife? I thought they were real tight.

LULU: Not anymore they're not. I've been a lousy mother, Barry, and this is my chance to make up for a lot.

BARRY: Bring her down to Washington. She can move in with us.

LULU: Right now she's in rehab. She's a bright kid and I'm sure she'll pull out of it.

BARRY: Fine. How long...?

LULU IN BABYLON

LULU: At this point, I don't know. But I want to be here for her. I want her to know that she has a home to come to.

BARRY: Fine. We have a home, don't we? And she's more than welcome. And, as far as rehabs are concerned...

LULU: Barry, I don't like Washington. I don't like the life style. I don't like the people.

BARRY: Are they any different than the people here in "la la land?" You find phonies anywhere you go.

LULU: It's not the phonies. It's the wheeling and dealing, the business of politics. I know, I know. But I can deal with it here.

BARRY: Then it isn't only your daughter.

LULU: Hollywood is home. This house is my home.

BARRY: Lulu, Myron is dead.

LULU: The part of me that belonged to Myron is not, and it never will be. That is me.

BARRY: And what part is that?

LULU: The movies, for one.

BARRY: And what about your responsibilities as a wife?

LULU: Do you love me, Barry?

BARRY: Well, of course, I love you.

LULU: Would you want me to be miserable? You have politics in your blood. I have movies in mine. It used to be just me. I wanted to be a movie star. I wanted the glory. I wanted the fame. I wanted the money.

BARRY: And now?

LULU IN BABYLON

LULU: It's the work. It's simply the joy I get from performing. It's taken me a long time to get to that point.

BARRY: In other words you've made up your mind. You're not coming back. You want a divorce? Is there anyone else?

LULU: No.

BARRY: No what?

LULU: No. There's no one else. And, as far as a divorce is concerned, that's up to you.

BARRY: It sure makes it awkward for me, Lulu. Not that a divorce is the end of the world.

LULU: We don't have to decide that right now, do we?

BARRY: What am I supposed to tell people?

LULU: Tell them the truth. I've got a family problem that I've got to deal with.

BARRY: And then what?

LULU: Let's take it one step at a time. Who knows what tomorrow will bring?

BARRY: What about Wayne? He's the girl's father, isn't he? He's running for mayor, isn't he? This won't do his campaign any good, will it? Nor will it do your career any good.

LULU: Drugs don't do anyone any good.

BARRY: I do love you, Lulu.

LULU: Yes, dear, I know you do. Unfortunately love isn't everything. It would be nice if it were, but it isn't. It took me a long time to learn that too. Oh, Honey, you'll find someone else. Someone more compatible.

LULU IN BABYLON

BARRY: What about you?

LULU: As a matter of fact, I need some time by myself, with myself. I was always afraid to be alone. Maybe it's because I grew up without a real family. I don't know.

BARRY: People think it's easy being a senator. But what are we really? We're servants, public servants. And everyone has an axe to grind. I went into politics because I thought I could do some good, help people. But it's impossible to please everyone. God knows, I try. I really do. I know it's a lot of work arranging all those parties and smiling at everyone and being charming even when you're dealing with idiots and morons...but that's politics.

LULU: I know, dear, I know.

BARRY: And I can't do it all alone. What I mean to say is this is a chance to do some good, to help people. To contribute. I know that the movies is a major industry. It gives a lot of work to a lot of people. And sure, it provides entertainment. People have to relax and get a good laugh. But this is a chance to do something really important with your life. You're an intelligent woman, Lulu. What are you smiling at? I mean it.

LULU: I know you do.

BARRY: But you don't care. You don't care about doing something with your life, something of value. I'm trying to help people. Don't you understand?

LULU: I'm people, too, dear.

BARRY: Okay, okay.

LULU: What are you laughing at?

BARRY: Nothing. I was just thinking of that old joke.

LULU: What joke is that?

LULU IN BABYLON

BARRY: "You can lead a whore to culture, but you can't make her think." Horticulture?

LULU: That's very funny.

BARRY: *(HE sighs.)* Well, I guess I better get back. Thank God for Mary. I don't know what I'd do without her.

LULU: She is a gem.

BARRY: There's no need to be sarcastic. No matter what, I know I can depend on her. I mean...

LULU: I know what you mean, dear.

BARRY: There's nothing going on between us.

LULU: I'm sure there isn't.

BARRY: She's not that kind of a girl...woman. Maybe you'll change your mind. And, please, don't let pride stand in your way. We all make mistakes. And it wasn't all bad, was it?

LULU: No, of course not.

BARRY: *(HE kisses her.)* I hope to see you soon.

> *(BARRY goes off. LULU sits with a sigh and is lost in thought. The phone rings. She answers it.)*

LULU: Hello? Yes, Kay. I came back a couple of days ago. Suzy is fine. That is, she's safe. I can't tell you that. Very well, I won't. I gave her my word. *(After a moment)* Hello? Yes, Wayne. I'm fine. A couple of days ago. He's fine. Washington is...Washington. Yes, the belle of the ball. She's okay. What I mean to say is everything's under control. Wayne, I'm not blaming you. I don't know what went on between the two of you, but she doesn't want to see you. I'm sorry. Not so far. What do you want me to tell them? Fine. *(After a moment.)* Yes, Kay, I'd love to come to

LULU IN BABYLON

dinner. Barry's in Washington. I'm sure it has, and it's all very unfortunate...for everyone. Friday will be fine. Me, too.

(LULU hangs up and stands thinking.)

Scene 3

Song: HOORAY FOR HOLLYWOOD

Subtitle: "KRAMER VS KRAMER" WINS TOP HONORS

Subtitle: LOEWS GRAND NOW A MULTIPLEX

Subtitle: LULU AND THE MAYOR

The lights come up on the sitting room. WAYNE HUDSON is seated, waiting impatiently. HE rises, goes to the phone and dials.

WAYNE: Did Lulu call? That woman will drive me nuts. The older she gets the nuttier she gets. She asked me to drop by on the way home from the office, as if I had nothing better to do, and she's nowhere in sight. You haven't heard from Suzy, have you? I thought there might be a problem with the baby. He did have that stomach condition, and all the news is funneled through Grandma. The way she carries on. As if no one else in the world has ever had a grandchild. Never mind. Madam has arrived. I'll be home soon. Yes, yes, I will. I'm expecting that call from Washington at seven thirty. *(HE hangs up.)* Lulu? Lulu?!

LULU: *(Offstage)* Coming.

WAYNE: So is Christmas.

    (LULU enters.)

LULU: What?

WAYNE: Never mind.

LULU: Have you been waiting long?

WAYNE: What's on your mind?

LULU: Let me catch my breath.

LULU IN BABYLON

WAYNE: Is the baby all right?

LULU: As far as I know. Why? Have you heard anything? I don't know where the time goes. I need a drink. Let me fix you a Scotch. Sit down, sit down. Are you touching up your hair? *(SHE pours two drinks.)*

WAYNE: Why? Does it look strange?

LULU: No, not at all. It's just that...

WAYNE: What?

LULU: Nothing.

WAYNE: Don't do that to me, Lulu.

LULU: If I told you you'd think I was flattering you.

WAYNE: I'll take that chance.

LULU: Maybe it's the light. Is it true?

WAYNE: What?

LULU: That you may be running for president.

WAYNE: It's all very nebulous.

LULU: Then it's true.

WAYNE: Would you vote for me, if I did decide to run.

LULU: God, no. You're a lousy actor, Wayne, and I think you'd make a lousy president. Here you are. *(SHE hands him his drink.)* How's Kay, by the way?

WAYNE: You saw her just yesterday.

LULU: That's why I ask. She was looking rather peaked.

LULU IN BABYLON

WAYNE: Is that what we're here to discuss, Kay's health?

LULU: It doesn't concern you?

WAYNE: Kay is fine. She's never been better. Lulu, I'm a busy man. Why have you dragged me here?

LULU: I'm organizing a benefit.

WAYNE: Put me down for two tickets. How much are they? *(After a moment)* Now wait a minute. I've got a town to run. People to see, things to do.

LULU: And since you may be running for president, I think you're the perfect man for the job.

WAYNE: What job?

LULU: I'd like you to be master of ceremonies, and chairman of the committee.

WAYNE: Chairman of what committee? What ceremonies?

LULU: All it means is your name on the letterhead and...

WAYNE: And what?

LULU: Make a few phone calls. That's all.

WAYNE: Is this another one of your charities?

LULU: It is, my dear, it is, and it's an important one. If it wasn't, I don't think Liz Taylor would be involved in it. Do you?

WAYNE: Stop beating about the bush.

LULU: You've heard about Rock Hudson.

WAYNE: Is this some sort of a joke?

LULU IN BABYLON

LULU: No, my dear. There's nothing funny about it.

WAYNE: We're talking about AIDS, are we not? And you expect me to get involved? Do you know what that would do to my chances...? Forget it. I have nothing against the gay community. It's a way of life I don't approve of, but live and let live I always say.

LULU: We're talking about our friends...and our peers. And there's been some cases reported outside of the so-called gay community. It could attack Suzy. It could attack our grandson.

WAYNE: I think that's highly unlikely.

LULU: Kay is willing to help out.

WAYNE: You've spoken to Kay about this? And what did she say?

LULU: She wouldn't do anything without your approval.

WAYNE: Good. And now, if you'll excuse me...

LULU: Just a moment.

WAYNE: What is it now?

LULU: I'd like you to take a look at something.

WAYNE: Really, Lulu...

LULU: It won't take a moment.

> *(SHE goes to a table, opens the drawer, takes out a letter and hands it to him.)*

WAYNE: What is it?

LULU: It's a letter.

WAYNE: Obviously.

LULU IN BABYLON

LULU: Read it.

WAYNE: *(HE takes the letter out of the envelope and starts to read it. After a moment HE sits down and continues to read. HE looks up.)* I'm sorry.

LULU: He was...is...a good friend, to both of us.

WAYNE: I was very fond of Harvey.

LULU: He was the one that brought us together, if you recall... For better or for worse.

WAYNE: We lost touch.

LULU: Yes, I know. You stopped writing. He always asks about you.

WAYNE: I often wonder what became of him.

LULU: It was easy enough to find out.

WAYNE: It's just that...

LULU: What?

WAYNE: We have nothing in common...anymore. And I never really did approve...

LULU: Of what?

WAYNE: His lifestyle.

LULU: Wayne...!

WAYNE: What?

LULU: You were lovers.

WAYNE: That's not true.

LULU IN BABYLON

LULU: You intend to deny it?

WAYNE: Is that what he told you?

LULU: Wayne...?!

WAYNE: If that's what you think, then you're mistaken. I'm sorry for the man. However, he made his bed...

LULU: You really are a son-of-a-bitch.

WAYNE: You're upset. I understand. And I feel sorry for him, too. But we all have a choice in life. Please give him my best when you write to him, and I assume you will.

LULU: Oh, I will. And I'll tell him how generous you're going to be, in helping out with my benefit.

WAYNE: You can tell him what you like. *(HE starts off.)*

LULU: Because you are, my dear.

WAYNE: *(HE stops and turns toward her.)* Is that a threat?

LULU: It's funny how people change. Ever since Harvey wrote me about his illness I've been thinking back, thinking about the past. It's taken me a long time but I've finally gotten to the point where I really like myself. As a matter of fact, maybe it's senility, but I look at people and they're all so...so beautiful. Civilization is a mess. All over the world people are killing each other. But when I look at a man or a woman or a child I see beauty. Why do you think that is?

WAYNE: I don't know, Lulu. I really don't know.

LULU: I think back to when we first met, how sweet you were, how charming, how eager, discovering love for the very first time. Except, of course, for Harvey. But that wasn't really love, you said. But it was, on his part...and you...well... So what does that make you?

LULU IN BABYLON

WAYNE: You know, Lulu, I don't think you're in any position to pass judgement on anyone.

LULU: I don't, and I never have. But I never pretended to be better than I really am. I don't know, maybe we do become our parents, eventually. I hope not, because my mother was a mess.

WAYNE: Will you please get to the point?

LULU: That is the point. Ever since the word's gotten out that you may be selected to run for president, I've been hounded by reporters. They want me to talk about you. After all, we were married for five years. Some people actually think that we're still married. And they want to know, these reporters... What was he like when you first met? Why did your marriage break up? How did you meet?

WAYNE: And what have you told them?

LULU: I haven't told them anything...as yet.

WAYNE: I see. If you remember, Lulu, the divorce was your idea, not mine. And, as far as Harvey is concerned, you know perfectly well how I feel.

LULU: How do you feel?

WAYNE: I don't give a damn what anybody does in the privacy of their own home. It's just that, politically speaking...

LULU: Politically speaking, whether you like it or not, my dear, you're going to have to take a stand. You may be surprised. They may respect you for it.

WAYNE: The people on your side of the fence, perhaps. *(After a moment)* And suppose I don't take part in this benefit of yours...?

LULU: It's not only mine. There are some very highly respected people associated with it.

LULU IN BABYLON

WAYNE: Not from my side of the fence.

LULU: Whosever side of the fence they're on, they all vote.

WAYNE: Sometimes, Lulu, I do things, not because I want to...

LULU: Because it's politically expedient. Like naming names?

WAYNE: The people whose names I gave to that committee were people who'd already been incriminated.

LULU: Incriminated?

WAYNE: Named. Investigated. Call it what you like. And it's not fair to bring that up. Those were very dark days. And besides I still think I did the right thing.

LULU: Very far right.

WAYNE: Let's not get into politics.

(LULU smiles. THEY both laugh.)

WAYNE: All right, all right. I've made mistakes. I'm not denying it. But I've paid for it, Lulu, I really have. I've lost Suzy.

LULU: Nonsense. You haven't lost her.

WAYNE: And I think I've lost my son. He's become an embarrassment.

LULU: The way his father was, at one time?

WAYNE: Well, I hope he straightens himself out. Anyway, he and Kay are still close. *(After a moment)* The funny thing is, I think I'm still a little in love with you. Believe it or not. But you frighten me. You always have.

LULU: In what way?

LULU IN BABYLON

WAYNE: You're...amoral.

LULU: I'm not sure what that means.

WAYNE: Neither am I.

LULU: Anyway, does it really matter?

WAYNE: There you are. That's a perfect example. Of course it matters. Everything matters.

LULU: Let's just say, we agree to disagree. And I'm sure you'll do a bang-up job as host. When you're at your charming best, my dear, you're irresistible. And if, as you say, you're still in love with me, of course you're going to be there.

WAYNE: Be where?

LULU: At the benefit that's planned as a tribute.

WAYNE: A tribute to whom?

LULU: To me, of course?

WAYNE: You're planning a tribute to yourself?

LULU: Who else is better equipped?

WAYNE: I've gotta go.

   (HE starts off.)

LULU: Incidentally, what would you like me to do with all those notes you and Jeffrey used to write to one another?

WAYNE: What notes?

LULU: You know perfectly well, what notes.

LULU IN BABYLON

WAYNE: I never wrote any notes.

LULU: Since they were hand written, you'll have a tough time denying them.

WAYNE: You can do what you like, Lulu. I will not be blackmailed, and good luck with your benefit. *(HE goes off.)*

(BLACKOUT)

Song: A PRETTY GIRL IS LIKE A MELODY

ANNOUNCER'S VOICE: It seems like only yesterday that a young girl from Kansas burst on the screen and lit a flame that still burns brightly in the hearts of moviegoers around the world.

(We see a montage of LULU in her various roles, with her various husbands and lovers. The last shot is one of LULU and WAYNE. The stage grows dark.)

WAYNE: Ladies and gentlemen, Miss Lulu Marsh.

(After a long pause LULU appears. SHE bows.)

LULU: Thank you. Ladies and gentlemen, I'd like to present the new chairman of the Committe to Prevent AIDS, and the next president of the United States, Mr. Wayne Hudson.

(WAYNE enters. THEY kiss, bow and take the curtain call together.)

THE DISINTEGRATION OF DELLA LONGSTREET

A Play In One Act

CAST OF CHARACTERS

Della Longstreet

Drew Longstreet

Dick Longstreet

Debbie Longstreet

SCENE

The living room and dining room of the Longstreet summer cottage
(A unit set)

ACT ONE

The adjoining living room, stage left, and dining room, stage right, of the Longstreet summer cottage. A door, upstage in the dining room, leads to the kitchen. A door, upstage in the living room, leads to the bedrooms. It is late afternoon. The phone is ringing in the living room. DELLA enters from the kitchen.

DELLA: Coming. *(SHE crosses into the living room and picks up the phone.)* Yes, Margaret? Oh, Lucy! How did you get this number? I see. Well, yes it is a secret. It's Drew's idea. He likes to have a place where we won't be disturbed. It's not the wilderness, dear, and I won't be alone. As a matter of fact, it's been a long time since we've all been together. Debbie and Dickie, of course, and Drew and I. Of course I was going to call you. How long will you be gone? I should be back by then. Have a good trip, dear. *(SHE hangs up, stands thoughtfully for a moment, then picks up the phone and dials.)* Oh, Margaret. Did you give this number to Mrs. Lancaster? No, you weren't. Well, for the future... What about? Where did you find it? What were you doing in Dickie's drawers? Well, he's not a boy any longer, and he is entitled to his privacy, and I don't think a picture book could ever hurt anyone. Be that as it may... All right. I said, all right. I'll look into it. Good-bye.

(SHE hangs up, stands looking troubled, then starts for the kitchen. The telephone rings just as SHE reaches the kitchen door. SHE returns to the living room and picks up the phone.)

DELLA: Hello? Margaret? Hello? Hello?!

(SHE slams the phone down, looking very upset. SHE stands trying to collect herself. SHE sits, closes her eyes and remains very still until SHE calms down, then goes off to the kitchen. DICK enters from the outside with his bag and tennis racquet.)

DICK: Hello? Anyone home?

(DELLA reenters.)

DELLA: Dickie? Is that you?

(SHE runs into the living room and THEY embrace.)

DICK: Mumsie.

THE DISINTEGRATION OF DELLA LONGSTREET

DELLA: It's so good to see you. My, my my, you've grown so big.

DICK: Have I? Where's everyone?

DELLA: They haven't arrived as yet. I came up early to get things ready.

DICK: And a good job, too. *(HE sets down his bag.)* How are we feeling today?

DELLA: I'm feeling fine.

DICK: Well, just in case, I've brought along some Valium.

DELLA: *(After a moment)* Did you have a nice trip, dear?

DICK: As well as could be expected, under the circumstances.

DELLA: What circumstances?

DICK: My car, Mumsie dear, my car. It's falling apart.

DELLA: But you just got it. Didn't you?

DICK: Two years ago. If it's money we're thinking about, it's really more economical to turn it in every year or so.

DELLA: I know nothing about cars, but that does seem like a needless extravagance.

DICK: As you say, Mother dear, you know nothing about cars. We are looking pretty today.

DELLA: Nonsense. I look a mess. I've been cleaning house all day.

DICK: Don't you have any help?

DELLA: Your father and I agreed that there would only be the four of us.

THE DISINTEGRATION OF DELLA LONGSTREET

DICK: Well, we don't want you exhausting yourself our first day out here. Now do we?

DELLA: Where's Debbie?

DICK: On her way, I imagine.

DELLA: Didn't you come up together?

DICK: I came directly from school.

DELLA: Yes, but...

DICK: But what?

DELLA: Well, since you both go to Helmsly, I should think...

DICK: That was last year, Mother.

DELLA: When did you switch?

DICK: I didn't switch, Mumsie. Debbie did. Don't you remember?

DELLA: What school is Debbie going to?

DICK: Beardsly.

DELLA: And you're going to...?

DICK: Helmsly. Now, what school is Debbie going to?

DELLA: Beardsly.

DICK: And what school am I going to?

DELLA: Helmsly.

DICK: There now. That's not too hard to remember. Now is it?

THE DISINTEGRATION OF DELLA LONGSTREET

DELLA: I would have remembered if I had known.

DICK: Of course, you would. Well, I guess I might as well unpack.

DELLA: There's no rush, dear. We see each other so seldom.

DICK: If we see each other at all.

DELLA: What is that supposed to mean?

DICK: Nothing.

DELLA: I wish you wouldn't say things like that and leave me hanging.

DICK: Now, now, now. You mustn't upset yourself.

DELLA: I am not upset. I just don't enjoy being treated like a child.

DICK: Yes, Mother dear. *(HE sighs and picks up his bag.)*

DELLA: Dickie...?

DICK: Yes, dear?

DELLA: I was just wondering. Well, you are a young man. What I mean to say is...you're not a boy any longer, and love is very important to the young, I suppose.

DICK: To the old as well, I should think. And I love you dearly.

DELLA: I'm not talking about that sort of love.

DICK: Oh, I see. And what would you like to know?

DELLA: Maybe it's your father that should be talking to you. He did have a talk with you once, didn't he?

DICK: Oh my, yes.

THE DISINTEGRATION OF DELLA LONGSTREET

DELLA: Then you do know...

DICK: How we fit? There's no need to be embarrassed, Mother. You can ask me anything you like?

DELLA: Well, the fact is...

DICK: Yes, dear?

DELLA: What I mean to say is... That is, I'm willing to answer any questions you might like to ask me.

DICK: *(HE sets down his bag.)* All right. Why haven't you and Daddy been sleeping together for all these years?

DELLA: Well, I... It hasn't been that long.

DICK: How long has it been?

DELLA: Three years, if you really must know.

DICK: You mean to tell me that you've gone without sex for three whole years?

DELLA: Well Dickie, dear, I am a middle-aged women.

DICK: Nonsense. You're young and attractive, and I really do think that we ought to do something about it. You're not frigid, by any chance?

DELLA: I think that you and Debbie are proof positive that I am not.

DICK: Not necessarily.

DELLA: Your father and I are still very fond of one another, but not in that way.

DICK: Why did you marry him?

DELLA: We were in love. But as you grow older...

THE DISINTEGRATION OF DELLA LONGSTREET

DICK: You are delicious, Mumsie dear.

(HE picks up his bag, kisses her, and goes off. DELLA sits, lost in thought. DEBBIE enters with her bag and tennis racquet.)

DEBBIE: There you are!

DELLA: Debbie, dear.

DEBBIE: Mumsie.

(DEBBIE sets down her bag and THEY kiss.)

DEBBIE: How lovely you look!

DELLA: And you, dear. You get prettier every day. *(After a moment)* Isn't that dress just a little bit too short?

DEBBIE: You think so? I was thinking of taking it up an inch or two.

DELLA: The color is very becoming.

DEBBIE: The place looks so fresh and cheerful. Are Daddy and Dickie here yet?

DELLA: Dickie just arrived.

DEBBIE: We're going to have such fun, all four of us together at last. You look so sad.

DELLA: Do I, dear?

DEBBIE: Is there anything wrong?

DELLA: Not really, dear. It's just that...

DEBBIE: What?

THE DISINTEGRATION OF DELLA LONGSTREET

DELLA: It's so confusing. I mean Life. It seems like only yesterday that you and Dickie were little babies, and now you're all grown up and now we're practically strangers. I feel it more with you than I do with Dickie. I mean mothers and daughters should grow closer as they grow older. They should be friends.

DEBBIE: That's why we're here, isn't it? Just the four of us. To grow closer.

DELLA: I understand you haven't been happy at school. Well, you did switch schools, didn't you?

DEBBIE: That was a year go.

DELLA: But why?

DEBBIE: It was purely academic. I should have gone to Beardsly in the first place, but Dickie and I wanted to be together our first year away from home.

DELLA: I'm so glad the two of you are so devoted to one another.

DEBBIE: I love Dickie, Mother.

DELLA: Yes, I know you do. And he loves you.

DEBBIE; There's nothing in the world as important as love. Is there, Mumsie? If only everyone loved each other the way we do. There would be no wars, there would be no killings, there would be no jealousy. If only people would understand that...

DELLA: What, dear?

DEBBIE: We're conceived in love. We're born with love and we desire nothing more that to give love and to receive it. And yet people put all sorts of restrictions on it. Do you think that's right?

DELLA: I'm not quite sure what you mean by restrictions.

THE DISINTEGRATION OF DELLA LONGSTREET

DEBBIE: Aren't you, dear?

DELLA: What I mean to say is... Well, we must never lose our self respect.

DEBBIE: Oh, Mumsie, you're so...old fashioned. That's what I love about Daddy. He's willing to admit that he feels something below the belt, and he's not afraid to express what he feels. I think that's beautiful.

DELLA: I'm glad you're fond of your father, dear.

DEBBIE: I worship him. Just as I do Dickie, in a different way, of course. Why do people put up defenses against one another? Physical defenses, emotional defenses. Why can't we be free and open with one another? Why can't we give what we have to give and receive just as openly? We're all dependant on one another. Why should we be ashamed of it? Take last week, for example.

DELLA: What happened last week?

DEBBIE: I ran out of money and I went out and I panhandled. Well, this dear, sweet little old lady came up to me and she said such vile things.

DELLA: What did she say?

DEBBIE: I don't think you want to hear them. I mean if someone needed money and I had it to give I would give it all to them?

DELLA: And then what would you do?

DEBBIE: Mother, if a child is starving you don't worry about the future.

DELLA: But you certainly have enough money, Debbie. You did receive your check last month.

DEBBIE: I'm always running short.

DELLA: What do you spend it on?

THE DISINTEGRATION OF DELLA LONGSTREET

DEBBIE: People. Things. I don't keep track.

DELLA: Well, you should.

DEBBIE: Why? It doesn't belong to me really. I never earned it. Why should I be miserly about something I don't really deserve? That's where the trouble starts. The earth belongs to everyone and so do the fruits thereof. That's why I'm grateful to you and Daddy. You've taught me to be unselfish and kind and good and generous, and that's why I think we're such an exceptional family.

DELLA: Unfortunately, dear, life is not that simple.

DEBBIE: Well, it should be. And maybe it would be if we lived it that way. It's just like war, for example. If no one went to war, there would be no wars.

DELLA: Unfortunately there is such a thing as evil.

DEBBIE: Like the Bible says, "Evil is in the eye of the beholder."

DELLA: I don't think that's in the Bible, dear.

DEBBIE: Well, wherever it is. I'm absolutely starved. When do we eat?

DELLA: As soon as your father arrives.

DEBBIE: Good.

>   *(SHE kisses DELLA, picks up her bag and goes off. The telephone rings. DELLA hesitates then answers it.)*

DELLA: Hello? Who is this?!

>   *(SHE slams the phone down. DREW enters a moment later.)*

DELLA: Oh, Drew!

DREW: What's the matter, Honey? Is there anything wrong?

THE DISINTEGRATION OF DELLA LONGSTREET

DELLA: It's those phone calls.

DREW: Not another one.

DELLA: Don't look at me like that. There was a phone call, and there was someone at the other end.

DREW: There always is. Now we're not going to get hysterical, are we?

DELLA: I am not hysterical. And there was someone there!

DREW: Della, dear, you do have a very vivid imagination.

DELLA: That phone call was real.

DREW: I'm sure it was.

DELLA: And it would have been real to you, if you'd been here.

DREW: But I never am.

DELLA: I suppose that's my fault, too?

DREW: Darling, please. We're here to have a nice, pleasant vacation. We all have our little demons, darling, but we mustn't give in to them.

DELLA: That's not what you said the other day.

DREW: What did I say the other day?

DELLA: You said the only way to get rid of ones demons is to give into them.

DREW: The word was temptation. And I think that was Oscar Wilde.

DELLA: I made that up, too, I suppose.

DREW: It's not important, Honey. The important thing is we're still here together, you and I, after all these years.

THE DISINTEGRATION OF DELLA LONGSTREET

DELLA: You really are a caution. What are you smiling at? What did I say now?

DREW: Those quaint phrases of yours. "You really are a caution." Even your parents never talked like that?

DELLA: How would you know, since you never met my parents?

DREW: I most certainly did.

DELLA: Drew, they were dead when we met.

DREW: Then obviously I must have met them before we met.

DELLA: You never mentioned it. Why?

DREW: The subject never came up.

DELLA: We've often spoken about my parents.

DREW: I'm sorry I mentioned it now.

DELLA: I'm glad you did...meet them, I mean. They were quite remarkable. When did you meet them, Drew? And how?

DREW: I couldn't have been more than twelve or so. We were up in Newport for the summer. I was playing tennis. My partner hit the ball into your garden, and I went after it. When I tried to pick it up I fell into your mother's flower bed. She was furious at first, but when she saw the expression on my face she laughed and invited us both to tea. And that's when I met your father as well.

DELLA: There was no tennis court near our home in Newport.

DREW: No public court, perhaps. But I was visiting a friend and the family had a court on the grounds in back of their house. It was adjacent to yours.

DELLA: I wonder where I was.

THE DISINTEGRATION OF DELLA LONGSTREET

DREW: I haven't the vaguest idea. As a matter of fact, I never knew of your existence until years later.

DELLA: Isn't that strange!

DREW: I don't see anything strange about it.

DELLA: My mother never worked in her garden. She was allergic to the sun.

DREW: I never said she did...work in her garden.

DELLA: You said you fell into her flower bed.

DREW: Della....

DELLA: I'm sorry. Please go on.

DREW: There's nothing more to tell.

DELLA: I'm sorry. I didn't mean to offend you.

DREW: What possible motive could I have for lying to you about a thing like that?

DELLA: I never said that you were lying.

DREW: Della, Della, Della...

DELLA: What?

DREW: What do you think has driven us apart?

DELLA: I really don't know.

DREW: Your suspicions, my dear. Your terrible suspicions. At any rate, I'm glad our children are not as cynical as you are.

DELLA: I am not cynical, Drew, and it's cruel of you to say that I am.

THE DISINTEGRATION OF DELLA LONGSTREET

DREW: Our little vacation hasn't even begun and I've been accused of being cruel as well as lying.

DELLA: Would you like me to stop my mind? Would you like me to be a vegetable?

DREW: Well, there's certainly something to be said for vegetables. Now Della, you're not going to go into your little shell.

DELLA: Vegetables don't have shells.

DREW: Della, Della, Della. What are we going to do with you?

DELLA: Are all your lady friends mindless, Drew? Is that how you like your women?

DREW: There have been times when we were happy together.

DELLA: Physically, perhaps. You're very good at lovemaking. Practice makes perfect, I suppose.

DREW: That was uncalled for.

DELLA: Oh, and here I thought you were proud of your sexual prowess.

DREW: Sex isn't a thing one is proud of. It's simply a thing one does.

DELLA: And does and does and does.

DREW: Not in your case, Della.

DELLA: Well, you've made up for it elsewhere.

DREW: As if one could possibly make up for anything in life.

DELLA: Our marriage was a mistake.

DREW: It needn't be. I'm willing to forget the past, if you are.

THE DISINTEGRATION OF DELLA LONGSTREET

DELLA: What does that mean?

DREW: Whatever you'd like it to mean.

DELLA: You really are a beast. I should have divorced you a long time ago.

DREW: Why didn't you?

DELLA: Oddly enough, because I'm still in love with you.

DREW: Now that really makes sense. You won't sleep with me because you're still in love with me.

DELLA: It makes sense to me.

DREW: I think I'll take a shower before dinner. Is there time?

DELLA: I think so yes.

   (DREW picks up his bag and goes off.)

DELLA: *(SHE stamps her foot.)* Damn! Damn, damn, damn, damn, damn!

   (DREW reenters.)

DREW: I am in the guest room, I presume.

DELLA: You are.

DREW: I wouldn't want to make a mistake our first night out.

DELLA: There's no danger of that, I assure you.

   (DREW goes off to his room. DELLA goes off to the kitchen. After a moment DICK reenters in sports clothes. HE picks up a magazine and sits on the sofa. DEBBIE enters in sports clothes, comes up behind DICK and covers his eyes with her hands.)

THE DISINTEGRATION OF DELLA LONGSTREET

DICK: Now who could that be?

> *(DELLA enters the dining room with a table cloth. SHE proceeds to set the table, taking the dishes and the silverware from the cabinet. SHE can't help but being aware of what's going on in the other room. DICK kisses Debbie's hand, rises and THEY kiss.)*

DEBBIE: Did you miss me?

DICK: Not really, no.

DEBBIE: Beast!

DICK: Is that a new sweater?

DEBBIE: Not really, no.

DICK: What's in it is new.

DEBBIE: You're not supposed to notice such things.

DICK: Who makes these rules?

DEBBIE: I'll bet you had a high old time as soon as I left.

DICK: And you?

DEBBIE: That's for you to wonder, and me to know. How did you make out in chemistry? I mean your grades.

DICK: Oh, that. How did you make out?

DEBBIE: Why should I tell you?

DICK: You could switch back, if you wanted to.

DEBBIE: I could, couldn't I?

THE DISINTEGRATION OF DELLA LONGSTREET

DICK: And we could get a room together, since we don't have to live in the dorms anymore.

DEBBIE: We could do exactly as we pleased. Dress, if we felt like it.

DICK: Or not, if we felt like it.

DEBBIE: Beardsly is really square. No pot to be had.

DICK: That's awful.

DEBBIE: I haven't had any pot since Christmas.

DICK: We can have some later.

DEBBIE: I think the FBI has infiltrated the school.

DICK: I know. There are spies everywhere.

DEBBIE: Remember our last night at Helmsly?

DICK: How could I forget?

DEBBIE: That was a red letter, day, so to speak.

DICK: I still have scars to prove it.

DEBBIE: Where?

DICK: Where do you think?

DEBBIE: Let's go for a swim.

DICK: I forgot my suit.

DEBBIE: Since when do we need suits? Come on! I'll race you to the lake.

DICK: You're on.

THE DISINTEGRATION OF DELLA LONGSTREET

(DEBBIE runs off, followed by DICK. DELLA sits down, deeply troubled. DREW enters in sports clothes.)

DREW: Hello? Where is everyone? *(HE goes into the dining room.)* Where are the kids?

DELLA: They went for a swim.

DREW: In the lake? It's kind of chilly, isn't it?

DELLA: Not for them, apparently. Don't be angry with me, please.

DREW: I'm not angry, Della. What's wrong now?

DELLA: I wish we could be friends, Drew. If only for the sake of the children?

DREW: Is that the only reason?

DELLA: You're closer to them than I am.

DREW: I wonder why that is.

DELLA: Maybe it's because you allow them to do as exactly as they please. But I wonder...in a few years from now...if they will thank you for it. Drew we've got to have a talk with them.

DREW: What have they done now?

DELLA: It's not what they've done exactly. It's just that...

DREW: What?

DELLA: And it's not my imagination. I'm sure you'll accuse me of that. But they're...

DREW: They're what?

THE DISINTEGRATION OF DELLA LONGSTREET

DELLA: They're just like...honeymooners. It's not funny, Drew. They're too...close.

DREW: How can they be too close? They hardly ever see each other anymore.

DELLA: I know what I'm talking about. I know you think that I dream these things up. But I'm cursed. It's like this searchlight that I have. I can see things with blinding clarity, things other people aren't even aware of, or refuse to be aware of...or prefer to ignore.

DREW: What are you trying to say? That our children are lovers? Is that what you're trying to say?

DELLA: Is that so impossible?

DREW: No. As a matter of fact I remember... When we were growing up, I had sort of a yen for my sister...and she for me.

DELLA: But you never followed through, did you?

DREW: I sometimes wonder what would have happened if we had.

DELLA: Drew, I want you to have a talk with them.

DREW: What would you want me to say?

DELLA: You're very good with words, my dear. I'm sure you'll find the right ones.

DREW: But, Della, you don't know for sure. You're just guessing.

DELLA: I know what I heard.

DREW: You mean you were eavesdropping?

DELLA: Drew, they were in the other room, a few feet away. I couldn't help but overhear.

THE DISINTEGRATION OF DELLA LONGSTREET

DREW: And what exactly did you hear?

DELLA: They want to room together, and walk around naked, and do exactly as they pleased. And something happened on their last night together at Helmsly. Dickie spoke about scars on his body. And he remarked about her sweater. How...

DREW: How what?

DELLA: If you insist on treating this lightly, I'll just have to have a talk with them myself.

DREW: I wouldn't, if I were you.

DELLA: Why not?

DREW: Because I think it will embarrass all of us and create...a rather uncomfortable scene. Unless you want to spoil our little get-together, unless you want to ruin our whole summer and make it miserable for everyone. Is that what you want?

DELLA: What do you suggest we do?

DREW: I suggest we let nature take it's course. Knowing Debbie, I'm sure she's knows enough to protect herself.

DELLA: What are you suggesting?

DREW: I'm not suggesting anything. What do you think I'm suggesting? You don't think our daughter's still a virgin, do you?

DELLA: I don't know.

DREW: What do you mean, you don't know?

DELLA: It hadn't occurred to me.

DREW: Haven't you had a talk with her?

THE DISINTEGRATION OF DELLA LONGSTREET

DELLA: I've been meaning to. It's just that I find the whole question of sex...

DREW: Hard to deal with.

DELLA: I just think that too much importance has been placed upon it.

DREW: There's no danger of that, as far as you're concerned.

DELLA: We're not talking about me. We're talking about our daughter, and our son. I am very concerned about them, and so should you be. Will you, or will you not have a talk with them?

DREW: Very well, my dear.

DELLA: What does that mean?

DREW: I will have a talk with them. How I'm going to word it I haven't the vaguest idea. Where are you going?

DELLA: I'm going to take a shower, if that's all right with you. Dinner should be ready shortly.

> *(DELLA goes off. DREW goes into the dining room, picks up the phone and dials.)*

DREW: Hello? Hello, Charles? How did we do? Oh, dear. Well, they're bound to go up. How much? Charles, you know I don't have that sort of money. That does sound reasonable though. Go ahead and buy them. Fine. I'll manage somehow. Have a good week-end. *(HE presses the button and dials another number.)* What are you doing? I told you. I'm with my family in our little hideaway. If I told you where it was, it wouldn't be a hideaway any longer. Now would it? We're going to do all the little things a family does when they get together? No, dear. I think Della's forgotten how. Mmmm. You make it sound very tempting. It's impossible. I'm not in town. I told you where I was. I've got to go. Arrivederci.

> *(HE hangs up as DEBBIE enters.)*

THE DISINTEGRATION OF DELLA LONGSTREET

DEBBIE: Daddy! Oh, Daddy! *(SHE throws her arms around his neck and kisses him.)*

DREW: How's my little girl? Mmmm. You smell so good.

DEBBIE: I don't smell.

DREW: All young people smell good, Baby.

DEBBIE: Oh, Daddy, it's so good to see you again.

DREW: Where's Dickie?

DEBBIE: He's swimming in the lake.

DREW: It's freezing out there.

DEBBIE: I guess we're both hot blooded. Oh, Daddy, it's so going to be such fun, all four of us, together again.

DREW: That was the idea.

DEBBIE: Where's Mumsie?

DREW: She's taking a shower.

DEBBIE: Daddy?

DREW: Yes, dear? What is it?

DEBBIE: I've simply got to have more money.

DREW: I'm sure you do. Unfortunately I do not hold the purse strings. Why don't we just wait and see? One never knows what's around the corner.

DEBBIE: It would be so much easier if we could just come to you.

DREW: I quite agree.

THE DISINTEGRATION OF DELLA LONGSTREET

DEBBIE: How much more would I get?

DREW: This much more. *(HE holds his hands far apart.)*

DEBBIE: *(SHE kisses him.)* You have my vote.

DREW: Unfortunately these things are not decided by an election.

DEBBIE: How are they decided?

DREW: It's often a case of sheer luck. Your mother was born rich. I was born poor.

DEBBIE: Poor but handsome.

DREW: Don't say that, Honey.

DEBBIE: Why not, if it's true?

DREW: It makes me sound like a gigolo. I did not marry your mother for her money.

DEBBIE: Why did you marry her?

DREW: We were in love. We still are, in a way.

DEBBIE: Poor, Mumsie! What a strange little creature she is!

DREW: Your mother isn't little and, as a matter of fact, she's a very passionate woman.

DEBBIE: Then...?

DREW: What?

DEBBIE: Then why do you have separate rooms? Why haven't you slept together in three years?

DREW: Who told you that?

THE DISINTEGRATION OF DELLA LONGSTREET

DEBBIE: Dickie.

DREW: And how would Dickie know?

DEBBIE: Mumsie told him.

DREW: Did she really? How interesting.

DEBBIE: I don't know how Mumsie can resist you.

DREW: That's my little dumpling. But then you're not a dumpling any longer, are you? Some people, you see, are afraid of their own sexuality.

DEBBIE: But why?

DREW: When you get a little older, I think you'll understand.

DEBBIE: Can't you tell me now?

DREW: Sometimes our desires can be...

DEBBIE: What?

DREW: Overwhelming.

DEBBIE: So?

DREW: Come here. Come close to Daddy.

> (DELLA appears in the doorway. DEBBIE moves close to DREW and HE puts his arm around her and kisses her.)

DREW: Now, I want you to tell me something, and I want you to tell me the truth.

DEBBIE: Yes, Daddy?

DREW: Does my little girl know how to take care of herself?

THE DISINTEGRATION OF DELLA LONGSTREET

DEBBIE: How do you mean?

DREW: I mean... Well, if Daddy were to make love to his little girl would she know how to prevent a little accident?

DEBBIE: Oh, Daddy!

DREW: That's all I want to know.

DEBBIE: Oh!

DREW: What is it?

DEBBIE: I promised to bring Dickie a towel.

DREW: Well, we mustn't forget little Dickie. You go get a towel and we'll go find Dickie together. But first give Daddy a kiss.

(THEY stand and kiss.)

DREW: That's my sweet little girl. Go on, go on.

(HE pats her on the behind and she starts off.)

DEBBIE: Oh, Mumsie! Isn't this fun? *(SHE kisses DELLA and runs off.)*

DREW: Well, I spoke to her.

DELL: Yes, I saw and heard.

DREW: Now what do you mean by that?

DELLA: I'd rather not say.

DREW: You must be mad.

DELLA: I sometimes think that would be preferable.

DREW: At any rate, there's nothing to worry about. Now stop it!

THE DISINTEGRATION OF DELLA LONGSTREET

DELLA: Please don't make a scene, Drew. We'll talk about this some other time.

DREW: We'll talk about it now.

DELLA: I haven't said a word.

DREW: You don't have to.

(DEBBIE reenters with a towel.)

DEBBIE: Are you coming, Daddy?

DREW: Yes, dear, of course.

DEBBIE: How soon is dinner, Mumsie?

DELLA: Not for while. Run along, dear. Run along, Drew.

DREW: We'll have a long talk after dinner.

DEBBIE: Come on, Daddy. Dickie's waiting for his towel.

(DEBBIE takes DREW by the hand and THEY go off. DELLA goes to a drawer, takes out a pill box and swallows a pill. SHE coughs as SHE tries to swallow the pill. SHE runs into the kitchen. The telephone rings. DELLA reenters the dining room with a glass of water in her hand.)

DELLA: No. No, please!

(SHE stands looking at the phone, as if hypnotized by it. SHE sits, sets the glass on the table and covers her ears. The phone continues to ring. She uncovers her ears and approaches the phone as if under a spell. SHE picks up the receiver and puts it to her ear. SHE listens for a moment, drops the receiver and falls to the floor in a faint. DICK enters.)

THE DISINTEGRATION OF DELLA LONGSTREET

DICK: I'm back. *(HE sees DELLA on the floor and runs over to her.)* Mumsie? Are you all right? Mumsie?

> *(HE runs off to the dining room, sees the glass of water on the table, picks it up and returns to DELLA. HE takes his handkerchief from his pocket, dips it into the water and applies it to Della's forehead. SHE opens her eyes.)*

DICK: Mumsie? Are you all right?

DELLA: Where am I? What happened?

DICK: We're at the cottage. You had one of your fainting spells. Shall I get you one of your pills?

DELLA: No. No.

DICK: What happened?

> *(SHE sits up and looks around. DICK notices the receiver and hangs it up.)*

DICK: One of those imaginary phone calls?

DELLA: It wasn't imaginary. It was real.

DICK: I'm sure it was. Now, Mumsie...

DELLA: Why must you call me Mumsie?

DICK: I've always called you Mumsie. I thought you liked it.

DELLA: I did, when you were a child.

DICK: And you certainly liked it when Daddy called you Mumsie.

DELLA: That was different.

DICK: In what way?

THE DISINTEGRATION OF DELLA LONGSTREET

DELLA: It was...sort of a pet name.

DICK: You mean like a lover's name?

DELLA: Well, yes.

DICK: But I love you, too. And so does Debbie.

DELLA: Do you, dear?

DICK: Of course, we do. You're the prettiest...mother in all the world. And sexy, too. Oops. I shouldn't have said that.

DELLA: I guess I am out of touch with the world.

DICK: You have your own private world. I guess we all do, Mumsie. Oops!

DELLA: Do you think I'm old-fashioned, Dickie?

DICK: I don't believe in fashions, Della. How's that? I'll call you Della. Is that all right. Here. Let me help you up.

(HE helps her up and onto the sofa.)

DELLA: Thank you, dear. I'm fine now.

DICK: You look better, too.

DELLA: I'm out of touch with the world. I know it. It's not the same world that I grew up in.

DICK: What world was that?

DELLA: A gentle world, a quite world, a respectful world. *(After a moment)* You grow more like your father every day.

DICK: I shall take that as a compliment.

THE DISINTEGRATION OF DELLA LONGSTREET

DELLA: Your father's a very charming man.

DICK: And handsome, too.

DELLA: Dickie?

DICK: Yes, dear?

DELLA: You and Debbie are very fond of one another, aren't you?

DICK: Yes, of course, we are. Why do you ask? Is there anything wrong in that?

DELLA: No, of course not.

DICK: Then why did you bring it up? You think that Debbie and I are too fond of one another.

DELLA: No, of course not. It's just that...

DICK: Just that what?

DELLA: It's just that you are a young man now and Debbie's...

DICK: A young woman.

DELLA: Exactly. What I'm trying to say, dear, is that you aren't children any longer.

DICK: Della, you're shocking me.

DELLA: I'm serious.

DICK: Because we're not children any longer, does that mean we've got to stop having fun?

DELLA: No, of course not, dear. What do you mean by fun?

DICK: What do you mean?

THE DISINTEGRATION OF DELLA LONGSTREET

DELLA: I asked you first.

DICK: I mean, do we have to stop loving one another. Because if that's what you mean... I mean, after all, love is what makes us tick. Do you remember Bill Fielding?

DELLA: Yes, of course, I do. He was a friend of yours.

DICK: One of the jolliest friends I ever had. He was always laughing and joking. Just to be around him made you happy. Well, I ran into Bill just a few months ago. I couldn't recognize him. He was like an old man. Apparently, someone told him that he mustn't. And he doesn't...anymore.

DELLA: Doesn't what, dear?

DICK: Love, Della. Love.

DELLA: How do you know? I mean that someone told him that he...mustn't?

DICK: He was like a corpse, a zombie. And he always used to be so warm and so affectionate. Is that what you want to me be? A zombie?

DELLA: No, of course not.

DICK: Because the world is full of zombies, Della.

DELLA: Isn't there something in between?

DICK: In between what? What are we talking about? Are we talking about sex, Della? Because sex is just an expression of love. Now isn't it?

DELLA: It should be, yes. But if that were the case...

DICK: Yes, dear? The world is changing, Della. And even if one doesn't change with it one must, at least, acknowledge the change.

DELLA: I find it all so...confusing. So frightening.

THE DISINTEGRATION OF DELLA LONGSTREET

DICK: That's because you think with your mind.

DELLA: What else is one to think with?

DICK: One's heart, my dear, one's heart.

DELLA: *(After a moment)* If I asked you a question would you answer me honestly?

DICK: What's the question?

DELLA: What did you and Debbie do together your last night at Helmsly?

DICK: Why do you ask?

DELLA: I was just curious.

DICK: We painted old Helmsly blue. The statue, that is.

DELLA: That's all?

DICK: And ourselves.

DELLA: That's all?

DICK: Isn't that enough?

DELLA: It sounded so...

DICK: So what?

DELLA: So sensual.

DICK: Everything I do is sensual. I'm a sensual person. Were you eavesdropping, Della?

THE DISINTEGRATION OF DELLA LONGSTREET

DELLA: I was in the next room. I couldn't help but overhear. If your father asked you the same question, is that what you'd tell him? That you painted yourselves blue?

DICK: Why would my answer be any different?

DELLA Your father is so much more...

DICK: More what?

DELLA: Permissive.

DICK: Mumsie... Sorry. Della, you're getting yourself all upset...over nothing.

DELLA: Would your answer be any different?

DICK: Yes.

DELLA: Why?

DICK: When it comes to Debbie, Daddy's rather...

DELLA: Rather what?

DICK: Jealous. Well, maybe jealous isn't the right word exactly. Possessive.

DELLA: Why should he be jealous?

DICK: You know how fathers are when it comes to their daughters. Though I'm sure that Debbie...

DELLA: What? You're sure that Debbie...what?

DICK: Mother, you're going to work yourself up into a lather.

DELLA: You're sure that Debbie...what?

THE DISINTEGRATION OF DELLA LONGSTREET

DICK: All I'm trying to say is that Debbie loves Daddy.

DELLA: Well, of course, she does. He's her father.

DICK: Do you really think it's possible to love with just one part of oneself?

DELLA: No, of course not...but...

DICK: But what?

DELLA: I don't know what you're trying to say. It's true that we all have desires. Primitive perhaps. But...but that's why we have civilization, to regulate these desires, to curb them What would become of us if we all gave into...our primitive desires?

DICK: Why not? As long as we're not hurting anyone? The truth of the matter is, Mumsie, dear, an act of love never hurt anyone. It's the nay sayers that do all the damage.

DELLA: You're not serious, are you? *(After a moment.)* Dickie, I want you to take me home.

DICK: When?

DELLA: Now.

DICK: Now?

DELLA: Yes, now.

DICK: But...

DELLA: No buts. I'm going to pack my things and I want you to have your car ready as soon as I'm finished.

DICK: It's almost dark. Those roads are treacherous.

THE DISINTEGRATION OF DELLA LONGSTREET

DELLA: I don't have my car. Maxwell drove me up. Otherwise I wouldn't need your help.

DICK: If you insist, I will take you home in the morning. If you still want to go, that is. What are you afraid of, Mother. Are you afraid of me? Of Debbie? Of Daddy? Or is it yourself that you're afraid of?

DELLA: What do you mean by that?

DICK: If you like, you can lock yourself in your room.

DELLA: There are no locks on the doors, in case you've forgotten. Your father saw to that.

DICK: Then you can shove your bureau in front of the door, if that will make you feel any safer.

DELLA: Dickie, please.

DICK: Mother, I will not risk your life and mine, because of a foolish whim.

DELLA: It's not a whim.

DICK: What is it then?

DELLA: It's a premonition. Something terrible is going to happen here tonight. I know it.

DICK: Like what?

DELLA: Dickie, please. I beg of you.

DICK: No. Once and for all I will not kill us both. Those roads are bad enough during the day. At night they are death traps.

DELLA: Then I shall have to call Maxwell.

DICK: You can call him if you like, but I doubt if he will come.

THE DISINTEGRATION OF DELLA LONGSTREET

DELLA: What's our number? My mind is a blank. What is our number? No, that's not it. Ah, yes. *(SHE picks up the phone and dials.)* Hello? Who is this? I must have the wrong number. *(SHE hangs up and dials again.)* Hello? Oh, Margaret. Is Maxwell there? Let me speak to him please. Well, fetch him. Yes, I'll wait.

DICK: Mother... *(HE sighs.)*

DELLA: Hello? Hello, Maxwell. No, nothing's wrong. Well, yes there is. The fact of the matter is I'm not feeling very well, and I've got to see the doctor in the morning. No, no, no. I want you to pick me up now. It's an emergency. Yes, Mr. Longstreet has his car. That's beside the point. Nonsense. You're an excellent driver. That's why you were hired. Maxwell? *(SHE turns to DICK.)* He hung up.

DICK: Well, of course he did. What did you expect? I really think you should take one of your pills.

DELLA: I just took one. *(SHE hangs up the phone.)*

DICK: Then how about some Valium?

DELLA: I don't want any Valium.

DICK: Then relax.

DELLA: If I knew how to drive, I would drive myself.

DICK: But you don't. And even if you did, I wouldn't let you. Nor would Daddy.

DELLA: This was his idea, wasn't it?

DICK: What?

DELLA: This so-called getaway or reunion or whatever you want to call it. Your father planned all this, didn't he?

THE DISINTEGRATION OF DELLA LONGSTREET

DICK: Well, of course, he did. You know that. Mumsie, you didn't have to come if you didn't want to.

DELLA: We don't even have electricity here.

DICK: We never have had. We've got plenty of candles though. Why don't we light some of the candles. It's beginning to get dark. Where are the candles?

DELLA: I don't know.

DICK: *(HE opens a drawer, then another.)* Ah. Here they are, where they always are. And here are the candlesticks. Come on, Della, help me light the candles. *(HE proceeds to light several candles and places them about the room.)*

DELLA: I never liked this place. It's so...so primitive. There's no electricity, no heat.

DICK: It's summer, Mother.

DELLA: Well, it does get chilly at night. If we have a telephone I see no reason on earth why we can't have electricity...and heat.

DICK: Why didn't you see to it?

DELLA: Because this was your father's project, not mine. I don't know what he had in mind when he built it, or had it built. Or maybe I do.

DICK: Now calm down, Della. Just calm down.

DELLA: I'm going to serve our dinner, and directly afterwards I'm going to my room, and I'm going to bed, and the three of you can do whatever you please.

DICK: We'll probably play a game of chess.

DELLA: Chess is a game for two.

THE DISINTEGRATION OF DELLA LONGSTREET

DICK: I meant Daddy and myself.

DELLA: He's your father. He's not your Daddy! Why don't you call him father or Drew? I'm sorry, dear, it's just that I've been cursed with this...this pure, unadulterated vision.

DICK: I'd say it's quite possible that your vision has gotten slightly tainted along the way.

DELLA: I am not imagining things, and don't you dare tell me that I am. Dinner will be ready shortly.

DICK: How long is that?

DELLA: I couldn't say, since I'm not used to cooking on that damn primitive stove.

>   *(DELLA goes off to the dining room and fusses at the table. DEBBIE enters.)*

DEBBIE: Is dinner ready yet?

DICK: What happened to my towel?

DEBBIE: We got waylaid along the way.

DICK: Who's we?

DEBBIE: Daddy and I. I've gotta change.

DICK: What's wrong with what you've got on?

DEBBIE: I've got grass stains all over my skirt.

>   *(DEBBIE goes off to her room. DREW enters.)*

DREW: Dickie boy!

DICK: Hello, Daddy.

THE DISINTEGRATION OF DELLA LONGSTREET

(DELLA goes off to the kitchen. DICK goes up to DREW and kisses him.)

DREW: Let me take a look at you. Mmhh.

DICK: What does that mean?

DREW: You're filling out.

DICK: Well, I should hope so.

DREW: Well, how was school this year?

DICK: Okay, Dad. Nothing spectacular. Say, Dad?

DREW: Yes, Son?

DICK: I spoke to Mother about a new car, but she doesn't seem to understand. I don't suppose you could help me out, could you?

DREW: I wish I could, Son.

DICK: What is she gonna do with all that money?

DREW: I'll see what I can do.

DICK: Maybe you can sweet talk her.

DREW: Your mother's a very righteous woman. She doesn't hold with all that nonsense.

DICK: As a matter of fact, she's pretty upset.

DREW: About what?

DICK: You know Mumsie. She wanted me to take her home tonight. She even got on the phone and tried to get Maxwell to come up here and get her.

THE DISINTEGRATION OF DELLA LONGSTREET

DREW: I hope she isn't headed for another breakdown. You know what the doctor said.

DICK: No. What?

DREW: If she cracked up again they might have to put her away for quite a while.

DICK: Poor Mumsie.

DREW: Well, your mother's always been sort of high strung. Your hair's getting kind of long, isn't it?

DICK: You think I oughta cut it?

DREW: No. I like it like that. Did your mother say anything to you about you and Debbie?

DICK: She asked me what Debbie and I did on our last night at Helmsly.

DREW: What did you tell her?

DICK: I told her we painted ourselves blue. Did she talk to you about it?

DREW: Your mother has a very vivid imagination.

DICK: Incidentally I wouldn't say anything to her about Debbie getting those grass stains on her dress.

DREW: Oh?

> (DELLA enters the dining room with a platter of food which she places on the table.)

DREW: I'm looking forward to taking one of our long hikes together. Get away from all these women folk.

DICK: I'd like that, Daddy. We sure had a lot of fun last year, didn't we?

THE DISINTEGRATION OF DELLA LONGSTREET

(In the dining room DELLA takes some candlesticks and candles from the drawer, places them around the room and lights the candles.)

DREW: It's good for us menfolks to get together every once in a while. Out there in the woods, communing with Nature. Do what we wanna do, when we wanna do it. Women are all right in their place but, let's face it, Son, it's what goes on between we men that make all the difference. I love you, Dickie. I want you to know that. And don't you think that just because I make a fuss over your sister every once in a while, that doesn't mean that I love you any the less.

(DELLA appears in the doorway just as DREW kisses DICK.)

DELLA: Dinner is on the table, if you two can tear yourselves away from one another. Where's Debbie?

DREW: She's in her room.

(DEBBIE reenters in another outfit.)

DEBBIE: Here I am. All set to go.

DELLA: What was wrong with what you had on?

DEBBIE: I got grass stains all over it.

DELLA: How did you manage that?

DEBBIE: By lying on the grass.

DREW: Shall we eat?

DELLA: We don't have any washing machines up here, you know.

DEBBIE: I'm aware of that, Mumsie.

DELLA: And even if we did, we don't have any electricity.

THE DISINTEGRATION OF DELLA LONGSTREET

DREW: What have we got for dinner?

DELLA: A roast.

DEBBIE: How duckie! Will you take me into dinner, Daddy?

DREW: Certainly, my love. Coming, Dickie?

DICK: I'm right behind you.

DEBBIE: How romantic. All this candlelight. Ah do declare. Two such handsome young men. I won't let either of you out of my sight for one little minute.

DELLA: An ounce of precaution is worth a pound of cure.

(The THREE of them look at her.)

DELLA: One of my quaint little sayings.

(DELLA goes off to the dining room and into kitchen. DREW, DICK and DEBBIE follow into the dining room as the lights come down.)

ACT TWO

The action is continuous. DREW, DEBBIE and DICK take their places at the dinner table DELLA reenters with the rest of the food, places it on the table and sits down.

DEBBIE: It all looks so good. Ah don't know where to start.

DELLA: There is no soup.

DEBBIE: No soup?

DICK: No soup?

DELLA: No soup!

DEBBIE: And I was so looking forward to having some soup.

DICK: So was I.

DELLA: I'm sure you'll find that there's more than enough here for everyone.

DEBBIE: May I give you some meat, Daddy dear?

DREW: Nothing would please me more.

DEBBIE: And you, Dickie?

DICK: I wouldn't pass it up for all the world?

DEBBIE: Mumsie?

DELLA: I can serve myself, thank you.

DEBBIE: That's not nearly as much fun.

DICK: Those little cherry tomatoes look mighty tempting.

DREW: I thought they were out of season.

THE DISINTEGRATION OF DELLA LONGSTREET

DICK: Cherry tomatoes are always a rarity.

DEBBIE: Those bananas look so big. I've never seen such big bananas. Where on earth did you get such big bananas?

DELLA: Where does one usually get bananas?

DEBBIE: I don't think I could get one in my mouth.

DICK: You'll just have to open wide.

DEBBIE: I haven't had a banana in ages.

DICK: Neither have I.

DREW: You're not eating, dear.

DELLA: I'm not very hungry.

DREW: It's all that snacking.

DELLA: One has to taste what one makes.

DEBBIE: I always do.

DICK: So do I?

DREW: Are you all right, dear?

DEBBIE: Where's the wine?

DELLA: It's in the kitchen. I'm afraid you'll have to excuse me. It's so close in here. I have to get some air. *(SHE rises and goes outside.)*

DEBBIE: I'll get the wine. *(SHE goes off to the kitchen.)*

DREW: Maybe you'd better look after your mother, Son.

DICK: Right.

THE DISINTEGRATION OF DELLA LONGSTREET

(DICK goes off. DEBBIE reenters with the wine. DREW opens the bottle and fills the glasses.)

DEBBIE: Where's Dickie?

DREW: He went to look after your mother.

(DREW and DEBBIE continue to eat. DEBBIE looks toward the outside door.))

DEBBIE: The food is getting cold.

DREW: I'll go see how your mother is doing.

(DREW goes off. DEBBIE continues to eat. DICK reenters.)

DICK: Poor Mumsie!

DEBBIE: Is she all right?

DICK: She was ready to take off all by herself.

DEBBIE: On foot? In the dark?

DICK: The dark is everywhere, she said. *(HE continues to eat.)* This roast is delicious.

(DREW reenters.)

DEBBIE: Where's Mother?

DREW: She'll be in, in a minute.

DEBBIE: Would you like some wine, Dickie?

DICKIE: Don't mind if I do.

(DEBBIE pours the wine. DICK drinks.)

THE DISINTEGRATION OF DELLA LONGSTREET

DICK: Nectar for the gods.

(DELLA reenters and takes her seat. DICK, DEBBIE and DREW continue to eat.)

DELLA: It's so dark out there. Not even a moon. I did see one little star though. It was so far away.

DREW: Would you like some wine, dear?

DELLA: Maybe just a little.

(DREW fills her glass.)

DELLA: So far away. It reminded me of the time when I was a little girl. I used to watch this one particular star from my window at night. It was the last thing I saw before I fell asleep. It wasn't always there though. I think everyone should have one particular star. Even if it isn't always visible. Don't you think so, Drew?

DREW: Most assuredly.

DELLA: My father used to sing me a song about a star. It was a nursery rhyme set to music. He used to put a tune to all the nursery rhymes and sing them to me.

DEBBIE: What was Grandpa like?

DELLA: He looked like Mark Twain with a full head of white hair and a lovely white beard. You've seen pictures of Mark Twain, haven't you?

DEBBIE: Was he funny like Mark Twain?

DELLA He had a wonderful sense of humor...about most things.

DEBBIE: Was he very strict?

DELLA: About some things, I suppose he was...by today's standards, that is. But things were different then.

THE DISINTEGRATION OF DELLA LONGSTREET

DICK: How were they different?

DELLA: Ask your father.

DICK: How were they different, Dad?

DREW: Well, for one thing, women's dresses were a little longer.

DELLA: A lot longer.

DREW: And things we talk about today and accept...didn't even exist.

DELLA: Of course, they existed. No one made a fuss about them, that's all. They just were. The world hasn't changed since the days of Adam and Eve.

DEBBIE: Now there was a pair for you, running around the garden of Eden without a stitch.

DREW: *(After a moment)* You really should eat something, dear.

DELLA: I'm not very hungry. Are we ready for dessert and coffee?

DICK: What's for dessert?

DELLA: Pineapple upside-down cake.

DEBBIE: My favorite.

DICK: Mine, too.

DELLA: I'll take your plates.

DEBBIE: Can I help?

DELLA: You can pour the coffee.

DEBBIE: Four coffees coming up.

THE DISINTEGRATION OF DELLA LONGSTREET

>(DEBBIE *goes into the kitchen.* DELLA *collects the empty plates and follows her off.*)

DICK: Mumsie seems much calmer now.

DREW: We must do our utmost to keep her that way, mustn't we?

DICK: By all means. Are you on for chess?

DREW: I most certainly am. Damn! I forget to bring the radio.

DICK: I brought mine.

DREW: Good thinking. There's nothing like music to soothe the savage breast.

DICK: Or any breast, for that matter.

>(DEBBIE *enters with the coffee and sets the cups on the table.*)

DEBBIE: Here we are. Daddy. Dickie. Mumsie. And last, but not least, little Debbie.

>(DELLA *enters with four plates of cake, which she places on the table.* DEBBIE *goes off to the kitchen.* DELLA *takes her seat.* DEBBIE *reenters with the milk and sugar and takes her seat. They proceed to eat.*)

DICK: What have you been up to, Mumsie?

DELLA: What do you mean?

DICK: What have you been doing, while we've been away, Debbie and I?

DELLA: Nothing special, really.

DREW: Your mother's very modest, Son. Mumsie's been doing a lot of charity work.

THE DISINTEGRATION OF DELLA LONGSTREET

DEBBIE: Really?

DELLA: Yes, really. I've been working for the cancer fund, and the war orphans and I've been invited to join the board of the Arts Center.

DEBBIE: Oh?

DELLA: Yes, indeed. We've housed and fed thousands of homeless children. There's been a breakthrough on the cure for cancer. And we've sponsored a series of free concerts for the underprivileged.

DREW: Your mother's been very generous with her time and her money.

DELLA: I believe in putting whatever little time we have here on earth to practical use.

DICK: Confucius say, "Charity begins at home."

DELLA: Confucius says lots of things.

DICK: Like what?

DELLA: "Like he who steals my purse, steals trash."

DEBBIE: That's an odd thing for him to say.

DELLA: Not as odd as painting oneself blue, I should think.

DEBBIE: Painting oneself blue?

DELLA: Isn't that what you and Dickie did your last night at Helmsly?

DEBBIE: Why, yes. Yes, of course.

DELLA: Don't you remember?

DEBBIE: Of course, I remember.

THE DISINTEGRATION OF DELLA LONGSTREET

DELLA: It was supposed to have been such a memorable evening. Or could it be that it never happened?

DICK: Of course, it did. I told you all about it.

DELLA: That doesn't necessarily make it so.

DEBBIE: Now, Mumsie, why would Dickie lie about a thing like that?

DELLA: I want the truth. What did you and Dickie do your last night at Helmsly.

DEBBIE: Like Dickie said, we painted ourselves blue. What do you think we did?

DREW: This cake is delicious. When did you have time to bake it?

DELLA: Would you care for some more?

DREW: Maybe later, if there's any left over.

DELLA: Dickie?

DICK: No, thank you.

DELLA: Debbie?

DEBBIE: I've got to watch my figure. I'm beginning to put on weight.

DELLA: That doesn't always come from food.

DEBBIE: Oh?

DELLA: No. They say that gaining weight is one of the side effects of the pill.

DEBBIE: Then again, it's possible to gain wight as a result of not taking the pill, is it not?

THE DISINTEGRATION OF DELLA LONGSTREET

DREW: That's true.

DEBBIE: Thank God for the pill.

DELLA: *(Ironically, half to herself)* Yes, thank God for the pill.

DREW: What's that, dear?

DELLA: Would anyone like some more coffee?

> *(DREW, DICK and DEBBIE shake their heads. DELLA rises and takes some dishes into the kitchen.)*

DEBBIE: I guess I should help Mumsie with the dishes, though I can't see why we can't have a dishwasher.

DICK: We'd need electricity for that.

DREW: Dickie and I will to the dishes. Won't we, Dickie?

DICK: What's that? Okay, if you say so.

DREW: I do. Come along. Let's clear the table.

> *(DREW and DICK gather up the rest of the dishes as DELLA reenters)*

DELLA: You don't have to do that. I can manage.

DREW: You're to sit down and rest. You've done enough work for the day. Dickie and I will finish up.

DEBBIE: Come along, Mumsie. We're being cast aside. The men are taking over. And it's about time, too.

DELLA: I'll just...

DREW: No, you won't.

THE DISINTEGRATION OF DELLA LONGSTREET

DELLA: I just want to put some tinfoil around the leftovers.

DREW: I think we can manage that, Dickie, don't you?

DICK: I think so.

DEBBIE: Come along, Mumsie. The ladies will retire to the drawing room.

>*(DEBBIE leads DELLA into the living room as DREW and DICK finish clearing off the table and take the things into the kitchen.)*

DELLA: I hope we have enough candles. I should hate to be stranded in the dark.

DEBBIE: We can always go into town in the morning.

DELLA: It's not the morning I'm concerned about.

DEBBIE: Would you like to play some scrabble?

DELLA: I don't think so, dear. I think I'll just work on my needlepoint.

DEBBIE: Needlepoint?

DELLA: I've taken up needlepoint. I find it relaxes me.

DEBBIE: You are a caution, Mumsie. Where is it? I'll get it for you.

DELLA: That's all right. I can get it myself. I'm not even sure where I put it. *(SHE picks up a candle.)* I do hope that next year we can have some electricity.

>*(DELLA goes off. DICK and DREW enter the dining room. DICK gathers up some dishes. DREW enters the living room.)*

DREW: Where's your mother?

DEBBIE: She went to get her needlepoint.

THE DISINTEGRATION OF DELLA LONGSTREET

DREW: You have a nice long talk with your mother. She's missed you both.

DEBBIE: Yes, Daddy.

> *(DICK takes some things into the kitchen. DREW goes into the dining room, clears the table and goes into the kitchen. DELLA reenters with her needlepoint and takes a seat.)*

DELLA: So, here we are?

DEBBIE: What are you sewing?

DELLA: It's a sampler.

DEBBIE: What's a sampler?

DELLA: It's a decorative piece that I'm going to frame and hang on the wall. They used to be very popular.

DEBBIE: May I see it?

DELLA: Yes, of course. It's not finished yet. The lettering, that is.

DEBBIE: What's it going to say?

DELLA: God Bless Our Home. You see? There's this little cabin with trees and flowers around it.

DEBBIE: It looks like this one, doesn't it?

DELLA: Why, yes. I suppose it does.

DEBBIE: There are no people though.

DELLA: Of course, there are.

DEBBIE: I don't see them.

THE DISINTEGRATION OF DELLA LONGSTREET

DELLA: That's because they're all inside.

DEBBIE: I see.

DELLA: My mother had this very same pattern. It hung in the kitchen. When I was a little girl I used to sit and stare at it every morning at breakfast. And I used to make up little stories about the house.

DEBBIE: What kind of stories?

DELLA: Oh, I don't know. Sometimes it was a happy house. Sometimes it was a sad house. Sometimes it was a cruel house. Sometimes it was a kind house.

DEBBIE: What about the people in the house? What were they like?

DELLA: That depended on my mood. If I was in a happy mood, there was a birthday party, or a ball with music and dancing. On rainy days, when I was sad or blue, everyone was grief-stricken. There was a death in the family, perhaps, and then there were candles all over the house, and everyone sat around the coffin weeping.

DEBBIE: What was a coffin doing in the house?

DELLA: What's that?

DEBBIE: I mean coffins are usually kept in a funeral parlor.

DELLA: When you're a little girl coffins can be anywhere you want them to be.

DEBBIE: *(After a moment)* Mumsie...

DELLA: Yes, dear?

DEBBIE: Why don't you take a lover?

DELLA: I beg your pardon.

THE DISINTEGRATION OF DELLA LONGSTREET

DEBBIE: Oh, Mumsie, come off it.

DELLA: I'm sorry, dear. I know that I'm old fashioned, but I find it embarrassing to talk about my personal life with my children.

DEBBIE: I'm not a child anymore. I'm a young woman.

DELLA: Almost, perhaps.

DEBBIE: You can't spend the rest of your life hiding your head in the sand.

DELLA: I'm not hiding my head anywhere.

DEBBIE: You're in the prime of your life. You should have some sort of a love life. You should have a lover.

DELLA: Should I? You're a young woman now. Have you a lover?

DEBBIE: At the moment, no.

DELLA: I'm relieved to hear it.

DEBBIE: That doesn't mean that I haven't had.

DELLA: Who is he? Who was he? What happened to him?

DEBBIE: Oh, Mumsie, you are naive.

DELLA: In what way?

DEBBIE: Never mind. I don't want to shock you.

DELLA: Have you had more than one? Lover?

DEBBIE: Yes, dear.

DELLA: In other words, you've been shopping around.

THE DISINTEGRATION OF DELLA LONGSTREET

DEBBIE: What a charming way of putting it. It's a new world, Mumsie, and life has so much to offer. Throw off your chains.

DELLA: And you think, instead of doing charity work, I should be hopping from bed to bed.

DEBBIE: There's no reason why you can't do both. Charity can take many forms, you know. And don't tell me that the charity work you're doing now is fulfilling.

DELLA: Of course it is, or I wouldn't be doing it. I happen to believe in fidelity, not only as a matter of principle, but as a matter of practicality.

DEBBIE: Then why don't you and Daddy go your separate ways?

DELLA: If your father wanted his freedom, I would certainly give it to him.

DEBBIE: And you have no desire to be free?

DELLA: But I am free, dear. I'm free to take a lover...or not.

DEBBIE: And you prefer...not.

DELLA: For the moment.

DEBBIE: But time is passing.

DELLA: Yes, dear, it has a way of doing that.

DEBBIE: But aren't you afraid...?

DELLA: Of missing out on something? I used to be, when I was your age. I married your father, you know, over the objection of most of my family.

DEBBIE: Why did your family object to Daddy?

THE DISINTEGRATION OF DELLA LONGSTREET

DELLA: My family objected to all the young men who weren't as wealthy as I was. So you see, my dear, I was really quite the rebel.

DEBBIE: Were you, Mumsie?

DELLA: I most certainly was. *(After a moment)* I have another sampler, dear, if you'd care to...

DEBBIE: Thank you, but no thanks. I'd rather sit here and look at you. You really are a beautiful woman, Mumsie.

DELLA: Why thank you, dear.

DEBBIE: It seems a shame to let all that beauty go to waste.

DELLA: I don't think it's going to waste. I often think that people are like flowers, and sometimes it's gratifying just to look at them. And, if I am nice to look at, and I look after myself properly, then, perhaps, I'm spreading joy in my own little way.

DEBBIE: *(After a moment)* What are you thinking about, Mumsie?

DELLA: I'm thinking about you, dear. Debbie Longstreet at various ages.

DEBBIE: Was I so different along the way?

DELLA: Everyone changes, dear, as they grow older.

DEBBIE: You're not getting one of your headaches, are you?

DELLA: No, no, no. I just feel a little tense, that's all. *(SHE rubs the back of her neck.)*

DEBBIE: Let me massage it for you. I'm very good at it. I do it for my room-mate all the time. *(SHE massages Della's neck.)*

DELLA: What is she like, your room-mate?

DEBBIE: Oh, she's all right.

THE DISINTEGRATION OF DELLA LONGSTREET

DELLA: What is she like?

DEBBIE: Oh, she's kind of attractive, I guess, in an offbeat sort of way.

DELLA: I mean her personality, her character.

DEBBIE: You wouldn't like her.

(DELLA looks puzzled)

DEBBIE: Oh, Mumsie, you are naive. Not that I have any objection to that sort of thing. But a little of that goes a long way with me, if you know what I mean. There. Is that any better?

DELLA: What? Oh, yes. That was fine.

DEBBIE: If you get undressed, I can give you a real massage. It never fails. Carrie swears by it.

DELLA: Who is Carrie?

DEBBIE: My room-mate. You don't have to get all undressed, if you don't want to. Just let down the top of your dress and slip out of your bra.

DELLA: Maybe later, dear.

DEBBIE: Okay. Are you upset about anything?

DELLA: No, no. I'm just fine.

DEBBIE: Oh, Mumsie. I wish we could spend more time together. Remember when you used to let me sleep with you. We used to have those long, long talks late into the night. Don't you remember?

DELLA: Yes, of course, I do. I don't remember what we talked about.

DEBBIE: I do. We talked about everything.

THE DISINTEGRATION OF DELLA LONGSTREET

DELLA: Did we, dear?

DEBBIE: And I used to sit and watch you undress. You had a beautiful body, Mumsie. You still do. *(DEBBIE sits beside her and places Della's free arm around her shoulder.)*

DELLA: I'll never finish this sampler, dear.

DEBBIE: What's more important, your sampler or your daughter? I hope my body is as nice as yours when I'm your age.

DELLA: Well, I'm not that old, dear.

DEBBIE: But you must do something with your hair.

DELLA: What's wrong with my hair?

DEBBIE: It's so old-fashioned. I mean the way you wear it. Now let me see. What can we do with it?

DELLA: Be careful, dear. I just had it set.

DEBBIE: Nonsense. It looks awful. There. That's much better.

DELLA: What does it look like?

DEBBIE: I'll get you a mirror.

DELLA: Never mind. I'll look at it later.

DEBBIE: On second thought... Let me see. I think it would look even better if you wore it just loose, like that.

DELLA: I couldn't wear my hair like that.

DEBBIE: Why not?

DELLA: That's for young girls.

THE DISINTEGRATION OF DELLA LONGSTREET

DEBBIE: You said yourself you're not that old. As a matter of fact, one of our teachers wears her hair like that and it's very becoming and I'm sure she isn't any younger than you are.

DELLA: Debbie?

DEBBIE: Yes?

DELLA: Will you be rooming with Carrie next year?

DEBBIE: I don't know yet. How are you at massaging necks?

DELLA: I don't know.

DEBBIE: Would you do mine?

DELLA: Yes, of course, dear.

DEBBIE: Mmmm. That feels good. Just a little harder. Mmm. Yes.

DELLA: There. How was that?

DEBBIE: Well, short, but sweet. Can I sleep with you tonight, Mumsie?

DELLA: Well, my bed is rather small.

DEBBIE: I don't mind. We can snuggle up close.

DELLA: We'll see, dear.

DEBBIE: I wonder what Dickie and Daddy are up to in there?

DELLA: What do you mean?

DEBBIE: I mean they've been doing those dishes for a long, long time. It really is a man's world, isn't it?

DELLA: Is it?

THE DISINTEGRATION OF DELLA LONGSTREET

DEBBIE: I mean they rule the roost. They can do just as they please. Are you uncomfortable.

DELLA: Well, you are rather crowding me.

DEBBIE: Oh, I'm sorry.

DELLA: That's quite all right. Why don't you go and see what Dickie and Daddy are up to?

DEBBIE: Must I? It's so comfortable here, with you. In a way, I hate growing up. If I ever have any children I shall never let them grow up. I'd want to keep them with me always.

DELLA: That might get to be a little awkward, after a certain age.

(DEBBIE snuggles up close)

DELLA: Please, dear.

DEBBIE: Am I hurting you?

DELLA: No, dear. But I would like to work on my sampler.

DEBBIE: Oh, very well. I know when I've been rejected.

DELLA: I'm not rejecting you.

DEBBIE: Of course, you are. I think I shall join Dickie and Daddy. Maybe they will appreciate me more. If you promise to behave, I might even let you have one of them.

(DEBBIE goes into the kitchen. DELLA works on her sampler, puts it down and feels her hair. DEBBIE's laughter is heard from the kitchen. DELLA sighs, picks up her sampler and continues to work on it. DICK enters.)

DICK: Mumsie, you've let down your hair.

THE DISINTEGRATION OF DELLA LONGSTREET

DELLA: That was Debbie's doing.

DICK: It's very becoming. I hope it's not symbolic.

DELLA: And what if it is?

DICK: Mumsie, what's come over you?

DELLA: Nothing's come over me. Everyone treats me as if I were the original prude, and nothing could be further from the truth.

DICK: Come. 'Fess up. What's the real you like, Mumsie?

DELLA: The real me is no different from...the real anyone else.

DICK: Don't tell me our goddess is made of clay.

DELLA: Don't talk nonsense. I'm not a goddess. What's more, I don't pretend to be.

(DEBBIE's laughter is heard.)

DELLA: What are your father and your sister doing in there?

DICK: Whatever it is, they seem to be enjoying it.

DELLA: Dickie...?

DICK: Yes, dear?

DELLA: What do you really think of me? As a person. Aside from the fact that I'm your mother.

DICK: I think you're very beautiful and very desirable. I think you're charming and intelligent.

DELLA: My, my, my, my, my. You do want that new car, don't you? I'm sorry. I didn't mean that. I know you wouldn't stoop to flattery to get what you want.

THE DISINTEGRATION OF DELLA LONGSTREET

DICK: But, of course, I would. A little flattery never hurt anyone.

DELLA: You're getting more and more like your father every day. You're very fond of your father, aren't you?

DICK: Don't you want me to be?

DELLA: Yes, of course, I do.

DICK: What are you sewing, Mumsie?

DELLA: A sampler.

DICK: Is that a new hobby of yours?

DELLA: Relatively new. What are your hobbies, dear?

DICK: You don't really want to know, do you?

DELLA: Why would I ask, if I didn't want to know?

DICK: Life is my hobby. I want to see, I want to taste, I want to enjoy everything there is to enjoy.

DELLA: Everything?

DICK: I intend to leave no stone unturned.

DELLA: There are some experiences that can be harmful. Take drugs, for example.

DICK: I never touch the hard stuff. But I do think it's a crime to go to ones grave having lived only half of ones life.

DELLA: Pleasure need not always be sensual.

DICK: Everything we experience is sensual. We cannot escape our bodies, Mumsie, no matter how hard we try. I don't believe you're as aloof as you pretend to be.

THE DISINTEGRATION OF DELLA LONGSTREET

DELLA: I'm not aloof at all. I'm just trying to hold on to my sanity in a world that seems to me to have gone completely mad. I should think that you, of all people, would understand me, Dickie.

DICK: But I do understand you, Mumsie, perhaps even better that you do yourself. Your desires aren't evil, Mumsie. They're beautiful.

DELLA: And how do you know what my "desires" are?

DICK: Are they any different from anyone else's? If only you weren't bound by so many rules.

DELLA: Oh, Dickie, if only we could be friends. I mean real friends.

DICK: We are, Mumsie, as far as I'm concerned.

DELLA: We used to be, when you were very young. Remember how we used to tell each other stories?

DICK: You mean continuation stories?

DELLA: Once there was a little girl. She was very pretty and very rich. She lived in a beautiful garden surrounded by high walls, and all she could see was the sky. She would play alone in that garden every day until...one day...

DICK: One day a big red rubber ball came flying over the wall. It landed right at her feet. She looked at the rubber ball, afraid to touch it. She kicked it gently with her toe. She looked closely at it. Finally she put her finger on it...and then...

DELLA: And then it turned into a beautiful young man. End of story.

DICK: But that's only the beginning.

DELLA: And they lived happily ever after.

DICK: You're copping out.

THE DISINTEGRATION OF DELLA LONGSTREET

DELLA: No one really wants to hear what happened after that.

DICK; The beautiful young man took the pretty young girl in his arms and he kissed her.

DELLA: And he promised her all sort of things. And they were married.

DICK: What did she promise him?

DELLA: To love, honor and obey.

DICK: And did she?

DELLA: Most honorably.

DICK: And she was betrayed.

DELLA: Most vilely.

DICK: And her revenge?

DELLA: She was not that sort. She sought no revenge.

DICK: Even upon herself?

DELLA: I don't want to play this game anymore.

DICK: What game shall we play?

DELLA: I don't want to play any games. No, please don't go.

DICK: I wasn't going. Oh, Mumsie. Poor Mumsie. *(HE puts his arm around her.)*

DELLA: If only you understood me, Dickie. If only someone understood me.

(DICK caresses her face and then kisses her as DREW enters.)

THE DISINTEGRATION OF DELLA LONGSTREET

DREW: What a pretty picture!

DICK: We were playing games, Mumsie and I.

DREW: So I see. Debbie said you brought along something to smoke.

DICK: Would you like some?

DREW: Why not?

DICK: Coming up. *(HE goes off.)*

DELLA: You're not going to smoke that awful stuff?

DREW: What's so awful about it?

DELLA: The smell is sickening.

DREW: You wouldn't mind the smell so much if you tried it once. Why don't you try it?

DELLA: My senses are sharp enough without artificial stimulation.

DREW: Obviously.

DELLA: What is that supposed to mean?

DREW: People in glass houses...

DELLA: You must be out of your mind!

DREW: Oh, stop it, Della!

(DICK reenters carrying a small box and a small portable radio.)

DICK: Here we are.

DREW: We'll smoke in the kitchen, Dickie. The smell disturbs your mother. Go on in. I'll join you in a minute.

THE DISINTEGRATION OF DELLA LONGSTREET

(DICK goes into the kitchen.)

DELLA: I'll forget you said what you said.

DREW: What did I say, Della? What did I say?

DELLA: What you implied.

DREW: At least I had the decency merely to imply it.

DELLA: It isn't true.

DREW: What isn't true" What I implied or what you said I implied.

DELLA: Any of it.

DREW: Then why are you getting so upset?

DELLA: Dickie merely...

DREW: What?

DELLA: Merely wanted to comfort me.

DREW: Isn't that a husband's job?

DELLA: Your mind is in the gutter.

DREW: I think you'd better take one of your pills to calm you down. Your imagination is beginning to work overtime.

DELLA: I saw what I saw and I heard what I heard.

DREW: You saw no more than I did when I came into this room.

DELLA: I'm leaving in the morning. I shouldn't have come up here in the first place.

(Ravel's "Bolero" is heard softly coming from the kitchen.)

THE DISINTEGRATION OF DELLA LONGSTREET

DELLA: Oh, that smell! That awful smell. Please, Drew, please. Let's not quarrel. I'm going to my room.

DREW: Well, go ahead.

DELLA: I don't know what's come over me.

DREW: Shall I tell you, my dear? Desire, Della. Pure and simple desire. It has you in its clutches.

(DEBBIE's laughter is heard.)

DELLA: Oh, Drew, I'm so unhappy.

DREW: Yes, dear, I know.

DELLA: I feel so alone.

DREW: Like the gods on Mount Olympus. Like Moses on the top of Mount Sinai.

DELLA: But I'm not like that at all.

DREW: I know you're not.

DELLA: I see such terrible things. I hear such terrible things, and it's destroying me.

DREW: If only you could learn to...

DELLA: What?

DREW: To share.

DELLA: How? By a meaningless act?

DREW: Must everything have a meaning, my dear?

THE DISINTEGRATION OF DELLA LONGSTREET

DELLA: I simply cannot believe that we are here on earth merely to satisfy our lusts.

DREW: If sex is pleasurable, perhaps there's a reason for it. Perhaps that's why flowers are beautiful.

DELLA: Sex is not just an animal function, and you will never convince me of that.

DREW: I'm not trying to convince you of anything, my dear, except that you can't go on like this.

DELLA: Like what?

DREW: We have been here less than four hours and you have accused us of all sorts of terrible things.

DELLA: I haven't accused anybody of anything. You're the one.

DREW: Did I accuse you, Della?

DELLA: Didn't you?

DREW: I only know what I saw.

DELLA: And what did you see?

DREW: I saw your son kiss you full on the lips with a kiss that was far from dutiful.

DELLA: He did not kiss me on the lips.

DREW: Now Della...

DELLA: He didn't. His back was turned to you when you came into the room. How could you possibly have seen where he kissed me. It was merely a kiss of affection.

DREW: Brought on by what?

THE DISINTEGRATION OF DELLA LONGSTREET

DELLA: I'm not quite sure.

DREW: Something he sensed, perhaps. Something he felt you wanted him to do. A need he felt you wanted fulfilled.

DELLA: I have never desired Dickie, never. Not in that way.

DREW: You may protest as much as you like, my dear, but you can't fool yourself. Not for very long, at any rate. Because you see, my dear, our libido has a way of catching up with us. Be my lover again. You won't regret it, Della, I promise you.

DELLA: Not anymore, Drew. Not anymore.

DREW: You want to be taken? Is that it.

DELLA: *(SHE moves away.)* Oh, that smell!

DREW: Then let go, Della. God damn you, let go of us.

DELLA: You'd like that, wouldn't you? You'd like me to cut you off without a penny.

DREW: I never married you for your money, and you know it.

DELLA: But you're used to living comfortably, aren't you, Drew? You're used to living beyond your means.

DREW: Is that how you get your kicks? By keeping us all on a string?

DELLA: I shouldn't have come here. I shouldn't have come.

DREW: Why, Della, why? Are you afraid of us? Afraid of your own family?

DELLA: I love you, Drew. I really do. And the children. More than life itself. What else is there for me?

DREW: Your charities, perhaps?

THE DISINTEGRATION OF DELLA LONGSTREET

DELLA: They're games, little games I play to pass away the time.

DREW: You live in a fantasy world, my dear. The truth of the matter is you're concerned with no one but yourself.

DELLA: Drew...please.

DREW: Please what? Please go? Please stay? Please leave me alone? Please take me?

DELLA: I'm going to my room. I don't want you to follow me.

(SHE rises and starts to sway. DREW catches her to prevent her from falling.)

DELLA: No, Drew, please.

(DREW kisses her gently as DICK and DEBBIE enters.)

DICK: Nuptial bliss.

DEBBIE: How divine?

DELLA: *(Weakly)* No, please.

DICK: Bless you, my children.

(DREW lifts her and starts off.)

DEBBIE: Oh, how romantic!

(DREW carries her off.)

DELLA: *(Softly)* Noooo.

DICK: What on earth do you think they're going to do?

DEBBIE: On such a lovely moonlit night.

THE DISINTEGRATION OF DELLA LONGSTREET

DICK: What a shame to be cooped up like this. *(HE starts to blow out the candles.)* Blow out your candles, Debbie.

> *(DEBBIE blows out the rest of the candles. DICK extends his hand to DEBBIE. SHE takes it and they run out of the house. "The Bolero" which has grown increasingly louder reaches its climax. Blackout. The lights come up. It's the following morning. The sun is shining brightly. DREW enters from the kitchen with a plate of food. HE sits at the table and proceeds to eat heartily. DICK enters from his room.)*

DREW: Good morning, Dickie.

DICK: Good morning, Daddy. And how are you this morning?

DREW: Bright as a copper penny. And you, Son?

DICK: I'm ready for a good game of tennis.

DREW: You'll need some energy first. I whipped up a batch of bacon and eggs.

DICK: Just what the doctor called for.

> *(DICK goes into the kitchen. DEBBIE enters from her room.)*

DEBBIE: Good morning, Daddy.

DREW: Good morning, dear. And how are you on this bright and cheery morning?

DEBBIE: Bright and cheery.

> *(SHE kisses DREW and goes into the kitchen. DICK enters with a plate of food, sits at the table and eats.)*

DREW: Did you sleep well last night?

DICK: Like a top. And you?

THE DISINTEGRATION OF DELLA LONGSTREET

DREW: This mountain is certainly invigorating.

DICK: You're an excellent cook, by the way.

DREW: Why, thank you, son.

DICK: I'm going to beat the pants off you.

DREW: We'll see about that.

(DEBBIE enters with a plate of food and sits at the table.)

DEBBIE: This does look good. Mumsie must have gotten up early to do all this.

DREW: Your Daddy cooked your breakfast, dear. Mumsie is still in her room.

DEBBIE: Oh? That is unusual, isn't it? She never sleeps late.

DREW: She's not sleeping, dear. She's getting ready to leave.

DICK: Oh? Is she going back home?

DREW: No, son. She's going away, for a long, long rest.

DICK: Oh?

DREW: Yes, indeed.

DICK: What a pity!

DREW: Your mother doesn't seem to thinks so. As a matter of fact, she seems very anxious to leave.

DEBBIE: Poor Mumsie! These eggs are delicious. We're going to have to let you cook breakfast every morning. We are staying on, are we not?

DREW: I don't see why not.

THE DISINTEGRATION OF DELLA LONGSTREET

DICK: I guess we'd better phone Maxwell. Or shall one of us drive her into town?

DREW: That's all taken care of, Dickie. I spoke to Dr. Pepper this morning. He's sending someone up to pick her up.

DICK: I see.

DREW: I think she'll be much happier there.

DEBBIE: How long...?

DREW: That's difficult to say.

> (THEY continue to eat. DELLA enters from her room, carrying an overnight bag. SHE sits on the sofa in the living room.)

DEBBIE: Maybe Mumsie would like some breakfast.

DREW: Why don't you go and ask her. And Debbie...

DEBBIE: Yes, Daddy?

DREW: You'd better not say that I cooked it.

> (DEBBIE nods. SHE goes into the living room.)

DEBBIE: There you are. All packed and ready to go.

DELLA: I'll send for the rest of my things.

DEBBIE: Would you like something to eat?

DELLA: A glass of water, please.

DEBBIE: *(SHE goes into the dining room.)* I'm getting Mumsie some water.

> (DEBBIE goes into the kitchen. DICK goes into the living room.)

THE DISINTEGRATION OF DELLA LONGSTREET

DICK: Good morning, Mumsie. Is there anything I can do for you?

(DELLA shakes her head.)

DICK: Would you like us to visit you?

DELLA: I suggest you talk to Dr. Pepper. Dickie, please...

DICK: Yes, dear?

DELLA: I'd like to be alone.

DICK: Yes, of course.

(DICK goes into the dining room. DEBBIE reenters the living room with a glass of water.)

DEBBIE: Here you are, Mumsie.

DELLA: *(SHE takes a sip of the water and hands the glass back to DEBBIE.)* Thank you.

DEBBIE: I hope you'll be coming back to us soon.

DELLA: I doubt if I shall ever come back.

DEBBIE: But we're your family.

DELLA: I have no family.

DEBBIE: You're going to isolate yourself from the rest of the world?

DELLA: I hope so, if I possibly can. The world has become a place I no longer find attractive or interesting. The world at large, that is.

DEBBIE: What other world is there?

DELLA: My world. My private world. Pure and unsoiled.

THE DISINTEGRATION OF DELLA LONGSTREET

(A car horn is heard. DELLA rises. DEBBIE reaches for the bag.)

DELLA: That's all right. I can manage.

DEBBIE: Don't you want to say good-bye to Dickie and Daddy?

DELLA: You do that for me, dear.

(DEBBIE moves to kiss her. DELLA shrinks back. The car horn is heard. DELLA turns toward the outside door, takes one last look around, collects herself and walks off, head held high. DREW and DICK enter the living room.)

DEBBIE: She's gone.

DREW: I'm sure she'll be much happier without us.

DEBBIE: I guess I'd better do the dishes.

DREW: There's plenty of time for that. I think we should take our morning constitutional. How does that strike you?

DICK: I'm up and ready.

DEBBIE: Me, too. I'll just get my sun glasses. *(SHE runs off to her room.)*

DICK: Now that Mother is gone for good...

DREW: Yes, dear boy?

DICK: I suppose it is too soon to speak about my new car.

DREW: I don't see why.

DICK: And an increase in my allowance.

DREW: Is negotiable.

THE DISINTEGRATION OF DELLA LONGSTREET

DICK: Thank you, Daddy.

(DICK kisses him. DEBBIE reenters.)

DREW: You, too.

DEBBIE: Me, too, what?

DICK: A bigger allowance.

DEBBIE: Oh, goody, goody!

(DEBBIE kisses DREW.)

DREW: Come along, children. The morning sun awaits us.

(DREW places his arms around DICK and DEBBIE. As THEY go off DREW pats them both on the rear. After a moment the phone rings several times and stops.)

I WENT TO A MARVELOUS PARTY

A Comedy In Two Acts

CAST OF CHARACTERS

Gertie Lennox

John Gordon

Fay Thorpe

Harriet Thorpe

Jeff Gordon

Barry Cousins

Jimmy Cousins

TIME

The summer of 1939

PLACE

New York City and Ottumwa, Iowa

ACT I

(Dance music is heard. New York City. GERTIE LENNOX appears.)

GERTIE: I went to a marvelous party. My own. The theme was lost love. Everyone came as star-crossed lovers...Romeo and Juliet, Hero and Leander, Pyramus and Thisbe. And that's where I met Barry Cousins.

(BARRY COUSINS enters and approaches GERTIE.)

BARRY: So, you're the famous Gertie Lennox.

GERTIE: I detested him instinctively.

BARRY: I'm Barry Cousins. I'm very big in grain and feed. My son is getting married next month. I'd like to throw a party to celebrate. Something different, something unique. Money is no object.

GERTIE: That's what they all say, at first.

(THEY dance.)

BARRY: Are you free?

GERTIE: No, I'm very expensive. And I'm leaving next week, for a trip around the world.

BARRY: It would be worth your while.

BARRY: Well?

GERTIE: Well, what?

BARRY: The party? In honor of my son's wedding?

GERTIE: Why isn't the bride giving the party?

BARRY: They're poor.

GERTIE: But Iowa!

I WENT TO A MARVELOUS PARTY

BARRY: It's not the end of the world. Twenty thousand. Twenty five.

GERTIE: As my fee? Plus expenses?

BARRY: You drive a hard bargain. Okay, okay.

GERTIE: No strings attached?

BARRY: What do you take me for?

GERTIE: A business man.

BARRY: Twenty five thousand, plus expenses.

GERTIE: *(SHE sighs)* The world will still be there, I suppose.

BARRY: I've a large house.

GERTIE: What about your wife? Don't you think...?

BARRY: She's dead.

(HE goes off. The music stops. The sound of a plane taking off.)

GERTIE: I'd never been to Iowa. Oh, I've flown across the American continent innumerable times. I've even been to Chicago. But America, for me, consists of two coasts, the East and the West. And, of course, there's Texas. I've given the maddest parties in Texas, so the flatness of Iowa did not dismay me. As a matter of fact, compared to Texas, Iowa is a scenic wonder, especially in June.

(BARRY enters.)

BARRY: You made it.

GERTIE: So it would appear. *(SHE turns around.)* Ne touchez pas! Ne touchez pas!

I WENT TO A MARVELOUS PARTY

(GERTIE runs off. HARRIET THORPE enters.)

HARRIET: Where is she going?

BARRY: I don't know. She's rather eccentric.

(GERTIE reenters, carrying an urn.)

GERTIE: Sons of bitches! Don't they understand English around here?

BARRY: English, yes. French, no. This is Harriet Thorpe, mother of the bride.

HARRIET: Oh, Miss Lennox...

GERTIE: Mrs. This is my husband, or what's left of him.

BARRY: Are you joking?

GERTIE: I never joke about Rupert.

BARRY: Isn't that rather ghoulish?

HARRIET: I think it's beautiful.

BARRY: You would. *(HE goes off.)*

GERTIE: Did he kill his wife?

HARRIET: Oh, no. She drank herself to death.

GERTIE: That figures. My, but you're pretty.

HARRIET: I was once. My daughter's the one. She was chosen Miss Fairfax, the prettiest girl in Fairfax County. She could have gone on to Miss Iowa, but my husband objected. He's Presbyterian. You don't have to stay with Barry, if you don't want to. You can stay with us. We've plenty of room. Of course, it isn't as elegant, but it's comfortable.

I WENT TO A MARVELOUS PARTY

(HARRIET and GERTIE go off. FAY THORPE is discovered in her room, writing.)

FAY: Dear John. *(SHE crosses it out.)* Dearest John. *(SHE crosses it out.)* John. I've been putting off this letter for weeks. I'm getting married. I know this will come as a shock to you, after all we've been to each other, but we're growing up now. Play time is over. *(SHE hesitates, then continues.)* I know you're going to rant and rave and, I suppose, I would do the same if I were you. This is the cowardly way, I know. I should be telling you this face to face, but I am a coward and a weakling, so you see, you're well rid of me.

(HARRIET enters the house.)

HARRIET: Fay, dear. Fay!?

FAY: I'm busy, mother.

(GERTIE enters the house, followed by BARRY.)

BARRY: You're not really going to stay here, are you?

GERTIE: Why not? It's a perfectly lovely house.

BARRY: Well, for one thing, Harriet is going to be busy for the next two weeks. She won't have time to look after you properly. And she has no servants.

GERTIE: I am perfectly capable of looking after myself. And I'll be pretty busy too, you know.

BARRY: Was this your idea, Harriet?

HARRIET: I merely offered. Mrs. Lennox is perfectly free to stay wherever she likes.

GERTIE: Gertie, please.

HARRIET: And we do have a guest room, Gertie.

I WENT TO A MARVELOUS PARTY

BARRY: It's more like a closet.

GERTIE: Why don't we take a look at it?

(HARRIET, GERTIE and BARRY go off.)

FAY: *(Writing)* Everything I say will sound like a platitude, I know, but we can still be friends. In Europe, Mama says, people are much more sensible about these things. People marry for practical purposes, and then there's love. I mean the two need not interfere with one another, if you know what I mean. I just can't go through life worrying about pennies. I'm sorry.

(GERTIE, HARRIET and BARRY reenter.)

GERTIE: It's a charming room.

BARRY: Well, whether you stay here or not, I'd like you to come out to the house. We have lots to talk about.

HARRIET: Fay and I have an appointment with the dressmaker.

BARRY: We'll be in touch with you after lunch.

GERTIE: It's a lovely house.

(BARRY and GERTIE go off. HARRIET approaches FAY.)

HARRIET: What are you doing, dear?

FAY: I'm writing a letter...to John.

HARRIET: Do you think it wise?

FAY: Mother, I haven't told him yet.

HARRIET: You resent me now, I know, but in a couple of years from now you'll be grateful to me. Men are all the same, my dear, Jimmy or John. After a couple of years you'll be faced with the very same problems

I WENT TO A MARVELOUS PARTY

no matter who you marry, and it's so much easier to solve ones problems in comfort and luxury. How many girls get to see Europe on their honeymoon? How many girls get to build their own home and furnish it with the best there is? And then when the children come... We couldn't even send you to college.

FAY: I don't want to go to college.

HARRIET: And you know why your father didn't want you to enter the Miss Iowa contest. We couldn't afford the expense.

FAY: I don't want to be Miss Iowa.

HARRIET: Your father has no imagination. That's why we live as we do. In order to be successful, one must have vision. One must be willing to risk everything. Your father is penny wise and pound foolish.

FAY: *(After a moment)* Mother...?

HARRIET: Yes, dear?

FAY: Were you in love with Daddy when you married him?

HARRIET: No.

FAY: Then why did you marry him?

HARRIET: I married your father because I thought he would be successful. He was ambitious and level headed and well organized.

FAY: What happened?

HARRIET: Your father's too well organized, too level headed and not ambitious enough.

FAY: Were you in love with anyone else?

HARRIET: Yes.

I WENT TO A MARVELOUS PARTY

FAY: Who?

HARRIET: John's father.

FAY: Was he in love with you?

HARRIET: Yes.

FAY: I never knew that.

HARRIET: There was no reason for you to know.

FAY: Have you ever regretted your decision?

HARRIET: Not really, no. Jeff Gordon is a fool. An attractive fool, a charming fool and a good for nothing fool. And his son, I regret to say, is exactly the same. At least your father is not the laughing stock of Ottumwa.

FAY: I'm very fond of Mr. Gordon.

HARRIET: So am I, dear. But I didn't marry him. Jeff is the sort of man you dream about, and promptly forget when you're awake. Come along. We're going to be late.

(HARRIET goes off. FAY sighs, and follows her. GERTIE appears, followed by BARRY.)

GERTIE: It's a charming town, absolutely charming. It reminds me of where I was born.

BARRY: Where was that?

GERTIE: Sussex, a little village in the Cotswolds. My father was a dairyman.

BARRY: Nonsense.

GERTIE: Are you calling me a liar?

I WENT TO A MARVELOUS PARTY

BARRY: You were born in London. Your father owned a pub, and you worked as a bar maid until you were sixteen.

GERTIE: You've been spying on me. How dare you? Actually I was born in Hammersmith. It's a suburb of London. I tended bar until I was fifteen. And I'm catching the next plane back to Los Angeles.

BARRY: Come back here. You're making a scene. Everyone is looking at us.

GERTIE: I will not be spied on.

BARRY: I'm not going to marry a woman I know nothing about. Jeff! Jeff Gordon! Where is that man?

GERTIE: Is this your store?

BARRY: One of them, yes.

GERTIE: How many do you have?

BARRY: A few. It's not where I make my money though.

(JEFF GORDON enters.)

JEFF: Mr. Cousins?

GERTIE: What a beautiful man!

BARRY: What was that?

GERTIE: Nothing, Mr. Cousins.

JEFF: I'm sorry, Mr. Cousins. I was out back.

BARRY: And stop calling me Mr. Cousins. My name is Barry. We went to school together. As a matter of fact, you're six months older than I am. And you're always out back. What do you do back there?

I WENT TO A MARVELOUS PARTY

JEFF: That's where we keep the feed.

BARRY: Have you got a customer back there?

JEFF: No.

BARRY: Then what are you doing? Counting the grain?

GERTIE: Aren't you going to introduce me?

BARRY: This is Gertie Lennox. Jimmy is getting married, you know.

JEFF: I didn't know it was official.

BARRY: It's official all right. The wedding's next week. Miss Lennox here...

GERTIE: Mrs. Lennox.

BARRY: Mrs. Lennox here is going to organize a fancy party to celebrate.

JEFF: Yes, I've read about you, Mrs. Lennox.

BARRY: I want to show Mrs. Lennox around. You're paid a full weeks wages for thirty-five hours of work. The least you could do is to mind the store. Or is that asking too much?

JEFF: No, sir.

BARRY: And stop calling me sir.

GERTIE: Oh, don't be such a bully, Barry. Maybe Mr. Gordon went to relieve himself. Or don't you allow that?

JEFF: I was out back reading. There was nothing to do so I was reading.

GERTIE: What were you reading, Mr. Gordon?

I WENT TO A MARVELOUS PARTY

JEFF: Plato?

GERTIE: "The Republic?"

JEFF: No. One of the dialogues.

GERTIE: There are other interests in life besides making money, Barry.

BARRY: Where would I be if I sat on my ass reading Plato? Watch that box! Here you better take my arm.

GERTIE: I can manage by myself. I'm not a cripple.

> *(GERTIE winks at JEFF and follows BARRY off. The phone rings. JEFF answers it.)*

JEFF: Hello? Yes, Carrie. How sick is she? Don't you worry about dinner. Just let me know when you get there, and give her my love.

> *(JEFF hangs up as BARRY reenters.)*

BARRY: Where's the key to the warehouse?

> *(JEFF hands him the key. BARRY winks at JEFF.)*

BARRY: Just trying to impress her.

> *(BARRY goes off. JIMMY COUSINS enters.)*

JIMMY: Hello, Mr. Gordon. Is my father around?

JEFF: Hello, Jimmy. Why yes, he's showing some lady around the warehouse.

JIMMY: What lady?

JEFF: Gertie Lennox. I understand she's here to take care of your wedding party.

I WENT TO A MARVELOUS PARTY

JIMMY: I see.

JEFF: What did you want to see him about?

JIMMY: He's been gone all day. There's all sorts of things I'd like to check with him.

JEFF: I wouldn't bother him now, if I were you.

   (JIMMY starts off.)

JEFF: Jimmy?

JIMMY: Yes, sir?

JEFF: Congratulations.

JIMMY: Thank you.

JEFF: This is all kind of sudden, isn't it? The wedding, I mean.

JIMMY: Not really, no. I've been back for seven months and Fay and I have know each other just about all our lives.

JEFF: I never knew the two of you were dating.

JIMMY: There's lots of things that you don't know, Mr. Gordon.

JEFF: Jimmy?

JIMMY: Yes, sir?

JEFF: What happened in New York?

JIMMY: What do you mean?

JEFF: You've come back a different person.

I WENT TO A MARVELOUS PARTY

JIMMY: I went away a boy and came back a man, corny as that may sound.

JEFF: Was it very disappointing?

JIMMY: What?

JEFF: New York?

JIMMY: New York is a city, just like any other city, only bigger. You were right to stay here in Ottumwa, Mr. Gordon. When's John due back?

JEFF: Some time next week, I guess.

JIMMY: I hope he doesn't decide to make any trouble.

JEFF: Look, boy, I used to carry you piggy-back. What's come over you?

JIMMY: Why did you encourage me to write poetry?

JEFF: I never told you to try and sell it.

JIMMY: You never told me not to.

JIMMY: I'm not a nay-sayer, Jimmy.

JIMMY: You are something else.

(JIMMY turns to go and comes face to face with FAY.)

FAY: Why, Jimmy. I thought you were still in Des Moines.

JIMMY: I got back last night. I was going to call you this afternoon. What are you doing here?

FAY: We just came from the dressmaker, and I just dropped in to say hello to Mr. Gordon.

JEFF: I'll be out back, if you want me. *(HE goes off.)*

I WENT TO A MARVELOUS PARTY

JIMMY: Have you told John yet?

FAY: I'm writing him a letter.

JIMMY: I thought you were going to call him.

FAY: I decided not to.

JIMMY: You have no intention of telling him, have you?

FAY: Of course, I have.

JIMMY: He'll be back next week. Are you going to wait until then?

FAY: I said I was writing him a letter.

JIMMY: It may not get to him in time.

FAY: Jimmy, the wedding is two weeks away.

JIMMY: Eleven days. Do you want me to tell him?

FAY: No.

JIMMY: You can still change your mind.

FAY: You keep saying that.

JIMMY: Only because you seem so hesitant.

FAY: He's still in love with me, Jimmy. I just don't know how to break it to him.

JIMMY: Are you still in love with him?

FAY: I'll always love John but no, I don't love him enough to marry him.

JIMMY: Then tell him now. Call him tonight.

I WENT TO A MARVELOUS PARTY

FAY: Okay, okay, I'll call him.

JIMMY: I just don't think it's fair to any of us, that's all.

FAY: Do you want to come over for dinner tonight?

JIMMY: I'll be over afterwards. Don't get yourself so upset. It'll all work out. But the sooner you tell him, the sooner it'll all be over.

FAY: You're right, I know it. I'll call him tonight.

JIMMY: That's my baby.

(JIMMY kisses her and goes off. FAY stands deeply troubled. The phone rings and startles her. SHE looks about then picks up the phone.)

FAY: Hello? Just a moment.

(FAY is about to set down the phone when JEFF reenters.)

FAY: It's for you, Mr. Gordon. *(SHE hands the phone to JEFF.)*

JEFF: Thank you. Hello? John?! Where are you calling from? Fay? Why...

(FAY shakes her head.)

JEFF: She just left. I guess she didn't recognize your voice. She just dropped in to say hello. Oh, she's fine. When did you get home? Your Aunt Meg isn't feeling too well, and your mother just left to look after her. I'm sure there's plenty of food in the house, if you're hungry. I'll be home in a few hours, or you can drop by here, if you like. All right, Son. I'll see you later. *(HE hangs up.)* He's going over to your house. I guess you'll have to tell him now. Or have you told him already?

FAY: No. *(After a moment)* Mr. Gordon?

JEFF: Yes, Fay?

I WENT TO A MARVELOUS PARTY

FAY: How did you take it when you and Mother broke up?

JEFF: She told you, did she?

FAY: How did you feel?

JEFF: That was a long time ago. Besides, John and I are two different people.

FAY: Do you find it hard to talk about it?

JEFF: No, child, of course not. Well, let me see. My first reaction was I wanted to kill myself. I never tried that. Then, as I remember, I wanted to kill your mother and your father. I never tried that. Then I decided to drink myself to death. I was drunk for a solid month, fell out of a second story window, broke a leg and a couple of ribs, and then I met Mrs. Gordon, while I was in the hospital, that is, and that was end of that. But, as I say, John and I are two different people.

FAY: How do you think he'll take it?

JEFF: I don't know, Fay. I really don't know.

(HARRIET enters.)

HARRIET: Fay, dear... Hello, Jeff.

JEFF: Hello, Harriet.

HARRIET: I've been waiting for you.

FAY: I'm sorry, Mother. I ran into Jimmy.

HARRIET: Yes, I saw Jimmy. Mrs. Edgewater is going to take us home. Why don't you see how she's doing? She's at Barton's, across the street.

FAY: I know where Barton's is, Mother. *(SHE goes off.)*

HARRIET: What did she say to you?

I WENT TO A MARVELOUS PARTY

JEFF: She just wanted to know how I thought John would take the news.

HARRIET: How <u>do</u> you think he'll take it?

JEFF: You know, John, Harriet. How do <u>you</u> think he'll take it?

HARRIET: I hope he won't do anything foolish. This isn't my doing. I assure you it isn't. I don't expect you to believe me, but Fay has a mind of her own. If she didn't want to marry Jimmy, she wouldn't. You can be assured of that.

JEFF: My dear Harriet, I don't have to be assured of anything.

HARRIET: John is your son. Aren't you concerned about him?

JEFF: Frankly, Harriet, I've always found John a little overpowering. I haven't felt protective about him since he was nine.

HARRIET: Well, I feel sorry for the boy. I really do. I've always been fond of John, and I think it's very unfair of Fay to have kept this from him.

JEFF: She's truly your daughter, isn't she?

HARRIET: For your information, I think she's truly in love with Jimmy.

JEFF: Just the way you were in love with Lester.

HARRIET: I don't regret a thing. We would never have been happy together, you and I.

JEFF: You're probably right.

HARRIET: But I am afraid for Fay.

JEFF: I wouldn't be, if I were you. The younger generation is far more resilient then we are.

HARRIET: When is John due back?

I WENT TO A MARVELOUS PARTY

JEFF: He is back. He just got in a little while ago. As a matter of fact, he's on his way over to your place right now.

HARRIET: Does Fay know?

JEFF: Yes.

HARRIET: Well, the sooner the better. Oh, don't look so contemptuous. Only a woman like Carrie would put up with you, and you're lucky to have found her. You live in a dream world. You're like a vegetable. How dare you pass judgement on others?!

> *(HARRIET goes off. JEFF smiles ruefully. GERTIE enters, slightly disheveled.)*

GERTIE: Oh, Mr. Gordon, I don't suppose you have any Scotch around here.

JEFF: No, Ma'am. I might be able to dig up a little whiskey.

GERTIE: A little whiskey would be most welcome.

JEFF: You wait right here. I'll get it for you.

> *(JEFF goes off. GERTIE takes a mirror from her purse and tries to repair the damage. JEFF reenters with a pint of whisky and a small glass.)*

JEFF: I hope you don't mind the plastic cup. I rinsed it out.

GERTIE: Alcohol is an antiseptic, my dear man. It kills all germs. *(SHE pours a drink and downs it. SHE tries to pour another.)*

JEFF: I'm afraid that's all there is. We keep it on hand in case of an accident.

GERTIE: That's very wise of you. Thank you very much. Mr. Cousins, by the way, fell down a chute. He may need some assistance.

I WENT TO A MARVELOUS PARTY

(GERTIE goes off. JEFF starts off and almost runs into BARRY.)

BARRY: Where is she?

JEFF: I don't know. She just left.

BARRY: What are you doing with that whiskey bottle?

JEFF: She needed a drink.

BARRY: You're fired.

> *(BARRY goes after GERTIE. JEFF shrugs and starts off back. BARRY reenters.)*

BARRY: I mean it.

> *(BARRY goes off again. JEFF nods and goes out back. BARRY reenters.)*

BARRY: Jeff? Jeff?!

> *(JEFF reenters, getting into his jacket.)*

BARRY: Where are you going?

JEFF: I'm going home. You said I was fired.

BARRY: Oh, don't be such a fool! Where would I find someone to work as cheaply as you do? She took my car. I'm going to phone the police.

JEFF: I wouldn't, if I were you.

BARRY: Why not?

JEFF: Was she driving it?

BARRY: Of course not. What do you think I pay Henry for?

I WENT TO A MARVELOUS PARTY

JEFF: Then I don't think you have much of a case.

BARRY: Maybe you're right. Well, there's no plane out of here today, and she's just missed the three o'clock train. She's probably on her way to the Thorpes. Damn it! I want to marry her.

JEFF: You're not very subtle about it, Barry.

BARRY: Since when have I ever been subtle about anything?

JEFF: Maybe it's about time you learned.

BARRY: What do you suggest I do?

JEFF: Treat her like a lady.

BARRY: That's what I thought I was doing. You think she's a lush?

JEFF: Now how on earth would I know that? Oh, that. Anybody might take a drink after an unnerving experience.

BARRY: What do you mean by that?

JEFF: I don't know, Barry. All I know is she came out here looking like she'd been through the wringer.

BARRY: I didn't lay a finger on her. She fought like a tiger. I just thought she was trying to be coy.

JEFF: That's what I mean, Barry. This is not exactly the place to court a lady.

BARRY: Maybe you're right. I'll call her up and apologize.

JEFF: Wherever she's going, I doubt if she's there yet.

> (BARRY *picks up the phone and dials. The phone rings at the Thorpe residence.*)

I WENT TO A MARVELOUS PARTY

BARRY: There's no one home.

(The phone continues to ring. JOHN GORDON enters the Thorpe living room and picks up the phone.)

JOHN: Hello?

BARRY: Hello? Who's this?

JOHN: John Gordon.

BARRY: John, boy! When did you get home?

JOHN: Mr. Cousins? I just got home a little while ago.

BARRY: I see. How have you been, son?

JOHN: Just fine, Mr. Cousins, just fine.

BARRY: Is anyone at home?

JOHN: No. There's no one here.

BARRY: Well, look, son. If Gertie Lennox should show up... Do you know what she looks like?

JOHN: I think I've seen pictures of her in the papers.

BARRY: Well, if she does show up, I want you to give her a message for me.

JOHN: Yes, sir.

BARRY: Just tell her that I apologize. You got that, son?

JOHN: Yes, sir.

BARRY: Just tell her that I apologize, and I expect her for dinner.

I WENT TO A MARVELOUS PARTY

JOHN: Yes, sir. You apologize and you expect her for dinner.

BARRY: Nice talking to you, son. I want to get together with you, by the way. Drop by my office tomorrow. Any time, son.

JOHN: Yes, sir.

BARRY: Good-bye, John.

JOHN: Good-bye, Mr. Cousins.

>   *(THEY hang up. JOHN sits and picks up a magazine.)*

BARRY: Why didn't you tell me John was home?

JEFF: I didn't know it myself until just a few minutes ago.

BARRY: He didn't waste any time getting over to Fay, did he? Does he know?

JEFF: No.

BARRY: I'm very fond of that boy. Got all sorts of plans for him. He is finished with school, isn't he?

JEFF: He's got another year to go.

BARRY: Waste of time. I don't suppose you wanna come to the wedding.

JEFF: Let me talk it over with Carrie.

BARRY: It's gonna be quite a bash. Let me know if you wanna come.

>   *(BARRY goes off. JEFF sighs, takes off his jacket and goes out back. In the Thorpe living room JOHN throws down the magazine and walks about. The doorbell rings. JOHN opens the door. GERTIE is discovered. SHE stares at JOHN)*

GERTIE: Who are you?

I WENT TO A MARVELOUS PARTY

JOHN: I'm John Gordon. I have a message for you, Miss Lennox. Mr. Cousins telephoned to say that he apologized, and that he expected you to dinner.

GERTIE: Oh, he does, does he?

JOHN: He must think a lot of you if he called to apologize. Mr. Cousins never apologizes to anyone.

GERTIE: What are you? His agent?

JOHN: I'm a friend of the family.

GERTIE: Which one? The Cousins or the Thorpes?

JOHN: I'm engaged to Fay.

GERTIE: Engaged?

JOHN: To be married. We've been going steady for a couple of years now.

GERTIE: I see. Does your father work for Mr. Cousins?

JOHN: That's right.

GERTIE: Yes. Well, so you're engaged to be married.

JOHN: Unofficially, that is. But I'm going to make it official this summer. I'm going to quit school. It's a waste of time. For me, that is.

GERTIE: What are you going to do?

JOHN: Well, eventually, I'd like to have my own farm. I'm gonna be a farmer. I like to make things grow. I like to work with my hands.

GERTIE: What were you studying at school?

I WENT TO A MARVELOUS PARTY

JOHN: Iowa State? Agriculture. Oh, I don't mean that there aren't things I can still learn at school. But I can always take an extra course, if I feel the need.

GERTIE: Why did you choose Iowa State?

JOHN: I got a scholarship there. A football scholarship.

GERTIE: You're an athlete.

JOHN: Well, I guess you might say that. I play for the fun of it. But I don't think of myself as an athlete. Why do you look at me like that?

GERTIE: Like what?

JOHN: So sad like.

GERTIE: You remind me of someone. He was somewhat of an athlete, too. An amateur athlete.

JOHN: A friend?

GERTIE: My husband. He's dead. Which reminds me. I have some things out on the porch. Would you get them for me? A bag and an urn. Be careful with the urn.

JOHN: Sure.

GERTIE: I'd better hold the door for you.

(THEY *go off and reenter, JOHN carrying a bag and the urn.*)

GERTIE: Just set them down anywhere. I'll take the urn.

(JOHN *sets the bag on the floor.* GERTIE *places the urn on the mantlepiece.*)

JOHN: What have you got in there? The family jewels?

I WENT TO A MARVELOUS PARTY

GERTIE: My husband. His ashes, that is.

JOHN: Are you kidding? I'm sorry. But it is rather unusual.

GERTIE: I'm an unusual woman.

JOHN: No, I can understand. It must be very hard to let go of someone you really loved.

GERTIE: He wasn't much older than you when he died.

JOHN: He must have been very remarkable.

GERTIE: He was an idiot, a beautiful idiot. If he hadn't been, he'd be alive today.

JOHN: How did he die? I'm sorry. Are you staying here? I mean, are you visiting the Thorpes?

GERTIE: I haven't quite decided...whether I'm staying here or not. I'm here on business.

JOHN: For the Thorpes?

GERTIE: Mr. Cousins. Barry has asked me to give a party. I met him in New York last month.

JOHN: And you came all the way out here to give a party?

GERTIE: That's my business, giving parties. Among other things.

JOHN: What things?

GERTIE: I do favors for people, for a fee, that is. Shopping, matchmaking. You name it. I'm really sort of a parasite. But then, that's the way of the world, is it not? I mean we're all dependant upon one another, in one way or another. Don't you agree?

I WENT TO A MARVELOUS PARTY

JOHN: I never thought of it in quite that way, but I guess you're right. Have you met my father?

GERTIE: Yes. A short while ago. A charming man. You're very much like him. You should be pleased. Or don't you approve of your father?

JOHN: I'm not quite sure. But then I haven't made up my mind about a lot of things.

GERTIE: Yes, you are at that age, aren't you?

JOHN: What age is that?

GERTIE: The age of decision. You've decided to marry Fay and be a farmer.

JOHN: You think that shows lack of ambition? Mr. Cousins thinks so, I know, and Mrs. Thorpe.

GERTIE: We can't all be wealthy or famous. Someone has got to bake the bread.

(HARRIET enters, followed by FAY.)

HARRIET: Well, hello John! Fay, dear, look who's here. It's John.

JOHN: Hi.

FAY: Hi.

HARRIET: And you haven't met Mrs. Lennox, dear. This is my daughter.

GERTIE: How do you do.

HARRIET: You've decided to stay with us.

GERTIE: For the time being.

I WENT TO A MARVELOUS PARTY

HARRIET: Fay, dear, why don't you show Mrs. Lennox to the guest room.

FAY: Why, yes, of course.

GERTIE: That's all right. I can manage the bag.

FAY: It's right this way.

GERTIE: Yes. Yes, I know.

HARRIET: Oh, Gertie...you'll want your urn, won't you?

GERTIE: Yes.

> *(GERTIE sets down the bag and picks up the urn. FAY takes the bag and goes off, followed by GERTIE who glances back at JOHN. SHE can sense what's coming next.)*

HARRIET: Well, this is a surprise!

JOHN: I'm only home a few days earlier.

HARRIET: How did you get in?

JOHN: The window was open and the phone was ringing, so I climbed in and answered it.

HARRIET: Who was it?

JOHN: Mr. Cousins. He was trying to get in touch with Mrs. Lennox.

HARRIET: John, I have some rather upsetting news for you. Fay is marrying Jimmy Cousins. She should have told you some time ago, but she didn't want to hurt your feelings.

JOHN: There must be some mistake.

I WENT TO A MARVELOUS PARTY

HARRIET: There's no mistake, and I hope you will take it sensibly. John? Did you hear what I said?

JOHN: I don't believe it.

(FAY reenters.)

HARRIET: I'd better start dinner. I imagine you'll be wanting to have dinner with your family, your first night home.

JOHN: What? Yes, yes.

(HARRIET goes off.)

JOHN: Is it true? Why?

FAY: I told you. I do not want to be a farmer's wife.

JOHN: You never told me that.

FAY: Well, I'm telling you now.

JOHN: I don't have to be a farmer. Mr. Cousins wants me to work for him. I can be a big executive, if that's what you want.

FAY: Is that what you want?

JOHN: What do you want?

FAY: I've been trying to write you for the past few weeks, trying to put it into words.

JOHN: Well, here I am. Tell me.

FAY: I was afraid you'd act like this.

JOHN: Like what?

FAY: Emotionally.

I WENT TO A MARVELOUS PARTY

JOHN: How did you expect me to act?

FAY: That's why I kept putting it off.

JOHN: Have you been...

FAY: No!

JOHN: Don't do it, Fay. Please, don't do it.

FAY: Ohhh! *(SHE stifles her sobs.)*

JOHN: I'll be anything you want me to be. Whatever I am, it won't mean anything without you. You won't be happy either. You love me. You know you do.

FAY: And what about ten years from now?

JOHN: Ten years from now? We may be dead ten years from now. My God! I mean, do you really think you can be happy with someone else? I know you, Fay. You need love and understanding. I know you have this thing about money and security. But people have always got to eat.

FAY: Oh, John, it isn't as if you couldn't find someone else. My goodness, every girl in Ottumwa High would give anything to be in my shoes.

JOHN: We're not in Ottumwa High anymore.

FAY: I don't expect you to understand now. Your feelings are hurt. That's understandable.

JOHN: This is your mother's doing, isn't it?

FAY: No. She may think it is, but it's not. I've always had a mind of my own.

JOHN: When are you getting married?

I WENT TO A MARVELOUS PARTY

FAY: Next week. A week from Sunday, that is.

JOHN: Isn't this rather sudden? I mean Jimmy's been away for over a year. When did all this happen?

FAY: Since he came back.

JOHN: Is Gertie Lennox here because of your wedding?

FAY: Mr. Cousins wants to throw a big party before the wedding, sort of an engagement and wedding party all in one. We certainly couldn't afford it.

JOHN: And that's what's so important? A big party?

FAY: I want to be able to give parties, yes.

   (HARRIET enters.)

HARRIET: I need your help, dear. Of course, if you want to stay for dinner, John, you're certainly welcome. Why don't you make yourself at home? Come along, dear.

   (FAY follows HARRIET off. JOHN sits down in a daze. GERTIE reenters.)

GERTIE: They've told you. Screw 'em, Honey.

   (The doorbell rings.)

HARRIET: *(Offstage)* Would you get that, please?

   (GERTIE opens the door. BARRY enters.)

BARRY: So, here you are. John, boy! How are you, Son?

   (JOHN rises automatically and shakes Barry's extended hand.)

JOHN: Excuse me, sir.

I WENT TO A MARVELOUS PARTY

(JOHN walks out the door, leaving it open. GERTIE closes it.)

GERTIE: He's just received some rather upsetting news.

BARRY: He'll get over it.

GERTIE: How do you know?

BARRY: Because he's a man. That's how I know. I'll make it up to him.

GERTIE: How?

BARRY: I'll give him something to occupy his mind.

GERTIE: And what about his heart?

BARRY: The heart's an organ that pumps blood.

GERTIE: Is that why you attacked me in your store?

BARRY: I didn't attack you.

(HARRIET enters.)

HARRIET: Why, Barry. Is there anything wrong?

BARRY: Why should there be anything wrong? I just came to speak to Gertie.

(FAY enters.)

FAY: Where's John?

GERTIE: He left.

HARRIET: Fay!

FAY: I can't let him go like that.

I WENT TO A MARVELOUS PARTY

BARRY: Your mother's right, Fay. It'll be easier for the both of you, if you just break clean.

GERTIE: And come out punching.

BARRY: What's that?

GERTIE: I'd like something to munch on. Is the kitchen in there?

HARRIET: Why, yes.

(GERTIE goes into the kitchen.)

BARRY: Leave John to me.

HARRIET: Mr. Cousins knows what's best, dear.

(FAY runs up to her room and throws herself onto her bed.)

HARRIET: Is there anything going on between you and Gertie Lennox?

BARRY: That's none of your business.

HARRIET: I never said that it was. As a matter of fact, you should have a wife. It's not good for a man to live alone.

BARRY: I do not live alone. I have a house full of servants, and a son.

HARRIET: But Jimmy won't be living with you.

BARRY: I hope Fay isn't marrying Jimmy for his money.

HARRIET: Why don't you ask her?

BARRY: The trouble with you, Harriet, is you're too clever for your own good.

HARRIET: Isn't that odd?! I've often heard that said about you. We would have made a great team.

I WENT TO A MARVELOUS PARTY

BARRY: So you've led me to believe.

HARRIET: You're no prize, Barry. I'm sure Edith would have testified to that.

BARRY: We had some fun, Harriet. Why don't we just leave it at that?

HARRIET: What makes you think I would have it otherwise?

> (*HARRIET starts for the kitchen and comes face to face with GERTIE in the doorway, munching on a stalk of celery.*)

HARRIET: I've got to get dinner ready. *(SHE goes off.)*

GERTIE: Who would have thought it? Even here in Ottumwa!

BARRY: What are you talking about?

GERTIE: Barry, dear, I do need the money.

BARRY: I know you do.

GERTIE: But I'm not for sale. I will stage this party of yours on one condition only...that you promise to behave yourself.

BARRY: I thought you found me attractive. I was mistaken.

GERTIE: I'm not in love with you.

BARRY: Who said anything about love?

GERTIE: I did.

BARRY: Love comes with time.

GERTIE: Then give me two weeks.

BARRY: That's a promise. At the end of two weeks, my dear, you will find yourself head over heels in love with me.

I WENT TO A MARVELOUS PARTY

GERTIE: You'll be the first to know. Until then, let's, as you Americans say, "cool it."

BARRY: I thought you were an American. An American citizen, at any rate.

GERTIE: I shall always be British at heart.

   (HARRIET enters.)

HARRIET: If you'd care to stay for dinner, Barry, you're welcome.

BARRY: No, thank you, Harriet. Gertie and I will be leaving now. Where are your things?

GERTIE: In the guest room. I've started to unpack.

BARRY: I'll give you a hand. Excuse us, Harriet.

HARRIET: Yes, of course.

BARRY: Shall we?

GERTIE: Why not?

   (GERTIE winks at Harriet and goes off with BARRY. FAY has picked up the phone in her room and dials. The phone rings in Jimmy's office. JIMMY enters and picks it up.)

JIMMY: Hello?

FAY: Jimmy?

JIMMY: Is anything wrong? You sound upset.

FAY: I've told John.

JIMMY: How'd he take it?

I WENT TO A MARVELOUS PARTY

FAY: I don't know.

JIMMY: What do you mean, you don't know? You were there, weren't you. I mean you told him in person, didn't you?

FAY: How do you know that?

JIMMY: My father said that he was over at your place.

FAY: Yes. Yes, he was here, and I told him.

JIMMY: And...?

FAY: I just wanted to let you know, that's all. Just in case...

JIMMY: In case what?

FAY: In case he should try to make any trouble.

JIMMY: Do you think he will? Try to make trouble, that is?

FAY: I don't know. He took it pretty hard.

JIMMY: I didn't expect him to be happy about it. Do you want me to come over?

FAY: No. I'll be all right. I'm just glad it's over with. That I've told him, I mean.

JIMMY: What did he say?

FAY: He begged me not to go through with it. Marrying you, I mean.

JIMMY: Did he say anything about me?

FAY: Not exactly.

JIMMY: Then what makes you think he's going to try and make trouble?

I WENT TO A MARVELOUS PARTY

FAY: I just don't see John giving up without some sort of a fight.

JIMMY: You think he'll want to beat me up?

FAY: I don't know. I just wanted to talk to you, that's all.

JIMMY: Well, don't you worry about me. I can take care of myself.

FAY: John is a professional athlete, almost.

JIMMY: Well, he better not try anything funny.

FAY: What will you do?

JIMMY: Never you mind.

FAY: You don't have a gun, do you?

JIMMY: Of course, not. Besides, John and I have always been friends. I'm sure we can talk it over, after he gets used to the idea. Besides, my father's going to give him a job, a good one. He won't want to mess that up. I'll see you later. I've got some things to attend to. Are you sure you're all right?

FAY: Yes, I'm fine.

JIMMY: I'll see you later then. Okay?

FAY: Okay.

JIMMY: Good-bye.

> *(JIMMY hangs up and goes off. FAY hangs up and sits lost in thought. JEFF has entered the warehouse and taken a seat. HE stands up and looks off.)*

JEFF: John?

> *(JOHN enters.)*

I WENT TO A MARVELOUS PARTY

JEFF: Hello, Son

JOHN: Hi.

JEFF: I thought you were over at Fay's.

JOHN: I was.

JEFF: I see.

JOHN: Did you know about Fay marrying Jimmy?

JEFF: I heard talk, but I didn't know for sure until this afternoon.

JOHN: Why didn't you tell me? Why didn't you write me?

JEFF: I said I didn't know for sure until this afternoon. Did she tell you herself?

JOHN: Her mother did. I'm not gonna let her do it.

JEFF: How are you gonna stop her?

JOHN: I don't know yet. Did Mom know about this, too?

JEFF: Not for certain, no. None of us did, for certain. And none of us ever did hold much for gossip. Did we, Son?

JOHN: Jimmy! I could break him in two. She's marrying him for his money, you know.

JEFF: I don't think it's as simple as that.

JOHN: You think she's in love with him?

JEFF: Maybe. Maybe not.

JOHN: You don't think it's important.

I WENT TO A MARVELOUS PARTY

JEFF: It becomes less important as the years go by.

JOHN: Nothing's important to you.

JEFF: That's not true, Son. You're important to me, and your mother.

JOHN: When did you ever lift a finger for me or for Mom?

JEFF: You and your mother were never hungry or cold.

JOHN: Oh, great! You think it's enough to have the necessities of life.

JEFF: No, Son, I don't. But, as far as that's concerned...

JEFF & JOHN: We're the richest family in town.

JOHN: Crap! We are poor. Mom has always had to count pennies. If I hadn't gotten a football scholarship I would never have been able to go to Iowa State. Why should Fay marry me? What have I got to offer her? Fay is a beautiful girl. She's bright and she's special. Why shouldn't she have the best that life has to offer. You think everyone's content to live like we do? On day dreams?

JEFF: No, Son, they're not. And that's why this world is getting ready to destroy itself.

JOHN: I don't want to hear anymore of your crap. You sent Jimmy off to New York on a wild goose chase. You encouraged me to be a farmer. You let Mom work like a dog, just to satisfy your ego. The sage of Ottumwa! Well, most people think you're really a fool, if you wanna know the truth. Mr. Cousins laughs at you behind your back, and he's not the only one. How many times has he fired you? And how many times have you begged him to take you back?

JEFF: I've never begged in my life.

JOHN: He felt sorry for you then. Or Mom begged him for you. And, whenever we did have any money, you lent it to someone or gave it away. I suppose you expect me to take care of you in your old age.

I WENT TO A MARVELOUS PARTY

JEFF: You wanna fight with me, Son? Is that it? Well, go ahead and hit me.

JOHN: I never hit a man when he's down. And you are down, down, down.

>*(JOHN stalks off. JEFF stands thinking for a moment, then picks up the phone and dials. The phone rings in Jimmy's office. JIMMY enters and picks up the phone.)*

JIMMY: Hello?

JEFF: Jimmy, it's Jeff Gordon.

JIMMY: Yes, Mr. Gordon?

JEFF: I think John is itching for a fight. There's no point in your getting hurt. I'd avoid him for a couple of days, if I were you. Until he cools down, that is.

JIMMY: Thank you for your advice, Mr. Gordon. Is there anything else?

JEFF: No, Son, that's it.

>*(JEFF hangs up and goes off. JIMMY hesitates for a moment then hangs up. HE sits lost in thought. The telephone rings in the Thorpe living room. HARRIET enters and answers it.)*

HARRIET: Hello? Where are you? Lester, we are expected at Barry's... Where are you calling from? I can hear music in the background. When will you be back? Well, your daughter's wedding is ten days off. I hope you can make it.

>*(HARRIET slams down the phone and stands fuming. JIMMY has just picked up the phone and dials. HARRIET starts for the kitchen when the phone rings again. SHE picks it up.)*

HARRIET: Yes? What is it?

I WENT TO A MARVELOUS PARTY

JIMMY: Mrs. Thorpe?

HARRIET: Oh, Jimmy!

JIMMY: May I speak to Fay, please?

HARRIET: She stepped out for a moment. Can I help you, dear?

JIMMY: I thought I might come over for dinner, if that's all right.

HARRIET: Yes, of course, dear. We were hoping you might come. As a matter of fact, we're having stuffed pork chops.

JIMMY: Oh, great. See you in a little while.

>(JOHN appears in the doorway to Jimmy's office. HE holds a small paper bag.)

JIMMY: Good-bye, Mrs. Thorpe. *(HE hangs up.)*

HARRIET: Jimmy...? Jimmy? *(SHE hangs up, hesitates, then looks up a phone number.)*

JOHN: Jimmy...

JIMMY: Hello, John.

JOHN: It's good to see you.

JIMMY: What have you got in the bag?

JOHN: Oh, this?

>(HARRIET has dialed and the phone rings in Jimmy's office.)

JIMMY: Excuse me.

JOHN: Certainly.

I WENT TO A MARVELOUS PARTY

JIMMY: *(HE picks up the phone.)* Hello?

JOHN: Jimmy, dear. It's Mrs. Thorpe. Would you mind very much picking up some cream and some butter?

JIMMY: Yes, of course.

HARRIET: A pint of cream and a pound of butter.

JIMMY: A pint of cream and a pound of butter.

HARRIET: Thank you, dear.

JIMMY: No problem. Good-bye.

HARRIET: Good-bye, dear.

> *(HARRIET hangs up and goes into the kitchen. JIMMY hangs up.)*

JOHN: Having dinner with the Thorpes?

JIMMY: Why, yes. As a matter of fact, I am. When did you get back?

JOHN: Just a little while ago.

JIMMY: Have you seen Fay yet?

JOHN: That's why I'm here.

JIMMY: I see. John, I know how you must feel.

JOHN: Do you?

JIMMY: It's just one of those things that just happened.

JOHN: I understand.

I WENT TO A MARVELOUS PARTY

JIMMY: It may be hard for you to accept, at first. And you know that the last thing either one of us would want to do would be to hurt you.

JOHN: *(HE takes a pint of whiskey out of the bag.)* Let's have a drink, Jimmy boy.

JIMMY: Sure, John, if you want to. I've got one glass here.

JOHN: I don't think we need any glasses. Remember that night we went to Greenville?

JIMMY: I sure do. John, you are my best friend, just about. I mean you've always been like one of the family. As a matter of fact, if the truth were known, I think my Dad likes you better than he does me.

JOHN: Have a drink, Jimmy. It's all right. It's just whiskey.

JIMMY: *(HE takes a swig from the bottle and hands it back to John.)* Kinda strong.

JOHN: *(HE wipes the neck of the bottle with his sleeve and takes a swig.)* It's awful. I don't know how your mother ever drank this stuff.

JIMMY: Mother drank wine.

JOHN: People do acquire a taste for it, don't they?

JIMMY: How was school?

JOHN: Okay, Jimmy. Okay. I'm not going back.

JIMMY: Why not? I mean...has your scholarship run out?

JOHN: Oh, no. It's a four year scholarship.

JIMMY: Is it because...?

JOHN: Oh, no. I made up my mind before I came home. This whole business of growing up, Jimmy, it's not easy. I mean one is a man long

I WENT TO A MARVELOUS PARTY

before Society accepts the fact. I mean we both know that one has to go on learning for the rest of ones life, but I think it's time for me to start living. You have, and you're even younger than I am.

JIMMY: One month.

JOHN: You've lived a whole life time.

JIMMY: You mean my year in New York?

JOHN: It was almost two, wasn't it? Jimmy, I think there's something that you don't know. I mean Fay and I might not have been married, but we are man and wife, if you know what I mean.

JIMMY: You mean you were lovers? I sort of figured you were.

JOHN: And it doesn't make any difference to you?

JIMMY: Well, I'm not a virgin. I don't see why Fay has to be.

JOHN: That's not what I meant. We think of each other as man and wife. We're part of one another. We know each others moods. We know everything about each other. Fay is like her mother in many ways, though she likes to think she's not. The Thorpes have always been poor. Not really, but from Mrs. Thorpes way of thinking they are impoverished. Fay was brought up to think that money, financial security, is all important.

JIMMY: You mean you think she's marrying me for my money?

JOHN: I don't think so, I know it. What Fay and I feel for each other happens only once in a lifetime. I know that sounds corny, but it's a fact.

JIMMY: What do you want me to do?

JOHN: I want you to postpone the wedding. Give Fay time to think.

JIMMY: She's had plenty of time to think. And even if I wanted to... I mean, it's up to Fay. If she wanted to postpone the wedding, of course, I'd respect her wishes.

I WENT TO A MARVELOUS PARTY

JOHN: Don't you see that she doesn't know what she wants.

JIMMY: Maybe she does, John, and you just don't want to admit it. You've had a trial marriage, so to speak, and Fay has made her choice.

JOHN: I told you, Jimmy, I know Fay. She'll come back to me, and how will you feel then?

JIMMY: John, did it ever occur to you that this is your trip to New York? You have my deepest sympathy, but football scholarships don't go on forever. Eventually we all come up against hard, cold facts. Romeo and Juliet died in their teens. You've had everything you've always wanted, but few people, if any, go through life that way. You're bigger than I am, and you're stronger than I am. You could beat me up, if you wanted to, but I wouldn't advise it...for two reasons I can think of offhand. My father can do a lot for you. And if you do beat me up Fay is bound to sympathize with me. I didn't want to fall in love with Fay. It just happened. I don't care why she's marrying me. I need her, and if she isn't in love with me now, she will be eventually. And now, if you'll excuse me...

JOHN: Jimmy, please... You don't understand. Fay and I, we're like one person. If I lose her, my life is over, and it's the same for her, only she doesn't realize it yet. Why do you think I'm quitting school? Because life has no meaning when I'm away from her. When Fay's not around, it's like part of me is missing. And she feels the same way. It doesn't matter whether she marries you or not. We'll find each other again. She'll leave you, Jimmy, even if she remains married to you, she'll leave you. She'll never leave me.

JIMMY: She's left you, John.

> *(JIMMY starts off. JOHN takes hold of his arm to prevent him from leaving.)*

JOHN: Jimmy, please...

JIMMY: Let go of me.

I WENT TO A MARVELOUS PARTY

(JIMMY takes a swing at him.)

JOHN: You son of a bitch!

(THEY fight. JIMMY lands on the floor and lets out a cry. JOHN rises.)

JOHN: Jimmy? Are you all right?

JIMMY: Leave me alone.

(JIMMY limps off clutching his arm.)

JOHN: Jimmy? Is there anything wrong with your arm? Jimmy?

(JOHN follows him off as the lights come down.)

ACT II

(The Cousins estate. The night of the party. Music is heard in the background. GERTIE is discovered as the lights come up.)

GERTIE: The party was a distinct success. One of my lesser triumphs, perhaps, but then Ottumwa, Iowa is not the sort of place to inspire one.

(BARRY enters.)

BARRY: You'll stay for the wedding, of course. You're not crying, are you?

GERTIE: I always cry at weddings. The very thought of one is enough to make me weep.

BARRY: I don't get you. You'll haggle over pennies. I've heard you. Yet you'll toss away a couple of thousand without blinking an eye. You pretend to be very cynical about love, and yet you behave sentimentally.

GERTIE: My dear Barry, what is there to understand? In the morning the sun comes up and the world is flooded with light. The sun goes behind a cloud and the world is in shadow. The sun sets and the world is dark. It's the same world.

BARRY: Did I offend you in anyway? Is it something I said? Is it something I did. If it is, I apologize.

GERTIE: I think you're fooling yourself. You don't care as deeply about me as you would like to believe.

BARRY: Now why on earth would I want to fool myself?

GERTIE: You're married to your work, Barry. You don't need a wife.

BARRY: Then why do I want to marry you?

GERTIE: You want a hostess, and I'm about as good as they come.

BARRY: I don't deny that's one of the reasons, but it's only one.

I WENT TO A MARVELOUS PARTY

GERTIE; I'm flattered, Barry. I really am, and I'm a fool for not accepting you before you change your mind. But, as I look back over my life, it seems to be nothing but one foolish mistake after another.

BARRY: Your life isn't over yet.

GERTIE: That part of it is.

BARRY: What nonsense! You're still a young woman.

GERTIE: Not inside. Inside this glamorous facade is a shriveled old harridan.

BARRY: I'm not giving up. There's no one else, is there?

GERTIE: Not a soul.

BARRY: That's all I want to know. *(HE goes off.)*

GERTIE: The most successful party can be spoiled by going on too long.

(The music stops. HARRIET enters, not too steadily.)

HARRIET: But, Gertie, they were paid...

GERTIE: We've gotten our money's worth.

HARRIET: I must apologize for Lester. Why are men such pigs?

GERTIE: The same reason, I suppose, that women are such bitches.

HARRIET: How I envy you! Are you going to marry Barry?

GERTIE: No.

HARRIET: Then he has asked you. It would be nice to have you around.

GERTIE: You must come and visit me some time, with Fay and Jimmy. Or even by yourself.

I WENT TO A MARVELOUS PARTY

HARRIET: I'm a prisoner here, and I hate it. One of these days I may just up and leave.

GERTIE: If you do, make sure you know where you're going.

HARRIET: That was my mistake from the very beginning. I always knew exactly where I was going. *(SHE goes off, unsteadily.)*

GERTIE: She's had a little too much to drink. But that's all right. My parties have often been the turning point in many a life. My last affair, the one where I met Barry, resulted in three divorces, one legendary romance, two pregnancies and Harry Ingram discovered he loved nothing better than parading about in his wife's undergarments. Life among the idle rich, you will say. Nonsense! The idle rich behave no different than you and I. Because of their money they may do things with a little more style. You would think, as a catalyst, for I'm nothing more than that, my life would be relatively simple. Wrong! Everyone seems to seek me out and, as a result, my life becomes unbearably complex. And that's when I know it's time to move on.

(GERTIE starts off. FAY enters.)

FAY: Gertie, I've got to talk to you.

GERTIE: What is it now, dear?

FAY: John just called. He's threatened to kill me and Jimmy and then himself.

GERTIE: Is this before or after the wedding?

FAY: I'm serious. He might just try it.

GERTIE: Where is he now?

FAY: I don't know. For all I know he might be somewhere on the premises.

GERTIE: I'll speak to the chief detective.

I WENT TO A MARVELOUS PARTY

FAY: I don't want him hurt.

GERTIE: Where's Jimmy?

FAY: I don't know.

GERTIE: Where are you going?

FAY: I don't know.

> (FAY goes off. GERTIE sighs and shakes her head. JIMMY enters, his arm in a sling.)

JIMMY: Have you seen Fay?

GERTIE: She went that-a-way.

JIMMY: It's a lovely party.

GERTIE: Thank you.

JIMMY: Did you know that the band was leaving?

GERTIE: I sent them home.

JIMMY: Oh? Well, I think Dad has asked them to stay. Gertie?

GERTIE: Yes, dear?

JIMMY: Are you going to marry my father?

GERTIE: No.

JIMMY: Why not?

GERTIE: I'm not in love with him.

JIMMY: Isn't that rather old-fashioned? I mean...marrying for love?

I WENT TO A MARVELOUS PARTY

GERTIE: On the contrary, my dear. Romance is all the rage.

JIMMY: Do you really believe in love?

GERTIE: When it happens, and it happens so rarely, I think it's wonderful.

JIMMY: I suppose you know all about John.

GERTIE: I've gotten the general idea.

JIMMY: I don't blame him for this. I really don't and I'm sure that, eventually, he'll come to his senses.

GERTIE: Don't be too sure.

JIMMY: Well, he can't go through life roaring drunk and breaking people's arms.

GERTIE: It's been done before.

JIMMY: I've told Fay that I was willing to step aside, if she changed her mind, that is.

GERTIE: And what did she say?

JIMMY: Well, right now, she isn't speaking to me. I mean it's certainly not my fault that John broke my arm. Maybe she thinks that I'm a weakling, I don't know. I've never had a grand passion, and I certainly respect it, but if falling in love means going through what John's going through right now, I hope it never happens to me.

GERTIE: Aren't you in love with Fay?

JIMMY: Oh, sure. But I'm not madly in love with her, like John. I did have a passion once for poetry, but I've outgrown that, thank God.

GERTIE: I know exactly how you feel.

I WENT TO A MARVELOUS PARTY

JIMMY: Do you think I'll be ruining Fay's life and mine, if I marry her?

GERTIE: Now how would I know that?

JIMMY: Well, you are a woman of the world, so to speak.

GERTIE: You make me sound like something out of Oscar Wilde. If you want to know the truth, my dear, I was wiser at nineteen than I am right now.

JIMMY: My mother was a very wise woman, but she was just a little too fragile. I used to think that the meek would inherit the earth, but that's just a myth. What do you think?

GERTIE: I think I need a drink. Give me your good arm and escort me to the bar, if we can find it.

JIMMY: I think I'd be happier married to an older woman.

GERTIE: A woman never grows old, my dear, only mature.

> *(JIMMY and GERTIE go off arm in arm. Music is heard in the background. FAY enters, stops and sighs. BARRY follows her on.)*

BARRY: Are you all right?

FAY: I'm just fine.

BARRY: Then why aren't you speaking to Jimmy?

FAY: That's none of your business.

BARRY: Now see here, young lady...

FAY: I'm an individual, and I'm entitled to my privacy. And if you think that you and your son are buying me, you are very much mistaken. You think because you're rich you own the world.

BARRY: That isn't true, Fay.

I WENT TO A MARVELOUS PARTY

FAY: My father drinks too much and he talks too loud, and my mother is as phoney as they come, but that doesn't mean that I'm like either one of them.

BARRY: I never said that you were.

FAY: I know all about you and my mother, and I don't intend to make the same mistakes. Once I've made a bargain, I intend to stick to it. I don't know whether I'm in love with Jimmy or not, but if I marry him...

BARRY: What do you mean "if?" The wedding's tomorrow morning. This morning, as a matter of fact. It's a hell of a time to be changing your mind.

FAY: I haven't changed my mind. I just haven't made it up yet.

BARRY: Have you two had a fight?

FAY: I think I'm going to be sick.

(FAY goes off. JIMMY and GERTIE enter arm in arm.)

BARRY: Jimmy, I'd like a word with you.

JIMMY: Would you excuse me for a moment?

BARRY: The band, by the way, was sneaking off when I caught them.

GERTIE: Good for you! *(SHE goes off.)*

BARRY: Is she drunk?

JIMMY: I don't think so.

BARRY: Well, too many people are. Those hicks out there don't know how to handle their liquor. Half of them shouldn't have been invited, and that includes that future father-in-law of yours. What a clod!

JIMMY: I find Lester rather amusing.

I WENT TO A MARVELOUS PARTY

BARRY: How's your arm?

JIMMY: It only hurts when I laugh.

BARRY: What's going on between you and Fay?

JIMMY: A wedding, I hope.

BARRY: What do you mean, you hope?

JIMMY: The deal isn't sealed until you've signed the contract.

BARRY: Jimmy?

JIMMY: Yes, Dad?

BARRY: Those ugly things you said to me after your mother died...

JIMMY: Forget 'em.

BARRY: That's easier said than done. Maybe there was a small grain of truth in what you said, but I never willfully wished your mother any harm.

JIMMY: I'd rather not talk about it, if you don't mind. I don't hold any grudge against you, Dad. I really don't.

BARRY: Marriage is a tricky business, Son. It's like...it's like riding a horse while standing on its back. *(HE chuckles.)* So you see, we all of us have a bit of the poet in us. Well, maybe that's not exactly a poetic image.

JIMMY: I've given up on my poetry.

BARRY: I don't see why you can't go on with it, for your own pleasure, I mean.

JIMMY: What's the point of fooling myself? I'm not a Shelley or a Keats.

I WENT TO A MARVELOUS PARTY

BARRY: Why should you be? We're all of us individuals and everyone has something individual to offer.

JIMMY: At this point, I don't have anything to offer.

BARRY: Well, I'm certainly not going to try to send you back to your poetry, but I do think everyone should have some sort of a hobby...to relax one.

JIMMY: I'm perfectly relaxed.

BARRY: I never knew how to reach your mother, or you for that matter. And it certainly wasn't because I didn't try. I took you fishing, didn't I? And fishing bores the hell out of me. I took you to a baseball game, and I hate baseball. I even took you to a concert once and you fell asleep.

JIMMY: I wasn't asleep. I was just closing my eyes.

BARRY: And your mother insisted on living in a world of her own. Life wasn't easy for her, I suppose, but it certainly wasn't easy or me either. I had to face the world as it is, without the help of alcohol. I think the number one curse of civilization today is alcohol. You can say what you like about me, but I have no crutches. I take life as it comes and, whether you realize it or not, you're a lot like me. I was against your going to New York it's true but, deep down underneath, I was really proud of you. It took guts to do what you did, and even more guts to come back here and admit that you were a failure.

JIMMY: I don't consider myself a failure. It's the world that's a failure. Or maybe I was just born at the wrong time. A poet, in a world that's prosaic.

BARRY: What do you want me to do about John?

JIMMY: I don't want you to do anything.

BARRY: Is Fay still in love with him?

JIMMY: You'll have to ask Fay.

I WENT TO A MARVELOUS PARTY

BARRY: It means a great deal to me to have you back, Son.

(BARRY pats him on the back and goes off. GERTIE reenters with two glass of champagne. SHE hands one to JIMMY.)

JIMMY: If a woman is unfaithful once, do you think it's likely that she'll be unfaithful again?

GERTIE: That all depends, I suppose.

JIMMY: On what?

GERTIE: On the woman.

JIMMY: I'm on my way to becoming a thorough cynic.

GERTIE: Welcome to the club.

(SHE touches glasses with JIMMY and drinks, then takes his arm. THEY stroll off together. HARRIET tiptoes on.)

HARRIET: John? John?

(JOHN appears from behind a bush.)

JOHN: What is it? What's the matter?

HARRIET: You poor boy! You poor, dear boy! How you must be suffering!

JOHN: Is there anything wrong? Has anything happened to Fay?

HARRIET: You must take her away from here.

JOHN: How?

HARRIET: By force, if necessary.

I WENT TO A MARVELOUS PARTY

JOHN: Did she ask you to send for me?

HARRIET: Yes...and no. No with her mouth. Yes with her heart.

JOHN: Have you been drinking, Mrs. Thorpe?

HARRIET: You mustn't blame her, John. The fault is mine, all mine. But it's not too late.

JOHN: She said she never wanted to see me again.

HARRIET: And you believed her! We fall in love only once. The rest is sham.

JOHN: What's gotten into you, Mrs. Thorpe? I've never seen you like this.

HARRIET: John, dear John, I'm being given another chance. Fay is my second chance. Do you know what it's like to spend your life without love? Without hope? I thought I was preparing my child for the realities of life.

JOHN: Mrs. Thorpe, Mr. Cousins said that if he ever caught me around here, he'd put me in jail.

HARRIET: That's where Fay is now, in jail. Don't you see? This is jail. Those walls. They're jailhouse walls. Those gates. They're prison gates.

JOHN: I think you've had too much to drink, Mrs. Thorpe.

HARRIET: Have you given up so easily? Then perhaps you don't deserve one another. Perhaps you don't deserve any happiness.

JOHN: Has Fay changed her mind?

HARRIET: She hasn't made it up yet. I've made it up. Jimmy's made it up. Mr. Cousins' made it up. But Fay has not. I'm her mother. I should know.

I WENT TO A MARVELOUS PARTY

JOHN: But on the phone...

HARRIET: Forget the phone. Forget what she said on the phone. You've got to talk to her in person...here and now.

JOHN: Now how am I going to manage that?

HARRIET: I'm going to help you, that's how. Wait here.

JOHN: But...

HARRIET: But what?

JOHN: If I'm not here, look for me in jail.

HARRIET: Oh ye of little faith...

>   *(HARRIET goes off. JOHN sighs and paces about. HE stops suddenly, turns around and stands face to face with GERTIE, who's just entered.)*

GERTIE: I thought it was you. You must be mad. What are you doing here? Don't look at me like that.

JOHN: Like what?

GERTIE: We've got to get you out of here. How on earth did you get in?

JOHN: I can't leave now.

GERTIE: You can and you will.

JOHN: Are you giving me orders?

GERTIE: Oh, don't be a fool! You're lucky you're not in jail.

JOHN: If you wanna give me away, you can, but I'm not leaving.

I WENT TO A MARVELOUS PARTY

GERTIE: If you had any chance at all, you've ruined it by breaking Jimmy's arm.

JOHN: I didn't mean to, but he deserves it..

GERTIE: Do you realize that this place is swarming with detectives, and everyone of them has a detailed description of you?

JOHN: I'm very flattered.

GERTIE: You needn't be. You're only incidental. They're here to guard the gifts, and various other valuables.

JOHN: Fay being one of them.

GERTIE: How did you get in here?

JOHN: Through that gate back there?

GERTIE: It was locked. Did Fay send for you? Did she?

JOHN: No.

GERTIE: Then how did you get in? You couldn't have climbed those walls. You would have been cut to pieces. Well, whichever way you got in, that's the way you're getting out.

JOHN: I'm not leaving until I see Fay.

GERTIE: Then she does know you're here.

JOHN: If you must know, Mrs. Thorpe phoned me and told me to come. I think she's drunk.

GERTIE: Get back out of sight.

(*JOHN dashes behind a bush. BARRY enters.*)

BARRY: What are you doing here all by yourself?

I WENT TO A MARVELOUS PARTY

GERTIE: I was looking at the moon.

BARRY: What's the point? I can give you everything you want.

GERTIE: At the moment my wants are simple. A glass of champagne.

BARRY: Come along then.

>(HE offers her his arm. SHE takes it and THEY stroll off. SHE glaces back as they leave. JOHN reenters cautiously. Hearing a noise HE dashes back out of sight. HARRIET reenters.)

HARRIET: John? John?

>(JOHN reenters.)

HARRIET: I can't find her. But you mustn't leave. Quickly. Get behind that bush.

>(JOHN dashes off. JIMMY reenters.)

JIMMY: Mrs. Thorpe...?

HARRIET: Yes, dear? What is it?

JIMMY: Have you seen Fay?

HARRIET: I believe she went upstairs.

JIMMY: Are you all right?

HARRIET: That's for me to know and you to guess.

JIMMY: That champagne is pretty potent.

HARRIET: If it's too strong for you, don't drink it. Go on, go on. I'll be all right.

>(JIMMY goes off. JOHN reenters cautiously.)

I WENT TO A MARVELOUS PARTY

HARRIET: Get back!

(JOHN dashes off. GERTIE reenters.

GERTIE: What are you going here?

HARRIET: I might ask the same of you.

GERTIE: Did you send for him?

HARRIET: Him? Who?

GERTIE: Isn't that boy in enough trouble, as it is?

HARRIET: You have no faith. That's the trouble with you.

GERTIE: John? John?

HARRIET: What are you doing?

(JOHN enters cautiously.)

GERTIE: Get back!

(JOHN runs back off. FAY enters.)

FAY: Mother? Are you all right?

HARRIET: Why shouldn't I be?

GERTIE: She's had a little too much to drink.

HARRIET: Too much, or not enough. Gertie is going to take care of me, aren't you, dear? No. I want Gertie to take care of me. You stay here. I...I lost my pin. The one with the fake diamond. Your father will never forgive me.

FAY: You weren't wearing it.

I WENT TO A MARVELOUS PARTY

HARRIET: That's how much you know. I dropped it here, I know.

FAY: All right, all right. I'll look for it.

GERTIE: *(SHE sighs.)* Come along, Cupid.

> *(HARRIET goes off, supported by GERTIE. FAY looks about. JOHN enters.)*

JOHN: Fay...

FAY: How did you get in?

JOHN: Your mother let me in. She sent for me. I swear it.

FAY: She's drunk. Why did you go and break Jimmy's arm?

JOHN: I didn't mean to.

FAY: You've spoiled everything.

JOHN: I've spoiled everything?!

FAY: Yes, you. We could have been friends, all three of us.

JOHN: Wouldn't that be cozy?

FAY: It's done all the time.

JOHN: Is that what you had in mind?

FAY: And what if it was?

JOHN: I'm not one for leftovers.

> *(SHE slaps him. HE starts off.)*

FAY: John! Oh, John, I don't want my life to go sour, like my mother's did.

I WENT TO A MARVELOUS PARTY

JOHN: And you think you can be happy with Jimmy?

FAY: I just wonder if anyone's really happy.

JOHN: My mother and father are.

FAY: That's because they've settled...they've settled for less.

JOHN: Do you really think that money is that important?

FAY: If only you hadn't broken Jimmy's arm. Mr. Cousins will never give you a job now. He used to be so fond of you. You said so yourself. You said you felt closer to him than you did to your own father.

JOHN: What do you want me to do, Fay? I'll do it.

FAY: Let me try and patch it up between you and Mr. Cousins.

JOHN: And then what? Tomorrow's the wedding.

FAY: You mean more to me than anyone else in the world. You always have and you always will.

JOHN: But you're still going to go ahead and marry Jimmy.

FAY: That doesn't mean that I have to stay married to him. You've got to trust me.

JOHN: Okay, Fay. Whatever you say.

FAY: Go home. I'll call you. *(SHE looks about then kisses him hastily.)*

JOHN: I love you.

FAY: And I love you.

(JOHN goes off. FAY watches him leave. HE reenters.)

FAY: What's the matter?

I WENT TO A MARVELOUS PARTY

JOHN: The gate is locked, and there's a padlock on it.

FAY: Stay here. There's a gate on the other side. I'll see if it's open.

(FAY goes off. JOHN paces about. Hearing a noise HE stops and runs off. BARRY and JEFF enter.)

JEFF: This is quite a place.

BARRY: You've never been here before? I thought you had.

JEFF: I've seen it from a distance.

BARRY: I had it brought over from Spain, brick by brick. It was built in the fourteenth century. That was before Shakespeare was even born. It cost me a fortune.

JEFF: It must have.

BARRY: That's what money's for. The man that owned this castle was the most powerful man in the country. There's a book that was written about him. I have it in the library. I'll show it to you. I just wanna enjoy life, while I'm living it. Most men sit and worry about their children and their grandchildren. The hell with them! If they want a fortune, let them get out there and earn it, like I did. I started from scratch.

JEFF: With a little help.

BARRY: Edith's money helped a little, but there wasn't that much of it, contrary to popular opinion. Anyway, that's neither here nor there. I am very disappointed in John. I had great plans for him.

JEFF: He'll pull out of it.

BARRY: He could have killed Jimmy. He might still try it. That's a terrible thing, to have to walk around in fear of your life. Well, if I catch him around here... I've got detectives all over the place, and they are armed.

I WENT TO A MARVELOUS PARTY

JEFF: I came over here to try and prevent any trouble.

BARRY: What makes you think he might be here?

JEFF: Bill Endicott phoned me and he said he saw John heading this way.

BARRY: Well, he won't get in now. I've had all the gates padlocked. Come on, I'll get you some champagne, now that you're here. I don't have anything against you personally.

JEFF: That's very big of you.

BARRY: Don't you get sarcastic with me! I'll kick you out on your ass. I'm trying to be a gentleman.

JEFF: The strain is beginning to show. *(HE goes off.)*

BARRY: You're fired! You son of a bitch, you're fired! And this time I mean it.

(BARRY follows JEFF off. FAY enters cautiously.)

FAY: John? John?

(JOHN enters.)

FAY: The other gate is locked. The only way out is through the house. Get back!

(JOHN runs off. FAY searches the ground. JIMMY enters.)

JIMMY: What are you looking for?

FAY: My mother said she lost a pin.

JIMMY: Fay, I've got to talk to you.

FAY: I'm listening.

I WENT TO A MARVELOUS PARTY

JIMMY: We're getting married tomorrow. Or are we?

FAY: That's up to you.

JIMMY: Well, we certainly won't have much of a married life not talking to one another.

FAY: We're talking.

JIMMY: Well, we're sure not communicating. I asked you a simple question, only because that was why John and I got into a fight. Were you sleeping with John when he was home during the Easter vacation? I'd like to know.

FAY: And what if I was?

JIMMY: But we were engaged.

FAY: Not officially.

JIMMY: Maybe we hadn't announced it, but we did have an understanding, or so I thought. I mean, the idea was that you were to tell John. I made it a point of deliberately being out of town, because you said you wanted to do it in your own way.

FAY: I have.

JIMMY: What is that supposed to mean?

FAY: Exactly what I said. John knows, doesn't he? I've told him, haven't I? You're not buying a shipment of grain, you know. If I don't have your respect, that's it. I'm not marrying you.

JIMMY: Well, you don't intend to go on seeing John after we're married, do you?

FAY: John is a friend. He's your friend, too. We're not going to give up all our friends, just because we're married, are we?

I WENT TO A MARVELOUS PARTY

JIMMY: No, of course not. But I don't think that John feels very friendly towards either one of us at this very moment.

FAY: Did you start the fight with John?

JIMMY: Well, technically...

FAY: Did you or didn't you?

JIMMY: Well, I guess I did hit him first.

FAY: Why didn't you tell your father that?

JIMMY; Well, that still doesn't change the fact that he broke my arm.

FAY: I want you to tell your father right now. I'll wait for you here. I've got to find my mother's pin.

JIMMY: I'll help you look for it.

(GERTIE enters.)

GERTIE: What are you two doing here?

JIMMY: Fay is looking for her mother's pin. She said she lost it.

GERTIE: You should be mingling with your guests. Go on, go on. I'll look for the pin. Go on!

(FAY, reluctantly, goes off with JIMMY.)

GERTIE: You can come out now.

(JOHN reenters.)

GERTIE: I suppose you know that all the gates are padlocked. You don't have a gun, do you?

JOHN: Of course, not.

I WENT TO A MARVELOUS PARTY

GERTIE: Did you threaten to kill Fay and Jimmy and yourself?

JOHN: I guess so. I just got carried away. I guess I'll have to stay here until morning, and then sneak out through the house while everyone's still asleep.

GERTIE: They may search the grounds. Besides you'll catch your death of cold. It's getting chilly and it's damp.

JOHN: Besides...

GERTIE: Besides what?

JOHN: Well, I didn't start the fight with Jimmy. Jimmy did. And I think he's going to tell his father.

GERTIE: I don't think his father is in any mood to hear anything, and besides, I wouldn't be too sure it would make any difference. Unless you want to end up in jail, or worse. Wait here, and keep your eyes open.

(GERTIE goes off. JOHN stands listening for a moment then runs off.)

HARRIET: Fay? Fay, dear?

(HARRIET enters leading JEFF by the hand.)

HARRIET: Fay?

JEFF: Harriet, what do you want to talk to me about?

HARRIET: They're gone.

JEFF: Who?

HARRIET: Fay...and John. They've run off together.

JEFF: Have you seen him?

I WENT TO A MARVELOUS PARTY

HARRIET: Of course, I've seen him. I sent for him. I knew they would make it up. Don't you see, Jeff? I did it for you. For us. For what might have been.

   (BARRY enters.)

BARRY: I thought I asked you to leave.

HARRIET: I asked him to stay.

BARRY: This is my house, my castle, and I want him out of here.

HARRIET: Who cares what you want? Just because you're rich you think you can buy and sell the world. Well, you can't buy my daughter. She doesn't love your son, and she's run off with the man she loves. So put that in your pipe and smoke it.

BARRY: You don't know what you're talking about.

HARRIET: Oh, don't I? I was the one that sent for him. I was the one that arranged the whole thing. So what are you going to do about that?

BARRY: You sent for John?

HARRIET: And he came, and he ran off with Fay.

BARRY: That's impossible.

HARRIET: That's what makes it so glorious.

BARRY: You're as nutty as a fruitcake.

   (JIMMY enters with FAY.)

JIMMY: Dad? Dad, I... What's going on?

BARRY: That's what I'd like to know. *(To Fay)* Have you seen John his evening? Here? On these grounds?

I WENT TO A MARVELOUS PARTY

FAY: What makes you think that?

BARRY: According to your mother...

FAY: My mother is obviously drunk, and I'm going to take her home. And Jimmy, you talk to your father. You tell him what you told me.

HARRIET: I don't understand.

   (FAY leads HARRIET off.)

BARRY: I think John is somewhere on the premises. If he tries anything funny, I will have him shot. *(HE stalks off.)*

JIMMY: Dad! Dad, I've got to talk to you.

   (JIMMY follows Barry off. JEFF is about to leave when GERTIE reenters wearing a long opera cloak with a hood.)

GERTIE: Don't worry about him.

JEFF: Have you seen him?

GERTIE: I'll hide him in my room until morning. When they all leave for church, he can sneak out.

JEFF: Aren't you taking a chance?

GERTIE: You gave me a drink when I needed it. The least I can do is return the favor.

JEFF: You're quite a remarkable woman.

GERTIE: The world is full of remarkable people, my dear. What a pity the timing is all wrong. Go home. Don't worry.

   (JEFF goes off. JOHN enters cautiously.)

JOHN: I never thought I'd end up a clown.

I WENT TO A MARVELOUS PARTY

GERTIE: You haven't started yet. *(SHE produces a wig.)* Here. Put this on.

JOHN: What is it?

GERTIE: What does it look like? And treat it gently. It's expensive.

JOHN: Must I?

GERTIE: Unless you prefer to go to jail, or get shot. You are trespassing on private property. Lovely! Now wrap this around you, and pull up the hood. As long as we keep in the shadows we're all right. This way.

JOHN: They're playing "Good Night Ladies."

GERTIE: My hearing is excellent.

BARRY: *(Offstage.)* Thank you for coming.

JOHN: That's Mr. Cousins.

GERTIE: He's looking the other way.

JOHN: I'm going to get you in trouble.

GERTIE: Shut up and keep moving.

> *("Good Night Ladies" is played as the lights come down, and THEY tiptoe off. The lights come up on Gertie's room. JOHN is seated, minus wig and cloak. Someone knocks three times on the door. JOHN approaches the door.)*

JOHN: Miss Lennox?

GERTIE: *(Offstage)* Open up.

> *(JOHN unlocks the door. GERTIE enters. JOHN locks the door behind her.)*

I WENT TO A MARVELOUS PARTY

GERTIE: And it's Mrs. Lennox.

JOHN: Have they all gone.

GERTIE: Just about.

(There's a knock at the door.)

GERTIE: Who is it?

BARRY: *(Offstage)* It's me, Barry. Open up.

(GERTIE motions to JOHN. HE goes off. GERTIE opens the door. BARRY enters.)

BARRY: Are you all right?

GERTIE: Why shouldn't I be?

BARRY: You're not leaving tomorrow, are you? Stay another week. Here's your check, by the way. No, it's not a mistake. I believe in paying for value received. It's certified, by the way, so I can't stop payment on it, even if I wanted to. I'm a lonely old man, Gertie. I need someone like you. Give me a chance. Stay on for a couple of weeks. No strings attached. When you get bored, you can leave. Or are you bored already?

GERTIE: If I am, the fault's not yours. We're too much alike, Barry.

BARRY: I should think that would work in my favor.

GERTIE; We'd cramp each other's style.

BARRY: You're tired.

GERTIE: A little.

BARRY: Get a good night's sleep. Tomorrow's a big day. We'll talk in the morning. May I kiss you good night?

I WENT TO A MARVELOUS PARTY

GERTIE: Yes, of course.

>(BARRY kisses her and goes off. GERTIE locks the door. After a moment JOHN pokes his head in.)

JOHN: All clear?

GERTIE: What's that? Oh, I'm sorry.

>(JOHN enters.)

JOHN: It's none of my business, but why don't you marry him?

GERTIE: I need a drink. How about you?

JOHN: Sure. Why not?

GERTIE: There's a glass in the bathroom.

>(JOHN gets the glass. GERTIE produces a bottle.)

GERTIE: There's only one glass. We'll have to share.

JOHN: I don't mind, if you don't.

GERTIE: I take it neat.

JOHN: That's okay.

>(GERTIE pours a drink, takes a sip and passes the glass to JOHN, who takes a sip.)

JOHN: That's good stuff.

GERTIE: I only drink the best.

JOHN: Not that I'm any sort of connoisseur.

GERTIE: You can have the bed. I'm not going to sleep.

I WENT TO A MARVELOUS PARTY

JOHN: I'm not sleepy either.

GERTIE: It's going to be a long night.

JOHN: I'm sorry.

GERTIE: Don't apologize.

JOHN: I could ruin everything with Mr. Cousins. I mean, if he ever found me here.

GERTIE: We're not all of us whores, my dear. I'm sorry. I shouldn't have said that. And besides, it's a lie. We all of us sell ourselves in one way or another. The world is a market place. What are you going to do when all this is over? Go back to school?

JOHN: I think not.

GERTIE: That's right. You want to be a farmer. Or don't you?

JOHN: I don't know. You're not crying, are you?

GERTIE: Don't mind me. I'm a little hysterical this evening. Throwing a party is not the easiest thing in the world. I don't just call a caterer and buy some paper hats. My parties are famous because they're unique, and they're unique because they're inspired...as a rule. I was not at my best tonight. Ottumwa, Iowa is not my milieu. I find your Middle West unbearably depressing. I get the feeling that all of you are sitting up at a wake, and none of you are quite sure who died. And the joke of it is the wake is your own. Not that you aren't cheerful about it. Maybe that's what makes it so depressing. You're all so goddamned cheerful, and you have nothing to be cheerful about. Where's that drink? Cheers! How about you?

(SHE passes the glass to JOHN who takes a sip.)

GERTIE: I can't wait to get out of here.

JOHN: Where do you go from here?

I WENT TO A MARVELOUS PARTY

GERTIE: The question is, where do **you** go from here?

JOHN: Maybe I oughta get out and see the world. I don't know.

GERTIE: I wish you'd stop saying that.

JOHN: Well, I don't.

GERTIE: Have another drink.

JOHN: Thank you. I will. *(HE drinks.)* You don't think much of Fay, do you?

GERTIE: The world is full of Fays.

JOHN: You're not like Fay, are you?

GERTIE: I'm an old lady, my dear.

JOHN: You're not that old. You couldn't be more than...thirty five.

GERTIE: I'll drink to that.

JOHN: Are you?

GERTIE: Now you know I'm not going to tell you my age, no matter how drunk we get.

JOHN: Why not? I'm not going to tell anyone.

GERTIE: I'm thirty six.

JOHN: That's not so old.

GERTIE: I quite agree. Thirty six is not very old.

JOHN: But you're not thirty six. You're forty six, fifty six, sixty six, seventy six, eighty six, one hundred and six.

I WENT TO A MARVELOUS PARTY

GERTIE: That's it! I'm one hundred and six. How old are you?

JOHN: One hundred and seven.

GERTIE: What's the matter? Is there anything wrong?

JOHN: I'm going to kiss you.

GERTIE: Is that a threat or an announcement?

JOHN: Do you mind?

GERTIE: There's only one way of finding out.

JOHN: *(HE kisses her.)* What was he like, your husband?

GERTIE: Why?

JOHN: I'd like to know. He must have meant a great deal to you.

GERTIE: He's been dead a long time.

JOHN: Fay wants me to stick around.

GERTIE: I don't blame her.

JOHN: Would you stick around, if you were me?

GERTIE: That's a personal choice, and you've got to make it.

JOHN: I guess I've been pretty spoiled. I've always had what I wanted. Not that I ever wanted very much. I've been taught not to want very much. We've always been poor, and I was taught to be proud of our poverty. Were you ever poor?

GERTIE: Oh my, yes.

JOHN: I don't believe you.

I WENT TO A MARVELOUS PARTY

GERTIE: I'm still poor, comparatively speaking. With me it's either feast or famine. Some days it's champagne and caviar. Others it's cheese and crackers.

JOHN: Does that bother you?

GERTIE: Hell, no! I enjoy living by my wits. And when they go, so do I. Have another drink.

JOHN: Thank you. I don't want to take advantage of you. I know that sounds funny but, after all, you are protecting me, and it would be unfair of me...well, to take advantage of the situation.

GERTIE: I'm old enough to be your mother.

JOHN: I'm almost twenty.

GERTIE: My, my, my, my, my!

JOHN: I could have lied to you and said I was older. Most people think I am. I could pass for twenty five, twenty six...and you could pass for thirty six.

GERTIE: When the lighting's right. Wait until morning, my dear.

JOHN: Ten years difference isn't very much.

GERTIE: I'll drink to that.

> *(SHE drinks. JOHN takes the glass from her and sets it down very carefully)*

GERTIE: What are you going to do?

JOHN: I'm going to make love to you.

GERTIE: Must you be so solemn about it?

I WENT TO A MARVELOUS PARTY

JOHN: Love is a very serious business. I'm very good at it. I am. And I can go on forever.

GERTIE: Well, just remember, there is ten years difference in our ages. Now what's the matter?

JOHN: I don't know anything about you.

GERTIE: What's that got to do with it?

JOHN: I can't make love to a stranger.

GERTIE: What do you want to know?

JOHN: Everything.

GERTIE: We've only got a couple of hours.

JOHN: Why won't you talk about your husband? You're still in love with him, aren't you? Isn't that a little obscene? It's like being in love with death.

GERTIE: You're very attractive, dear boy. Don't push your luck.

JOHN: Have you ever really given yourself to anyone, since he died?

GERTIE: I said...

JOHN: I heard what you said. You can kick me out, if you want to.

GERTIE: Why do you want to know about my husband?

JOHN: Because he's part of you and, I'm beginning to think, the most important part of you. You've got him caged up in that jar...

GERTIE: It's not a jar. It's an urn.

JOHN: Why don't you set him free? And yourself?

I WENT TO A MARVELOUS PARTY

GERTIE: Free to do what? And what makes you think I'm not free?

JOHN: Are you free to love me?

GERTIE: What are you? Some sort of creep? All we're going to do is spend the night together. Then you go your way and I go mine.

JOHN: I want to go with you.

GERTIE: Go with me? Go where?

JOHN: Wherever you go. I'll pay my own way.

GERTIE: How?

JOHN: If you can live by your wits, so can I.

GERTIE: What are you doing?

JOHN: I'm going to free your husband.

GERTIE: Put that down!

JOHN: It's empty!

GERTIE: So what?

JOHN: Why do you carry around an empty urn?

GERTIE: It was full once.

JOHN: What happened to him?

GERTIE: Some maid came and emptied him when I was out of the room. But he's still in there, as far as I'm concerned.

JOHN: Then I'm going to set him free.

GERTIE: What are you doing?

I WENT TO A MARVELOUS PARTY

(JOHN sends the urn crashing to the floor.)

GERTIE' You fool! You goddamned fool! You crazy son of a bitch! *(SHE springs at him and tries to scratch him.)*

BARRY: *(Offstage)* Gertie? Gertie?!

JOHN: It's Mr. Cousins.

BARRY: *(Offstage)* Gertie, are you all right?

GERTIE: Get back in there. Do as I say.

(JOHN goes off. GERTIE opens the door. BARRY enters.)

BARRY: Are you all right?

GERTIE: I'm terribly sorry. I broke the urn.

BARRY: Have you been drinking?

GERTIE: As a matter of fact, I have.

BARRY: I'll send for the maid.

GERTIE: No, please. Leave it alone.

BARRY: You'll cut yourself.

GERTIE: I'll take care of it.

BARRY: Do you often get like this?

GERTIE: Whenever I choose.

BARRY: I see.

GERTIE: Good night, Barry.

I WENT TO A MARVELOUS PARTY

BARRY: Be careful you don't cut yourself.

(BARRY goes off. GERTIE locks the door. JOHN reenters.)

JOHN: Mr. Cousins has a thing about liquor. His wife drank herself to death. That's what they say, anyway. I'm sorry. Are you all right?

(GERTIE sits on the bed. JOHN sits beside her. HE strokes her hair and brushes the tears away.)

JOHN: Don't cry. Please don't cry. It was empty anyway.

GERTIE: *(SHE kisses him.)* Who are you? No, don't tell me. You're the past come to haunt me.

JOHN: What was he like? How did he die?

GERTIE: Must we?

(HE nods.)

GERTIE: He was like quicksilver. Adored by everyone. And he was mine, all mine. Oh, how they envied me. We were on our honeymoon, on the Riviera. And then, on that fatal night. It was a Friday, Friday the thirteenth. We'd made love. We were insatiable. We couldn't get enough of one another. And then we quarreled. There was this yacht. It was anchored on the sea just outside the harbor. "It's the Duke of Westminster's," "I said. "It most certainly is not," he said. "It most certainly is," I said. "I'll prove it to you," he said. And he jumped out of bed, stark naked. He ran across the grass and dove into the sea, and I never saw him again, alive that is. Four days later his body was washed ashore. His beautiful body, all bloated and bruised, and I never loved again.

JOHN: Until now. *(HE squeezes her arms.)* Until now. *(HE kisses her.)*

GERTIE: Oh, Rupert!

JOHN: John. John, John, John.

I WENT TO A MARVELOUS PARTY

GERTIE: No....

JOHN: John, John, John.

GERTIE: You're hurting me. John, John, John, John.

(THEY kiss.)

GERTIE: Oh, John!

(JOHN reaches for the light and turns it off. Darkness.)

GERTIE: John, John, John.

(Church bells are heard. The following morning. HARRIET enters her living room, followed by FAY.)

HARRIET: I refuse to put up with your father any longer. I will not spend another night in this house.

FAY: Where will you go?

HARRIET: I haven't the vaguest idea.

FAY: Mother, you must have some idea where you're going.

HARRIET: New York.

FAY: What will you do there?

HARRIET: I'll get a job.

FAY: But what can you do?

HARRIET: I can do anything. I can type. I took typing in high school I can be a receptionist. Maybe Gertie can help me find something. She knows all sorts of people.

FAY: But won't you be lonely?

I WENT TO A MARVELOUS PARTY

HARRIET: And what do you think I've been all these years? There was only you, up until now. And now you're leaving.

FAY: I'm not so sure.

HARRIET: I'm sorry. I'm sorry I interfered.

FAY: You needn't be. Whether I marry Jimmy or not, the decision will be mine.

HARRIET: You don't have very much time, dear. We should be starting for the church right now. *(SHE goes to the foot of the stairs.)* Lester! Lester get a move on!

(The doorbell rings.)

HARRIET: That must be your father-in-law to be.

(HARRIET opens the door. JOHN is discovered.)

HARRIET: Come in, John. Come in. *(To Fay)* I'd better see to your father. We don't have much time. *(SHE goes up the stairs.)*

FAY: I couldn't sleep all night for worrying about you. How did you manage?

JOHN: Gertie helped me. She hid me in her room until morning.

FAY: I see.

(THEY speak at the same time. JOHN: Fay, I... FAY: John...)

JOHN: I'm sorry...

FAY: No. What were you going to say?

JOHN: What were **you** going to say?

FAY: Do you think we could make a go of it? John...?

I WENT TO A MARVELOUS PARTY

JOHN: No. I'm sorry, Fay, but we couldn't.

FAY: I meant...

JOHN: I know what you meant, and the answer is "no."

FAY: Well, you needn't be so vehement about it. Why have you suddenly changed your mind? Or has someone changed it for you?

JOHN: Yes. You have.

FAY: Last night...

JOHN: Was last night.

FAY: Have you had a better offer?

JOHN: I'm going away with Gertie.

FAY: What do you mean, you're going away with Gertie?

JOHN: Exactly what I said.

FAY: You're not going to marry her"

JOHN: I doubt it.

FAY: Are you going to live with her?

JOHN: Possibly.

FAY: She's old enough to be your grandmother.

JOHN: Not really. She's really very young, and quite naive.

FAY: Did you go to bed with her? That old crone? She is. She's an old crone. John... Don't be foolish. We're in love with each other. Aren't we?

JOHN: No, Fay. We're just afraid to let go, that's all.

I WENT TO A MARVELOUS PARTY

FAY: I suppose you're in love with Gertie.

JOHN: I think I could be. Maybe I am. I don't know.

FAY: You're doing this out of spite.

JOHN: I've come to say good-bye.

FAY: What about me?

JOHN: You'll manage. Good-bye, Fay.

(HE extends his hand. SHE ignores it.)

JOHN: I'll send you picture postcards.

FAY: From where?

JOHN: Wherever... *(HE goes off.)*

FAY: John! John, you come back here. John!!!

(FAY runs off after him. At a room in the church GERTIE enters, followed by BARRY.)

BARRY: You're acting like a madwoman. First you have me drive you down here to the church. Now you say you don't want to stay for the wedding. What's gotten into you?

GERTIE: Are you in the habit of giving your guests the third degree? I've changed my mind.

BARRY: About what?

GERTIE: Unless, of course, you want to make it a double wedding. Don't worry, I won't hold you to your offer.

BARRY: Whiskey is a disease. I can tolerate anything but a lush.

I WENT TO A MARVELOUS PARTY

GERTIE: I'd like to make a phone call before I leave.

BARRY: There's a phone right in front of you. The car will be waiting outside. Good luck, Gertie.

GERTIE: Thank you, Barry. You, too.

(BARRY goes off. GERTIE picks up the phone and dials.)

GERTIE: Operator, can you give me the phone number for the Gordon residence? I imagine it's listed under Jeffrey. That must be it. Would you ring it for me, please. Thank you.

(The phone rings in the Gordon living room. JEFF enters and picks it up.)

JEFF: Hello?

GERTIE: Hello, Mr. Gordon. It's Gertie. Gertie Lennox.

JEFF: Yes, Mrs. Lennox?

GERTIE: John should be getting home very shortly. I want you to keep him there.

JEFF: I'm afraid I don't understand.

GERTIE: He wants to come with me. It's an impossible situation. You can see that, can't you?

JEFF: What do you want me to say to him?

GERTIE: Nothing. Just keep him there, so I can get away.

JEFF: I'll do my best.

GERTIE: Thank you, Mr. Gordon.

JEFF: Good luck, and thank you.

I WENT TO A MARVELOUS PARTY

GERTIE: *(SHE hangs up.)* Oh, merde!

(GERTIE goes off. JEFF hangs up as JOHN enters.)

JEFF: Oh, John...

JOHN: I don't have much time.

JEFF: John...

JOHN: Yes, sir?

JEFF: Where are you going?

JOHN: I'm running off...with a lady.

JEFF: Mrs. Lennox?

JOHN: Why, yes.

JEFF: There's not much future in it.

JOHN: I'm not concerned with the future. I used to be, but not anymore.

JEFF: But surely you're not in love with her?

JOHN: She needs me, and I need her. I don't have time to explain. I'll write you.

JEFF: John...

(JOHN goes off, followed by JEFF. At the church FAY enters followed by JIMMY.)

FAY: You're not supposed to see me before the ceremony.

JIMMY: So what?

FAY: What is it? What's the matter?

I WENT TO A MARVELOUS PARTY

JIMMY: What's gotten into your mother? Is she still drunk?

FAY: Is that what you wanted to talk to me about?

JIMMY: No, but she is acting strangely.

FAY: She's leaving my father, and she seems to be very happy about it.

JIMMY: I see.

FAY: Jimmy, they're waiting for us.

JIMMY: Let them wait.

FAY: What's gotten into you?

JIMMY: I haven't told my father that I started the fight with John, and I don't intend to. I don't want him around. I don't want you seeing him, publicly or privately. Is that understood?

FAY: If it means that much to you, of course, dear.

JIMMY: You mean it?

(SHE kisses him.)

JIMMY: You won't pull anything funny, will you?

FAY: My word of honor! It was all a misunderstanding.

JIMMY: I love you, Fay.

FAY: And I love you.

(THEY kiss. Music is heard. BARRY enters.)

BARRY: Let's make it legal, kids, shall we?

I WENT TO A MARVELOUS PARTY

(JIMMY and BARRY go off. The wedding march is heard. FAY takes a deep breath and, head erect, SHE walks slowly off. A train whistle is heard in the distance. GERTIE enters the train platform holding an overnight bag. SHE sets down the bag and waits impatiently. JOHN enters hurriedly, carrying a large suitcase. HE sets down the suitcase next to Gertie's bag.)

JOHN: You forgot to wait for me.

GERTIE: How did you get here?

JOHN: By cab. I know, I know. You spoke to my father.

GERTIE: And...?

JOHN: He helped me pack. He believes in people finding their own way.

GERTIE: I'm forty seven. I'll be forty eight in October.

JOHN: October what?

GERTIE: What difference does it make?

JOHN: I'll want to buy you a birthday present.

GERTIE: I suppose you think you're very clever, and very sophisticated.

JOHN: Oh, Gertie, do shut up!

GERTIE: Don't you talk to me like that. I know you mean well...

JOHN: Are you concerned about me, or about yourself?

GERTIE: And suppose I am? How long will it last?

JOHN: What difference does it make? I'm certainly better than an empty urn.

I WENT TO A MARVELOUS PARTY

GERTIE: I'll be going back to London eventually. There's bound to be a war. It's inevitable.

JOHN: Then let's make the most of it. I love you, Gertie...and you love me.

GERTIE: You may regret it.

JOHN: Then again, I may not.

> *(The train is heard pulling into the station. GERTIE picks up her bag.)*

GERTIE: Well, if we're going to go, let's go. Let's get out of this godforsaken wilderness.

> *(GERTIE goes off. JOHN picks up his suitcase and runs after her.)*

CONDUCTOR: *(Offstage)* All aboard. All aboard.

> *(As the lights come down the train is heard pulling out of the station.)*

DANCING IN THE DARK

CAST OF CHARACTERS

Jessica Courtney

Calvin Courtney

Ben Brady

SCENE

The living room of the Courtney apartment in Greenwich Village in New York City. Spring 1954

(*Late afternoon. The radio is playing soft dinner music. The doorbell rings. JESSICA COURTNEY, a slim, attractive woman in her late thirties, enters from the kitchen. SHE turns down the radio then checks her appearance in the mirror. The doorbell rings again.*)

JESSICA: Just a moment.

(*JESSICA straightens the pillows on the sofa, takes a last look around the room then opens the door. BEN BRADY, a rugged looking man in his late forties, is discovered in the doorway.*)

JESSICA: Hello.

BEN: I'm sorry I'm late.

JESSICA: That's quite all right. I wasn't expecting you at any special time. Won't you come in? Did you have any difficulty finding us?

BEN: I know the Village pretty well. Haven't been here in quite some time, but it all comes back.

JESSICA: Well! I'm terribly excited about working with you, Mr. Brady.

BEN: You can call me Ben.

JESSICA: Jessica.

BEN: And your friends call you Jessie. That's what Lester calls you at any rate. Do you know Lester well?

JESSICA: We're sort of cousins...somewhere along the line. We've never quite figured out where.

BEN: Shrewd little man.

JESSICA: Yes, he is that.

(*CALVIN COURTNEY, a thin, pleasant looking man in his early forties materializes in the shadows.* **Actually he's in JESSICA's imagination.**)

DANCING IN THE DARK

CALVIN: Well, get on with it.

JESSICA: Can I get you a drink? I've mixed a batch of Whiskey Sours.

BEN: That'll be fine.

>*(CALVIN vanishes.)*

JESSICA: Are you hungry by any chance?

BEN: These nuts will do fine for now.

>*(BEN takes some nuts from a dish on the coffee table. JESSICA goes into the kitchen. BEN walks about the room, taking it in, then stands at the window looking out into the street. JESSICA reenters with two drinks. SHE gives one to BEN.)*

JESSICA: I'm afraid there's not much to see out there.

BEN: Have you lived here long?

JESSICA: Nine years. We keep saying it's temporary. It is convenient, however, and inexpensive.

BEN: By "we" you mean...?

JESSICA: My husband and myself.

BEN: Lester never mentioned whether you were married or not.

JESSICA: Does that make a difference?

BEN: It does to you, I imagine. You are British, aren't you?

JESSICA: I was born in England.

BEN: And your husband?

JESSICA: He's Canadian. Is your drink all right?

DANCING IN THE DARK

BEN: Fine. What does your husband do?

JESSICA: He's an editor. He works for "The Spectator." It's a weekly trade paper.

BEN: Do you work with him? On the paper, I mean.

JESSICA: Oh, no. I'm not that ambitious. I take an assignment now and then. Otherwise I'm just a housewife. And you? Are you married?

BEN: Divorced.

JESSICA: I'm sorry.

BEN: That's all right. I should be used to it by now. It's been three long years. I envy people who can make a go of it. I really do. It isn't easy.

(CALVIN *materializes.*)

CALVIN: The understatement of the century.

JESSICA: How long will you be in town?

BEN: One never knows. Actually I've come back to the States for a vacation.

JESSICA: From...? Where?

BEN: You name it.

JESSICA: Have you any children?

BEN: No. And you?

JESSICA: No.

BEN: *(HE takes a pipe from his pocket.)* Do you mind?

JESSICA: Not really, no.

DANCING IN THE DARK

BEN: If you do...

JESSICA: That's quite all right. I'll get you an ashtray.

> (*BEN fills his pipe and lights up while JESSICA crosses the room to find an ashtray.*)

CALVIN: We could have a child, you know. We could adopt one.

JESSICA: I don't think so.

CALVIN: Of course, there's always artificial insemination. They don't tell you who the father is.

JESSICA: It wouldn't be ours, would it?

> (*CALVIN vanishes.*)

BEN: Have you ever had that feeling...? You know what I mean?

JESSICA: It's called "deja vu." That feeling of having been somewhere before.

BEN: Have we ever met?

JESSICA: Not that I know of.

BEN: We used to live in the Village, my wife and I. On Barrow Street.

JESSICA: That's not very far from here.

BEN: Yes, I know. Would you excuse me for a moment? Where is it? The "john"? The "head"?

JESSICA: It's right through there. Off the bedroom.

BEN: Thank you.

> (*BEN goes off. After a moment CALVIN materializes.*)

DANCING IN THE DARK

CALVIN: Are you going to bed with him or not?

JESSICA: How should I know?

CALVIN: Well, you'd better get on with it. One never knows when I might pop up.

(*The telephone rings.*)

CALVIN: There I am.

JESSICA: (*SHE picks up the phone.*) Hello? Yes, Cal. He just arrived. I don't know. If I'm not home I'll leave the meat loaf on the stove. I love you too. Don't work too hard. How does it look? Well, it won't be the first time.

(*SHE hangs up as BEN reenters.*)

BEN: Was that the phone?

JESSICA: My husband.

BEN: Checking up on you?

CALVIN: You bet your ass.

BEN: I was expecting a call. I left this number. I hope you don't mind.

JESSICA: No, of course not.

BEN: Lester thought it might be a good idea if we met beforehand. I'm not quite sure why.

JESSICA: Lester moves in mysterious ways.

BEN: He thinks very highly of you. The exhibit opens tomorrow, by the way. We can attend the opening, if you like. I understand it's going to be a very posh affair. You can wear your best bib and tucker.

DANCING IN THE DARK

JESSICA: That might be nice.

BEN: On the other hand, it's bound to be very dull.

JESSICA: Why do you say that?

BEN: The very rich are very boring. Has Lester spoken to you about the article?

JESSICA: Oh, yes. I think I know what he wants.

BEN: Good. Well, I don't know what else we have to talk about, and you probably have things you want to do.

    (The telephone rings.)

BEN: That might be for me. Do you mind?

JESSICA: Go right ahead. *(SHE moves toward the side of the room.)*

BEN: *(HE picks up the phone.)* Hello? Yes, Penny...

    (The radio is playing "Dancing In The Dark." CALVIN takes JESSICA in his arms and THEY dance.)

JESSICA: What do you mean, the rich are boring?

CALVIN: There are exceptions to the rule.

JESSICA: If you mean me, I'm not that rich.

CALVIN: Well, you carry yourself like a duchess. I can see you playing croquet and entertaining the queen.

JESSICA: Are you a Communist?

CALVIN: I don't disapprove of royalty. In your case, however, it would make no difference.

DANCING IN THE DARK

JESSICA: What is that supposed to mean?

BEN: *(On the phone)* I see.

CALVIN: It means you're a lady, whether you were born in a castle or in a hovel.

JESSICA: And you're full of malarkey.

CALVIN: What's your name?

JESSICA: Jessica...Warrington.

CALVIN: <u>The</u> Jessica Warrington.

JESSICA: <u>A</u> Jessica Warrington.

BEN: *(On the phone)* Well, what about tonight?

CALVIN: Calvin Courtney. <u>The</u> Calvin Courtney.

JESSICA: Which one is he?

CALVIN: The one that's thinking about marrying you.

JESSICA: You've been reading too many novels.

CALVIN: No, my dear. Writing them.

BEN: *(On the phone)* Shall I call you?

JESSICA: I'm engaged to be married. Just in case you're interested.

CALVIN: Is there a mind that goes with this body?

JESSICA: I'm sure you think you're awfully clever.

CALVIN: Yes, I think I shall.

DANCING IN THE DARK

JESSICA: There's someone I must talk to.

CALVIN: Marry you, that is.

JESSICA: Will you excuse me?

CALVIN: I'll call you tonight.

JESSICA: You don't have my number.

CALVIN: But I know where I can get it.

JESSICA: You're wasting your time, you know.

BEN: *(On the phone)* A bientot. *(HE hangs up and turns to JESSICA.)* I'm sorry.

(CALVIN vanishes.)

JESSICA: Is she busy?

BEN: She's married.

JESSICA: Happily?

BEN: That's difficult to say.

JESSICA: Have you known her long?

BEN: We're old friends. Penny's always been lots of fun. People are always taking advantage of her.

JESSICA: You're welcome to stay for dinner, if you like.

BEN: That's very kind of you.

JESSICA: Unless, of course, you have something better to do.

BEN: I feel like a stranger here in America. Isn't that odd?

DANCING IN THE DARK

JESSICA: I know the feeling.

BEN: I guess the only anchor we really have is in the past, and that exists only in our mind.

JESSICA: I think you need another drink.

BEN: Good idea.

> (*JESSICA takes his glass and goes into the kitchen. BEN notices a photograph which HE picks up and studies. JESSICA reenters with the refill which SHE hands to him.*)

JESSICA: That was taken on our honeymoon.

BEN: You look very happy. (*HE accepts the drink.*) Thank you. You must have been very much in love.

JESSICA: Yes, we were.

BEN: And still are, I imagine.

JESSICA: People stay together for many reasons.

BEN: Such as?

JESSICA: Loyalty. Habit.

BEN: Are you a creature of habit?

JESSICA: Aren't we all creatures of habit?

BEN: I guess you've been told that you're a very attractive woman.

JESSICA: Thank you.

BEN: I think I'd better be going.

JESSICA: Please stay.

DANCING IN THE DARK

(HE puts down his glass and takes her in his arms. SHE is trembling.)

BEN: Are you all right?

(SHE nods and HE kisses her. SHE responds passionately, almost violently.)

BEN: Okay, Honey, okay. It's going to be all right. It's going to be all right.

JESSICA: Give me a minute.

(SHE goes off to the bedroom. BEN locks the outside door, takes a swig of his drink then goes into the bedroom. The lights grow dim. The music continues. The song ends.)

RADIO ANNOUNCER: Stolen hours of bliss. Which was the greater thrill? The ecstasy of love or the risk of being discovered? The maddening kisses, the frantic tussle, and all the while she listens intently for the familiar step, the rattle of the doorknob. She was a "Part Time Wife." Now out in paperback.

(The music continues. The light come up. BEN reenters from the bedroom in his shirtsleeves, adjusting his tie. HE turns on a lamp then unlocks the outside door. HE checks his appearance in the mirror. JESSICA reenters from the bedroom with Ben's jacket. She helps him into it.)

BEN: Thank you.

(BEN turns around, takes her in his arms and kisses her. SHE stiffens.)

JESSICA: Shall I refresh your drink?

BEN: I'm fine.

(SHE picks up her glass and goes into the kitchen. HE picks up

DANCING IN THE DARK

his pipe and relights it. JESSICA reenters with a fresh drink.)

BEN: Thank you.

JESSICA: For what?

BEN: There are so few women that really know how to enjoy...making love.

JESSICA: Is that what we were doing?

BEN: Do you do this often? I'm sorry. I don't mean to pry, but it's difficult to make small talk after our...little session in there.

JESSICA: You mustn't think...

BEN: What?

JESSICA: Never mind.

BEN: What were you going to say?

JESSICA: You mustn't think that what went on in there was any more than...what went on in there.

BEN: If that's the way you want it.

JESSICA: Tell me about yourself.

BEN: What would you like to know?

JESSICA: What makes you travel from place to place taking pictures of the world?

BEN: It pays very well, for one thing, and it certainly beats setting at a desk from nine to five.

JESSICA: Have you always wanted to be a photographer?

DANCING IN THE DARK

BEN: I've always been interested in photography, as a hobby, that is.

JESSICA: How did you get into it professionally?

BEN: My wife entered one of my pictures in a contest. I won the contest...and lost the marriage. Ironic, isn't it?

JESSICA: Why did you break up?

BEN: She wanted to stay at home and knit.

JESSICA: Like Penelope.

BEN: Penelope?

JESSICA: Or did she sew?

BEN: Oh. Yes, well I'm afraid she wasn't that patient.

JESSICA: Do you still see her?

BEN: No. Not since the divorce.

JESSICA: You don't correspond?

BEN: We have nothing to say to one another...except perhaps recrimination.

JESSICA: What a pity!

BEN: She's probably remarried by now, or so rumor has it. She liked married life.

JESSICA: And you?

BEN: I got used to it.

JESSICA: Why haven't you remarried?

DANCING IN THE DARK

BEN: Are you thinking of writing an article about me?

JESSICA: I'm sorry...I...

BEN: And you? What's your story?

JESSICA: I'm afraid it's even duller than yours.

BEN: You are incredibly lovely. Does that disturb you? To be told how attractive you are?

JESSICA: Don't look too close.

(CALVIN materializes.)

BEN: I've told you my story.

CALVIN: Don't you tell him!

BEN: Why did you hop into bed with me? You don't strike me as someone that sleeps around.

JESSICA: What makes you so sure of that?

BEN: Is your husband gay?

JESSICA: *(SHE laughs.)* Really!

BEN: Is he? Come on, let's cut the crap. I've been honest with you.

JESSICA: I enjoy sex. Let's just leave it at that.

CALVIN: Don't you tell him!

BEN: Okay, Honey, if that's the way you want it...

JESSICA: Where are you going?

BEN: I think I've served my purpose.

DANCING IN THE DARK

JESSICA: Don't be a fool!

BEN: We're going to work together. I'd like to be your friend.

CALVIN: You promised!

(BEN starts for the door. SHE bars his way.)

JESSICA: Please stay.

BEN: I don't like devious women.

JESSICA: I'm not devious. It's just that...

BEN: What? Good Lord, woman, whatever you say won't go any further.

JESSICA: Please. Sit down.

(THEY sit.)

CALVIN: Don't you dare! You promised. You promised.

JESSICA: My husband was wounded in the war. He was...incapacitated.

CALVIN: How could you? How could you? *(HE vanishes.)*

BEN: How long ago was that?

JESSICA: Ten years. It was three years after our marriage. I've never told anyone. Not even my family. They never approved of Cal.

BEN: Is that why you've stuck by him? Because of your family? *(After a moment)* It was a love match.

JESSICA: Oh, yes.

BEN: And you're still in love with him?

JESSICA: You must be starved.

DANCING IN THE DARK

BEN: Or is it pity?

JESSICA: Is there a difference?

BEN: Why do you just sit at home and keep house for him?

JESSICA: I keep house for myself as well.

BEN: You know what I mean. I've read one of your articles.

JESSICA: You mean I should be out there making a career for myself?

BEN: I think you could do better than an occasional assignment.

JESSICA: I'm quite content the way things are.

BEN: Are you? *(HE caresses her face than kisses her gently.)*

JESSICA: Don't. Please.

(HE kisses her again.)

JESSICA: No, please.

(HE kisses her. SHE responds. HE rises and takes her hand.)

BEN: What time does he get back?

JESSICA: Not till late. Tonight's the night they put the paper to bed.

BEN: Come on.

(SHE rises. HE goes to lock the door.)

JESSICA: No, don't. We'll leave the bedroom door open.

(HE follows her into the bedroom. The song on the radio ends.)

RADIO ANNOUNCER: The cool morning mist. The warm tropical sun.

DANCING IN THE DARK

Jamaica in the Spring.

> *(The music continues. The outside door opens. CALVIN enters. HE is about to call out, but stops apprehensively. HE sees the two glasses on the table, the pipe in the ashtray. HE walks to the radio and turns it off. HE stands for a moment, then goes into the kitchen. JESSICA enters from the bedroom.)*

JESSICA: Cal? Are you home?

> *(CALVIN enters from the kitchen with a glass of water.)*

CALVIN: In the flesh.

JESSICA: You must be starved.

CALVIN: I guess I'd better wash up.

JESSICA; We have a guest. Ben Brady.

CALVIN: I'll have to wait my turn.

JESSICA: Can I get you a drink?

CALVIN: One of your famous whiskey sours?

JESSICA: Is that all right?

CALVIN: Why not?

JESSICA: You sit right here. I'll fetch you one.

> *(JESSICA goes into the kitchen. CALVIN sits. SHE reenters with a drink.)*

CALVIN: What a foul smelling pipe!

JESSICA: You're home early.

DANCING IN THE DARK

CALVIN: I can always go back.

JESSICA: Don't be silly. How's the drink?

CALVIN: *(HE takes a sip.)* Superb, as always. Why is it so dark in here? *(HE turns on a lamp.)* There. Now I can see you.

JESSICA: How do I look?

CALVIN: The question is...how do you feel. There are days when I look in the mirror...sick as a dog...and I look wonderful. And there are days when I feel quite chipper and, for some reason or other, I look rather sallow.

JESSICA: I'd better get Ben a towel.

(JESSICA goes off to the bedroom. CALVIN sets down his drink and covers his eyes with his hand. JESSICA reenters.)

JESSICA: *(After a moment)* Is it raining out? I thought I heard some thunder.

CALVIN: The rain has stopped.

JESSICA: I'd better start the meat loaf. Would you get the table, dear? I've asked Ben to stay for dinner. Is that all right?

CALVIN: Yes. Yes, of course.

(CALVIN takes the drop-leaf table from the corner, places it in the center of the room and opens it. BEN enters from the bedroom.)

CALVIN: How do you do. You must be Ben.

BEN: How do you do.

CALVIN: I'm Calvin. Jessica's husband. You're joining us for dinner.

DANCING IN THE DARK

BEN: I hope I'm not intruding.

> (*CALVIN goes into the kitchen. BEN sits and lights his pipe. JESSICA reenters.*)

JESSICA: Are you all right?

BEN: Yes, I'm fine.

> (*CALVIN reenters with place mats and napkins.*)

JESSICA: Well, the meat loaf's on. And now for the salad. We eat very lightly. Would you care for a vegetable? I think we might have a potato or two.

BEN: I'm not particular.

JESSICA: It won't be long.

> (*JESSICA goes into the kitchen. CALVIN lays out the place mats and the napkins.*)

BEN: Can I help?

CALVIN: You're a guest.

BEN: What sort of paper do you work for?

CALVIN: "The Spectator."

BEN: I don't know it.

CALVIN: It's a weekly for the intelligentsia.

BEN: Does it do well?

CALVIN: That's not my department.

BEN: What's your position on the paper?

DANCING IN THE DARK

CALVIN: I'm the editor.

BEN: Of what? What department?

CALVIN: There are no departments. It's a very small paper. How long will you be in town?

BEN: I'm not quite sure.

CALVIN: You're working for Lester.

BEN: Just this one assignment.

CALVIN: And then what?

BEN: Well, I have some family in Michigan. I'm hoping to spend some time with them.

CALVIN: You're married.

BEN: Divorced.

CALVIN: What a pity!

> (*CALVIN goes into the kitchen. BEN rises and walks about restlessly.*)

CALVIN: (*Offstage*) I don't see why. (*HE reenters with some plates which HE places on the table.*) You get the best china.

BEN: I'm honored.

CALVIN: It's not that good. We live humbly. I'm sure you're accustomed to all sorts of exotic dishes.

BEN: Not really, no.

CALVIN: We don't eat much. What we do eat is nourishing.

DANCING IN THE DARK

BEN: Sounds good to me. Americans are notorious for overeating.

CALVIN: We're not Americans. Not by birth, at any rate. We consider ourselves citizens of the world.

BEN: Interesting. So do I.

CALVIN: Yes, well, I'm sure you've seen much more of the world than we have.

BEN: People are pretty much the same the world over.

CALVIN: You think so?

BEN: Don't you? Underneath.

CALVIN: I seldom get underneath.

(CALVIN starts for the kitchen as JESSICA reenters.)

JESSICA: We've run out of coffee.

BEN: Why don't I run out and get some? Please. I could use the walk.

JESSICA: We usually take Martinson's. The drip grind.

CALVIN: This should cover it. *(HE offers BEN a bill.)*

BEN: Let me.

CALVIN: You're a guest.

(BEN hesitates. JESSICA nods at him imperceptibly. BEN takes the bill.)

BEN: Is there anything else? Milk? Sugar? Bread?

JESSICA: We don't usually eat any bread. We do have some rice cakes.

DANCING IN THE DARK

BEN: I'll pick up some rolls. Butter? Anything else? How about dessert?

JESSICA: We have fresh fruit.

BEN: There is a little store around the corner, isn't there?

CALVIN: That's the closest one.

JESSICA: The A and P is open until ten. That's two blocks north on Seventh Avenue.

BEN: I'll find it.

JESSICA: It's getting rather chilly.

BEN: I'll be fine. *(HE goes off.)*

> *(CALVIN goes into the kitchen. JESSICA straightens the dishes on the table. CALVIN reenters with the silverware.)*

CALVIN: Aren't I neat enough for you?

JESSICA: I was just straightening things out.

> *(JESSICA goes into the kitchen. CALVIN begins to lay out the silverware. HE stops and starts to sob. HE stops, continues with the silverware but is overcome. HE sits sobbing. JESSICA reenters with a chair, which she sets at the table.)*

JESSICA: I can do that.

> *(HE turns away from her, clutching the knives and fork.)*

JESSICA: You must be tired.

> *(SHE lays her hand on his shoulder. HE removes it brusquely. SHE goes into the kitchen. CALVIN recovers and finishes laying out the silverware. JESSICA reenters.)*

DANCING IN THE DARK

JESSICA: There's nothing much to be done. I think I'll take a quick shower.

CALVIN: That's an excellent idea.

JESSICA: Was it very bad today?

CALVIN: Wednesdays are always hectic.

JESSICA: You can sleep late tomorrow.

CALVIN: So I can.

JESSICA: I won't be long.

> (SHE goes off. HE sits looking lost and forlorn then goes to the window and stands looking out. HE turns on the radio.)

RADIO ANNOUNCER: The budget will be balanced by the end of the year. In regard to the tax situation...

> (CALVIN changes the station and dinner music is heard. The song ends and "Dancing In The Dark" is played. The lights come up brightly, and we are in the past. CALVIN takes a sip of his drink.)

JESSICA: (Offstage, brightly) I won't be long. (SHE materializes in a negligee.)

CALVIN: Now that was worth waiting for.

JESSICA: You're drinking without me.

CALVIN: Dance first. Drink later.

> (THEY dance.)

JESSICA: Did it ever occur to you that we two are perfect, you and I?

DANCING IN THE DARK

CALVIN: Often.

JESSICA: Look at us there in the mirror.

CALVIN: I fully intend to.

JESSICA: Oh, Calvin!

CALVIN: What we do is beautiful, and we're beautiful doing it.

JESSICA: It's not really, you know. It's awkward and it's clumsy.

CALVIN: Speak for yourself, madam.

JESSICA: I want some champagne.

CALVIN: Keep dancing and I'll bring you some.

> *(JESSICA dances by herself. CALVIN pours invisible champagne in an invisible glass and hands it to her. THEY continue dancing.)*

JESSICA: I'm getting dizzy.

CALVIN: Too much champagne.

JESSICA: It's the dancing. *(SHE breaks away, sits at the table and lifts an invisible lid.)* That's not pheasant.

CALVIN: Pheasants are for peasants.

JESSICA: But we are peasants.

CALVIN: Poverty does not a peasant make.

JESSICA: What does?

CALVIN: Gluttony. *(HE kisses her on the neck.)*

DANCING IN THE DARK

JESSICA: Cal?

CALVIN: Mmmm?

JESSICA: Aren't we being just a little bit foolish?

JESSICA & CALVIN: We must think of the future.

JESSICA: I mean it. Suppose you should die and leave me with...five children?

CALVIN: Serve you right!

JESSICA: No, seriously.

CALVIN: I'm sure your family would grasp the opportunity to clutch you to their bosom.

JESSICA: Well, I'm not quite sure I'd want to be clutched, not after the way they behaved. Our marriage has got to be the most successful marriage that ever was, if only to spite my family.

CALVIN: You're so frivolous.

JESSICA: Me? Whose idea was it to spend our last penny on this decadent honeymoon.

CALVIN: Honeymoons are meant to be decadent...and memorable.

JESSICA: Well, I shall certainly remember this one. What's the matter?

CALVIN: I hope I'm not a disappointment to you.

JESSICA: You haven't been...so far.

CALVIN: I'm not speaking about our nights. I'm speaking about day to day, week to week, year to year.

JESSICA: When you become a successful novelist...

DANCING IN THE DARK

CALVIN: *(HE puts his finger to her lips.)* You mustn't say that...ever again. You've read my novel.

JESSICA: You have nowhere to go but up.

CALVIN: I'm not an ambitious man. I never have been. I'm afraid my only claim to fame will be that I captured the glamorous Jessica Warrington. And my only ambition is to make her happy.

JESSICA: My, my, my, my, my. Such pretty speeches. I do believe there's an ulterior motive behind all that flattery.

CALVIN: I'm the luckiest man in the world, and I can't, for the life of me, think why I should deserve such happiness.

JESSICA: Were you good to your mother?

CALVIN: Not to hear her tell it.

JESSICA: Calvin?

CALVIN: Yes, my love?

JESSICA: Suppose one day we should fall out of love? That is possible, isn't it?

CALVIN: Then I shall take a mistress and you shall take a lover, but we must keep up appearances.

JESSICA: Why?

CALVIN: For the sake of the children.

JESSICA: Oh, dear. How many are there?

CALVIN: Five, at last count.

JESSICA: Let's tuck them in.

DANCING IN THE DARK

(SHE starts toward the bedroom. There is a knock at the door.)

CALVIN: Jessie...?

JESSICA: *(SHE turns towards him.)* Yes, dear?

CALVIN: I just wanted to look at you.

JESSICA: Idiot!

> *(JESSICA goes off to the bedroom. A louder knock at the door. The lights change. CALVIN goes to the door and opens it. BEN enters with a large bag.)*

CALVIN: That was quick.

BEN: Speedy Gonzales they used to call me.

CALVIN: Jessica's taking a shower. She'll be out in a moment.

BEN: I bought a few extras, just in case.

CALVIN: Thank you.

> *(CALVIN takes the bag into the kitchen. JESSICA enters.)*

JESSICA: Back already?

BEN: Yes. I brought some milk and things.

JESSICA: What's it like out?

BEN: Cool and wet.

JESSICA: It's not still raining, is it?

BEN: No.

JESSICA: I'd better put things away.

DANCING IN THE DARK

(JESSICA goes into the kitchen. BEN sits. CALVIN reenters.)

CALVIN: Do you play cribbage?

BEN: Afraid not.

CALVIN: Bridge?

BEN: I do play chess.

CALVIN: We have a set somewhere. Jessie?

JESSICA: *(Offstage)* Yes, dear?

CALVIN: Do you remember where we put that chess set? Jessie?

JESSICA: *(SHE reenters.)* You're not going to play chess, are you?

CALVIN: Why not?

JESSICA: Dinner will be ready soon.

CALVIN: Then we'll stop.

JESSICA: It's in the chest, I believe. *(SHE goes off.)*

BEN: Maybe we'd better not.

CALVIN: Nonsense. *(HE starts rummaging through the chest.)* Where did all this junk come from?

JESSICA: *(Offstage)* Did you say something, dear?

CALVIN: Never mind.

BEN: I don't want to put you to any trouble.

CALVIN: Haven't played in years. I used to be pretty good. Here's the board. The men were in a little brown box.

DANCING IN THE DARK

BEN: Is this a copy of "The Spectator"?

CALVIN: What's that? Yes, that's last week's edition.

BEN: May I look at it?

CALVIN: Help yourself.

> (BEN *browses through the paper. CALVIN continues his search. The lights come up and we are in the past. JESSICA materializes.*)

JESSICA: What on earth are you doing?

CALVIN: Looking for my gloves.

JESSICA: When do you leave?

CALVIN: I don't know exactly.

JESSICA: I'm going to write Mother that you're coming.

CALVIN: You can't do that.

JESSICA: Why not?

CALVIN: Censorship. Besides, I'm not really sure where they'll be shipping us.

JESSICA: You will be careful, won't you?

CALVIN: Have no fear. God looks after fools and sinners.

JESSICA: And which are you?

CALVIN: Both.

JESSICA: I love you, damnit! And you've got to come back.

DANCING IN THE DARK

CALVIN: I will, my dear, I will.

JESSICA: *(SHE clings to him.)* Oh, God!

CALVIN: Now, now, now. Now get your coat. And your hat. You're going to walk me to the bus. Go on, go on.

> *(The lights change as JESSICA goes off. CALVIN comes up with a small brown box.)*

CALVIN: Aha! I knew it was in there somewhere.

BEN: What's that?

CALVIN: The chess set.

BEN: Are we going to play?

CALVIN: Unless you don't want to.

BEN: I don't mind.

> *(JESSICA enters from the kitchen with a plate of canapés.)*

JESSICA: What are you making so much noise about?

CALVIN: The chess set. I knew it was in there somewhere.

JESSICA: You can munch on these until dinner's ready.

CALVIN: When will that be?

JESSICA: Shortly. *(To BEN)* Thank you for the wine. And the dessert.

BEN: You're quite welcome. It should be kept chilled, by the way.

JESSICA: I put it in the fridge. Did you see the lovely pie Ben bought?

CALVIN: Thank you. What sort of cheese is that?

DANCING IN THE DARK

JESSICA: Blue.

CALVIN: Blue cheese is hard to digest.

JESSICA: Would you reach the wine glasses for me?

(CALVIN goes into the kitchen.)

JESSICA: You don't have to play if you don't want to.

BEN: I don't mind.

JESSICA: I hope this isn't too boring for you.

BEN: On the contrary. I was just reading this article of yours in "The Spectator."

JESSICA: What article is that?

BEN: In last week's paper.

JESSICA: Oh, that one.

BEN: It's very funny.

(CALVIN reenters with the wine glasses.)

CALVIN: What's funny?

JESSICA: My article...in last weeks' paper. Oh, darling, those glasses have got to be washed. Here let me take them. *(SHE goes off to the kitchen with the glasses.)*

BEN: You really should encourage Jessie to do more writing.

CALVIN: Jessie...has never needed any encouragement.

BEN: We all need encouragement from time to time.

DANCING IN THE DARK

CALVIN: If someone has something to say they'll say it. Choose. *(HE holds out his fist enclosing two chess pieces.)*

BEN: What? Oh. *(HE points to one hand.)*

CALVIN: You're black. I'm white.

> *(CALVIN opens the board and THEY set up the pieces.)*

CALVIN: What happened to your wife?

BEN: She's remarried...I think.

CALVIN: Where do you make your home?

BEN: That's a good question. I've lived in London, Rome, Tokyo... I had a nice little apartment in Paris once. This place reminds me of it.

CALVIN: It's your move.

BEN: What's that?

CALVIN: I moved.

BEN: So you did.

> *(BEN moves his piece. CALVIN sits studying the board, shifts position, sighs, shifts position again.)*

CALVIN: I play very slowly. I like to think out my moves.

BEN: Very commendable. Would you mind very much? I'd like to make a call.

CALVIN: Go right ahead.

> *(BEN goes to the phone and dials. The lights come up and we are in the past. JESSICA materializes.)*

DANCING IN THE DARK

JESSICA: Calvin...?

CALVIN: What are you doing here?

JESSICA: I've come to visit you.

CALVIN: Didn't you get my letter? I asked you not to come. I thought I made myself clear.

JESSICA: You've gained a little weight.

CALVIN: I want to die.

JESSICA: Oh, darling, it's not the end of the world.

CALVIN: Our world, it is.

JESSICA: Nonsense.

CALVIN: Don't you understand? We can never have a child.

JESSICA: We can always adopt.

CALVIN: It's not the same.

JESSICA: Nothing is ever the same...from minute to minute, from day to day.

CALVIN: Can't you see? I'm dead. I died out there.

JESSICA: How much longer will they keep you?

CALVIN: They're discharging me at the end of the week.

JESSICA: Al Pierce is starting a newspaper in New York. There's a place for you, if you want it. We could start all over again. New city, new job, new life.

CALVIN: Maybe the gods are punishing us for having been so smug. We used to think we were perfect, you and I.

JESSICA: And so we are.

CALVIN: Not anymore. The doctors have assured me that I'll be able to lead a normal life. Normal! You haven't told anyone, have you?

JESSICA: You asked me not to.

CALVIN: Not even your family?

JESSICA: Least of all my family.

CALVIN: Actually they were very nice to me. Your father, especially.

JESSICA: Is that a bandage on your wrist?

CALVIN: I...cut myself.

JESSICA: Both wrists? Oh, Cal...you fool!

CALVIN: There's a whole ward full of us. Did you know that? We make all sorts of jokes about it. But when we're alone...somehow or other...it's just not that funny.

JESSICA: We'll manage, my dear. We'll manage.

CALVIN: You say that now.

JESSICA: I must look a mess. Where can I wash up?

CALVIN: There's a ladies' room right down the corridor, to the left.

JESSICA: I'll be right back. You won't go away?

CALVIN: Where on earth would I go?

> *(JESSICA goes off. The lights change. BEN hangs up the phone and joins CALVIN.)*

DANCING IN THE DARK

BEN: Have you made your move?

CALVIN: I'm sorry. *(HE moves a piece.)* Did you make your call?

BEN: Yes.

> *(BEN moves a piece. The radio plays a loud jazz song. CALVIN rises, shuts it off, returns to his seat and studies the board.)*

CALVIN: So, that's what you're up to.

> *(JESSICA enters with the salad.)*

JESSICA: We might as well start on the salad. The meat loaf should be ready soon. Come along. You must be famished, the both of you.

> *(SHE sits at the table and dishes out the salad. CALVIN and BEN join her at the table.)*

JESSICA: There's oil and vinegar.

BEN: Thank you.

JESSICA: We do have French dressing...

BEN: This'll be fine.

JESSICA: Shall we open the wine, or would you prefer to have it with your meat?

BEN: It's all the same to me.

JESSICA: Calvin?

CALVIN: Where's the grated cheese?

JESSICA: Oh, I'm sorry. I'll get it. *(SHE goes off to the kitchen.)*

CALVIN: We use grated cheese on our salad.

DANCING IN THE DARK

(JESSICA reenters with the grated cheese.)

JESSICA: Here we are.

CALVIN: *(HE sprinkles the cheese on his salad.)* Would you care for some?

BEN: Why not? *(HE sprinkles the cheese on his salad, then hands it to JESSICA.)*

JESSICA: Thank you. Did you turn off the radio? I wanted to hear the news.

CALVIN: It's too late for the news.

JESSICA: It will come on again.

CALVIN: Not until eight. I don't know why you have to play the radio incessantly. I've never seen anything like it. The moment you come into the house you turn on the radio.

JESSICA: It's off now, dear, so let's drop the subject.

CALVIN: This passion for noise...I've never understood it. As if you didn't have enough noise...sound...whatever you want to call it...living in a city like New York.

JESSICA: If you have an aversion to noise why do you chatter so?

CALVIN: I don't think intelligent conversation can be considered noise.

JESSICA: Nor do I. Eat your salad.

(There is silence while they eat.)

CALVIN: What's it like, living in Paris?

BEN: It's not the places you remember, it's the people.

DANCING IN THE DARK

CALVIN: What are the women like in Paris...as compared to those in Tokyo, for example?

JESSICA: I don't think we know Ben well enough to ask him about his personal life.

CALVIN: That was not a personal question.

JESSICA: I think I'd better serve the meat loaf in the kitchen. May I have your plates? *(SHE takes the plates into the kitchen.)*

CALVIN: You mustn't mind Jessie. She gets a little crotchety at times.

BEN: I feel as if I'm intruding.

CALVIN: Nonsense. It's good for us to have a little company now and then.

>*(THEY eat in silence. JESSICA reenters with two plates of meat loaf.)*

JESSICA: It's hot, so be careful. *(SHE sets the plates down and goes back into the kitchen.)*

CALVIN: We might as well start. No use letting the food get cold.

>*(CALVIN starts to eat. JESSICA reenters with her plate.)*

CALVIN: This meat is cold.

JESSICA: Nonsense, dear. You can see the steam.

CALVIN: It's raw. Can't you see? It's hot on the outside and the inside is raw.

JESSICA: It isn't raw. It's just not well done.

CALVIN: I don't like raw meat.

DANCING IN THE DARK

JESSICA: How's yours?

BEN: Mine is fine.

CALVIN: Well, mine is raw.

JESSICA: Take mine. I think it's a little darker. How's that?

CALVIN: It's not quite as raw. Where did you get this meat?

JESSICA: Why?

CALVIN: It's not very fresh.

JESSICA: Of course, it's fresh. I got it yesterday.

CALVIN: I know fresh meat when I taste it. Where did you get it?

JESSICA: At the A and P.

CALVIN: You're always saving pennies. I told you not to buy our meat at the A and P. We have an excellent butcher around the corner.

JESSICA: You said you didn't like their meat. You said the meat at the A and P was fresher and cheaper. *(To BEN)* Calvin is very fussy about his food.

CALVIN: Why shouldn't I be? It's one of the few pleasures I have in life.

(BEN and JESSICA's eyes meet. CALVIN notices the exchange.)

CALVIN: And after a hard day's work I like to eat well. Is there anything wrong with that? *(HE rises.)*

BEN: I quite agree.

JESSICA: Where are you going?

CALVIN: I'm going to make myself a sandwich. *(HE goes into the*

DANCING IN THE DARK

kitchen.)

JESSICA: He's always like this on Wednesdays.

BEN: As a matter of fact, the meat loaf isn't bad.

JESSICA: You don't have to be polite.

BEN: This is the worst meat loaf I've ever eaten. You really ought to smile more often. Are you a Libra by any chance?

JESSICA: I'm not quite sure. I know what I'm not.

BEN: And what is that?

JESSICA: A good cook.

(JESSICA giggles uncontrollably. CALVIN reenters.)

CALVIN: What's so funny?

JESSICA: Nothing, dear.

CALVIN: Where's the mustard?

JESSICA: The mustard, my dear, is where it always is.

CALVIN: You needn't get up. Just tell me where it is.

JESSICA: Sit down, Calvin, please. I'll make you a sandwich.

CALVIN: You can take the meat loaf with you, unless you intend to finish it.

(SHE goes into the kitchen.)

CALVIN: I took out the ham and the bread.

JESSICA: *(Offstage)* I can see that, dear.

DANCING IN THE DARK

CALVIN: You don't have to eat that, if you don't want to.

BEN: All it needs is a little salt. *(HE continues to eat.)*

(JESSICA reenters with a sandwich.)

JESSICA: Here you are, dear.

CALVIN: It's customary to cut a sandwich in half. Never mind. I can do it myself.

JESSICA: That knife isn't sharp enough.

CALVIN: So I see. *(HE goes into the kitchen and reenters with a bread knife.)* This bread is as hard as a rock.

JESSICA: Of course, it is. We've had it for weeks.

CALVIN: Why on earth do you keep it that long?

JESSICA: I use it for stuffing. And I put some in the meat loaf.

CALVIN: No wonder it tastes stale.

JESSICA: Are we ready for coffee?

CALVIN: I am.

JESSICA: Ben bought a lovely fruit pie.

CALVIN: So you said.

JESSICA: Don't eat the bread. Just eat the ham.

CALVIN: That's what I'm doing.

BEN: We have those rolls.

CALVIN: That's all right.

DANCING IN THE DARK

(JESSICA collects the salad plates and bowl and takes them into the kitchen. BEN and CALVIN eat in silence. JESSICA reenters with two cups of coffee.)

JESSICA: How do you take your coffee?

BEN: Saccharin. No milk.

(JESSICA sets down the coffee, picks up the grated cheese and dressing and takes them into the kitchen. SHE reenters with another coffee and the saccharin.)

JESSICA: I hate to cut the pie. It's so lovely. *(SHE goes off.)*

CALVIN: Have you ever worked for Lester before?

BEN: Just once, a few years ago.

CALVIN: I don't like him very much.

BEN: Frankly, neither do I.

(JESSICA enters with three plates of pie.)

JESSICA: Here we are. I'll take your plates. *(SHE goes off with the plates and the condiments.)*

BEN: Does Jessica work for Lester often?

CALVIN: Now and then. She does have other things to do, you know. I mean the house...and that sort of thing.

BEN: Yes, of course.

(JESSICA reenters with dessert forks, and THEY start on the pie.)

JESSICA: This pie is excellent.

CALVIN: Have we any aspirins?

DANCING IN THE DARK

JESSICA: I'm sure we do.

CALVIN: Excuse me. *(HE goes off to the bedroom.)*

BEN: I'll leave after dinner.

JESSICA: You don't have to.

    (CALVIN reenters.)

CALVIN: We're out of aspirins. I just took the last two. *(HE swallows the aspirins with his coffee.)* Be sure to put it on the list.

JESSICA: Yes, dear.

CALVIN: When do you two start?

BEN: What's that? Oh, yes, well... we are planning to attend the preview tomorrow.

CALVIN: I'm surprised that Lester chose you for the assignment. I mean Jessie. She knows absolutely nothing about ancient Egypt.

JESSICA: I'll just have to read up on it, won't I? Would anyone care for more pie?

BEN: I'll have a little piece.

JESSICA: Cal?

CALVIN: Thank you, no.

    (JESSICA takes Ben's plate, goes into the kitchen and returns with another piece of pie.)

BEN: Thank you.

    (CALVIN starts to rise.)

DANCING IN THE DARK

JESSICA: That's all right, dear. I can manage. *(To BEN)* Take your time. There's no rush. *(SHE takes the empty pie plates and cups and saucers into the kitchen.)*

CALVIN: We can finish our chess game. Unless you have other plans.

BEN: Not at the moment.

    (JESSICA reenters.)

CALVIN: We're going to finish our chess game.

JESSICA: All right, dear. *(SHE gathers up the rest of the of the dishes and takes them into the kitchen.)*

CALVIN: It's your move, isn't it?

BEN: I think it's yours.

    (THEY move to the game.)

CALVIN: So it is.

    (JESSICA reenters with a damp cloth and wipes the place mats.)

BEN: Can I help?

JESSICA: You can put the table away. It belongs in that corner.

    (SHE goes into the kitchen with the place mats.)

CALVIN: The leaves drop down.

BEN: So I see. *(BEN drops the table leafs and puts the table in place.)*

    (JESSICA reenters.)

JESSICA: That chair goes into the kitchen.

DANCING IN THE DARK

BEN: Let me help with the dishes. I insist.

CALVIN: What about the game?

BEN: We can finish it afterwards.

JESSICA: There's really not much to do. Cal, are you all right?

> *(CALVIN doesn't respond. JESSICA goes into the kitchen, followed by BEN. After a moment her laughter is heard. CALVIN sits lost in thought, then rises and paces about. HE sits again then rises and looks out the window. The phone rings. Once. Twice.)*

JESSICA: *(Offstage)* Cal? *(SHE appears in the kitchen doorway.)* The phone's ringing, dear. That's all right. I'll get it. *(SHE picks up the phone.)* Hello? Yes, Al. Just a moment. *(To CALVIN)* It's Al, dear. *(SHE hands the phone to CALVIN.)*

CALVIN: Hello? *(HE sighs)* I'll be right down. *(HE hangs up.)*

JESSICA: What is it?

CALVIN: We've got to redo the whole front page.

JESSICA: Oh, dear. I'll get your coat. *(SHE goes off to the bedroom and reenters with his jacket.)* Shall I wait up for you?

> *(HE takes the jacket and goes off, leaving the door open behind him.)*

JESSICA: Cal?

> *(SHE closes the door slowly and stands lost in thought. BEN reenters.)*

JESSICA: Thank you. You don't have to stay if you don't want to.

DANCING IN THE DARK

BEN: Are you trying to get rid of me?

JESSICA: We forgot the wine. Would you care for some?

BEN: Not right now. Have you been to bed with Lester?

JESSICA: Why do you ask?

BEN: I was just curious. Were you in love with him?

JESSICA: Lester? Good lord, no.

BEN: Was he in love with you?

JESSICA: I don't think that Lester has ever been in love with anyone. Certainly not his wife.

JESSICA: Then he was safe.

JESSICA: Would you care to go for a walk?

BEN: I'd like some more coffee.

> (SHE goes into the kitchen. BEN paces about. JESSICA enters with two cups of coffee.)

JESSICA: Isn't there anyone else you can call?

BEN: There was one other. I tried her this morning.

JESSICA: And?

BEN: She died last year.

JESSICA: I am sorry.

BEN: She couldn't have been more than thirty five. A school teacher. She stayed with me for several weeks in Paris.

DANCING IN THE DARK

JESSICA: Were you fond of her?

BEN: She was a nice lady.

JESSICA: Tell me about your travels.

BEN: What would you like to know?

JESSICA: What's Paris like now?

BEN: Have you ever been to Paris?

JESSICA: Years ago.

BEN: Then you probably saw her at her best. There is no avant garde anymore. There are no rebels. Everything is respectable now.

JESSICA: What a pity!

BEN: The way of all flesh, I suppose. How many of us have the courage to follow the dreams of our youth? Don't you ever have any regrets?

JESSICA: About what?

BEN: About what might have been.

JESSICA: What would be the point? Weren't you supposed to call Penny?

BEN: I'm getting a little tired of being the odd man out.

JESSICA: I'm sure she doesn't think of you that way.

BEN: Maybe not. Women hate to let go, don't they?

JESSICA: What makes you think so?

BEN: It's true, isn't it? They cling to the past.

DANCING IN THE DARK

JESSICA: More so than men?

BEN: I think so, yes.

JESSICA: Maybe it's just that they're a little more loyal than men.

BEN: You don't happen to have any Scotch, do you?

JESSICA: As a matter of fact, I think we do. *(SHE goes into the kitchen and reenters with a fresh bottle of Scotch and a glass.)* It's been there since Christmas. Last Christmas. Neither of us drink Scotch. Would you care for some ice?

BEN: No.

JESSICA: You're not angry, are you?

BEN: Yes, I am.

JESSICA: At me? Why?

BEN: I'm so tired of hypocrisy. What are you smiling at?

JESSICA: I don't think that any of us are completely free from hypocrisy.

BEN: *(HE pours himself a healthy drink and downs it.)* You think I'm hypocritical?

JESSICA: You say you're envious of those who enjoy married life, and yet you haven't remarried. Why?

BEN: I hadn't met you...until today.

JESSICA: You know nothing about me.

BEN: I feel as if I've known you all my life. Does that sound corny?

JESSICA: And you think I'm hypocritical.

DANCING IN THE DARK

BEN: I think you're deceiving yourself.

JESSICA: In what way?

BEN: In believing that you and your husband are indispensable to one another.

JESSICA: None of us is indispensable, my dear.

BEN: Then why do you stick it out?

JESSICA: Because we took each other for better or worse.

BEN: "Till death do you part." There are all forms of death. You can still be friends and not be married to one another. What do you get out of all this? He won't even let you have a career.

JESSICA: If I wanted a career I would have one.

BEN: You're afraid of hurting his pride, so as a result you sit around punishing one another. He's eaten up with guilt. He had to be...depriving you of a rich, full life.

JESSICA: And what does that consist of?

BEN: Sex, for one thing.

JESSICA: We do have sex.

BEN: And a family.

JESSICA: I don't know of any relationship that's perfect. Do you?

BEN: Oh, come on, Jessie. I thought you'd tear me apart when I touched you. Not that I'm complaining... You might be of much more use to one another as friends.

JESSICA: It's very kind of you...

DANCING IN THE DARK

BEN: It's nothing of the sort. I'm lonely. I'm not asking you to make a decision right now. Look, I'm going up to Michigan to visit my sister, and then I'll be coming back to New York. Think about it. Okay? Excuse me.

(BEN goes off to the bedroom. JESSICA sighs and sits lost in thought. The lights changes. CALVIN materializes.)

CALVIN: Where have you been?

JESSICA: I've been shopping.

CALVIN: Do you know what time it is?

JESSICA: It's after six.

CALVIN: Exactly.

JESSICA: I ran into Betty Conroy and we had some coffee. You don't usually get home until six thirty.

CALVIN: Is that what you were counting on?

JESSICA: I'll start dinner.

CALVIN: I've eaten already, and you've just had some coffee, so why bother?

JESSICA: I'm sorry.

CALVIN: What have you been doing all day?

JESSICA: I told you. I went shopping.

CALVIN: And that was it?

JESSICA: I bought some groceries in the morning. I straightened up the apartment...and I went shopping.

DANCING IN THE DARK

CALVIN: Absolutely amazing! How you can spend the entire day and accomplish absolutely nothing. Is it too much to ask to have a meal waiting for me at the end of the day? Not an elaborate mean, just a very simple one. I don't know what groceries you bought because the fridge is half empty. And by straightening the apartment, I assume you must mean shifting the dust from one corner to another. Look at this bookcase. It hasn't been dusted in weeks. The place is filthy. There is no food. And you call yourself a housewife?

JESSICA: I don't call myself a housewife.

CALVIN: What do you call yourself?

JESSICA: A woman.

CALVIN: And by that I suppose you mean that you're entitled to spend half the day on the phone. I called you twice this morning to let you know I'd be coming home early, and twice the line was busy. I tried you twice this afternoon and you were gone.

JESSICA: You're not helpless, Cal. You can help yourself to dinner for once.

CALVIN: Am I supposed to clean the apartment, too?

JESSICA: Would that be so terrible?

CALVIN: What else would you like me to do? Run your bath for you? Lay out your clothes?

JESSICA: All right, Cal. You've made your point. I'm lazy. I'm selfish, and I'm of no use to anyone.

CALVIN: I never said that.

JESSICA: Well, it's the truth. I'm of no use to you. I'm of no use to myself. All right. You want to know what I did for most of the day? I sat in the park. I sat in the park like a goddamned fool, staring at the trees and staring at the sky and wondering what the hell it was all about.

DANCING IN THE DARK

(CALVIN starts for the kitchen.)

JESSICA: Where are you going?

CALVIN: I'm going to wash the dishes.

JESSICA: Leave the dishes.

CALVIN: I don't mind.

JESSICA: I said leave them!

(CALVIN Continues toward the kitchen. JESSICA rises, grabs him by the arms and starts to shake him.)

JESSICA: Did you hear what I said? I said leave them!

(HE slaps her.)

CALVIN: I'm sorry, Jessie. I'm sorry. I didn't mean that. Oh, God!

(CALVIN goes into the kitchen. JESSICA sits and starts to sob. The lights change. JESSICA wipes her eyes as BEN reenters.)

BEN: You're out of... Is it something I've said?

JESSICA: No.

BEN: Do you want to talk about it?

JESSICA: We've been talking about it all evening.

BEN: I'm sorry. I've made a pest of myself.

JESSICA: He tried to kill himself once.

BEN: Because of you? Come on, Jessie. He's made his adjustment by now. You're the one that's crippled. There's a world outside this apartment, another life, just waiting to be lived.

DANCING IN THE DARK

JESSICA: With you?

BEN: I'm game, if you are.

JESSICA: It's a little late for me to start dreaming.

BEN: Life is over when one stops dreaming.

JESSICA: Well, maybe it is...for me.

BEN: You are not Calvin and Calvin isn't you. You've been making demands on yourself...and Calvin...that you have no right to make. *(HE sits beside her, takes her hand and kisses it, then kisses her on the cheek, the lips.)*

JESSICA: No. Please.

BEN: *(HE goes to the door and locks it, then returns to JESSICA and holds out his hand.)* Come on.

    (JESSICA turns away.)

BEN: Let's go to my place. Leave him a note. We had some stuff to go over. I love you, Jessie. I know it sounds crazy, but I do.

JESSICA: I've got to think.

BEN: Don't. Just do. Come on, let's go. Let's just get out of here. Let's get some air.

JESSICA: Let me get my bag.
    (JESSICA goes into the bedroom. BEN unlocks he door. JESSICA reenters with her pocketbook.)

BEN: Ready?

JESSICA: As ready as I'll ever be.

    (SHE turns off one of the lamps. BEN opens the door. JESSICA

DANCING IN THE DARK

goes off, followed by BEN. The lights come down. The lights come up. The outside door is opened and CALVIN enters.)

CALVIN: Jessie? *(HE hesitates, then goes into the bedroom and comes out.)* Jessie? *(HE goes into the kitchen, comes out then turns on the other lamp. HE sees the bottle of Scotch, picks it up then sets it down. HE sits on the sofa, rises and paces about. HE goes to the phone, hesitates, then dials.)* Hello? It's Calvin, Lester. I hope I didn't wake you. Yes, I know. I just got in. Do you have Ben Brady's number? Ben Brady. Well, where's he staying. The what? You're sure. No, that's all right. I can look it up. Thank you. No nothing's wrong. Go back to sleep. *(HE hangs up, hesitates, then pulls out the phone book. HE changes his mind, sets down the phone book, goes into the kitchen and returns with a glass. HE pours himself some Scotch and downs it, then sits thinking.)*

(The lights come up.)

JESSICA: *(Offstage)* Calvin? Is that you?

CALVIN: Yes, dear.

(JESSICA enters rather shakily. SHE is slightly disheveled and holds a piece of raw meat to her eye.)

CALVIN: What happened? Are you all right?

JESSICA: Don't scold me, please.

CALVIN: I'm not going to scold you. Just tell me what happened.

JESSICA: It was a business acquaintance of Lester's. He asked me out for a drink. He seemed quite harmless. And then he said he was expecting a call. It was a perfectly respectable hotel...the Bedford, as a matter of fact.

CALVIN: What happened?

JESSICA: We were waiting for this call and having a drink when this friend of his arrived. They both were drinking and they began to get abusive. I tried to leave...but they wouldn't let me.

CALVIN: Let's see the eye.

(HE inspects the eye and touches her cheek. SHE winces.)

JESSICA: It looks awful, doesn't it?

CALVIN: Your neck is all bruised.

JESSICA: And look at my dress. It's the only smart frock I have.

CALVIN: Oh, Jessie!

JESSICA: I know, I know. Where are you going?

CALVIN: I was going to make us a pot of tea.

JESSICA: Let me. I've got to keep busy. *(SHE starts off, winces and stops.)*

CALVIN: Are you all right?

JESSICA: I'm fine. I'll be fine.

(SHE goes into the kitchen. CALVIN sits and buries his face in his hands. JESSICA reenters and comes up to him.)

JESSICA: Calvin...?

CALVIN: Yes? What is it?

JESSICA: Don't panic, dear. But I think there's something wrong. I have this pain in my side.

CALVIN: Where?

JESSICA: Right here.

DANCING IN THE DARK

CALVIN: *(HE touches her side.)* Where?

JESSICA: Ouch! I think I may have a broken rib.

CALVIN: We better take you to the hospital. I'll get a cab.

JESSICA: I can walk. It's only a couple of blocks.

CALVIN: Are you sure?

JESSICA: I'll get my coat.

(SHE goes into the bedroom very slowly. A thud is heard.)

CALVIN: Jessie? *(HE runs into the bedroom.)* Jessie? *(HE reenters quickly, picks up the phone and dials.)* I need an ambulance. Right away. 36 Charles Street. Apartment One A. Courtney. Calvin Courtney. Hurry, please.

(The lights return to normal. CALVIN is still on the phone.)

CALVIN: Hello? Yes. Can you tell me...? Is Ben Brady staying with you? No, no, no. That's all right. Do you know if he's in right now? No, no, no. Never mind. Thank you.

(HE hangs up and stands thinking. The phone rings. HE picks it up quickly.)

CALVIN: Hello? Oh, Lester. Yes, yes, everything's fine. She's gone to bed. Everything is fine. Thank you. Good night.

(HE hangs up, stands thinking, then picks up the phone. HE hears something, hangs up and goes into the kitchen. The door is opened and JESSICA enters.)

JESSICA: Calvin?

(HE reenters from the kitchen.)

DANCING IN THE DARK

CALVIN: I thought you were asleep. Have you been out?

JESSICA: I walked Ben to the subway, and it was such a lovely night...I went for a walk.

CALVIN: I was just getting ready to go to bed.

JESSICA: Would you care for some milk?

CALVIN: That might be nice.

JESSICA: Did everything work out all right?

CALVIN: It always does, doesn't it?

>   *(HE hesitates, then goes off to the bedroom. JESSICA sits, looking troubled and confused. The lights change. BEN materializes and sits beside her.)*

BEN: I think it's time I settled down. New York's as good a place as any, don't you think? Though I would like some trees and grass.

JESSICA: We had a lovely country house...in Cornwall. I used to love to work in the garden.

BEN: I spent my summers on a farm when I was a kid.

JESSICA: Did you?

BEN: What are you thinking?

JESSICA: Nothing in particular.

BEN: How did you and Calvin meet?

JESSICA: What's that? Oh. At a dinner dance...in Toronto. He was living there and I was visiting some friends.

BEN: Was it love at first sight?

DANCING IN THE DARK

JESSICA: He claims it was. He was awfully arrogant. So was I, for that matter. We were both very full of ourselves. Where did you meet your wife?

BEN: In college. Michigan State.

JESSICA: Did you know right away?

BEN: Not really, no. She wanted to get out and see the world. I was quite content to spend the rest of my life in Michigan. Now she's back in Michigan...or so I've been told...and here I am roaming about the face of the earth. Do you believe in fate? I mean that our destinies are all mapped out for us?

JESSICA: I don't know. Do you?

BEN: I like to think we have something to say about our lives, but I sometimes wonder. What would you change, if you were given another chance?

JESSICA: I would change the world.

BEN: Did you and Calvin want children?

(JESSICA rises and stands looking out the window.)

JESSICA: Look, there's a shooting star.

BEN: Where? *(HE joins her at the window.)*

JESSICA: It's gone.

BEN: Did you make a wish? You're supposed to make a wish.

JESSICA: All right. *(SHE closes her eyes.)*

BEN: It's too late now.

JESSICA: I'm going to make it anyway.

DANCING IN THE DARK

BEN: What did you wish? No, you mustn't tell me.

JESSICA: I wasn't going to.

> *(SHE returns to the sofa as the lights become normal. BEN remains in the shadows by the window. CALVIN reenters in pajamas and robe.)*

CALVIN: The bathroom's clear.

JESSICA: Thank you, dear.

CALVIN: Where's the milk?

JESSICA: Oh...I'm sorry.

CALVIN: I'll do it. Stay right where you are. Are you all right?

JESSICA: Yes, I'm fine.

CALVIN: He seems awfully nice.

JESSICA: What?

CALVIN: Ben. Ben Brady. He seems awfully nice.

JESSICA: Yes...yes, he is.

CALVIN: I feel sorry for him though. He seems sort of lost...and lonely. Don't you think?

JESSICA: Quite possibly.

> *(CALVIN goes into the kitchen. The lights brighten. BEN sits beside JESSICA.)*

BEN: I'd like you to meet my sister. I know the two of you would hit it off.

DANCING IN THE DARK

JESSICA: Is she anything like you?

BEN: She's better looking. But she doesn't have my personality. Her husband's nice, too. And the kids...well...

(The phone rings.)

BEN: Excuse me. I don't know who that could possibly be. I'm not expecting any calls. *(HE picks up the phone.)* Hello? Right. Right. Thank you. *(HE hangs up.)*

JESSICA: Anything important?

BEN: I don't know. Excuse me. *(HE dials.)* Hello, Jack? It's Ben. I'm fine. I see... Well, yes. I see. Well, tell me this. Could I take someone with me? A writer? Right. I see. Well, look, can I get back to you? All right. All right. First thing in the morning. Right. Talk to you soon. *(HE hangs up.)* How'd you like to go to China?

JESSICA: China?!

BEN: Have you a passport? That's all right. They can take care of all that. You might have to get some shots. Have you been to the Orient? You'd love it.

JESSICA: I'd have to think about this.

BEN: Take your time. Okay. What do you think? It's the chance of a lifetime. And it would pay well. It's for Life magazine. What do you say?

JESSICA: I'd have to talk this over...

BEN: Yes, of course. But I don't see how he could possibly stand in your way. Not for something like this.

JESSICA: I'd need clothes.

BEN: Overalls. Blue jeans. A parka. Things that are comfortable and warm. We can pick them up on the way. What do you say?

DANCING IN THE DARK

JESSICA: Ben...

BEN: Okay. I understand. Call me in the morning.

(SHE rises.)

BEN: You're not going, are you?

JESSICA: I must.

BEN: Stay. Please stay. I have this thing about sleeping alone.

JESSICA: I've never spent a night away. He'd be worried.

BEN: Give him a call.

JESSICA: What would I say?

BEN: We'll think of something. Don't go. Please.

JESSICA: I've got to. Besides, I'd have to pack. Get things organized.

BEN: Okay, okay. I'll put you in a cab.

(The lights return to normal as BEN goes off. CALVIN enters from the kitchen with two glasses of milk.)

CALVIN: Here we are, milady. Careful. It's hot.

JESSICA: Thank you.

CALVIN: I'll get some biscuits.

JESSICA: Calvin...?

CALVIN: Yes? What is it?

JESSICA: Nothing.

DANCING IN THE DARK

CALVIN: Drink your milk.

(HE goes off to the kitchen. JESSICA rises, looks about then goes to the radio and turns it on. Dinner music is heard. SHE returns to the sofa as CALVIN enters with the biscuits.)

JESSICA: I'll turn it off if it bothers you.

CALVIN: It's all right.

JESSICA: Calvin...

CALVIN: Yes?

JESSICA: Ben has asked me to come to China with him. He's going there for Life magazine. It could pay very well. What do you think?

CALVIN: Well, it's certainly something to think about. How long would you be gone? Do you know?

JESSICA: I don't know. A few weeks, I imagine.

CALVIN: It would certainly be a great opportunity. Whatever happened to that nightgown you bought?

JESSICA: What nightgown?

CALVIN: The one you bought last week. The sexy one.

JESSICA: Oh, that one. I'm taking it back.

CALVIN: Why?

JESSICA: It's much to expensive, for one thing.

CALVIN: Let me be the judge of that. Let's see what it looks like. I haven't seen it on.

JESSICA: Now?

DANCING IN THE DARK

CALVIN: It's nighttime isn't it? What better time to try on a nightgown?

JESSICA: Really, Cal.

CALVIN: Yes, really. Come on, please.

JESSICA: You know what time it is?

CALVIN: I don't have to get up early, nor do you. Pretty please, with sugar on it.

JESSICA: You are ridiculous. You're like a child.

(SHE goes into the bedroom. HE sighs, looks about the room, sighs, then paces.)

JESSICA: *(Offstage)* Calvin? Did you say something, dear?

CALVIN: What's that?

JESSICA: *(Offstage)* I said...

CALVIN: No. Jessie?

JESSICA: *(Offstage)* Yes, dear?

CALVIN: What did you say to Ben? About China?

(There's a moment of silence as CALVIN waits impatiently for the answer. The phone rings. CALVIN stares at it. It continues to ring.)

JESSICA: *(Offstage)* Is that the phone?

CALVIN: I'll get it. *(HE picks up the phone.)* Hello? Oh, Ben. Yes, she's here. Just a moment. *(HE lays down the phone.)* Jessie, it's Ben.

JESSICA: *(Offstage)* I'll be right out.

DANCING IN THE DARK

CALVIN: *(HE picks up the phone.)* She'll be right with you.

(HE sets down the phone, hesitates, then goes off to the kitchen. JESSICA enters wearing an attractive negligee. SHE picks up the phone.)

JESSICA: Hello? Yes, I got home fine. We were just sitting here, Calvin and I. We're drinking hot milk. My passport? *(SHE glances down and sees the pad next to the phone and picks it up.)* I haven't had a chance to look. Ben, what's the number of your hotel? I see. Ben, I've been thinking... This just isn't a very good time. No, I've thought it over. I'm sorry. Good night. *(SHE hangs up.)* Calvin? Where are you?

(CALVIN enters. Their eyes meet. SHE smiles.)

JESSICA: Well? What do you think?

CALVIN: Now that was worth waiting for.

JESSICA: Cal...

CALVIN: Yes, dear?

JESSICA: I've decided not to go. To China.

CALVIN: You sure?

JESSICA: Oh, my love, I'm not sure of anything. Are you?

CALVIN: Yes.

JESSICA: Our milk is getting cold.

CALVIN: Dance first, drink later.

(THEY melt into each others arms and dance. SHE rests her head on his shoulder. His eyes shine triumphantly, then a look of uncertainly creeps into them. THEY cling to one another and continue to dance as the lights fade.)

ABOUT THE AUTHOR

As an actor Norman Beim has appeared on Broadway in "Inherit The Wind" with the legendary Paul Muni, Off Broadway with Morgan Freeman at Joe Papp's Public Theatre, in various regional theatre productions and in film and on television. He is a director, a playwright and a novelist. His debut novel, "Hymie And The Angel," recently received excellent reviews. His plays have won numerous awards and have been produced in The Netherlands, Belgium and Canada and at theatres across the country. "Women Laid Bare" is the seventh collection of Mr. Beim's plays to be published. He is a member of the Dramatist Guild, Actors Equity, the Screen Actors Guild and AFTRA. He lives in New York City.

Printed in the United States
202974BV00003B/229-246/A